SURVIVAL OF THE FILTHIEST

SURVIVAL OF THE FILTHIEST

a GET FUZZY collection

by darby conley

Andrews McMeel
Publishing, LLC
Kansas City • Sydney • London

Other *Get Fuzzy* Books

The Dog Is Not a Toy (House Rule #4)

Fuzzy Logic: Get Fuzzy 2

The Get Fuzzy Experience: Are You Bucksperienced

I Would Have Bought You a Cat, But . . .

Blueprint for Disaster

Say Cheesy

Scrum Bums

I'm Ready for My Movie Contract

Take Our Cat, Please!

Ignorance, Thy Name Is Bucky

Dumbheart

Masters of the Nonsenseverse

Treasuries

Groovitude: A Get Fuzzy Treasury

Bucky Katt's Big Book of Fun

Loserpalooza

The Potpourrific Great Big Grab Bag of Get Fuzzy

Treasury of the Lost Litter Box

Get Fuzzy is distributed internationally by Universal Uclick.

Andrews McMeel Publishing, LLC
an Andrews McMeel Universal company
1130 Walnut Street
Kansas City, Missouri 64106
www.andrewsmcmeel.com

12 13 14 15 16 RR2 10 9 8 7 6 5 4 3 2 1

ISBN: 978-1-4494-2190-8

Library of Congress Control Number: 2012934477

Get Fuzzy can be viewed on the Internet at
www.gocomics.com/getfuzzy

DO YOU SMELL SOMETHING?
LIKE 800 THINGS. CAN YOU BE MORE SPECIFIC?
WHAT DO I SMELL IN HERE?
OPEN FACE DECADENCE, MY FRIEND.
WHAT IS MY SHAMPOO DOING IN THE KITCHEN? AND ALL MY DVDS? IS...IS THAT A HENDRIX DISC IN THE TOASTER ?!
A TOKEN OF YOUR CORRUPTED ETHICALS IS BEING PURIFIED, YES.
DUDE! STOP MELTING MY STUFF!
YOUR MORALIPIT IS DECREPITIED! I AM CLEANSING YOUR SOULS, ROBERT WILCO!
darb
IN FACT, I JUST DID THEM.
...YOU'RE ACTUALLY HOLDING A MEDIEVAL BURNING OF MY VANITIES ?!
TECHNICALLY, HE'S TOASTING YOUR VANITIES.

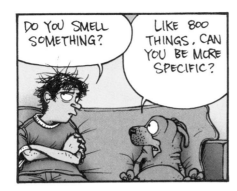

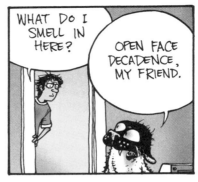

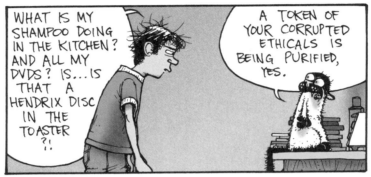

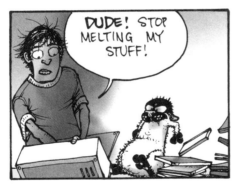

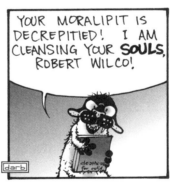

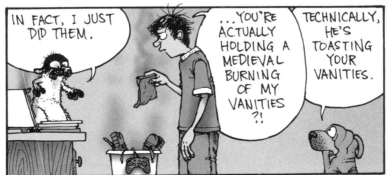

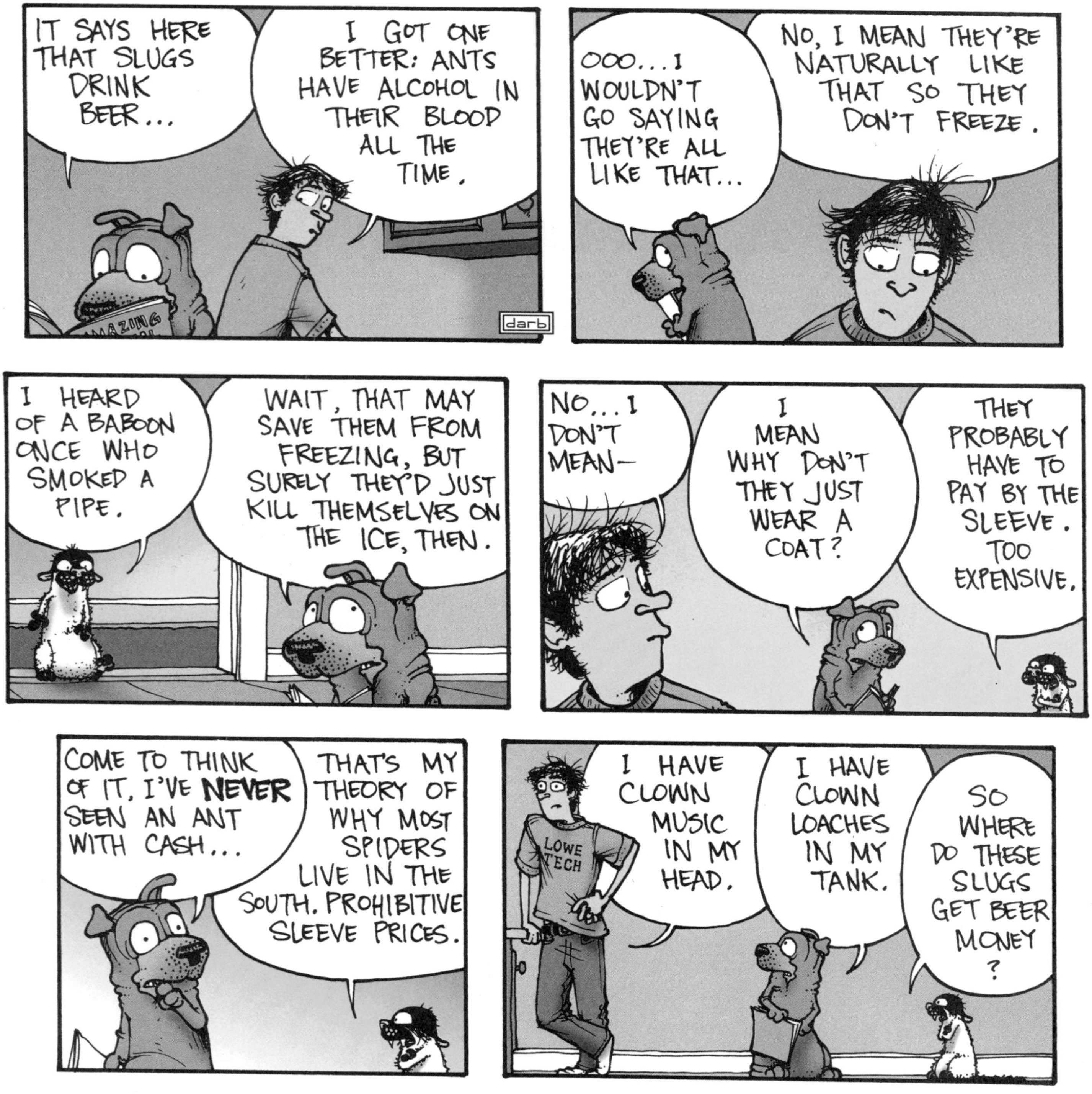
IT SAYS HERE THAT SLUGS DRINK BEER...
I GOT ONE BETTER: ANTS HAVE ALCOHOL IN THEIR BLOOD ALL THE TIME.
OOO... I WOULDN'T GO SAYING THEY'RE ALL LIKE THAT...
NO, I MEAN THEY'RE NATURALLY LIKE THAT SO THEY DON'T FREEZE.
I HEARD OF A BABOON ONCE WHO SMOKED A PIPE.
WAIT, THAT MAY SAVE THEM FROM FREEZING, BUT SURELY THEY'D JUST KILL THEMSELVES ON THE ICE, THEN.
NO... I DON'T MEAN—
I MEAN WHY DON'T THEY JUST WEAR A COAT?
THEY PROBABLY HAVE TO PAY BY THE SLEEVE. TOO EXPENSIVE.
COME TO THINK OF IT, I'VE **NEVER** SEEN AN ANT WITH CASH...
THAT'S MY THEORY OF WHY MOST SPIDERS LIVE IN THE SOUTH. PROHIBITIVE SLEEVE PRICES.
LOWE TECH
I HAVE CLOWN MUSIC IN MY HEAD.
I HAVE CLOWN LOACHES IN MY TANK.
SO WHERE DO THESE SLUGS GET BEER MONEY?

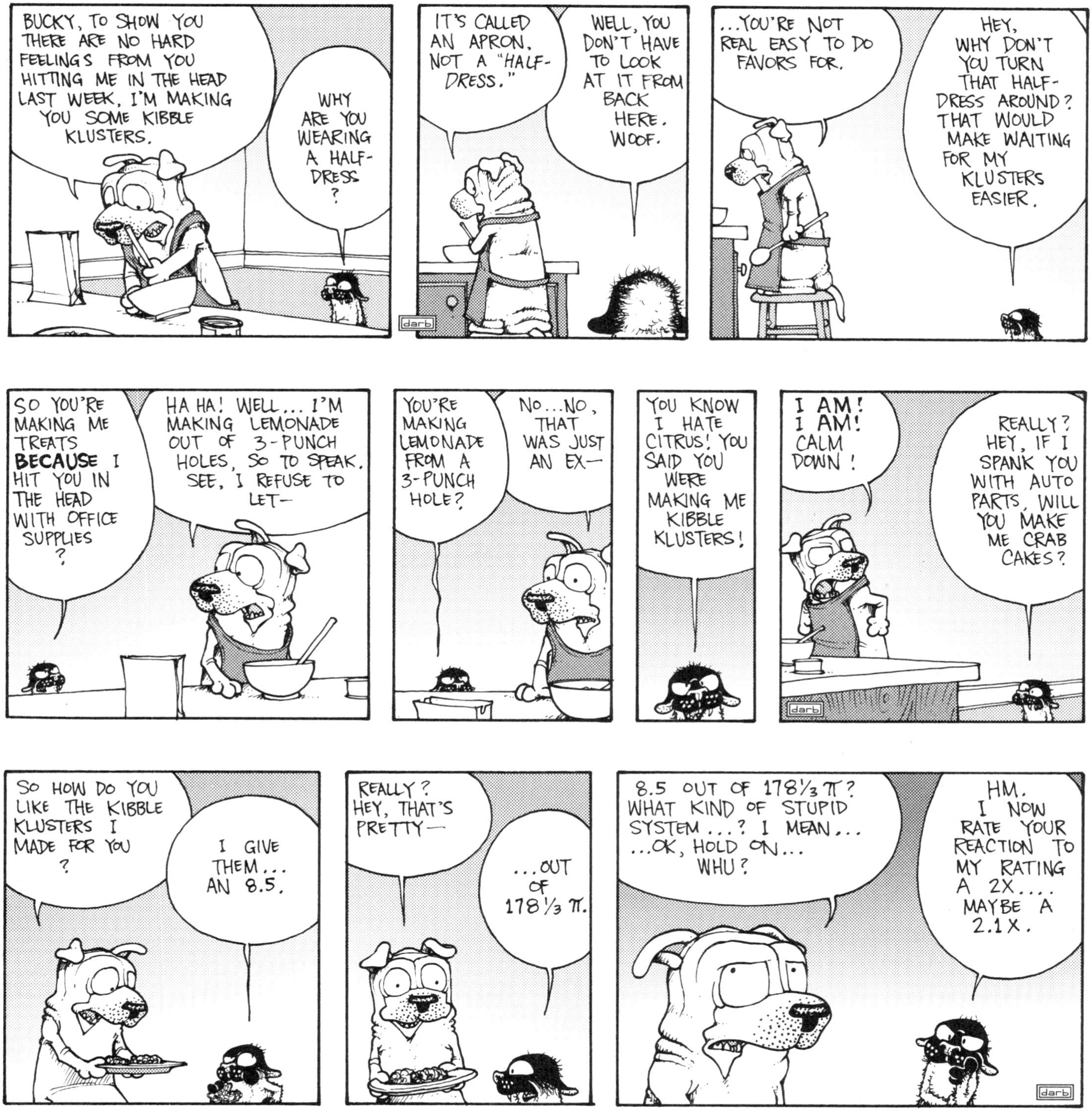
BUCKY, TO SHOW YOU THERE ARE NO HARD FEELINGS FROM YOU HITTING ME IN THE HEAD LAST WEEK, I'M MAKING YOU SOME KIBBLE KLUSTERS.
WHY ARE YOU WEARING A HALF-DRESS?
darb
IT'S CALLED AN APRON. NOT A "HALF-DRESS."
WELL, YOU DON'T HAVE TO LOOK AT IT FROM BACK HERE. WOOF.
...YOU'RE NOT REAL EASY TO DO FAVORS FOR.
HEY, WHY DON'T YOU TURN THAT HALF-DRESS AROUND? THAT WOULD MAKE WAITING FOR MY KLUSTERS EASIER.
SO YOU'RE MAKING ME TREATS **BECAUSE** I HIT YOU IN THE HEAD WITH OFFICE SUPPLIES?
HA HA! WELL... I'M MAKING LEMONADE OUT OF 3-PUNCH HOLES, SO TO SPEAK. SEE, I REFUSE TO LET—
YOU'RE MAKING LEMONADE FROM A 3-PUNCH HOLE?
NO...NO, THAT WAS JUST AN EX—
YOU KNOW I HATE CITRUS! YOU SAID YOU WERE MAKING ME KIBBLE KLUSTERS!
I AM! I AM! CALM DOWN!
REALLY? HEY, IF I SPANK YOU WITH AUTO PARTS, WILL YOU MAKE ME CRAB CAKES?
darb
SO HOW DO YOU LIKE THE KIBBLE KLUSTERS I MADE FOR YOU?
I GIVE THEM... AN 8.5.
REALLY? HEY, THAT'S PRETTY—
...OUT OF 178⅓ π.
8.5 OUT OF 178⅓ π? WHAT KIND OF STUPID SYSTEM...? I MEAN... ...OK, HOLD ON... WHU?
HM. I NOW RATE YOUR REACTION TO MY RATING A 2X.... MAYBE A 2.1X.
darb

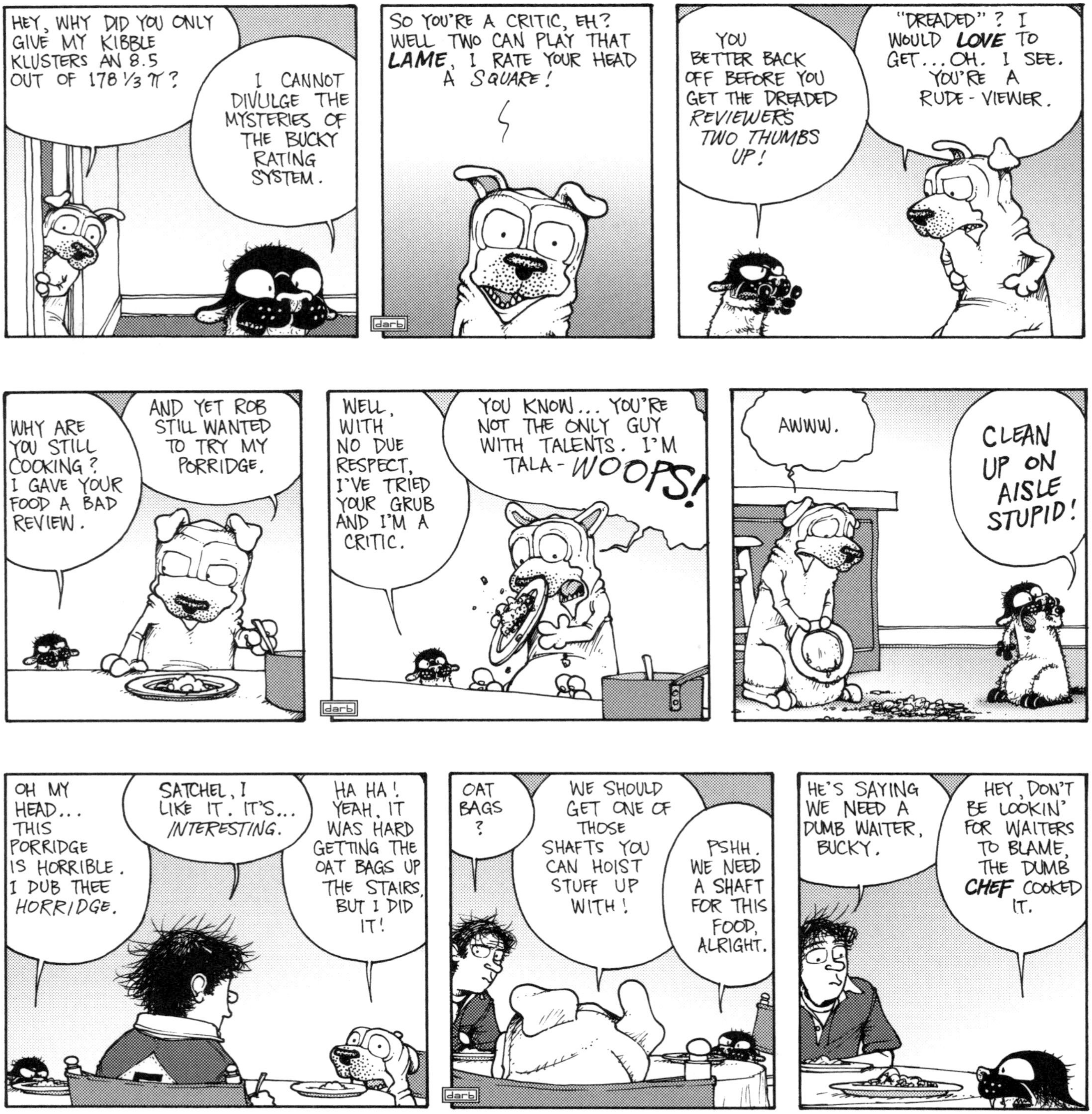
HEY, WHY DID YOU ONLY GIVE MY KIBBLE KLUSTERS AN 8.5 OUT OF 178 1/3 π?
I CANNOT DIVULGE THE MYSTERIES OF THE BUCKY RATING SYSTEM.
SO YOU'RE A CRITIC, EH? WELL TWO CAN PLAY THAT LAME, I RATE YOUR HEAD A SQUARE!
YOU BETTER BACK OFF BEFORE YOU GET THE DREADED REVIEWER'S TWO THUMBS UP!
"DREADED"? I WOULD LOVE TO GET... OH. I SEE. YOU'RE A RUDE-VIEWER.
WHY ARE YOU STILL COOKING? I GAVE YOUR FOOD A BAD REVIEW.
AND YET ROB STILL WANTED TO TRY MY PORRIDGE.
WELL, WITH NO DUE RESPECT, I'VE TRIED YOUR GRUB AND I'M A CRITIC.
YOU KNOW... YOU'RE NOT THE ONLY GUY WITH TALENTS. I'M TALA- WOOPS!
AWWW.
CLEAN UP ON AISLE STUPID!
OH MY HEAD... THIS PORRIDGE IS HORRIBLE. I DUB THEE HORRIDGE.
SATCHEL, I LIKE IT. IT'S... INTERESTING.
HA HA! YEAH, IT WAS HARD GETTING THE OAT BAGS UP THE STAIRS, BUT I DID IT!
OAT BAGS?
WE SHOULD GET ONE OF THOSE SHAFTS YOU CAN HOIST STUFF UP WITH!
PSHH. WE NEED A SHAFT FOR THIS FOOD, ALRIGHT.
HE'S SAYING WE NEED A DUMB WAITER, BUCKY.
HEY, DON'T BE LOOKIN' FOR WAITERS TO BLAME, THE DUMB CHEF COOKED IT.
darb

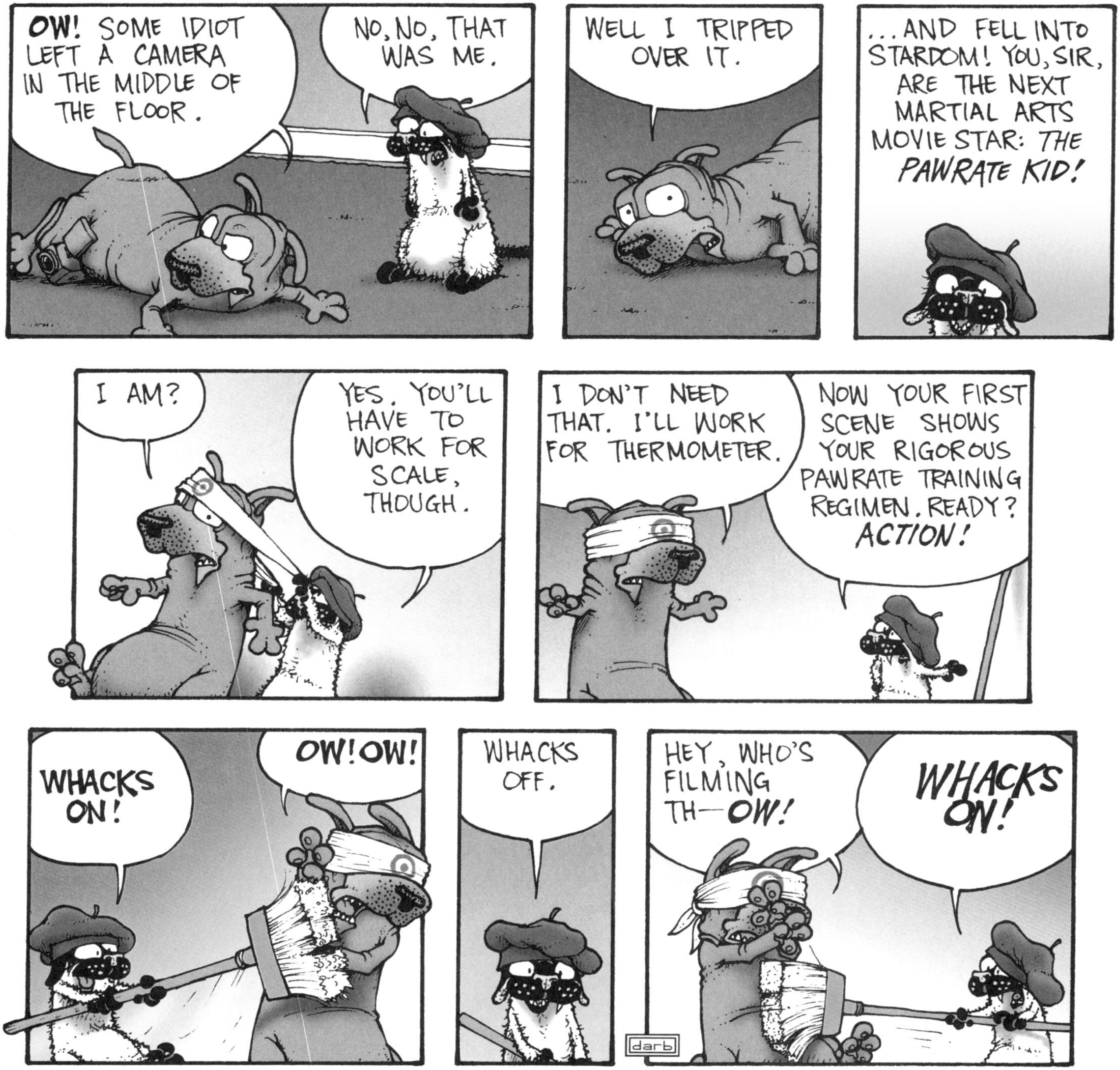
OW! SOME IDIOT LEFT A CAMERA IN THE MIDDLE OF THE FLOOR.
NO, NO, THAT WAS ME.
WELL I TRIPPED OVER IT.
...AND FELL INTO STARDOM! YOU, SIR, ARE THE NEXT MARTIAL ARTS MOVIE STAR: THE PAWRATE KID!
I AM?
YES. YOU'LL HAVE TO WORK FOR SCALE, THOUGH.
I DON'T NEED THAT. I'LL WORK FOR THERMOMETER.
NOW YOUR FIRST SCENE SHOWS YOUR RIGOROUS PAWRATE TRAINING REGIMEN. READY? ACTION!
WHACKS ON!
OW! OW!
WHACKS OFF.
HEY, WHO'S FILMING TH—OW!
WHACKS ON!
darb

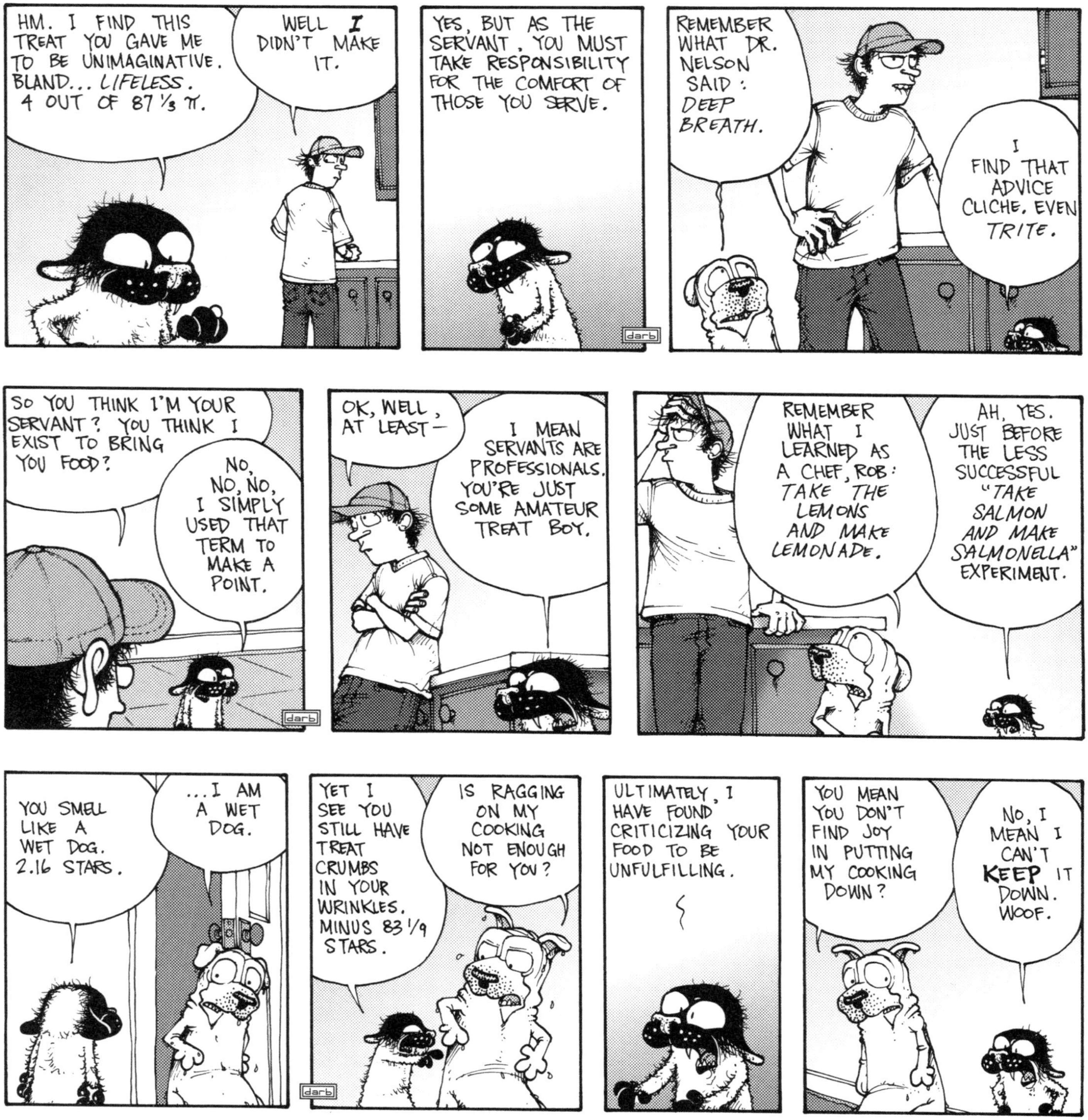
HM. I FIND THIS TREAT YOU GAVE ME TO BE UNIMAGINATIVE. BLAND... *LIFELESS.* 4 OUT OF 87 1/3 π.
WELL *I* DIDN'T MAKE IT.
YES, BUT AS THE SERVANT, YOU MUST TAKE RESPONSIBILITY FOR THE COMFORT OF THOSE YOU SERVE.
darb
REMEMBER WHAT DR. NELSON SAID: *DEEP BREATH.*
I FIND THAT ADVICE CLICHE. EVEN *TRITE.*
SO YOU THINK I'M YOUR SERVANT? YOU THINK I EXIST TO BRING YOU FOOD?
NO, NO, NO, I SIMPLY USED THAT TERM TO MAKE A POINT.
darb
OK, WELL, AT LEAST—
I MEAN SERVANTS ARE PROFESSIONALS. YOU'RE JUST SOME AMATEUR TREAT BOY.
REMEMBER WHAT I LEARNED AS A CHEF, ROB: *TAKE THE LEMONS AND MAKE LEMONADE.*
AH, YES. JUST BEFORE THE LESS SUCCESSFUL "*TAKE SALMON AND MAKE SALMONELLA*" EXPERIMENT.
YOU SMELL LIKE A WET DOG. 2.16 STARS.
...I AM A WET DOG.
darb
YET I SEE YOU STILL HAVE TREAT CRUMBS IN YOUR WRINKLES. MINUS 83 1/9 STARS.
IS RAGGING ON MY COOKING NOT ENOUGH FOR YOU?
ULTIMATELY, I HAVE FOUND CRITICIZING YOUR FOOD TO BE UNFULFILLING.
YOU MEAN YOU DON'T FIND JOY IN PUTTING MY COOKING DOWN?
NO, I MEAN I CAN'T **KEEP** IT DOWN. WOOF.

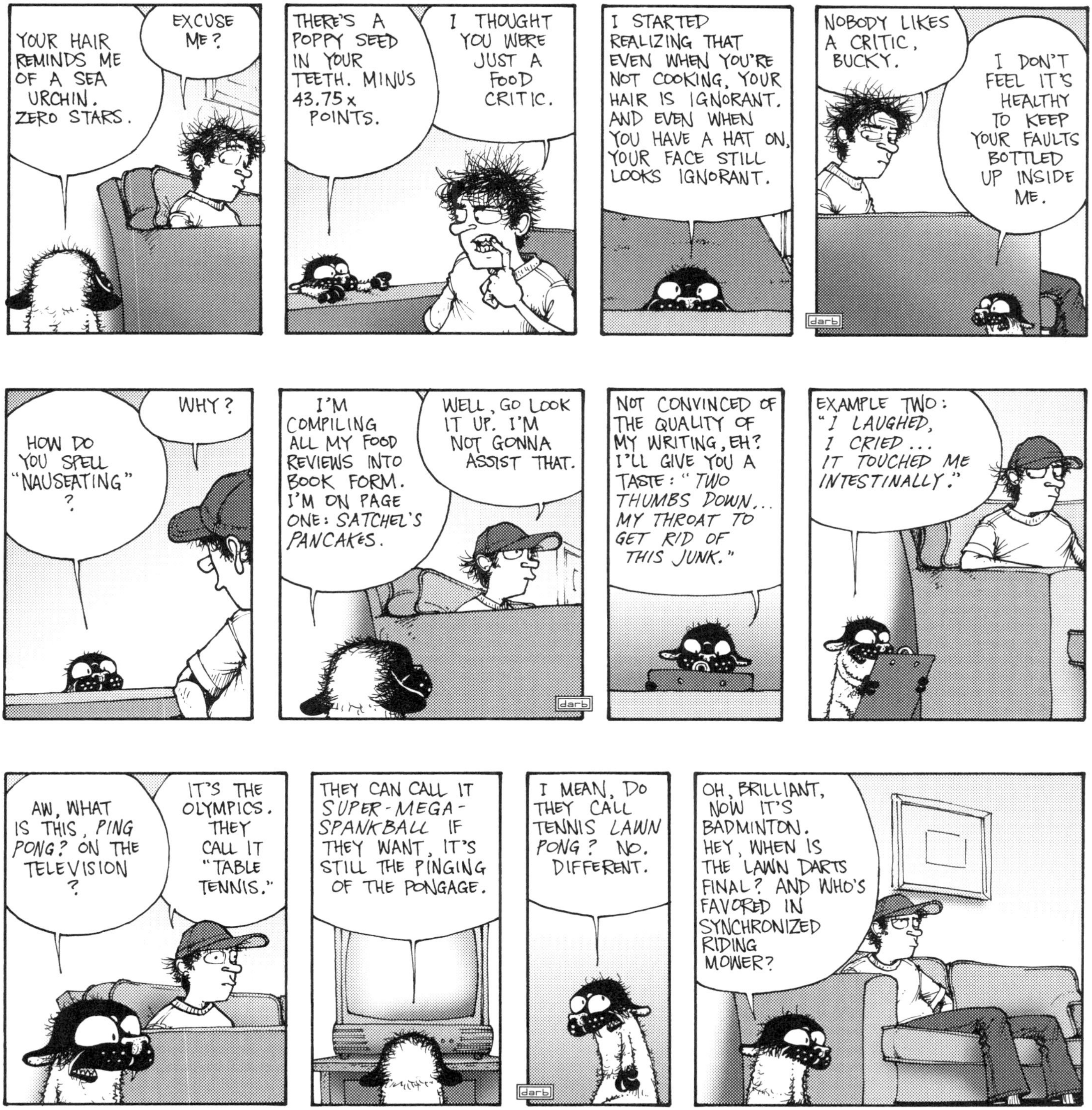
YOUR HAIR REMINDS ME OF A SEA URCHIN. ZERO STARS.
EXCUSE ME?
THERE'S A POPPY SEED IN YOUR TEETH. MINUS 43.75 x POINTS.
I THOUGHT YOU WERE JUST A FOOD CRITIC.
I STARTED REALIZING THAT EVEN WHEN YOU'RE NOT COOKING, YOUR HAIR IS IGNORANT. AND EVEN WHEN YOU HAVE A HAT ON, YOUR FACE STILL LOOKS IGNORANT.
NOBODY LIKES A CRITIC, BUCKY.
I DON'T FEEL IT'S HEALTHY TO KEEP YOUR FAULTS BOTTLED UP INSIDE ME.
darb
HOW DO YOU SPELL "NAUSEATING"?
WHY?
I'M COMPILING ALL MY FOOD REVIEWS INTO BOOK FORM. I'M ON PAGE ONE: SATCHEL'S PANCAKES.
WELL, GO LOOK IT UP. I'M NOT GONNA ASSIST THAT.
NOT CONVINCED OF THE QUALITY OF MY WRITING, EH? I'LL GIVE YOU A TASTE: "TWO THUMBS DOWN... MY THROAT TO GET RID OF THIS JUNK."
EXAMPLE TWO: "I LAUGHED, I CRIED... IT TOUCHED ME INTESTINALLY."
darb
AW, WHAT IS THIS, PING PONG? ON THE TELEVISION?
IT'S THE OLYMPICS. THEY CALL IT "TABLE TENNIS."
THEY CAN CALL IT SUPER-MEGA-SPANKBALL IF THEY WANT, IT'S STILL THE PINGING OF THE PONGAGE.
I MEAN, DO THEY CALL TENNIS LAWN PONG? NO. DIFFERENT.
OH, BRILLIANT, NOW IT'S BADMINTON. HEY, WHEN IS THE LAWN DARTS FINAL? AND WHO'S FAVORED IN SYNCHRONIZED RIDING MOWER?
darb

this yer kid
darb
this yer kid on munky
CARE TO SIGN OUR MONKEY-BANNING PETITION, MA'AM?
I THOUGHT YOU GAVE UP ON THAT.
I SCORED A CELEBRITY ENDORSEMENT. I'LL GIVE YOU A HINT... SHE'S NAMED AFTER AN EXOTIC EUROPEAN CITY AND A WELL-KNOWN RESORT...
....YOU GOT PARIS HILTON?
keep kidz off MUNKY!
NO, NO, HERE. THIS PROMO SHOT TELLS ALL ABOUT HER.
"MS. VLADIVOSTOK RED ROOF"?
WELL... I'M NOT MADE OF MONEY.
MUNSKI NYET!

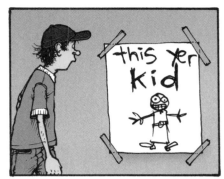

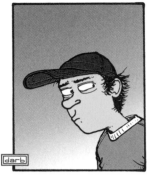

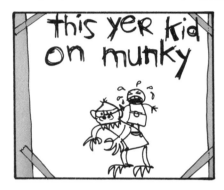

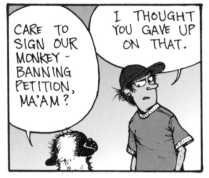

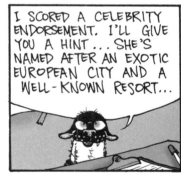

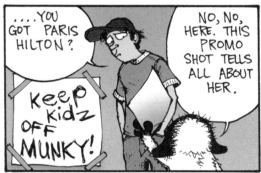

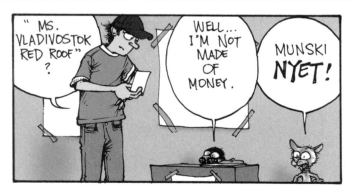

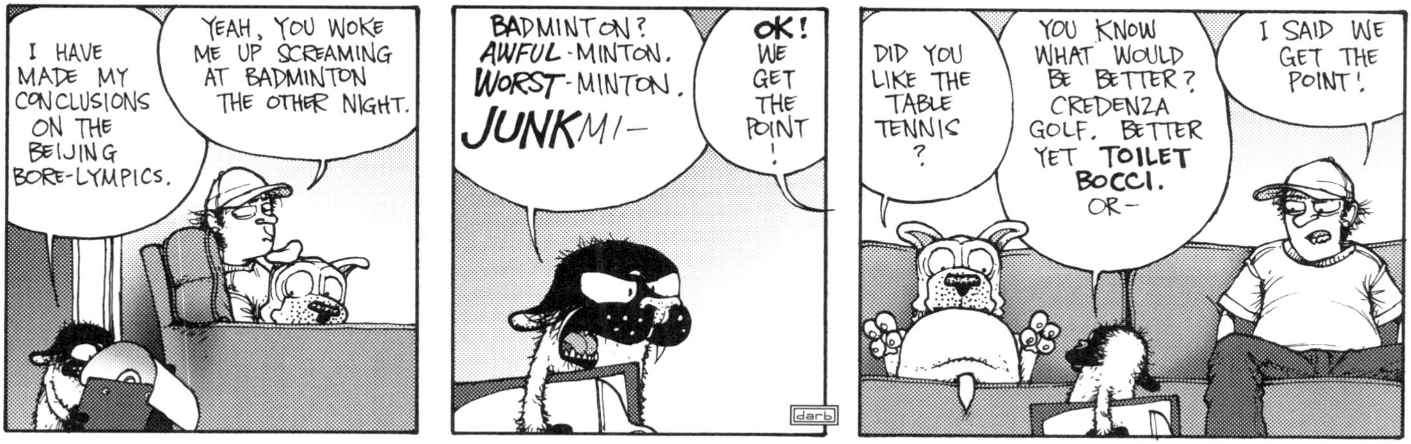
I HAVE MADE MY CONCLUSIONS ON THE BEIJING BORE-LYMPICS.
YEAH, YOU WOKE ME UP SCREAMING AT BADMINTON THE OTHER NIGHT.
BADMINTON? AWFUL-MINTON. WORST-MINTON. JUNKMI—
OK! WE GET THE POINT!
DID YOU LIKE THE TABLE TENNIS?
YOU KNOW WHAT WOULD BE BETTER? CREDENZA GOLF. BETTER YET TOILET BOCCI. OR—
I SAID WE GET THE POINT!
darb

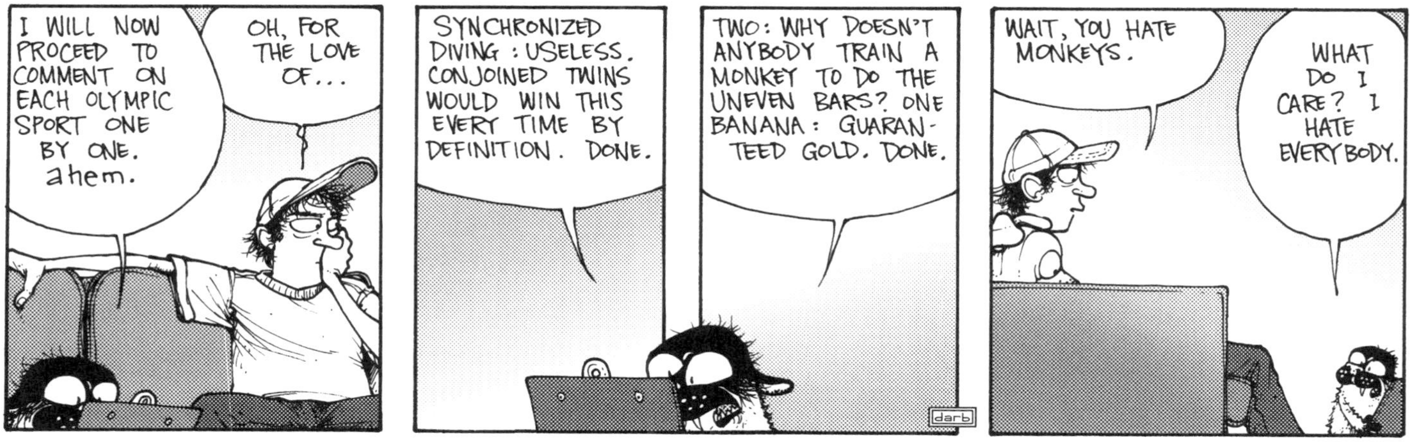
I WILL NOW PROCEED TO COMMENT ON EACH OLYMPIC SPORT ONE BY ONE. ahem.
OH, FOR THE LOVE OF...
SYNCHRONIZED DIVING: USELESS. CONJOINED TWINS WOULD WIN THIS EVERY TIME BY DEFINITION. DONE.
TWO: WHY DOESN'T ANYBODY TRAIN A MONKEY TO DO THE UNEVEN BARS? ONE BANANA: GUARANTEED GOLD. DONE.
darb
WAIT, YOU HATE MONKEYS.
WHAT DO I CARE? I HATE EVERYBODY.

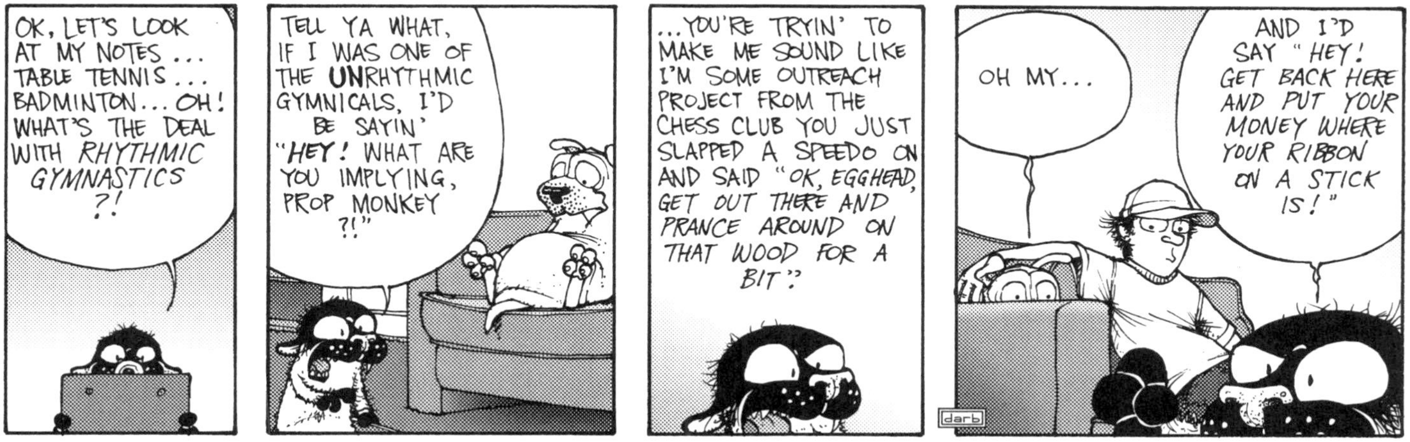
OK, LET'S LOOK AT MY NOTES... TABLE TENNIS... BADMINTON... OH! WHAT'S THE DEAL WITH RHYTHMIC GYMNASTICS?!
TELL YA WHAT, IF I WAS ONE OF THE UNRHYTHMIC GYMNICALS, I'D BE SAYIN' "HEY! WHAT ARE YOU IMPLYING, PROP MONKEY?!"
...YOU'RE TRYIN' TO MAKE ME SOUND LIKE I'M SOME OUTREACH PROJECT FROM THE CHESS CLUB YOU JUST SLAPPED A SPEEDO ON AND SAID "OK, EGGHEAD, GET OUT THERE AND PRANCE AROUND ON THAT WOOD FOR A BIT".
darb
OH MY...
AND I'D SAY "HEY! GET BACK HERE AND PUT YOUR MONEY WHERE YOUR RIBBON ON A STICK IS!"

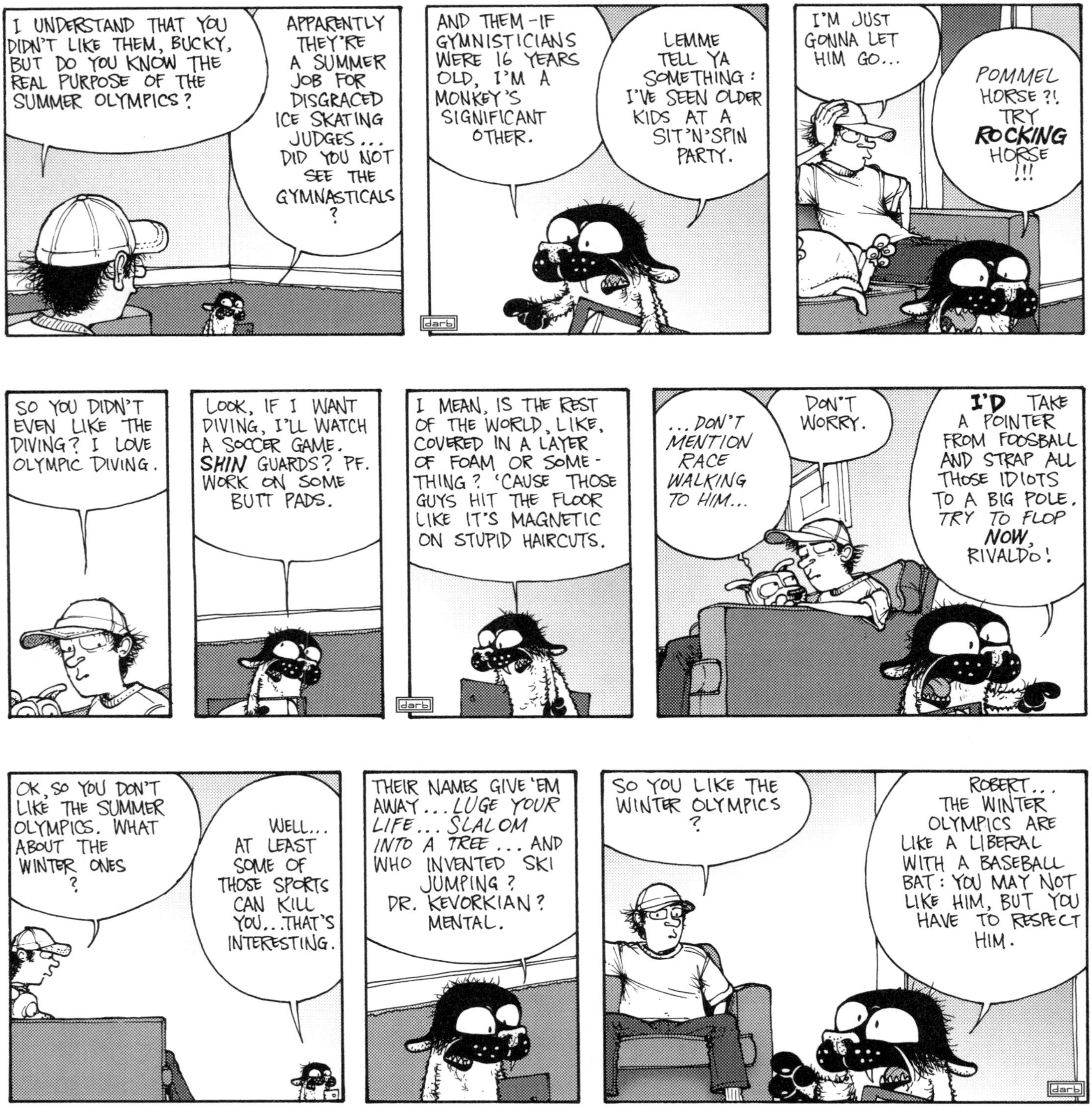
I UNDERSTAND THAT YOU DIDN'T LIKE THEM, BUCKY, BUT DO YOU KNOW THE REAL PURPOSE OF THE SUMMER OLYMPICS?
APPARENTLY THEY'RE A SUMMER JOB FOR DISGRACED ICE SKATING JUDGES... DID YOU NOT SEE THE GYMNASTICALS?
AND THEM - IF GYMNISTICIANS WERE 16 YEARS OLD, I'M A MONKEY'S SIGNIFICANT OTHER.
LEMME TELL YA SOMETHING: I'VE SEEN OLDER KIDS AT A SIT'N'SPIN PARTY.
darb
I'M JUST GONNA LET HIM GO...
POMMEL HORSE?! TRY ***ROCKING*** HORSE!!!
SO YOU DIDN'T EVEN LIKE THE DIVING? I LOVE OLYMPIC DIVING.
LOOK, IF I WANT DIVING, I'LL WATCH A SOCCER GAME. **SHIN** GUARDS? PF. WORK ON SOME BUTT PADS.
I MEAN, IS THE REST OF THE WORLD, LIKE, COVERED IN A LAYER OF FOAM OR SOME-THING? 'CAUSE THOSE GUYS HIT THE FLOOR LIKE IT'S MAGNETIC ON STUPID HAIRCUTS.
darb
...DON'T MENTION RACE WALKING TO HIM...
DON'T WORRY.
I'D TAKE A POINTER FROM FOOSBALL AND STRAP ALL THOSE IDIOTS TO A BIG POLE. *TRY TO FLOP* ***NOW***, RIVALDO!
OK, SO YOU DON'T LIKE THE SUMMER OLYMPICS. WHAT ABOUT THE WINTER ONES?
WELL... AT LEAST SOME OF THOSE SPORTS CAN KILL YOU... THAT'S INTERESTING.
THEIR NAMES GIVE 'EM AWAY... *LUGE YOUR LIFE... SLALOM INTO A TREE...* AND WHO INVENTED SKI JUMPING? DR. KEVORKIAN? MENTAL.
SO YOU LIKE THE WINTER OLYMPICS?
ROBERT... THE WINTER OLYMPICS ARE LIKE A LIBERAL WITH A BASEBALL BAT: YOU MAY NOT LIKE HIM, BUT YOU HAVE TO RESPECT HIM.
darb

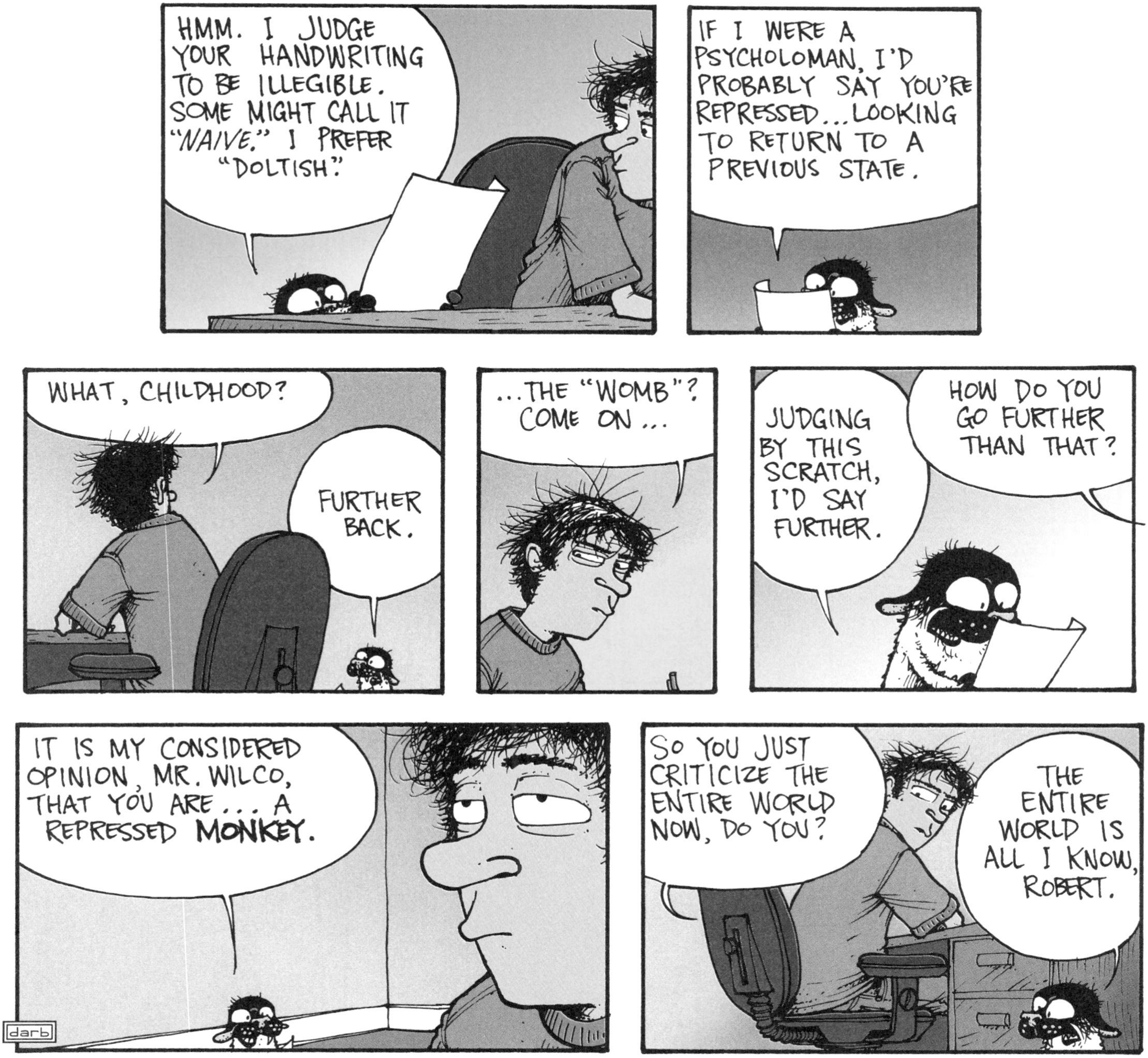
HMM. I JUDGE YOUR HANDWRITING TO BE ILLEGIBLE. SOME MIGHT CALL IT "*NAIVE*." I PREFER "DOLTISH."
IF I WERE A PSYCHOLOMAN, I'D PROBABLY SAY YOU'RE REPRESSED... LOOKING TO RETURN TO A PREVIOUS STATE.
WHAT, CHILDHOOD?
FURTHER BACK.
...THE "WOMB"? COME ON...
JUDGING BY THIS SCRATCH, I'D SAY FURTHER.
HOW DO YOU GO FURTHER THAN THAT?
IT IS MY CONSIDERED OPINION, MR. WILCO, THAT YOU ARE... A REPRESSED **MONKEY**.
darb
SO YOU JUST CRITICIZE THE ENTIRE WORLD NOW, DO YOU?
THE ENTIRE WORLD IS ALL I KNOW, ROBERT.

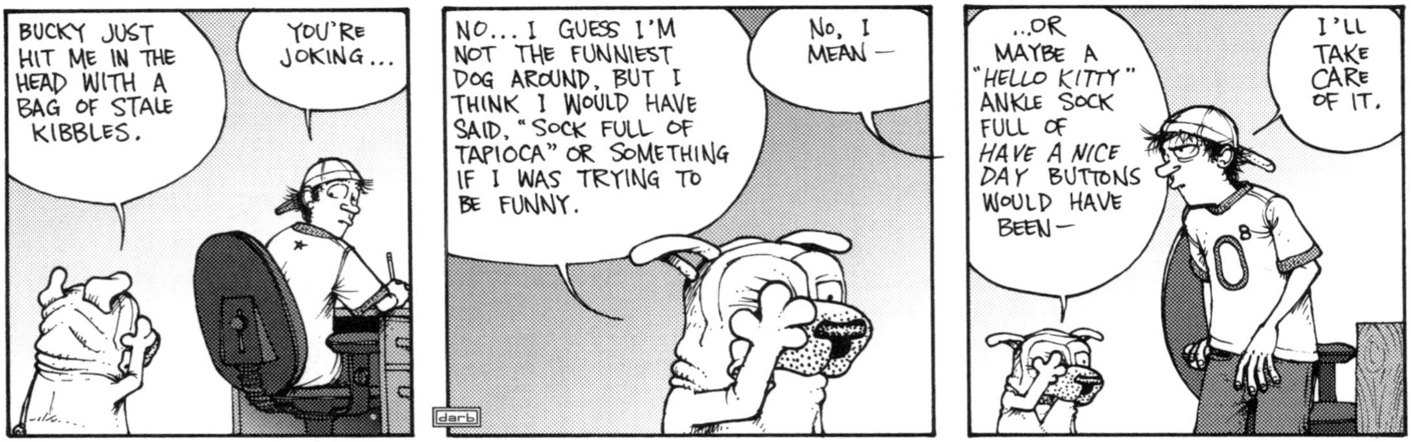
BUCKY JUST HIT ME IN THE HEAD WITH A BAG OF STALE KIBBLES.
YOU'RE JOKING...
NO... I GUESS I'M NOT THE FUNNIEST DOG AROUND, BUT I THINK I WOULD HAVE SAID, "SOCK FULL OF TAPIOCA" OR SOMETHING IF I WAS TRYING TO BE FUNNY.
NO, I MEAN—
...OR MAYBE A "HELLO KITTY" ANKLE SOCK FULL OF HAVE A NICE DAY BUTTONS WOULD HAVE BEEN—
I'LL TAKE CARE OF IT.

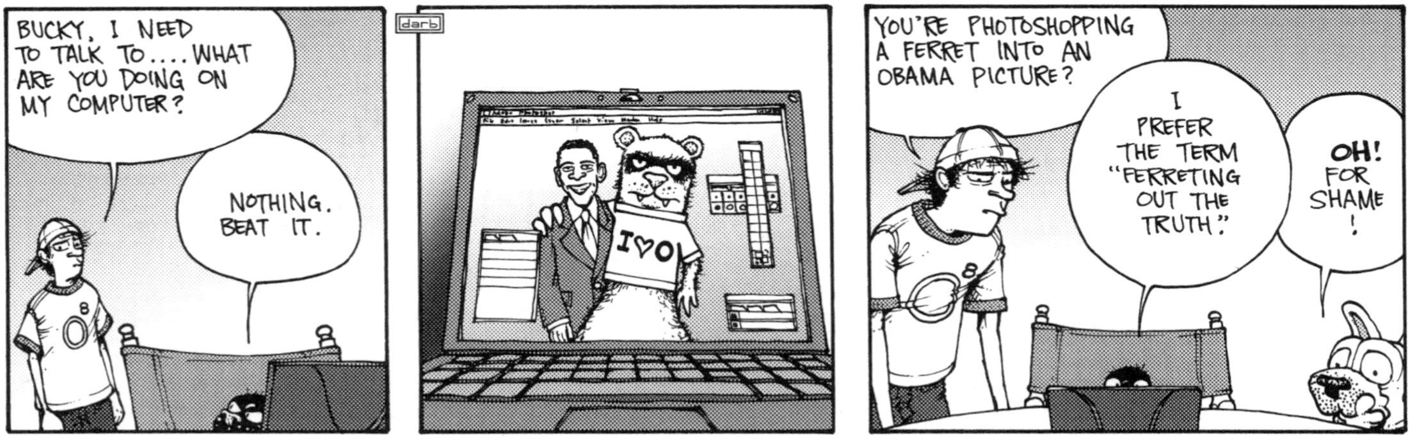
BUCKY, I NEED TO TALK TO.... WHAT ARE YOU DOING ON MY COMPUTER?
NOTHING. BEAT IT.
I♡O
YOU'RE PHOTOSHOPPING A FERRET INTO AN OBAMA PICTURE?
I PREFER THE TERM "FERRETING OUT THE TRUTH."
OH! FOR SHAME!

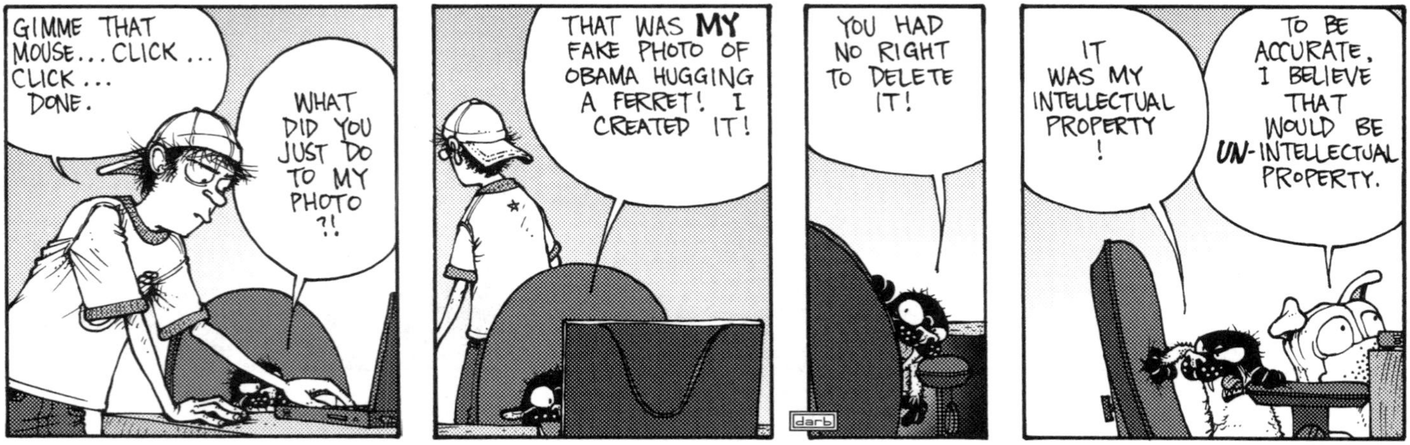
GIMME THAT MOUSE... CLICK... CLICK... DONE.
WHAT DID YOU JUST DO TO MY PHOTO?!
THAT WAS MY FAKE PHOTO OF OBAMA HUGGING A FERRET! I CREATED IT!
YOU HAD NO RIGHT TO DELETE IT!
IT WAS MY INTELLECTUAL PROPERTY!
TO BE ACCURATE, I BELIEVE THAT WOULD BE UN-INTELLECTUAL PROPERTY.

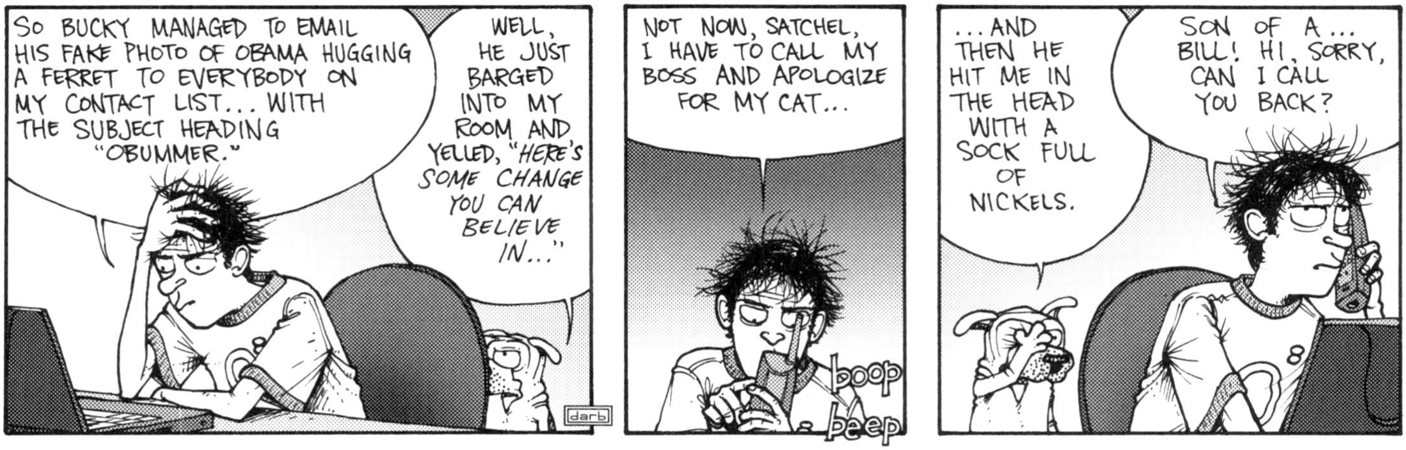
SO BUCKY MANAGED TO EMAIL HIS FAKE PHOTO OF OBAMA HUGGING A FERRET TO EVERYBODY ON MY CONTACT LIST... WITH THE SUBJECT HEADING "OBUMMER."
WELL, HE JUST BARGED INTO MY ROOM AND YELLED, "HERE'S SOME CHANGE YOU CAN BELIEVE IN..."
NOT NOW, SATCHEL, I HAVE TO CALL MY BOSS AND APOLOGIZE FOR MY CAT...
boop
beep
...AND THEN HE HIT ME IN THE HEAD WITH A SOCK FULL OF NICKELS.
SON OF A... BILL! HI, SORRY, CAN I CALL YOU BACK?
darb

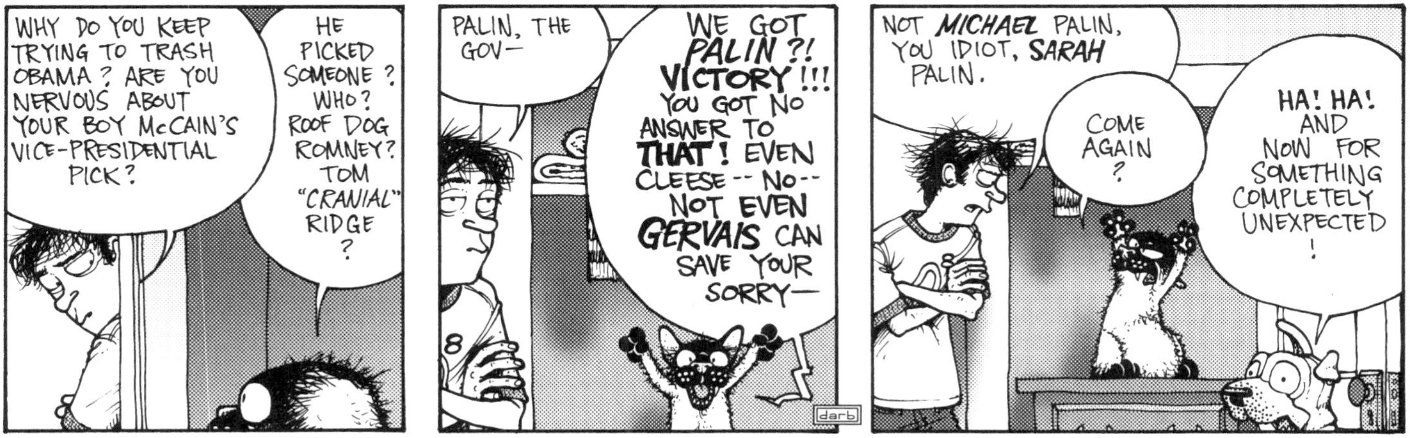
WHY DO YOU KEEP TRYING TO TRASH OBAMA? ARE YOU NERVOUS ABOUT YOUR BOY McCAIN'S VICE-PRESIDENTIAL PICK?
HE PICKED SOMEONE? WHO? ROOF DOG ROMNEY? TOM "CRANIAL" RIDGE?
PALIN, THE GOV—
WE GOT PALIN?! VICTORY!!! YOU GOT NO ANSWER TO THAT! EVEN CLEESE-- NO-- NOT EVEN GERVAIS CAN SAVE YOUR SORRY—
darb
NOT MICHAEL PALIN, YOU IDIOT, SARAH PALIN.
COME AGAIN?
HA! HA! AND NOW FOR SOMETHING COMPLETELY UNEXPECTED!

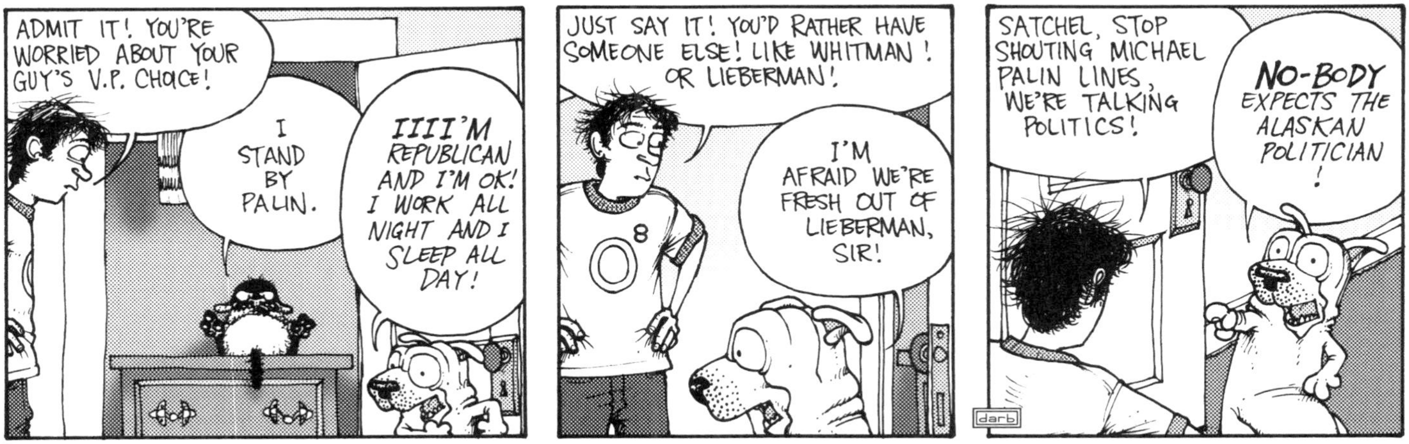
ADMIT IT! YOU'RE WORRIED ABOUT YOUR GUY'S V.P. CHOICE!
I STAND BY PALIN.
IIII'M REPUBLICAN AND I'M OK! I WORK ALL NIGHT AND I SLEEP ALL DAY!
JUST SAY IT! YOU'D RATHER HAVE SOMEONE ELSE! LIKE WHITMAN! OR LIEBERMAN!
I'M AFRAID WE'RE FRESH OUT OF LIEBERMAN, SIR!
SATCHEL, STOP SHOUTING MICHAEL PALIN LINES, WE'RE TALKING POLITICS!
NO-BODY EXPECTS THE ALASKAN POLITICIAN!
darb

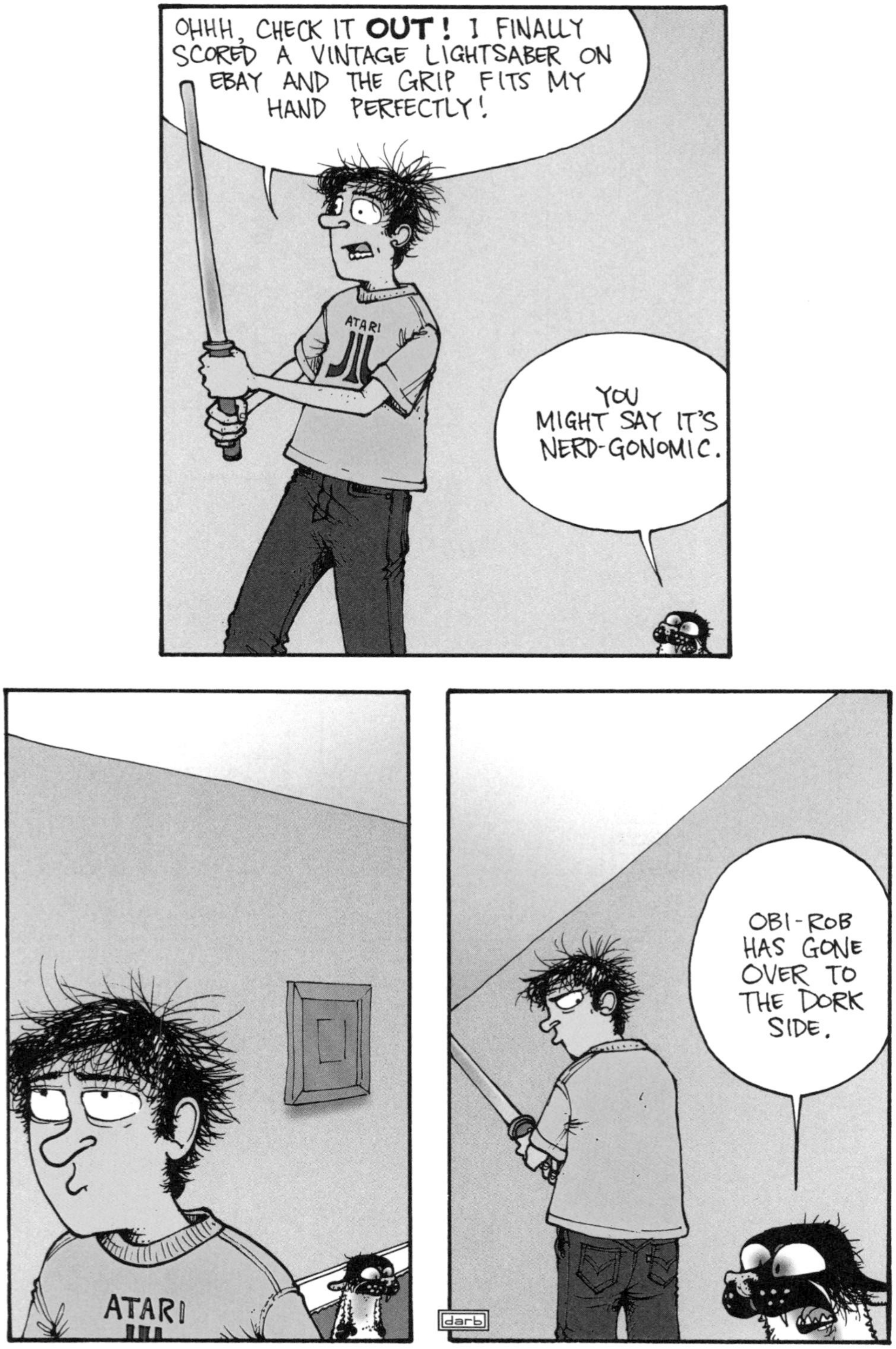
OHHH, CHECK IT **OUT!** I FINALLY SCORED A VINTAGE LIGHTSABER ON EBAY AND THE GRIP FITS MY HAND PERFECTLY!
YOU MIGHT SAY IT'S NERD-GONOMIC.
ATARI
ATARI
OBI-ROB HAS GONE OVER TO THE DORK SIDE.
darb

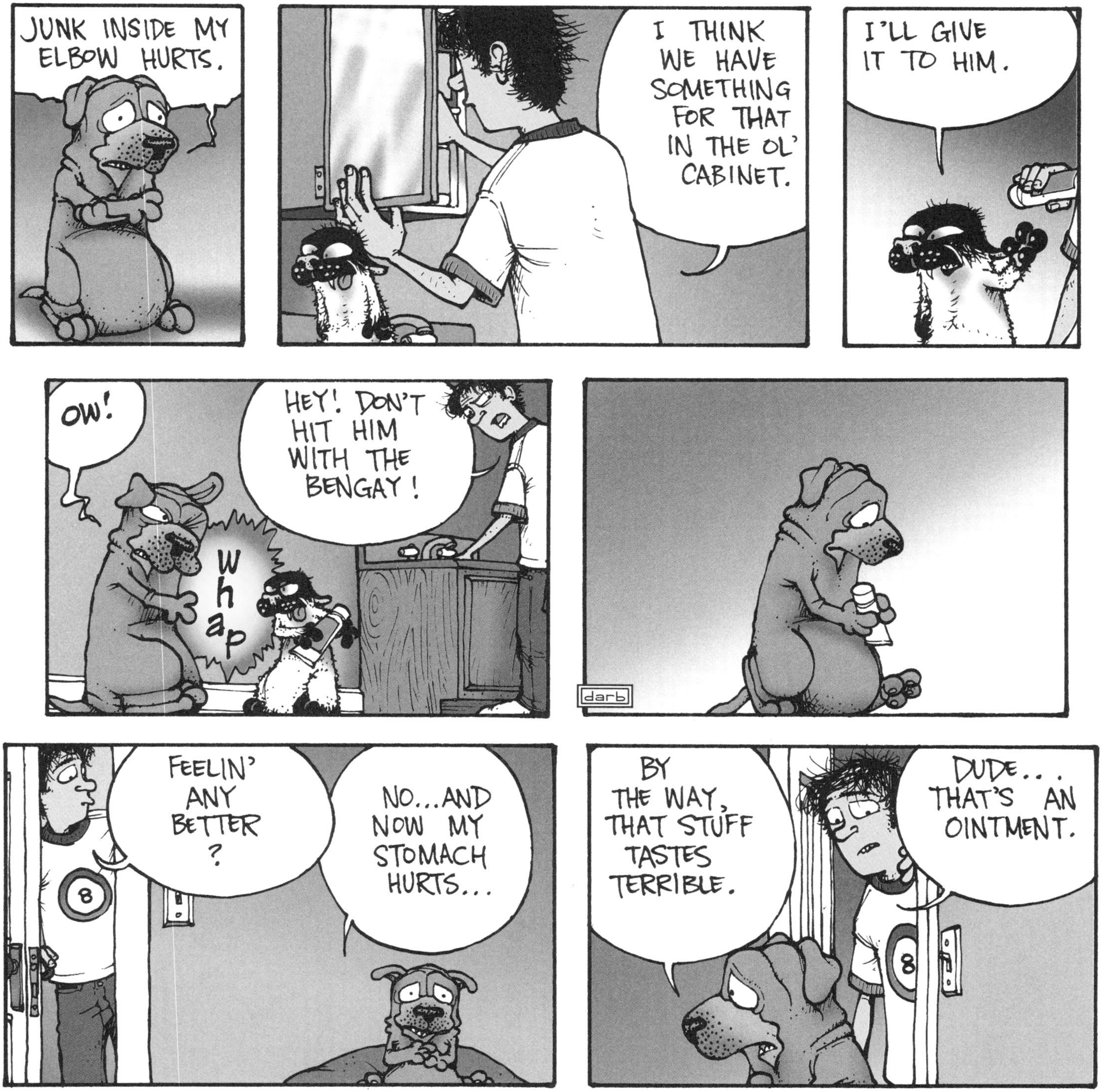
JUNK INSIDE MY ELBOW HURTS.
I THINK WE HAVE SOMETHING FOR THAT IN THE OL' CABINET.
I'LL GIVE IT TO HIM.
OW!
HEY! DON'T HIT HIM WITH THE BENGAY!
Whap
darb
FEELIN' ANY BETTER ?
NO...AND NOW MY STOMACH HURTS...
BY THE WAY, THAT STUFF TASTES TERRIBLE.
DUDE... THAT'S AN OINTMENT.

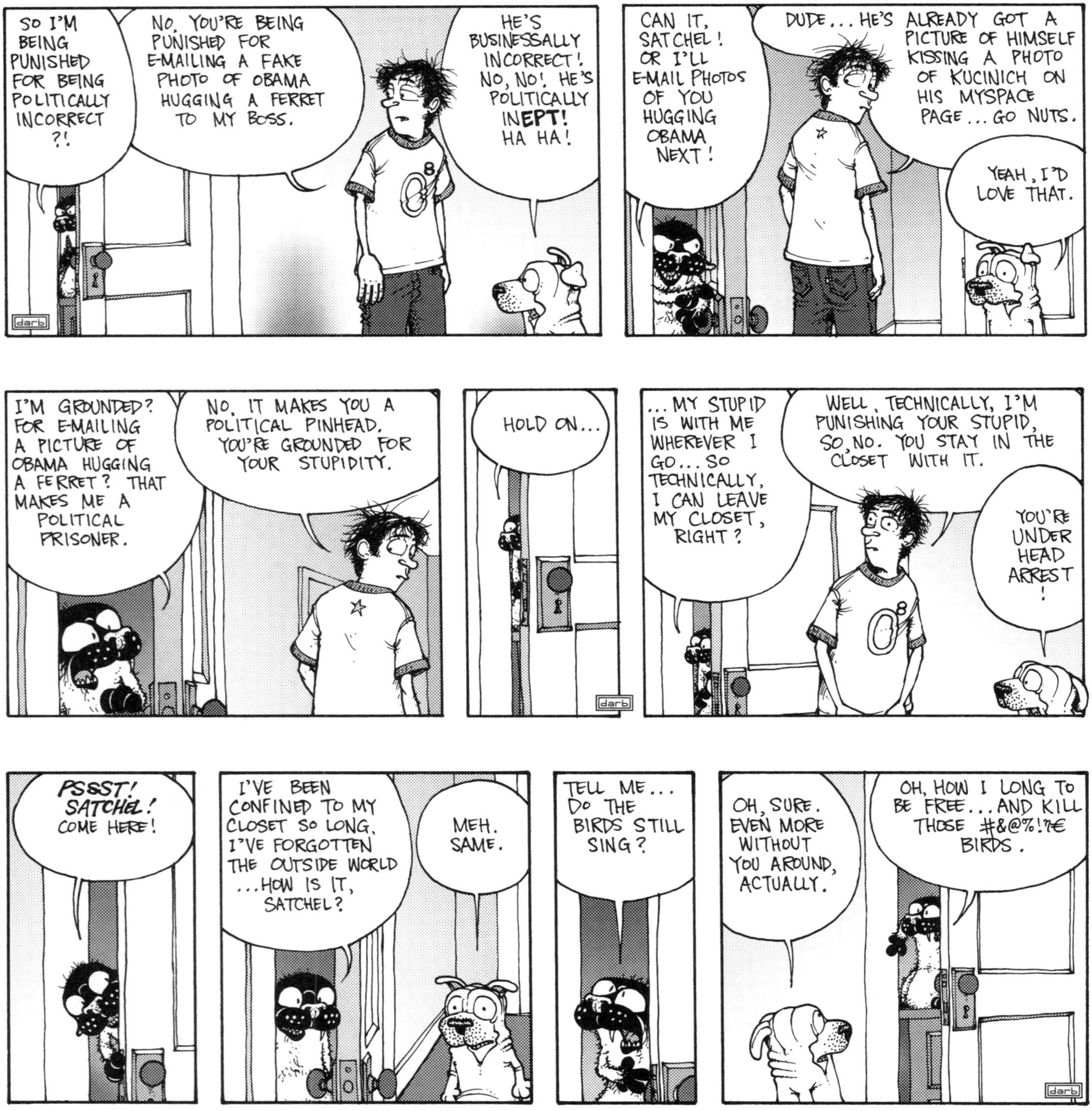
SO I'M BEING PUNISHED FOR BEING POLITICALLY INCORRECT ?!
NO, YOU'RE BEING PUNISHED FOR E-MAILING A FAKE PHOTO OF OBAMA HUGGING A FERRET TO MY BOSS.
HE'S BUSINESSALLY INCORRECT! NO, NO! HE'S POLITICALLY INEPT! HA HA!
darb
CAN IT, SATCHEL! OR I'LL E-MAIL PHOTOS OF YOU HUGGING OBAMA NEXT!
DUDE... HE'S ALREADY GOT A PICTURE OF HIMSELF KISSING A PHOTO OF KUCINICH ON HIS MYSPACE PAGE... GO NUTS.
YEAH, I'D LOVE THAT.
I'M GROUNDED? FOR E-MAILING A PICTURE OF OBAMA HUGGING A FERRET? THAT MAKES ME A POLITICAL PRISONER.
NO, IT MAKES YOU A POLITICAL PINHEAD. YOU'RE GROUNDED FOR YOUR STUPIDITY.
HOLD ON...
darb
...MY STUPID IS WITH ME WHEREVER I GO... SO TECHNICALLY, I CAN LEAVE MY CLOSET, RIGHT?
WELL, TECHNICALLY, I'M PUNISHING YOUR STUPID, SO, NO. YOU STAY IN THE CLOSET WITH IT.
YOU'RE UNDER HEAD ARREST!
PSSST! SATCHEL! COME HERE!
I'VE BEEN CONFINED TO MY CLOSET SO LONG, I'VE FORGOTTEN THE OUTSIDE WORLD ...HOW IS IT, SATCHEL?
MEH. SAME.
TELL ME... DO THE BIRDS STILL SING?
OH, SURE. EVEN MORE WITHOUT YOU AROUND, ACTUALLY.
OH, HOW I LONG TO BE FREE... AND KILL THOSE #&@%!?€ BIRDS.
darb

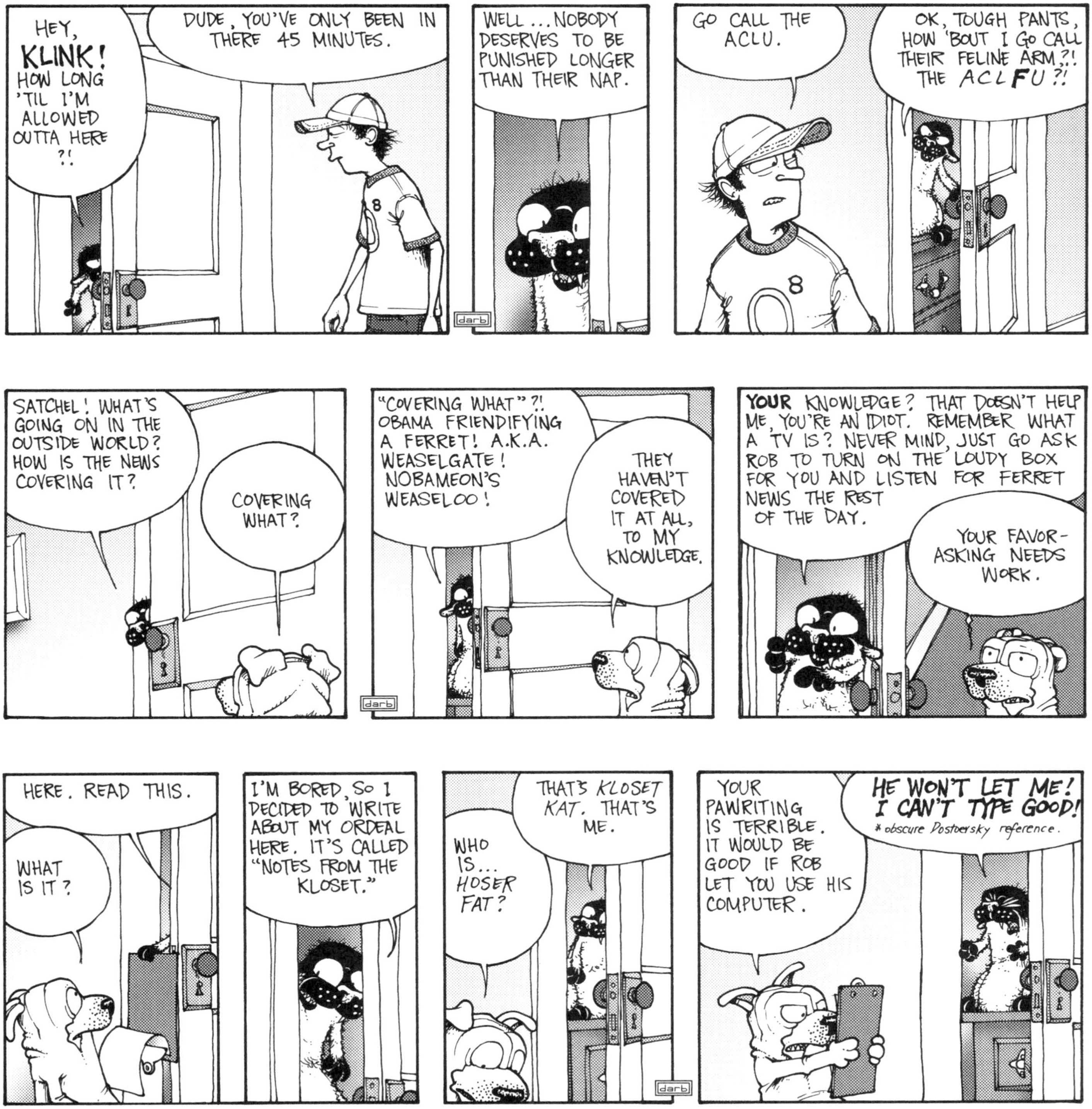
HEY, KLINK! HOW LONG 'TIL I'M ALLOWED OUTTA HERE ?!
DUDE, YOU'VE ONLY BEEN IN THERE 45 MINUTES.
WELL... NOBODY DESERVES TO BE PUNISHED LONGER THAN THEIR NAP.
GO CALL THE ACLU.
OK, TOUGH PANTS, HOW 'BOUT I GO CALL THEIR FELINE ARM ?! THE ACLFU ?!
SATCHEL! WHAT'S GOING ON IN THE OUTSIDE WORLD? HOW IS THE NEWS COVERING IT?
COVERING WHAT?
"COVERING WHAT"?! OBAMA FRIENDIFYING A FERRET! A.K.A. WEASELGATE! NOBAMEON'S WEASELOO!
THEY HAVEN'T COVERED IT AT ALL, TO MY KNOWLEDGE.
YOUR KNOWLEDGE? THAT DOESN'T HELP ME, YOU'RE AN IDIOT. REMEMBER WHAT A TV IS? NEVER MIND, JUST GO ASK ROB TO TURN ON THE LOUDY BOX FOR YOU AND LISTEN FOR FERRET NEWS THE REST OF THE DAY.
YOUR FAVOR-ASKING NEEDS WORK.
HERE. READ THIS.
WHAT IS IT?
I'M BORED, SO I DECIDED TO WRITE ABOUT MY ORDEAL HERE. IT'S CALLED "NOTES FROM THE KLOSET."
WHO IS... HOSER FAT?
THAT'S KLOSET KAT. THAT'S ME.
YOUR PAWRITING IS TERRIBLE. IT WOULD BE GOOD IF ROB LET YOU USE HIS COMPUTER.
HE WON'T LET ME! I CAN'T TYPE GOOD!
* obscure Dostoevsky reference.

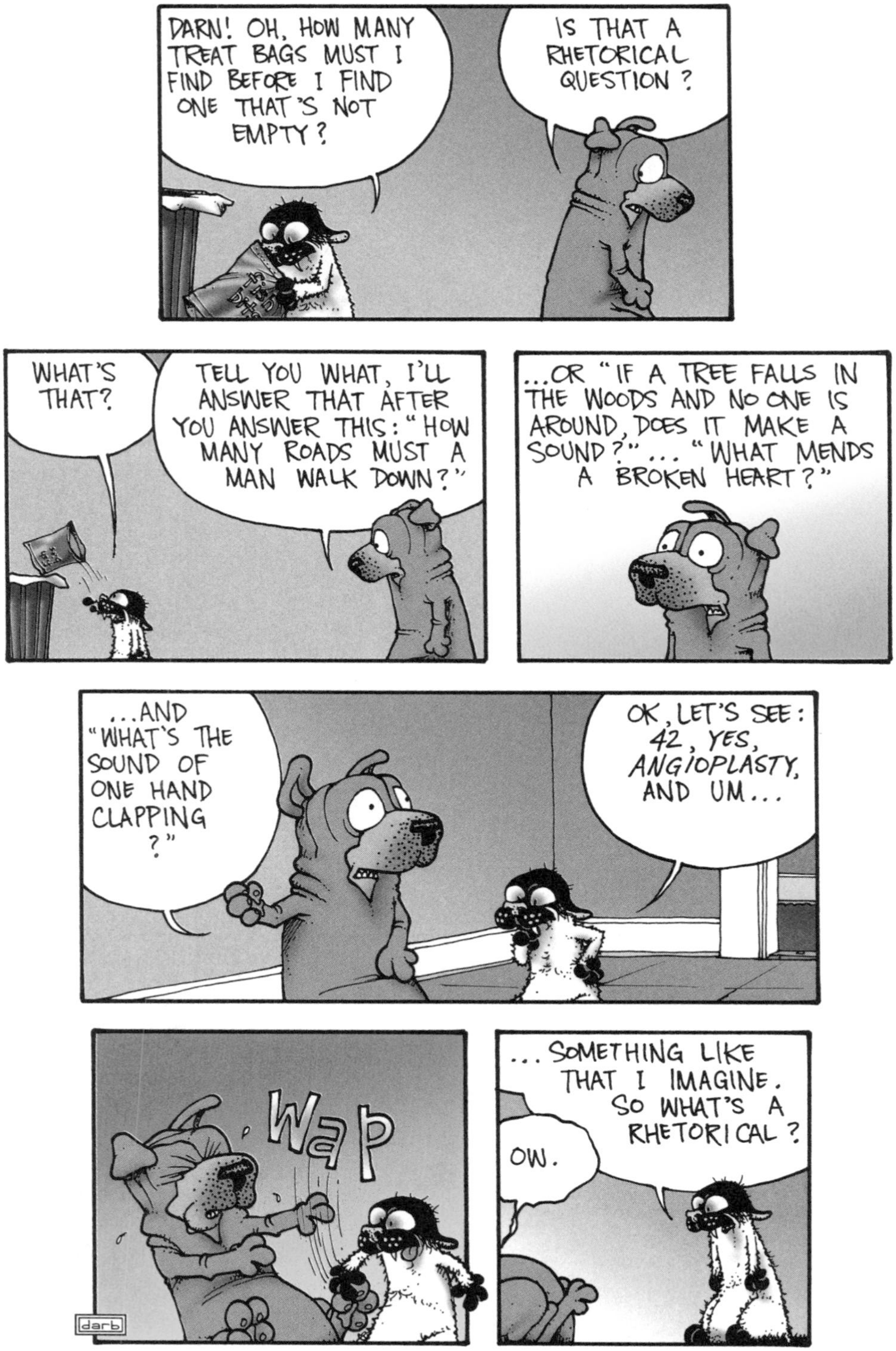
DARN! OH, HOW MANY TREAT BAGS MUST I FIND BEFORE I FIND ONE THAT'S NOT EMPTY?
IS THAT A RHETORICAL QUESTION?
WHAT'S THAT?
TELL YOU WHAT, I'LL ANSWER THAT AFTER YOU ANSWER THIS: "HOW MANY ROADS MUST A MAN WALK DOWN?"
...OR "IF A TREE FALLS IN THE WOODS AND NO ONE IS AROUND, DOES IT MAKE A SOUND?" ... "WHAT MENDS A BROKEN HEART?"
...AND "WHAT'S THE SOUND OF ONE HAND CLAPPING?"
OK, LET'S SEE: 42, *YES*, *ANGIOPLASTY*, AND UM...
WaP
darb
... SOMETHING LIKE THAT I IMAGINE. SO WHAT'S A RHETORICAL?
OW.

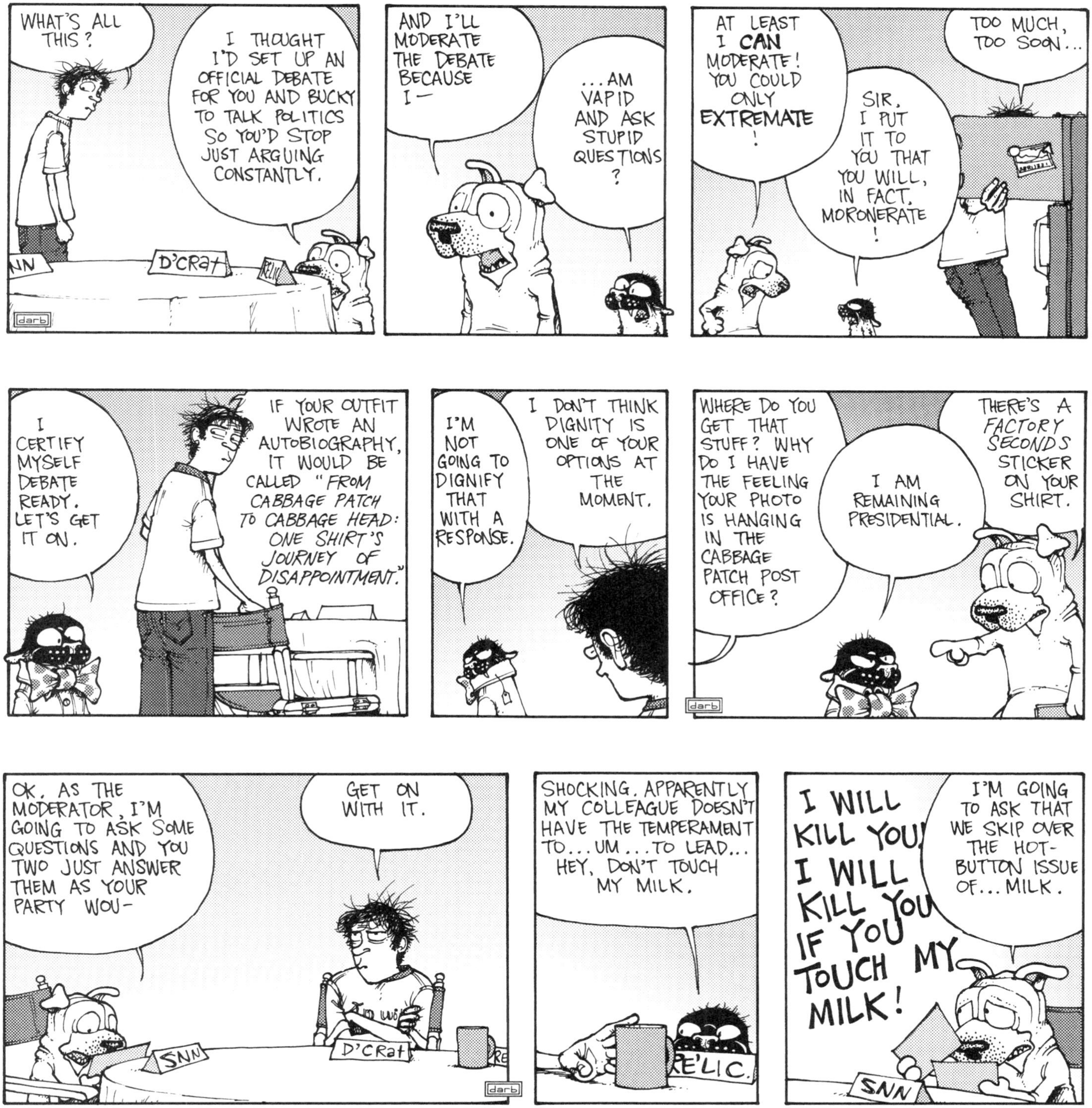
WHAT'S ALL THIS?
I THOUGHT I'D SET UP AN OFFICIAL DEBATE FOR YOU AND BUCKY TO TALK POLITICS SO YOU'D STOP JUST ARGUING CONSTANTLY.
D'CRAT
AND I'LL MODERATE THE DEBATE BECAUSE I—
...AM VAPID AND ASK STUPID QUESTIONS?
AT LEAST I **CAN** MODERATE! YOU COULD ONLY **EXTREMATE**!
SIR, I PUT IT TO YOU THAT YOU WILL, IN FACT, MORONERATE!
TOO MUCH, TOO SOON...
I CERTIFY MYSELF DEBATE READY. LET'S GET IT ON.
IF YOUR OUTFIT WROTE AN AUTOBIOGRAPHY, IT WOULD BE CALLED "*FROM CABBAGE PATCH TO CABBAGE HEAD: ONE SHIRT'S JOURNEY OF DISAPPOINTMENT.*"
I'M NOT GOING TO DIGNIFY THAT WITH A RESPONSE.
I DON'T THINK DIGNITY IS ONE OF YOUR OPTIONS AT THE MOMENT.
WHERE DO YOU GET THAT STUFF? WHY DO I HAVE THE FEELING YOUR PHOTO IS HANGING IN THE CABBAGE PATCH POST OFFICE?
I AM REMAINING PRESIDENTIAL.
THERE'S A *FACTORY SECONDS* STICKER ON YOUR SHIRT.
OK, AS THE MODERATOR, I'M GOING TO ASK SOME QUESTIONS AND YOU TWO JUST ANSWER THEM AS YOUR PARTY WOU-
GET ON WITH IT.
SNN
D'CRAT
SHOCKING. APPARENTLY MY COLLEAGUE DOESN'T HAVE THE TEMPERAMENT TO... UM... TO LEAD... HEY, DON'T TOUCH MY MILK.
RE'LIC.
I WILL KILL YOU! I WILL KILL YOU IF YOU TOUCH MY MILK!
I'M GOING TO ASK THAT WE SKIP OVER THE HOT-BUTTON ISSUE OF... MILK.
SNN

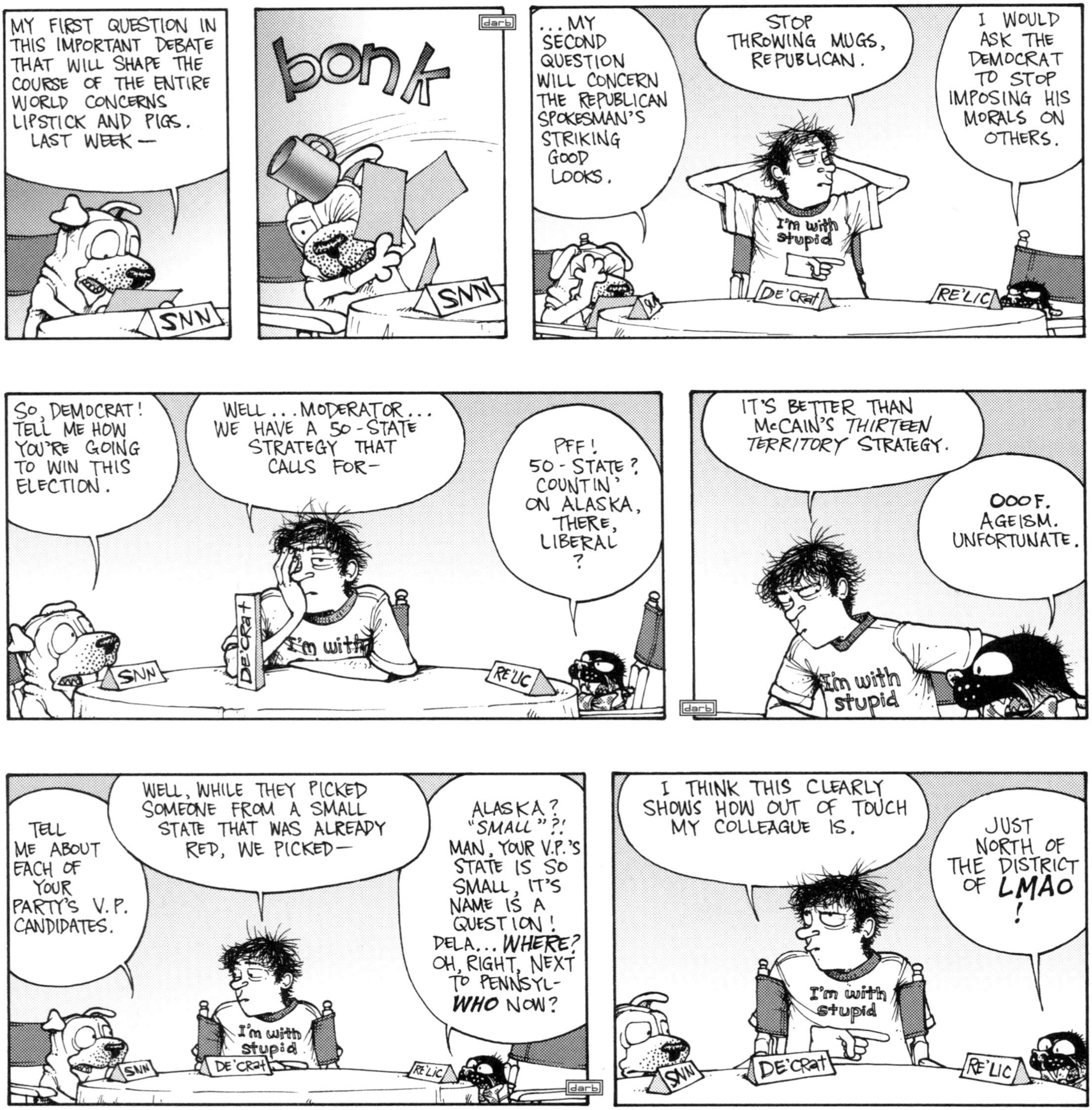
MY FIRST QUESTION IN THIS IMPORTANT DEBATE THAT WILL SHAPE THE COURSE OF THE ENTIRE WORLD CONCERNS LIPSTICK AND PIGS. LAST WEEK—
SNN
bonk
SNN
. . . MY SECOND QUESTION WILL CONCERN THE REPUBLICAN SPOKESMAN'S STRIKING GOOD LOOKS.
STOP THROWING MUGS, REPUBLICAN.
I WOULD ASK THE DEMOCRAT TO STOP IMPOSING HIS MORALS ON OTHERS.
I'm with stupid
DE'CRAT
RE'LIC
SO, DEMOCRAT! TELL ME HOW YOU'RE GOING TO WIN THIS ELECTION.
WELL . . . MODERATOR . . . WE HAVE A 50-STATE STRATEGY THAT CALLS FOR—
PFF! 50-STATE? COUNTIN' ON ALASKA, THERE, LIBERAL?
SNN
DE'CRAT
I'm with
RE'LIC
IT'S BETTER THAN McCAIN'S *THIRTEEN TERRITORY* STRATEGY.
OOOF. AGEISM. UNFORTUNATE.
I'm with stupid
TELL ME ABOUT EACH OF YOUR PARTY'S V.P. CANDIDATES.
WELL, WHILE THEY PICKED SOMEONE FROM A SMALL STATE THAT WAS ALREADY RED, WE PICKED—
ALASKA? "*SMALL*"?! MAN, YOUR V.P.'S STATE IS SO SMALL, IT'S NAME IS A QUESTION! DELA... **WHERE?** OH, RIGHT, NEXT TO PENNSYL-**WHO** NOW?
I'm with stupid
SNN
DE'CRAT
RE'LIC
I THINK THIS CLEARLY SHOWS HOW OUT OF TOUCH MY COLLEAGUE IS.
JUST NORTH OF THE DISTRICT OF **LMAO**!
I'm with stupid
SNN
DE'CRAT
RE'LIC

HOW'S MY HAIR NOW? BETTER?
PERFECT! YOU'RE A CHICK MAGNET!
"CHICK MAGNET"? SORRY, BUT UNLESS YOU'RE HITTIN' ON EGGS WRAPPED IN IRON WIRE, KEEP COMBIN'.
I MEAN, IF YOU WERE MAGNETIC, YOU'D BE POINTING TOWARD *TRUE NERD*.
darb
ANYTHING ELSE?
WELL... I SUPPOSE SOME TYPES OF CHICKS MIGHT BE DRAWN TO YOU...
...HOMELY PIGEONS, FOR EXAMPLE. OR MOCKINGROBS... SLEAZ-A-DEES...
BEER-BELLIED WOODN'TPECKERS. REFLUX-THROATED HURLINGBIRDS. ...UM...
YOU DONE?
SATCHEL, YOU'RE SO UGLY, YOU CAN'T EVEN GET A DATE ON FLEA-BAY.
OK, SATCH. LET'S GO.
WHAT'D **I** DO?!

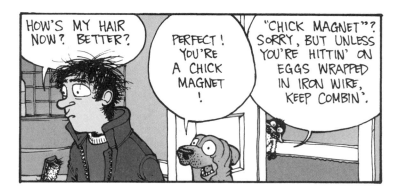

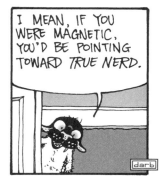

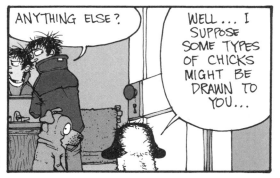

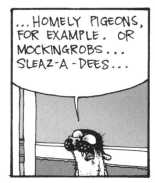

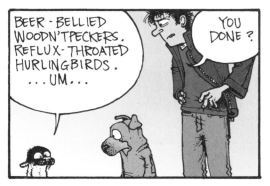

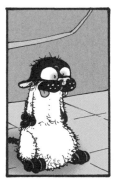

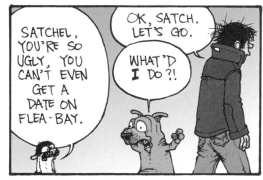

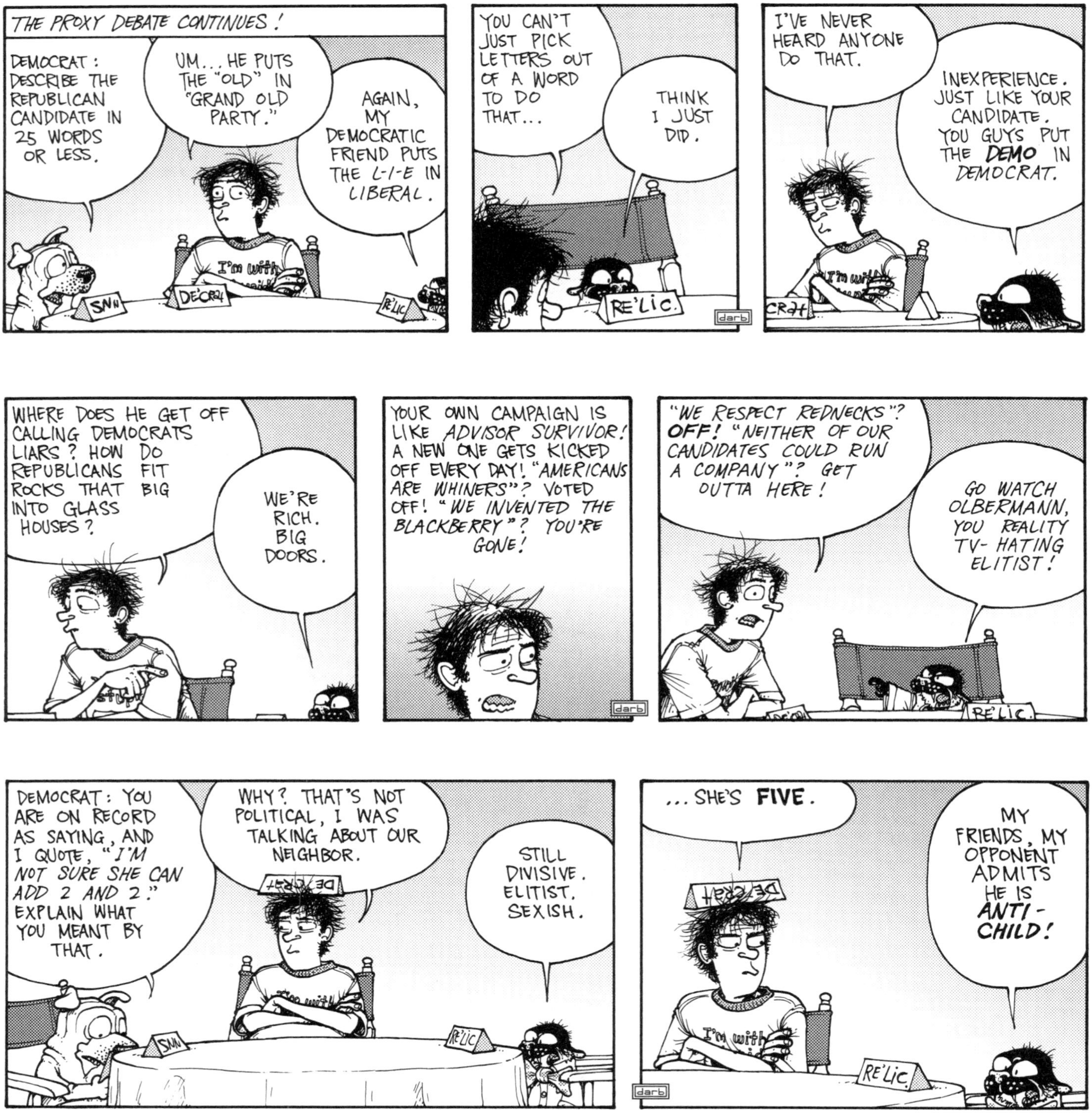
THE PROXY DEBATE CONTINUES!
DEMOCRAT: DESCRIBE THE REPUBLICAN CANDIDATE IN 25 WORDS OR LESS.
UM... HE PUTS THE "OLD" IN "GRAND OLD PARTY."
AGAIN, MY DEMOCRATIC FRIEND PUTS THE L-I-E IN LIBERAL.
YOU CAN'T JUST PICK LETTERS OUT OF A WORD TO DO THAT...
THINK I JUST DID.
RE'LIC.
I'VE NEVER HEARD ANYONE DO THAT.
INEXPERIENCE. JUST LIKE YOUR CANDIDATE. YOU GUYS PUT THE **DEMO** IN DEMOCRAT.
WHERE DOES HE GET OFF CALLING DEMOCRATS LIARS? HOW DO REPUBLICANS FIT ROCKS THAT BIG INTO GLASS HOUSES?
WE'RE RICH. BIG DOORS.
YOUR OWN CAMPAIGN IS LIKE *ADVISOR SURVIVOR!* A NEW ONE GETS KICKED OFF EVERY DAY! "*AMERICANS ARE WHINERS*"? VOTED OFF! "*WE INVENTED THE BLACKBERRY*"? *YOU'RE GONE!*
"*WE RESPECT REDNECKS*"? ***OFF!*** "*NEITHER OF OUR CANDIDATES COULD RUN A COMPANY*"? *GET OUTTA HERE!*
GO WATCH OLBERMANN, YOU REALITY TV-HATING ELITIST!
DEMOCRAT: YOU ARE ON RECORD AS SAYING, AND I QUOTE, "*I'M NOT SURE SHE CAN ADD 2 AND 2.*" EXPLAIN WHAT YOU MEANT BY THAT.
WHY? THAT'S NOT POLITICAL, I WAS TALKING ABOUT OUR NEIGHBOR.
STILL DIVISIVE. ELITIST. SEXISH.
... SHE'S **FIVE**.
MY FRIENDS, MY OPPONENT ADMITS HE IS ***ANTI-CHILD!***

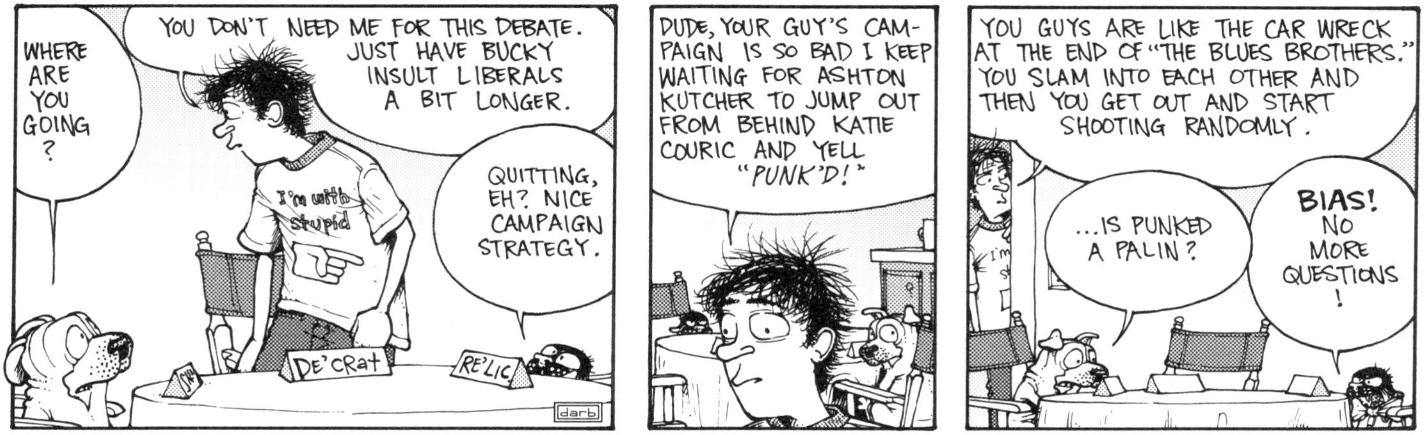
WHERE ARE YOU GOING?
YOU DON'T NEED ME FOR THIS DEBATE. JUST HAVE BUCKY INSULT LIBERALS A BIT LONGER.
I'm with stupid
DE'CRat
QUITTING, EH? NICE CAMPAIGN STRATEGY.
RE'LIC
darb
DUDE, YOUR GUY'S CAMPAIGN IS SO BAD I KEEP WAITING FOR ASHTON KUTCHER TO JUMP OUT FROM BEHIND KATIE COURIC AND YELL "*PUNK'D!*"
YOU GUYS ARE LIKE THE CAR WRECK AT THE END OF "THE BLUES BROTHERS." YOU SLAM INTO EACH OTHER AND THEN YOU GET OUT AND START SHOOTING RANDOMLY.
...IS PUNKED A PALIN?
BIAS! NO MORE QUESTIONS!

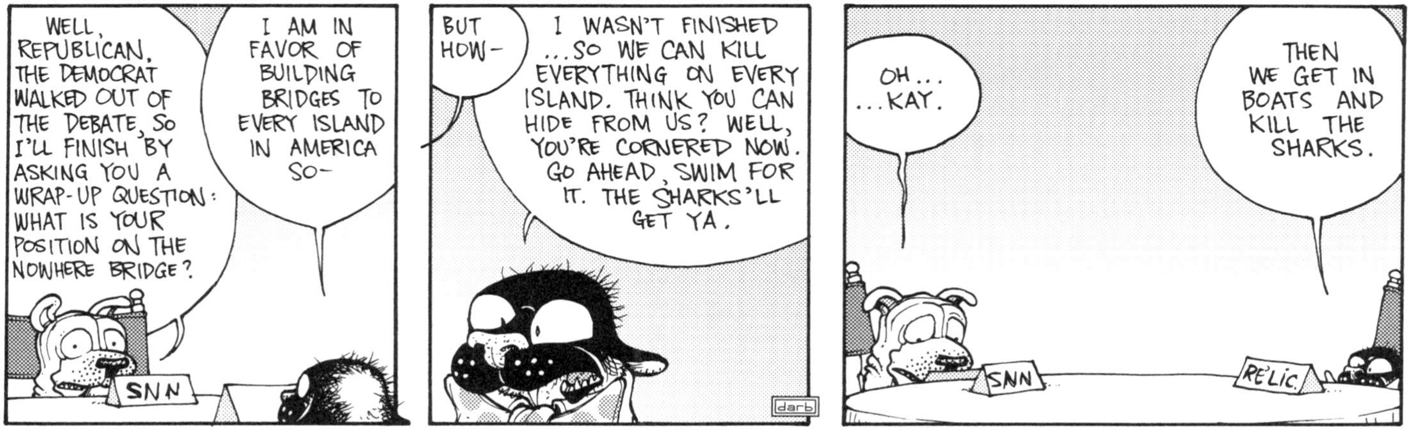
WELL, REPUBLICAN, THE DEMOCRAT WALKED OUT OF THE DEBATE, SO I'LL FINISH BY ASKING YOU A WRAP-UP QUESTION: WHAT IS YOUR POSITION ON THE NOWHERE BRIDGE?
I AM IN FAVOR OF BUILDING BRIDGES TO EVERY ISLAND IN AMERICA SO-
SNN
BUT HOW-
I WASN'T FINISHED ...SO WE CAN KILL EVERYTHING ON EVERY ISLAND. THINK YOU CAN HIDE FROM US? WELL, YOU'RE CORNERED NOW. GO AHEAD, SWIM FOR IT. THE SHARKS'LL GET YA.
darb
OH... ...KAY.
THEN WE GET IN BOATS AND KILL THE SHARKS.
SNN
RE'LIC

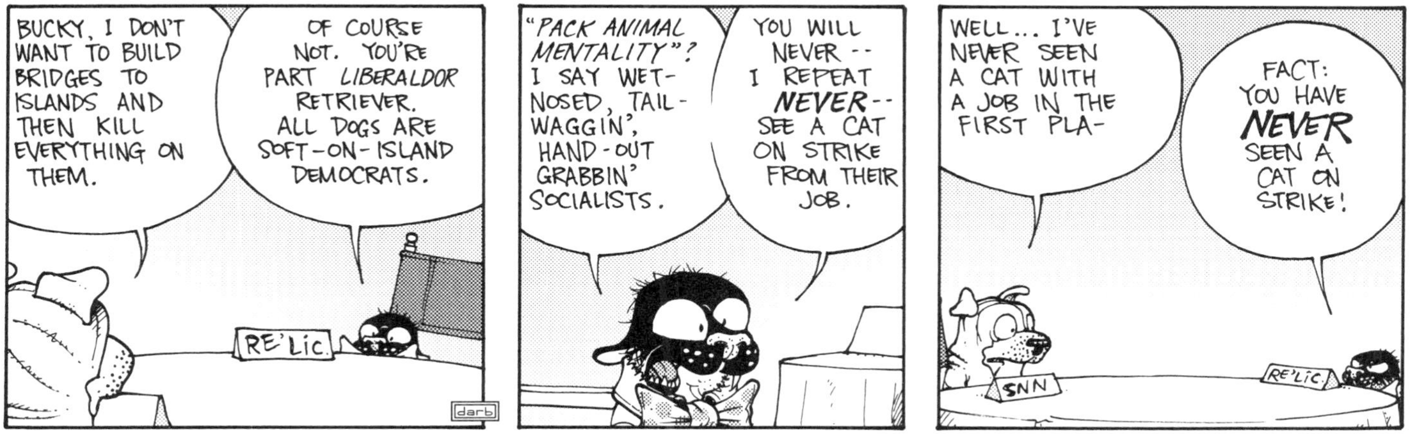
BUCKY, I DON'T WANT TO BUILD BRIDGES TO ISLANDS AND THEN KILL EVERYTHING ON THEM.
OF COURSE NOT. YOU'RE PART *LIBERALDOR* RETRIEVER. ALL DOGS ARE SOFT-ON-ISLAND DEMOCRATS.
RE'Lic
darb
"*PACK ANIMAL MENTALITY*"? I SAY WET-NOSED, TAIL-WAGGIN', HAND-OUT GRABBIN' SOCIALISTS.
YOU WILL NEVER -- I REPEAT ***NEVER*** -- SEE A CAT ON STRIKE FROM THEIR JOB.
WELL... I'VE NEVER SEEN A CAT WITH A JOB IN THE FIRST PLA-
FACT: YOU HAVE ***NEVER*** SEEN A CAT ON STRIKE!
SNN
RE'LIC

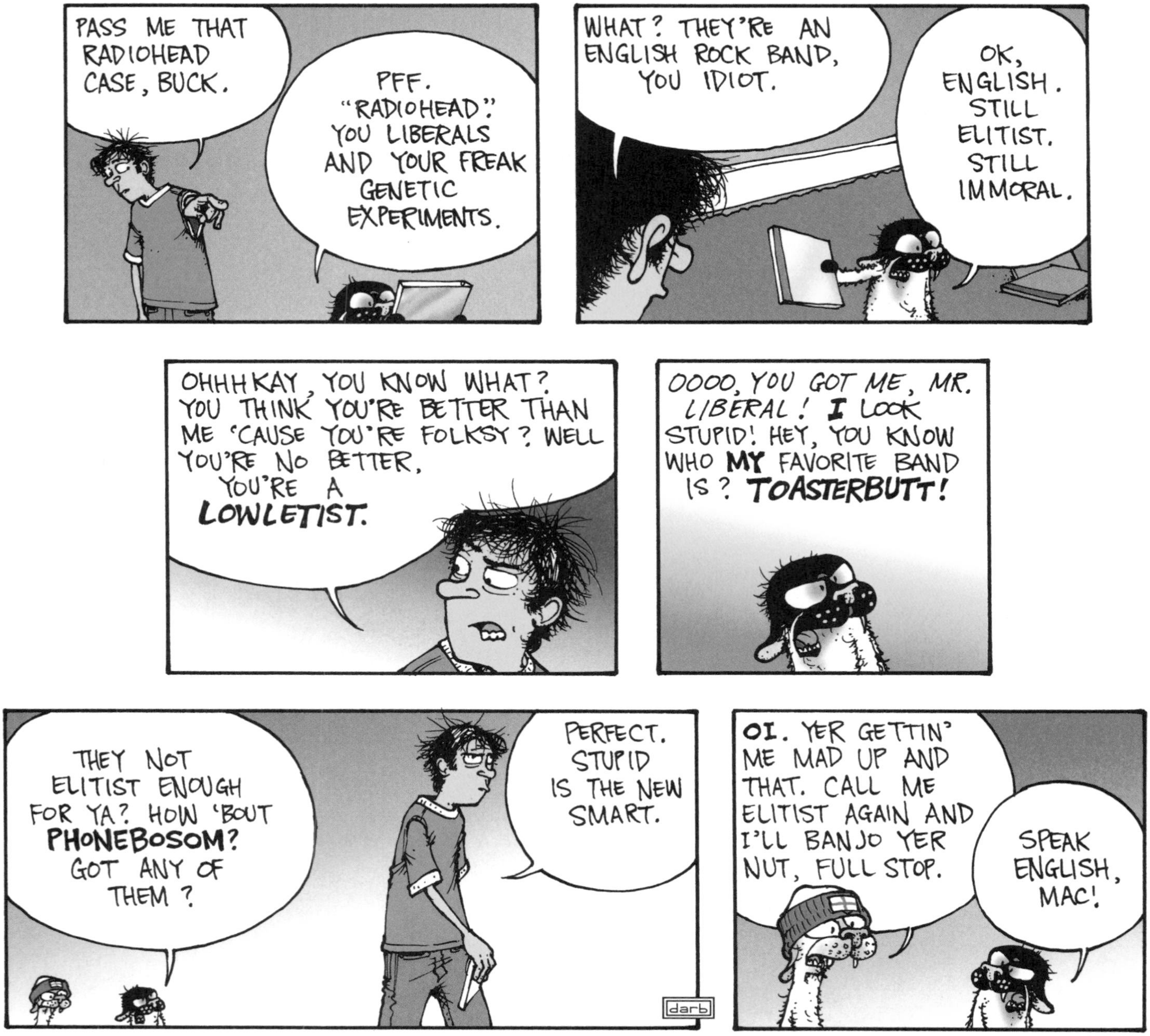
PASS ME THAT RADIOHEAD CASE, BUCK.
PFF. "RADIOHEAD." YOU LIBERALS AND YOUR FREAK GENETIC EXPERIMENTS.
WHAT? THEY'RE AN ENGLISH ROCK BAND, YOU IDIOT.
OK, ENGLISH. STILL ELITIST. STILL IMMORAL.
OHHHKAY, YOU KNOW WHAT? YOU THINK YOU'RE BETTER THAN ME 'CAUSE YOU'RE FOLKSY? WELL YOU'RE NO BETTER. YOU'RE A **LOWLETIST.**
OOOO, YOU GOT ME, MR. LIBERAL! **I** LOOK STUPID! HEY, YOU KNOW WHO **MY** FAVORITE BAND IS? ***TOASTERBUTT!***
THEY NOT ELITIST ENOUGH FOR YA? HOW 'BOUT **PHONEBOSOM?** GOT ANY OF THEM?
PERFECT. STUPID IS THE NEW SMART.
darb
OI. YER GETTIN' ME MAD UP AND THAT. CALL ME ELITIST AGAIN AND I'LL BANJO YER NUT, FULL STOP.
SPEAK ENGLISH, MAC!

WHAT'CHA WRITIN'?

A LIST OF EVERYONE WHO NEEDS TO BE SLAPPED UPSIDE THE HEAD.

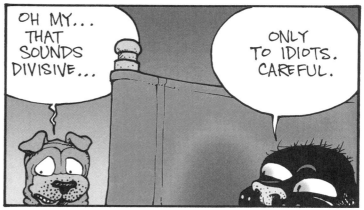

OH MY... THAT SOUNDS DIVISIVE...

ONLY TO IDIOTS. CAREFUL.

WHAT I AM PROPOSING IS A STANDARDIZED METHOD OF IDENTIFYING IDIOTS... *IDIOTIFICATION,* IF YOU WILL.

darb

THE PURPOSE OF MY HEAD SLAP WILL BE TWOFOLD: FIRST, TO AFFIX A STICKER IDENTIFYING THE SLAPEE AS AN IDIOT, A SORT OF IDIOT LETTER, IF YOU WILL, AND B: IT WILL AMUSE ME.

BUT HOW DO YOU **FIGURE OUT** WHO'S AN IDIOT? IT DOESN'T SOUND *DOABLE!*

INTERESTING. ARE YOU IMPASSIONED ABOUT THIS ENOUGH TO, SAY, RECITE AN ESSAY ABOUT YOUR FEELINGS ON PUBLIC RADIO?

YES...YES, I THINK I AM.

FAIR ENOUGH. UNFORTUNATELY, THAT WOULD EARN YOU A SLAP UPSIDE THE HEAD.

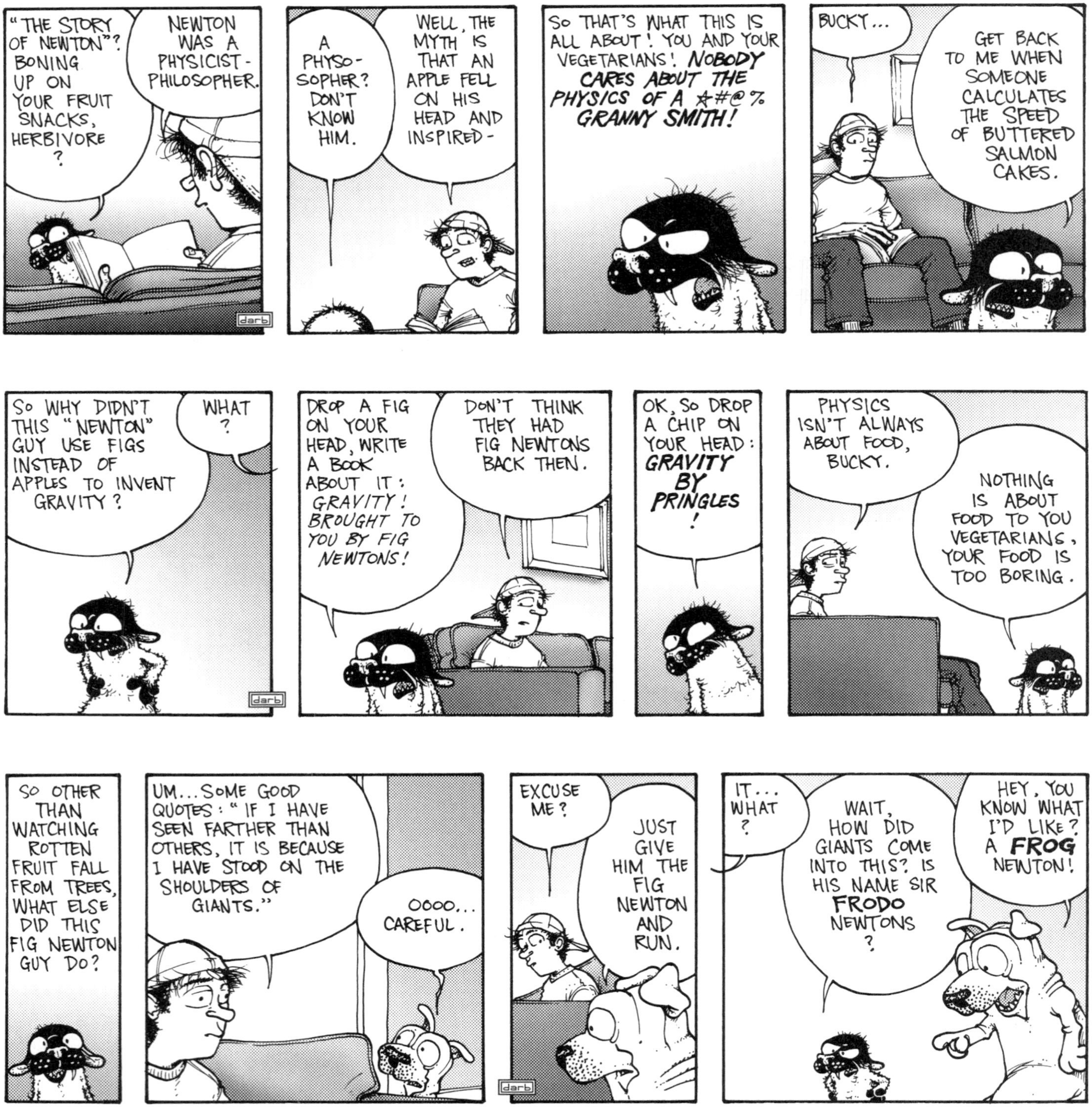
"THE STORY OF NEWTON"? BONING UP ON YOUR FRUIT SNACKS, HERBIVORE?
NEWTON WAS A PHYSICIST-PHILOSOPHER.
A PHYSO-SOPHER? DON'T KNOW HIM.
WELL, THE MYTH IS THAT AN APPLE FELL ON HIS HEAD AND INSPIRED-
SO THAT'S WHAT THIS IS ALL ABOUT! YOU AND YOUR VEGETARIANS! **NOBODY CARES ABOUT THE PHYSICS OF A ☆#@% GRANNY SMITH!**
BUCKY...
GET BACK TO ME WHEN SOMEONE CALCULATES THE SPEED OF BUTTERED SALMON CAKES.
darb
darb
SO WHY DIDN'T THIS "NEWTON" GUY USE FIGS INSTEAD OF APPLES TO INVENT GRAVITY?
WHAT?
DROP A FIG ON YOUR HEAD, WRITE A BOOK ABOUT IT: *GRAVITY! BROUGHT TO YOU BY FIG NEWTONS!*
DON'T THINK THEY HAD FIG NEWTONS BACK THEN.
OK, SO DROP A CHIP ON YOUR HEAD: **GRAVITY BY PRINGLES!**
PHYSICS ISN'T ALWAYS ABOUT FOOD, BUCKY.
NOTHING IS ABOUT FOOD TO YOU VEGETARIANS, YOUR FOOD IS TOO BORING.
darb
SO OTHER THAN WATCHING ROTTEN FRUIT FALL FROM TREES, WHAT ELSE DID THIS FIG NEWTON GUY DO?
UM... SOME GOOD QUOTES: "IF I HAVE SEEN FARTHER THAN OTHERS, IT IS BECAUSE I HAVE STOOD ON THE SHOULDERS OF GIANTS."
OOOO... CAREFUL.
EXCUSE ME?
JUST GIVE HIM THE FIG NEWTON AND RUN.
IT... WHAT?
WAIT, HOW DID GIANTS COME INTO THIS? IS HIS NAME SIR **FRODO** NEWTONS?
HEY, YOU KNOW WHAT I'D LIKE? A **FROG** NEWTON!
darb

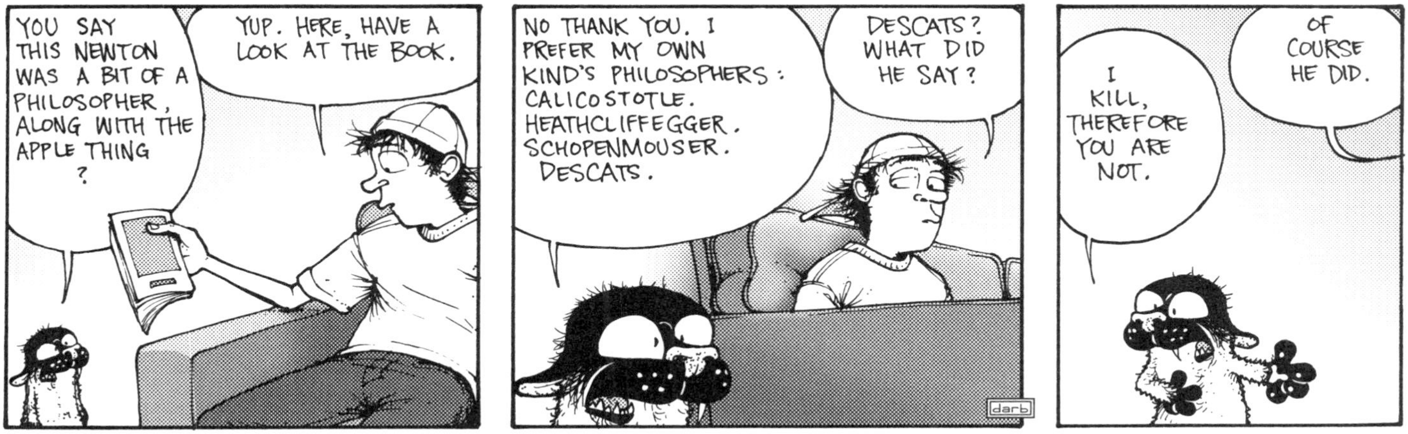
YOU SAY THIS NEWTON WAS A BIT OF A PHILOSOPHER, ALONG WITH THE APPLE THING ?
YUP. HERE, HAVE A LOOK AT THE BOOK.
NO THANK YOU. I PREFER MY OWN KIND'S PHILOSOPHERS: CALICOSTOTLE. HEATHCLIFFEGGER. SCHOPENMOUSER. DESCATS.
DESCATS? WHAT DID HE SAY?
darb
I KILL, THEREFORE YOU ARE NOT.
OF COURSE HE DID.

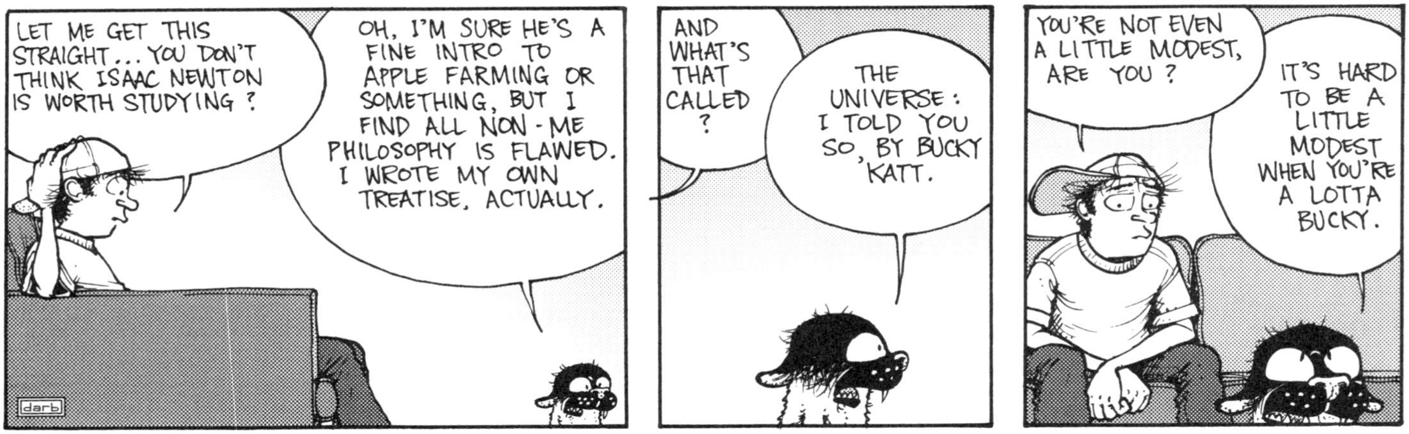
LET ME GET THIS STRAIGHT... YOU DON'T THINK ISAAC NEWTON IS WORTH STUDYING ?
OH, I'M SURE HE'S A FINE INTRO TO APPLE FARMING OR SOMETHING, BUT I FIND ALL NON-ME PHILOSOPHY IS FLAWED. I WROTE MY OWN TREATISE, ACTUALLY.
darb
AND WHAT'S THAT CALLED ?
THE UNIVERSE: I TOLD YOU SO, BY BUCKY KATT.
YOU'RE NOT EVEN A LITTLE MODEST, ARE YOU ?
IT'S HARD TO BE A LITTLE MODEST WHEN YOU'RE A LOTTA BUCKY.

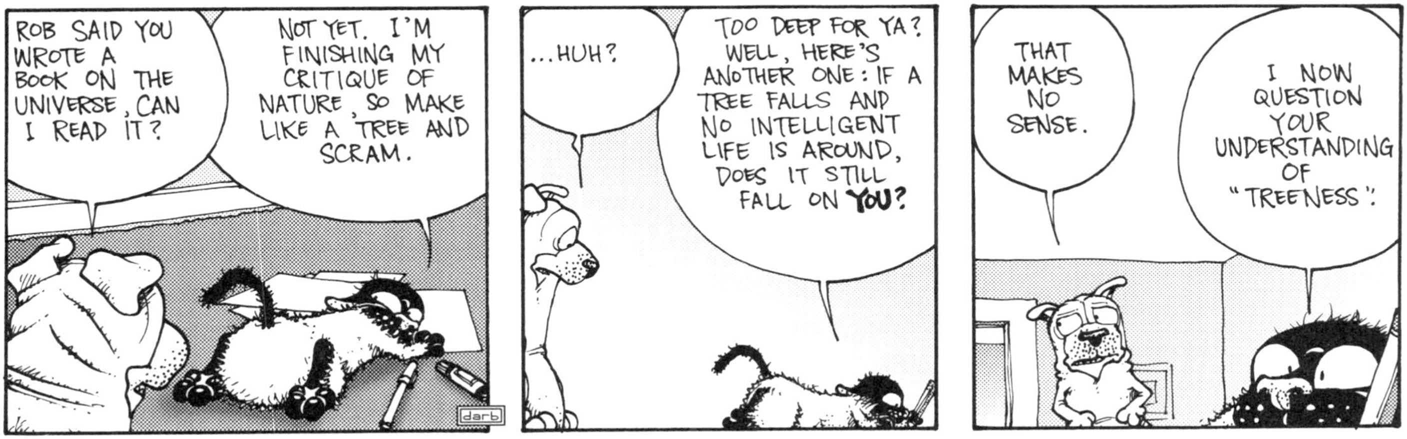
ROB SAID YOU WROTE A BOOK ON THE UNIVERSE, CAN I READ IT?
NOT YET. I'M FINISHING MY CRITIQUE OF NATURE, SO MAKE LIKE A TREE AND SCRAM.
darb
...HUH?
TOO DEEP FOR YA? WELL, HERE'S ANOTHER ONE: IF A TREE FALLS AND NO INTELLIGENT LIFE IS AROUND, DOES IT STILL FALL ON **YOU**?
THAT MAKES NO SENSE.
I NOW QUESTION YOUR UNDERSTANDING OF "TREENESS".

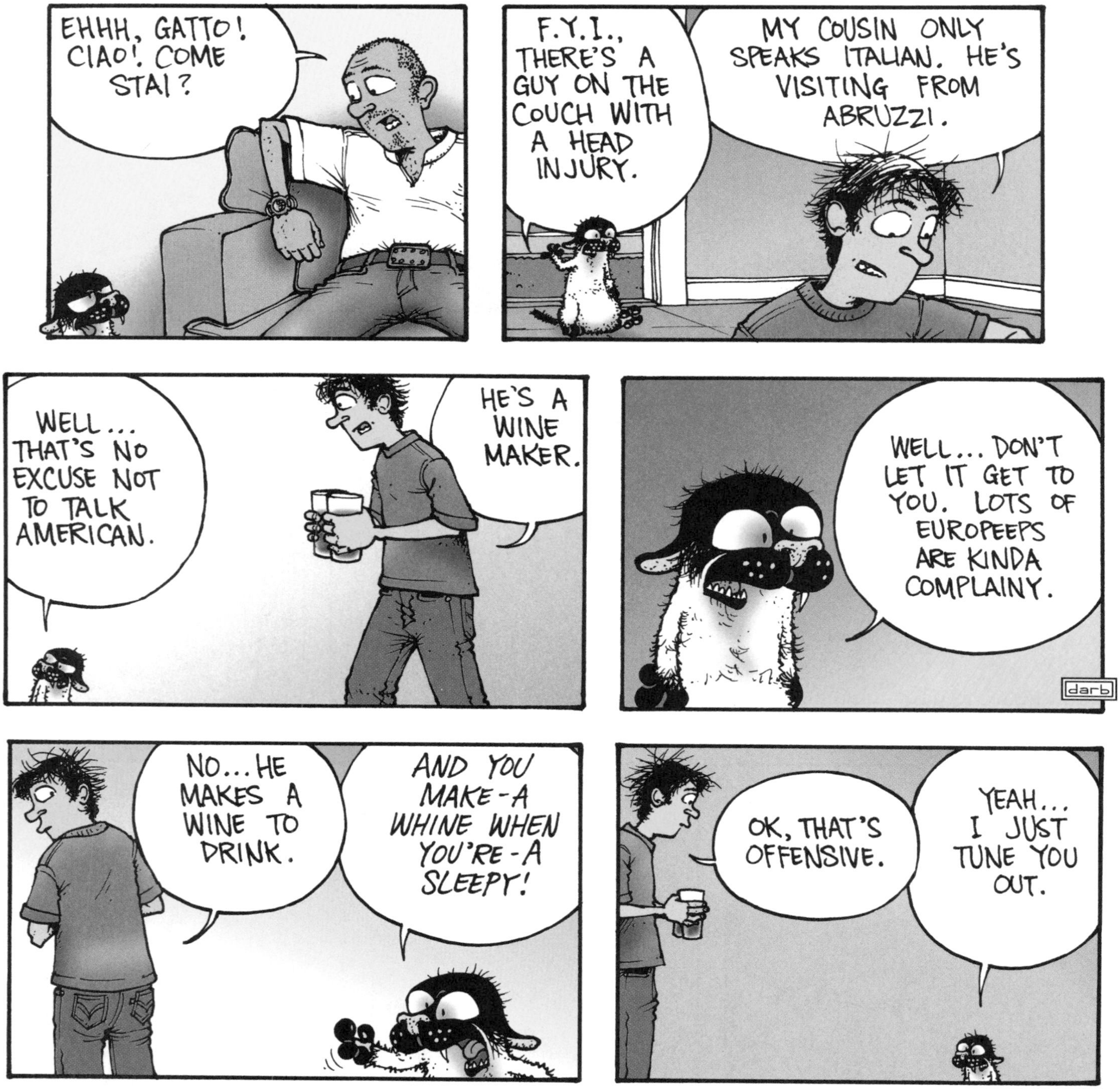
EHHH, GATTO! CIAO! COME STAI?
F.Y.I., THERE'S A GUY ON THE COUCH WITH A HEAD INJURY.
MY COUSIN ONLY SPEAKS ITALIAN. HE'S VISITING FROM ABRUZZI.
WELL... THAT'S NO EXCUSE NOT TO TALK AMERICAN.
HE'S A WINE MAKER.
WELL... DON'T LET IT GET TO YOU. LOTS OF EUROPEEPS ARE KINDA COMPLAINY.
darb
NO... HE MAKES A WINE TO DRINK.
AND YOU MAKE-A WHINE WHEN YOU'RE-A SLEEPY!
OK, THAT'S OFFENSIVE.
YEAH... I JUST TUNE YOU OUT.

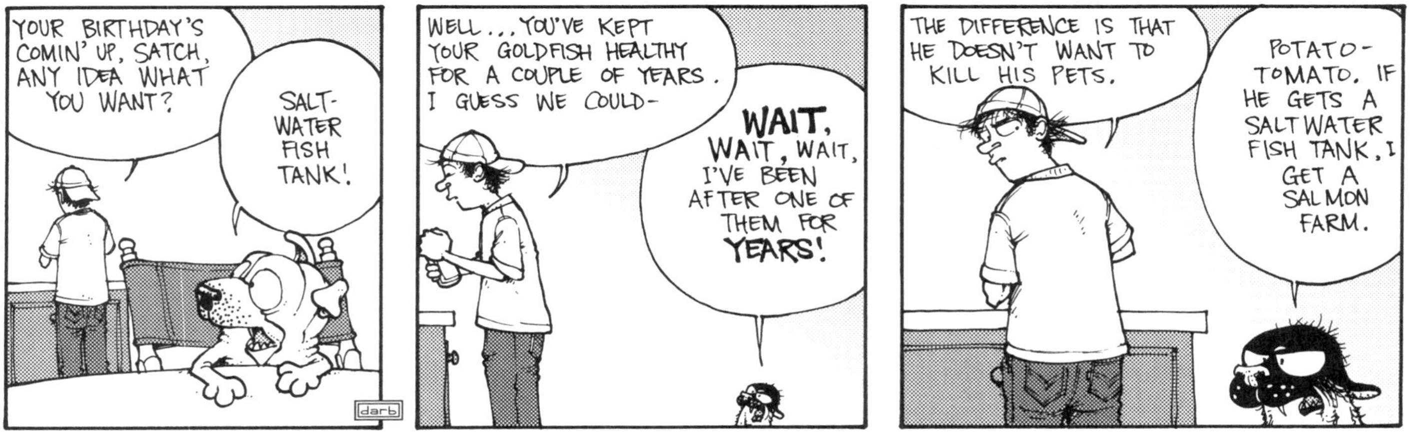
YOUR BIRTHDAY'S COMIN' UP, SATCH, ANY IDEA WHAT YOU WANT?
SALT-WATER FISH TANK!
WELL... YOU'VE KEPT YOUR GOLDFISH HEALTHY FOR A COUPLE OF YEARS. I GUESS WE COULD-
WAIT, WAIT, WAIT, I'VE BEEN AFTER ONE OF THEM FOR YEARS!
THE DIFFERENCE IS THAT HE DOESN'T WANT TO KILL HIS PETS.
POTATO-TOMATO. IF HE GETS A SALT WATER FISH TANK, I GET A SALMON FARM.
darb

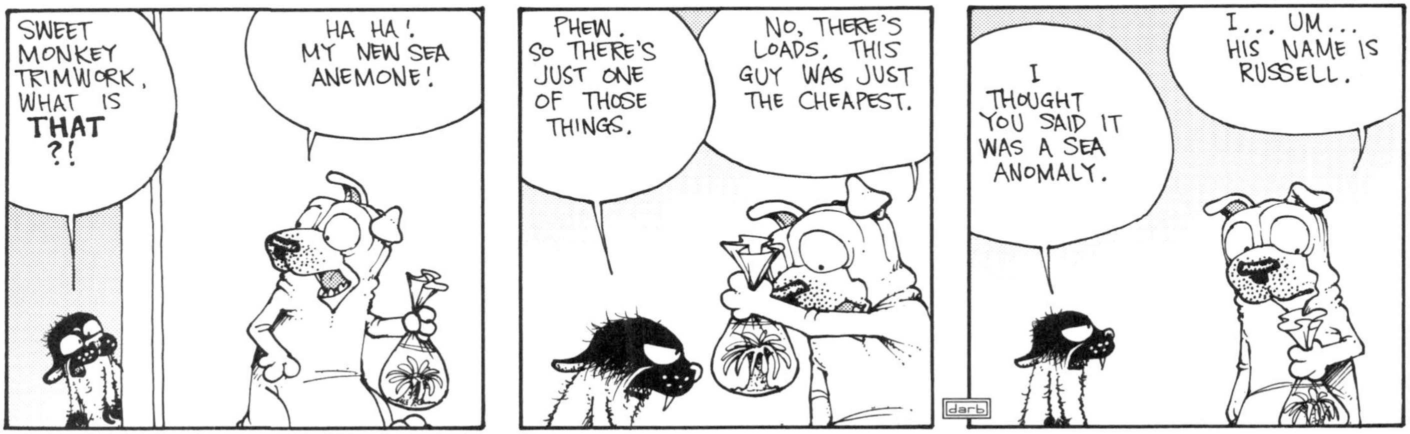
SWEET MONKEY TRIMWORK, WHAT IS THAT ?!
HA HA! MY NEW SEA ANEMONE!
PHEW. SO THERE'S JUST ONE OF THOSE THINGS.
NO, THERE'S LOADS. THIS GUY WAS JUST THE CHEAPEST.
I THOUGHT YOU SAID IT WAS A SEA ANOMALY.
I... UM... HIS NAME IS RUSSELL.
darb

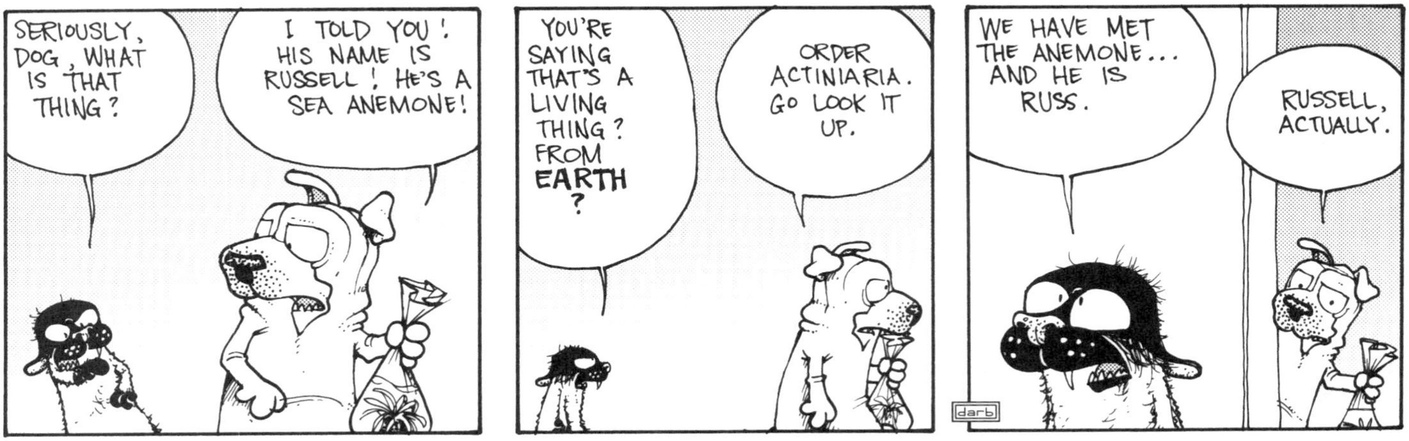
SERIOUSLY, DOG, WHAT IS THAT THING?
I TOLD YOU! HIS NAME IS RUSSELL! HE'S A SEA ANEMONE!
YOU'RE SAYING THAT'S A LIVING THING? FROM EARTH ?
ORDER ACTINIARIA. GO LOOK IT UP.
WE HAVE MET THE ANEMONE... AND HE IS RUSS.
RUSSELL, ACTUALLY.
darb

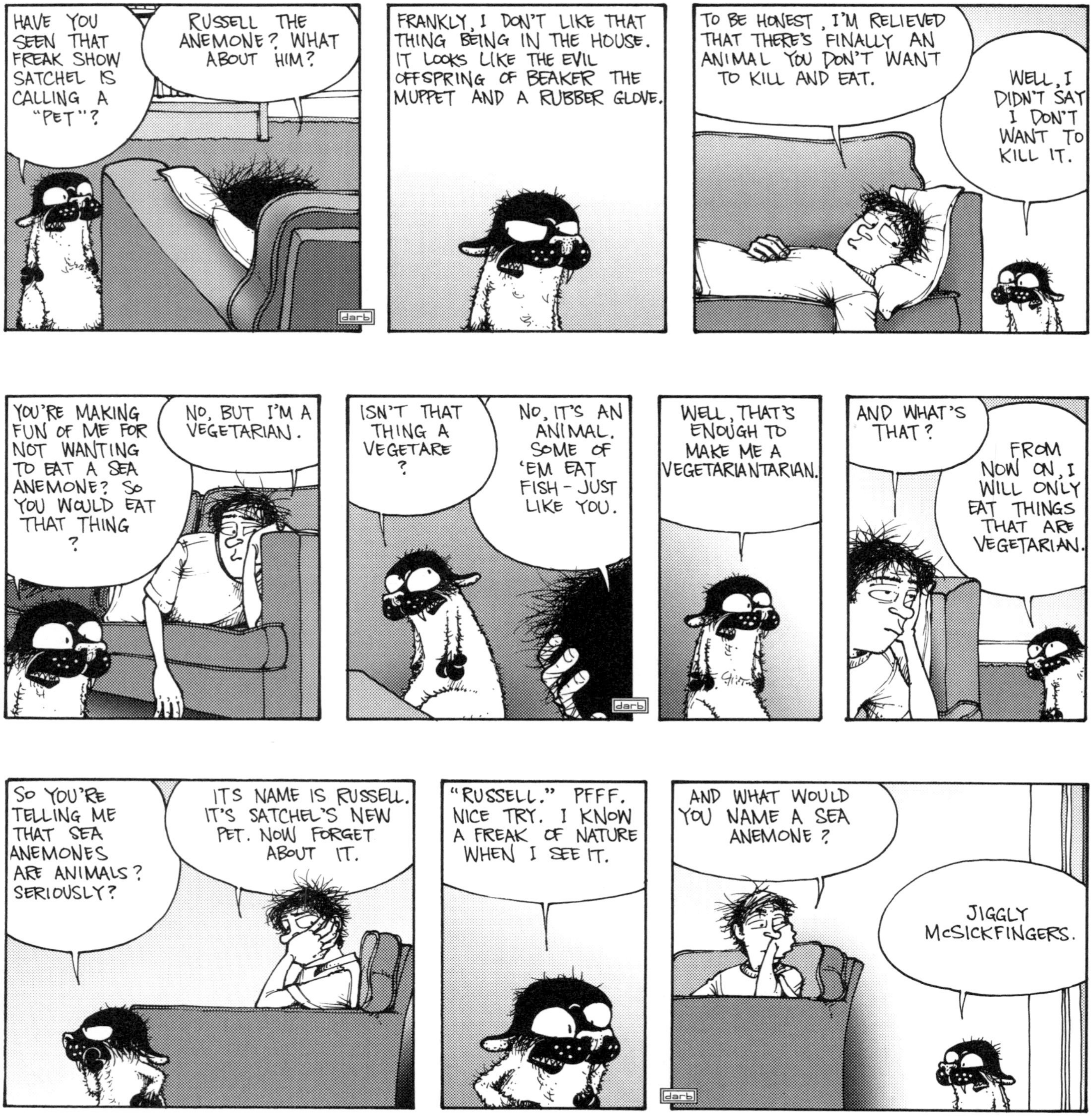
HAVE YOU SEEN THAT FREAK SHOW SATCHEL IS CALLING A "PET"?
RUSSELL THE ANEMONE? WHAT ABOUT HIM?
FRANKLY, I DON'T LIKE THAT THING BEING IN THE HOUSE. IT LOOKS LIKE THE EVIL OFFSPRING OF BEAKER THE MUPPET AND A RUBBER GLOVE.
TO BE HONEST, I'M RELIEVED THAT THERE'S FINALLY AN ANIMAL YOU DON'T WANT TO KILL AND EAT.
WELL, I DIDN'T SAY I DON'T WANT TO KILL IT.
darb
YOU'RE MAKING FUN OF ME FOR NOT WANTING TO EAT A SEA ANEMONE? SO YOU WOULD EAT THAT THING?
NO, BUT I'M A VEGETARIAN.
ISN'T THAT THING A VEGETARE?
NO, IT'S AN ANIMAL. SOME OF 'EM EAT FISH - JUST LIKE YOU.
WELL, THAT'S ENOUGH TO MAKE ME A VEGETARIANTARIAN.
AND WHAT'S THAT?
FROM NOW ON, I WILL ONLY EAT THINGS THAT ARE VEGETARIAN.
darb
SO YOU'RE TELLING ME THAT SEA ANEMONES ARE ANIMALS? SERIOUSLY?
ITS NAME IS RUSSELL. IT'S SATCHEL'S NEW PET. NOW FORGET ABOUT IT.
"RUSSELL." PFFF. NICE TRY. I KNOW A FREAK OF NATURE WHEN I SEE IT.
AND WHAT WOULD YOU NAME A SEA ANEMONE?
JIGGLY McSICKFINGERS.
darb

WOULD YOU LIKE TO SIGN MY PETITION TO ABOLISH SEAL CLUBBING?
HEY, WHO AM I TO JUDGE HOW SEALS LIKE TO SPEND A NIGHT OUT?
THEY, UMM... HM.
DIDN'T EVEN KNOW THEY COULD DANCE, WHAT WITH THOSE FLIPPER THINGS THEY GOT GOIN'.
MAYBE YOU'D BE MORE INTERESTED IN THIS ONE. DID YOU KNOW THAT IT TAKES AN ENTIRE BLACK BEAR TO MAKE ONE BRITISH ROYAL GUARD'S FUR HAT?
WELL, HIRE MORE BEARS.
MM-HM. MM-HM. COULD WE TALK ABOUT ANIMAL RIGHTS LAWS FOR A SEC?
BE GONE, OR I'LL SMACK YOU WITH MY OWN PERSONAL FIRST AMENDMENT.
darb

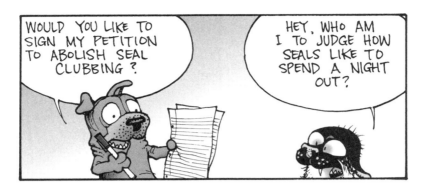

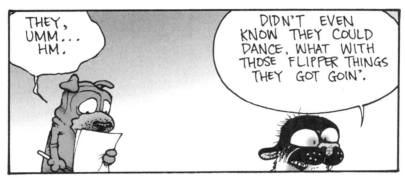

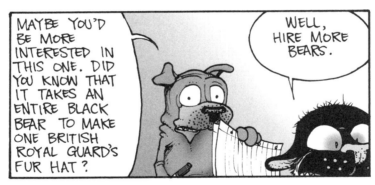

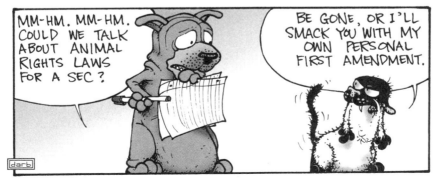

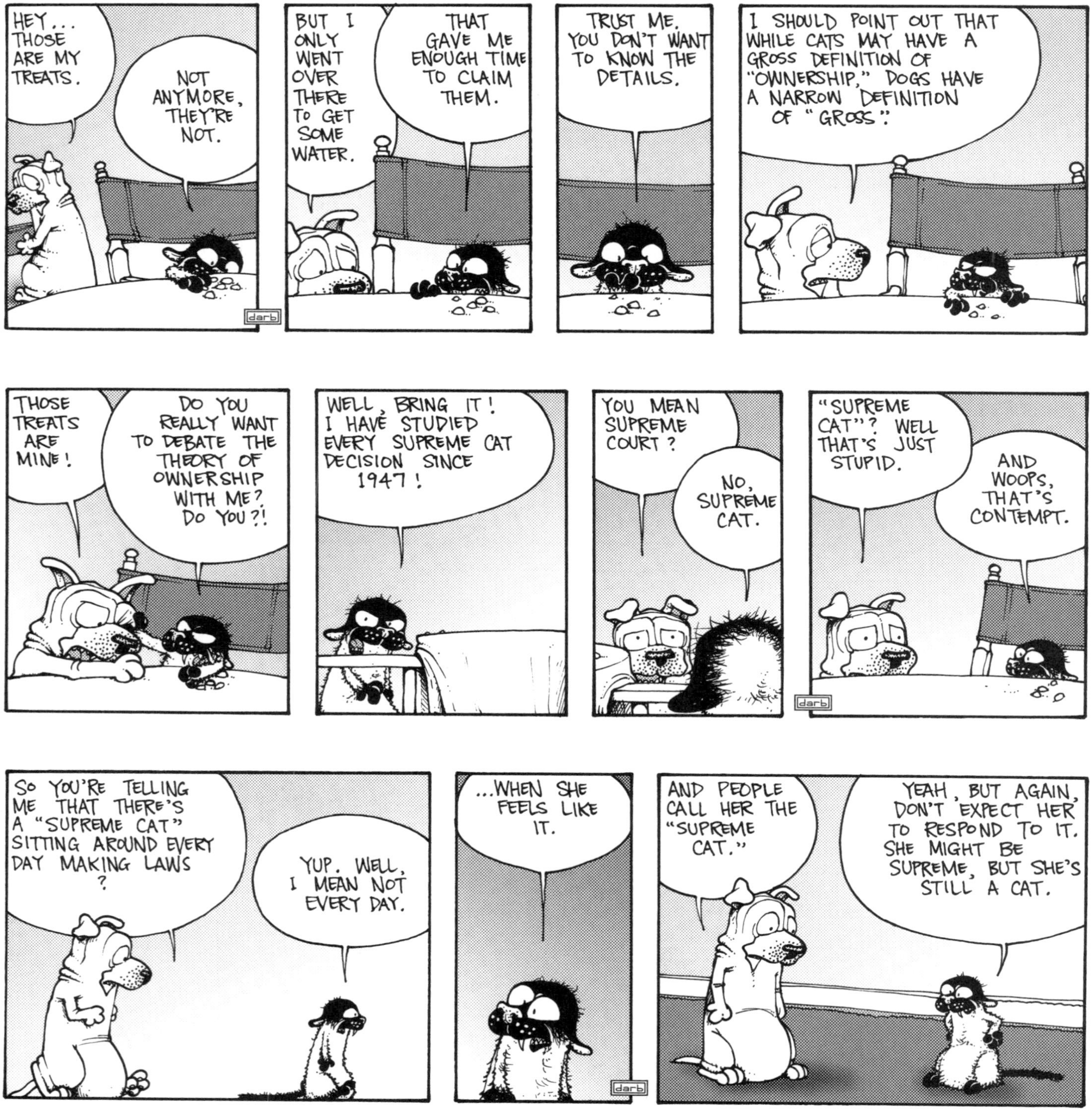
HEY... THOSE ARE MY TREATS.
NOT ANYMORE, THEY'RE NOT.
BUT I ONLY WENT OVER THERE TO GET SOME WATER.
THAT GAVE ME ENOUGH TIME TO CLAIM THEM.
TRUST ME. YOU DON'T WANT TO KNOW THE DETAILS.
I SHOULD POINT OUT THAT WHILE CATS MAY HAVE A GROSS DEFINITION OF "OWNERSHIP," DOGS HAVE A NARROW DEFINITION OF "GROSS."
darb
THOSE TREATS ARE MINE!
DO YOU REALLY WANT TO DEBATE THE THEORY OF OWNERSHIP WITH ME? DO YOU?!
WELL, BRING IT! I HAVE STUDIED EVERY SUPREME CAT DECISION SINCE 1947!
YOU MEAN SUPREME COURT?
NO, SUPREME CAT.
"SUPREME CAT"? WELL THAT'S JUST STUPID.
AND WOOPS, THAT'S CONTEMPT.
darb
SO YOU'RE TELLING ME THAT THERE'S A "SUPREME CAT" SITTING AROUND EVERY DAY MAKING LAWS?
YUP. WELL, I MEAN NOT EVERY DAY.
...WHEN SHE FEELS LIKE IT.
darb
AND PEOPLE CALL HER THE "SUPREME CAT."
YEAH, BUT AGAIN, DON'T EXPECT HER TO RESPOND TO IT. SHE MIGHT BE SUPREME, BUT SHE'S STILL A CAT.

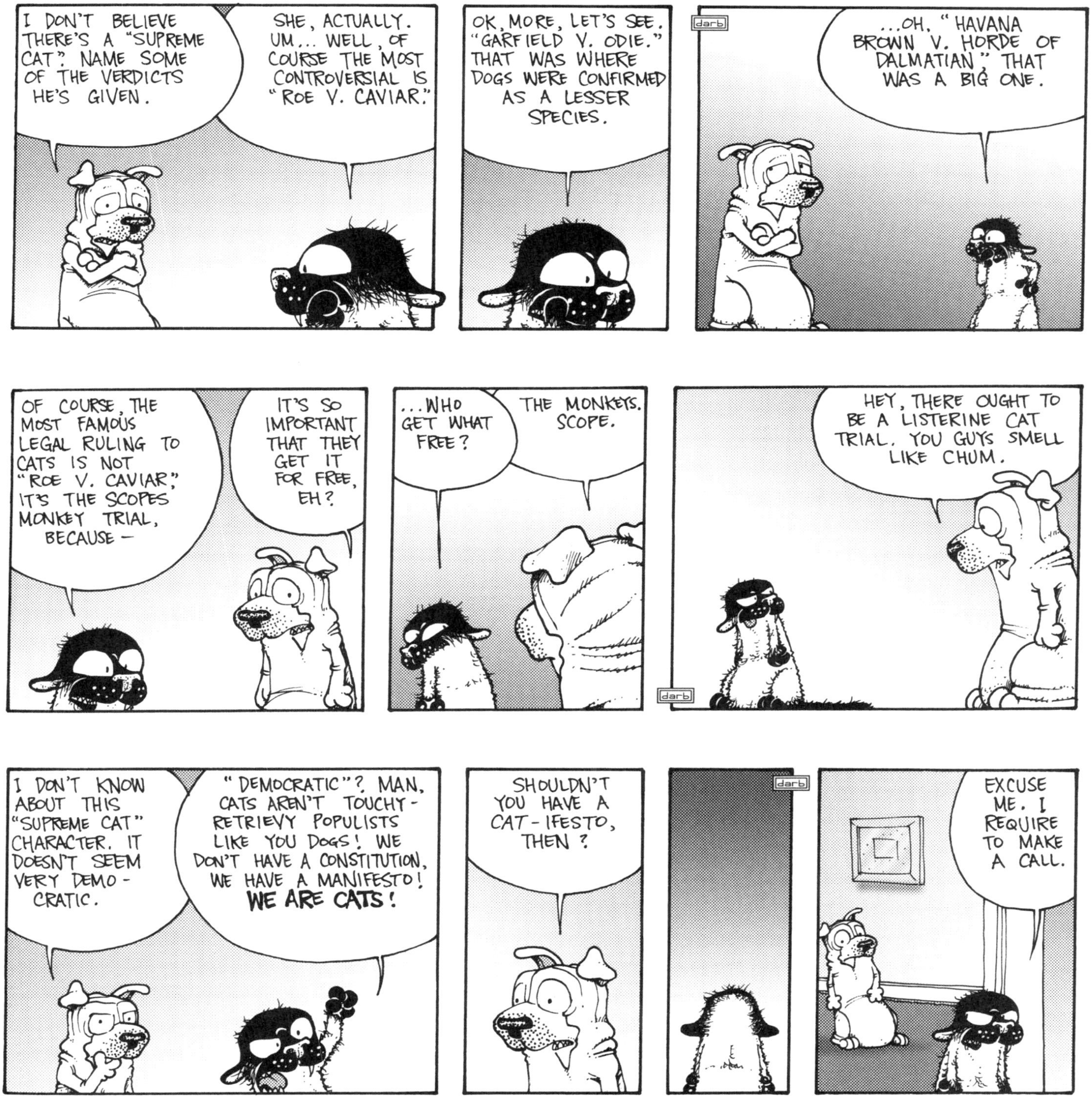
I DON'T BELIEVE THERE'S A "SUPREME CAT." NAME SOME OF THE VERDICTS HE'S GIVEN.
SHE, ACTUALLY. UM... WELL, OF COURSE THE MOST CONTROVERSIAL IS "ROE V. CAVIAR."
OK, MORE, LET'S SEE. "GARFIELD V. ODIE." THAT WAS WHERE DOGS WERE CONFIRMED AS A LESSER SPECIES.
...OH, "HAVANA BROWN V. HORDE OF DALMATIAN," THAT WAS A BIG ONE.
OF COURSE, THE MOST FAMOUS LEGAL RULING TO CATS IS NOT "ROE V. CAVIAR," IT'S THE SCOPES MONKEY TRIAL, BECAUSE —
IT'S SO IMPORTANT THAT THEY GET IT FOR FREE, EH?
...WHO GET WHAT FREE?
THE MONKEYS. SCOPE.
HEY, THERE OUGHT TO BE A LISTERINE CAT TRIAL. YOU GUYS SMELL LIKE CHUM.
I DON'T KNOW ABOUT THIS "SUPREME CAT" CHARACTER. IT DOESN'T SEEM VERY DEMOCRATIC.
"DEMOCRATIC"? MAN, CATS AREN'T TOUCHY-RETRIEVY POPULISTS LIKE YOU DOGS! WE DON'T HAVE A CONSTITUTION, WE HAVE A MANIFESTO! WE ARE CATS!
SHOULDN'T YOU HAVE A CAT-IFESTO, THEN?
EXCUSE ME. I REQUIRE TO MAKE A CALL.

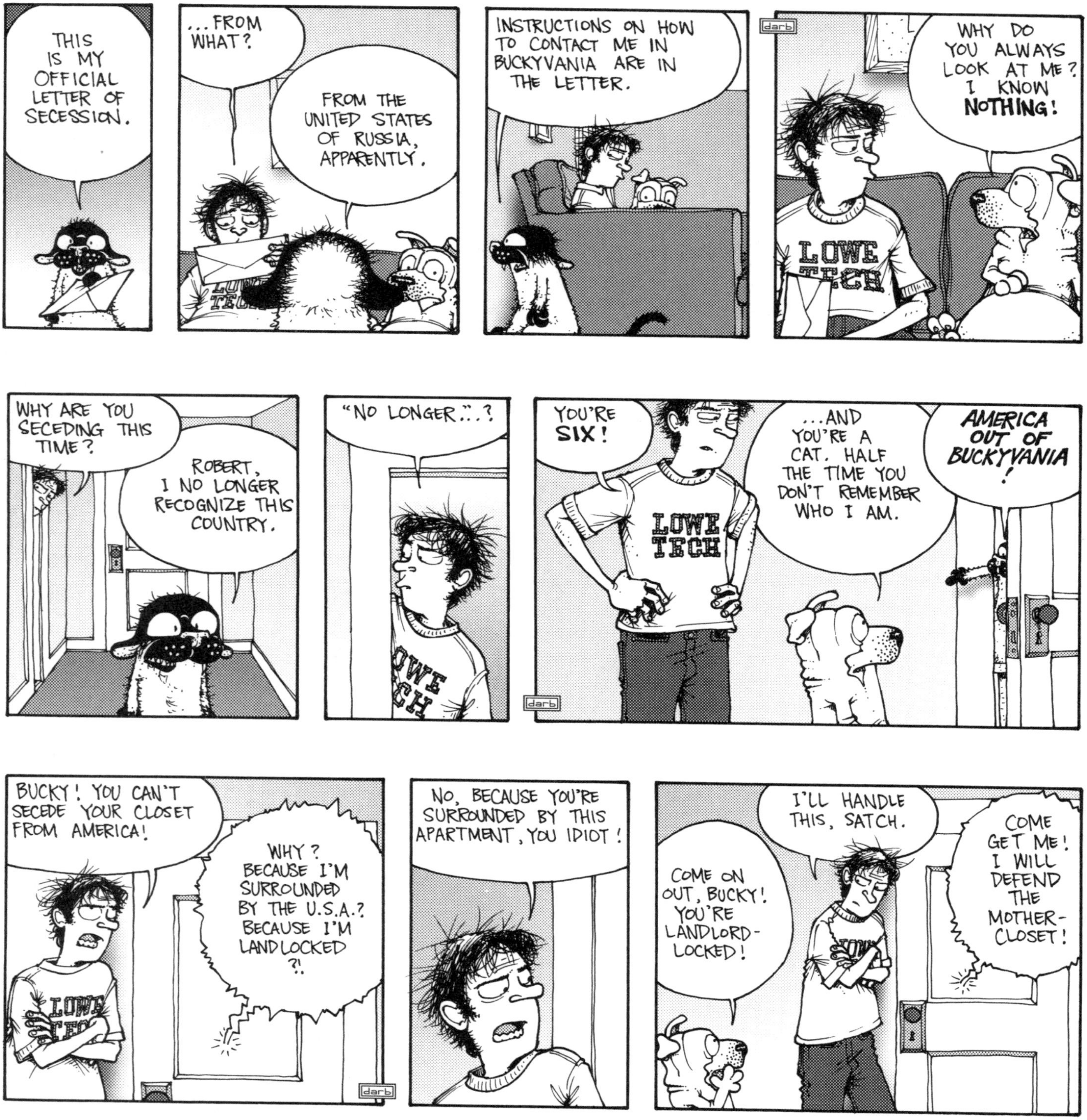
THIS IS MY OFFICIAL LETTER OF SECESSION.
...FROM WHAT?
FROM THE UNITED STATES OF RUSSIA, APPARENTLY.
INSTRUCTIONS ON HOW TO CONTACT ME IN BUCKYVANIA ARE IN THE LETTER.
darb
WHY DO YOU ALWAYS LOOK AT ME? I KNOW **NOTHING**!
LOWE TECH
WHY ARE YOU SECEDING THIS TIME?
ROBERT, I NO LONGER RECOGNIZE THIS COUNTRY.
"NO LONGER..."?
darb
YOU'RE **SIX**!
...AND YOU'RE A CAT. HALF THE TIME YOU DON'T REMEMBER WHO I AM.
AMERICA OUT OF BUCKYVANIA!
BUCKY! YOU CAN'T SECEDE YOUR CLOSET FROM AMERICA!
WHY? BECAUSE I'M SURROUNDED BY THE U.S.A.? BECAUSE I'M LANDLOCKED?!
darb
NO, BECAUSE YOU'RE SURROUNDED BY THIS APARTMENT, YOU IDIOT!
I'LL HANDLE THIS, SATCH.
COME ON OUT, BUCKY! YOU'RE LANDLORD-LOCKED!
COME GET ME! I WILL DEFEND THE MOTHER-CLOSET!

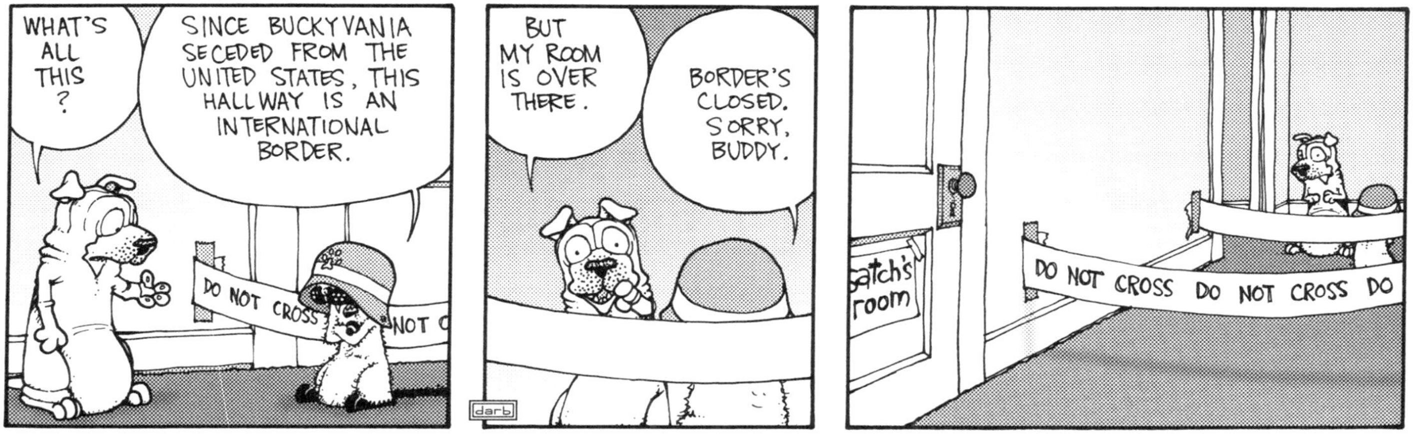
WHAT'S ALL THIS ?
SINCE BUCKYVANIA SECEDED FROM THE UNITED STATES, THIS HALLWAY IS AN INTERNATIONAL BORDER.
DO NOT CROSS
BUT MY ROOM IS OVER THERE.
BORDER'S CLOSED. SORRY, BUDDY.
darb
Satch's room
DO NOT CROSS DO NOT CROSS DO

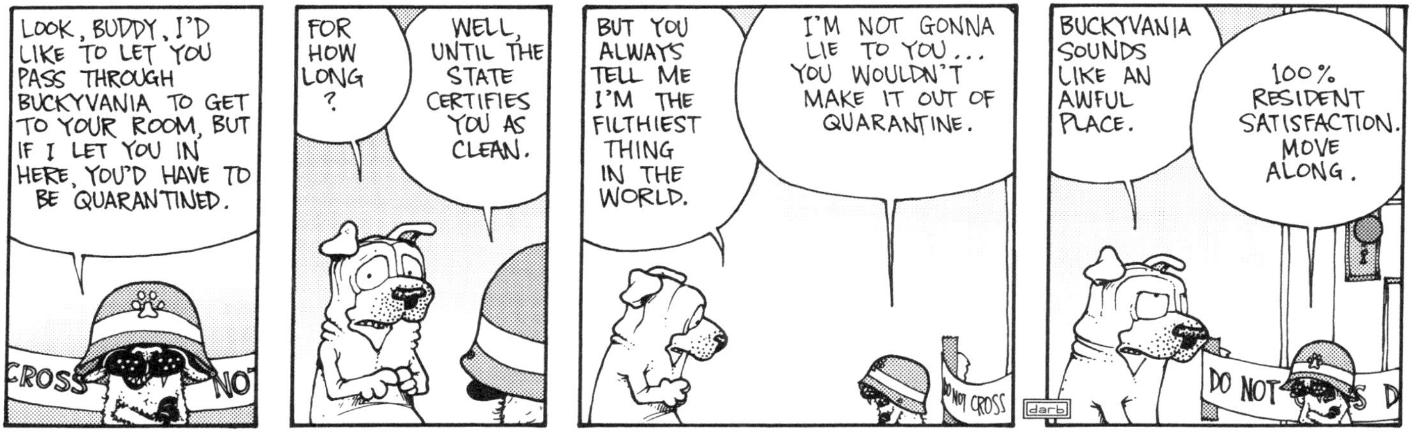
LOOK, BUDDY, I'D LIKE TO LET YOU PASS THROUGH BUCKYVANIA TO GET TO YOUR ROOM, BUT IF I LET YOU IN HERE, YOU'D HAVE TO BE QUARANTINED.
FOR HOW LONG ?
WELL, UNTIL THE STATE CERTIFIES YOU AS CLEAN.
BUT YOU ALWAYS TELL ME I'M THE FILTHIEST THING IN THE WORLD.
I'M NOT GONNA LIE TO YOU... YOU WOULDN'T MAKE IT OUT OF QUARANTINE.
DO NOT CROSS
darb
BUCKYVANIA SOUNDS LIKE AN AWFUL PLACE.
100% RESIDENT SATISFACTION. MOVE ALONG.
DO NOT

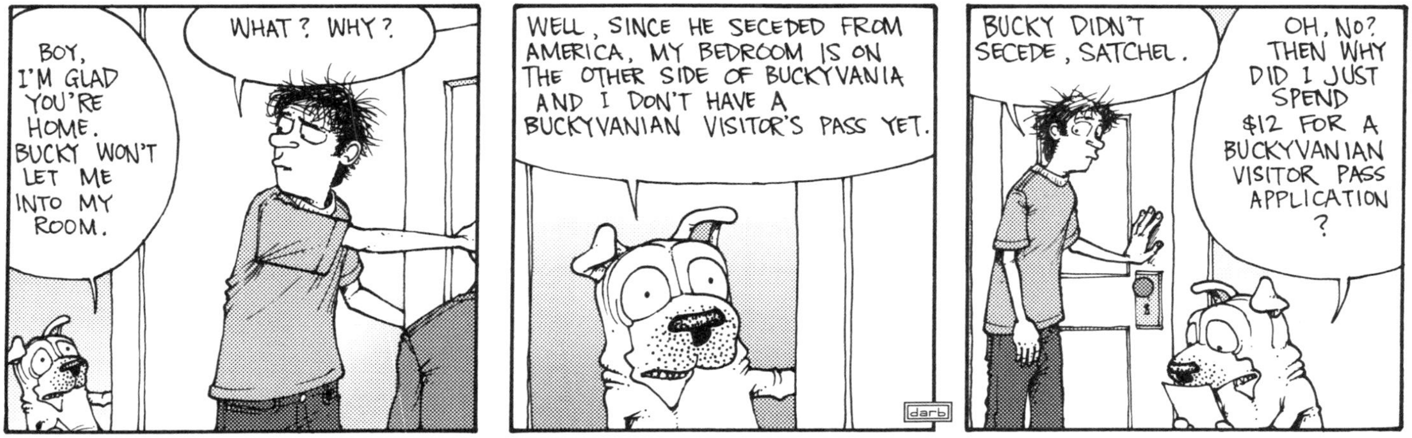
BOY, I'M GLAD YOU'RE HOME. BUCKY WON'T LET ME INTO MY ROOM.
WHAT? WHY?
WELL, SINCE HE SECEDED FROM AMERICA, MY BEDROOM IS ON THE OTHER SIDE OF BUCKYVANIA AND I DON'T HAVE A BUCKYVANIAN VISITOR'S PASS YET.
darb
BUCKY DIDN'T SECEDE, SATCHEL.
OH, NO? THEN WHY DID I JUST SPEND $12 FOR A BUCKYVANIAN VISITOR PASS APPLICATION ?

MORNING.
HA HA! YOU LOOK LIKE SOMETHING THE CAT DRAGGED IN!
HEY, DON'T IMPLICATE ME IN THAT TRAIN WRECK.
I'M SICK.
OF WHAT, BATHING?
No, I FEEL SICK.
YOU FEEL SICK? I HAVE TO EAT MY BODY DIRT. I HACK UP CLUMPS OF FUR LIKE IT'S A MEDIEVAL FESTIVAL.
BUT I DO IT EVERY DAY, MAN, 'CAUSE I HAVE PRIDE IN MY APPEARANCE.
darb
I'M ILL, BUCKY.
ILL-WHAT? ILL...? F...ILL? FILL? FILTHY?
WAIT, ARE YOU HERE TO SAVE ME MONEY ON CAR INSURANCE?
GOOD DAY.

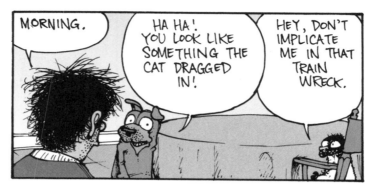

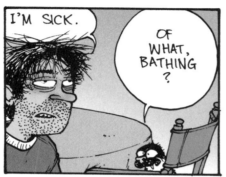

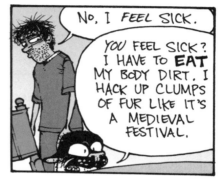

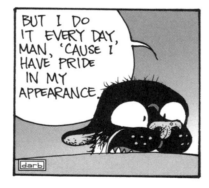

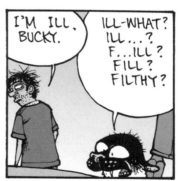

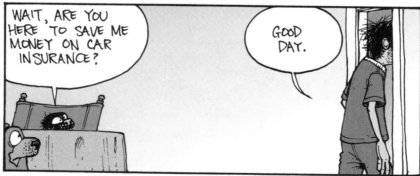

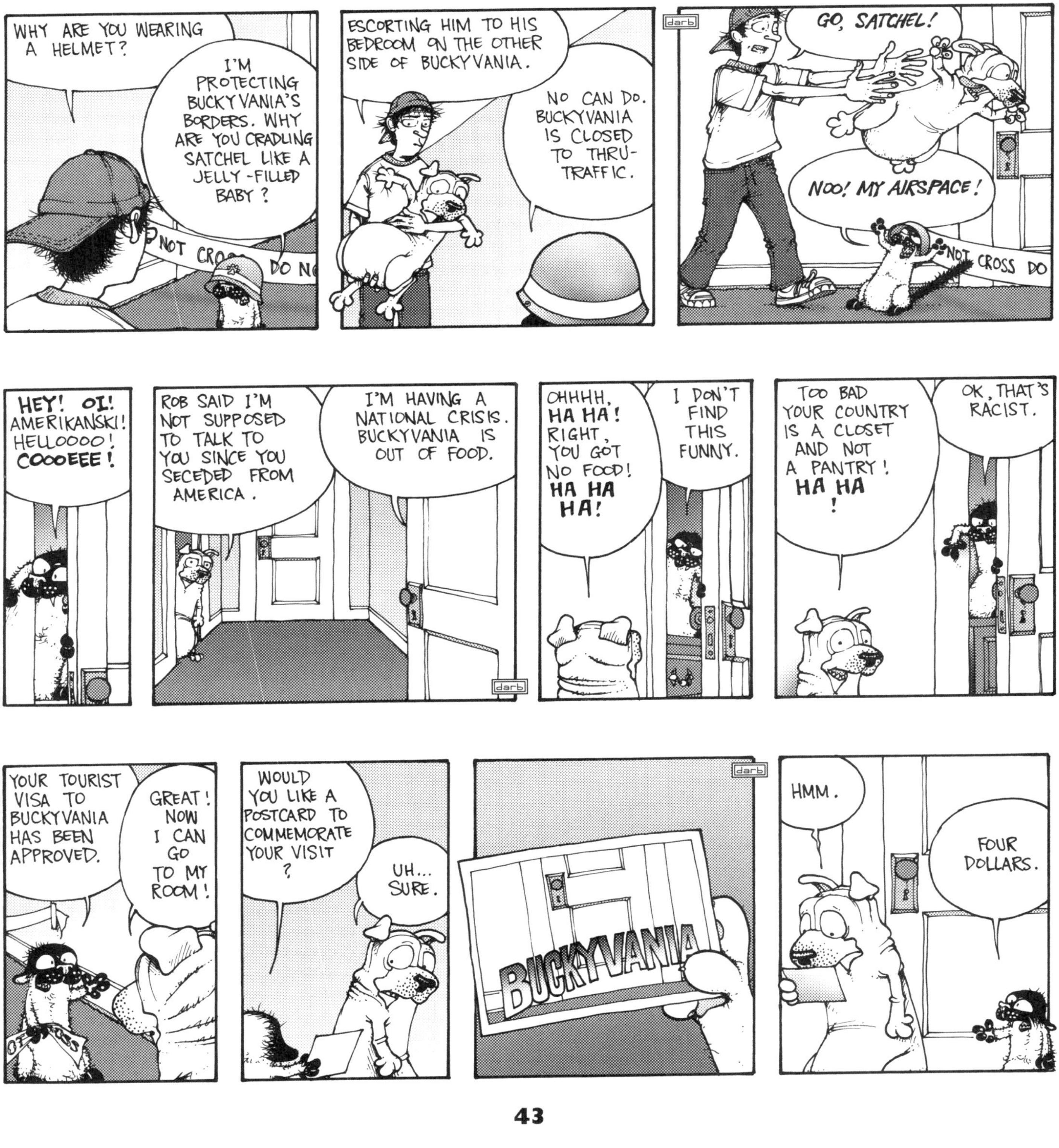
WHY ARE YOU WEARING A HELMET?
I'M PROTECTING BUCKYVANIA'S BORDERS. WHY ARE YOU CRADLING SATCHEL LIKE A JELLY-FILLED BABY?
NOT CROSS DO NO
ESCORTING HIM TO HIS BEDROOM ON THE OTHER SIDE OF BUCKYVANIA.
NO CAN DO. BUCKYVANIA IS CLOSED TO THRU-TRAFFIC.
darb
GO, SATCHEL!
NOO! MY AIRSPACE!
NOT CROSS DO
HEY! OI! AMERIKANSKI! HELLOOOO! COOOEEE!
ROB SAID I'M NOT SUPPOSED TO TALK TO YOU SINCE YOU SECEDED FROM AMERICA.
I'M HAVING A NATIONAL CRISIS. BUCKYVANIA IS OUT OF FOOD.
darb
OHHHH, HA HA! RIGHT, YOU GOT NO FOOD! HA HA HA!
I DON'T FIND THIS FUNNY.
TOO BAD YOUR COUNTRY IS A CLOSET AND NOT A PANTRY! HA HA!
OK, THAT'S RACIST.
YOUR TOURIST VISA TO BUCKYVANIA HAS BEEN APPROVED.
GREAT! NOW I CAN GO TO MY ROOM!
WOULD YOU LIKE A POSTCARD TO COMMEMORATE YOUR VISIT?
UH... SURE.
darb
BUCKYVANIA
HMM.
FOUR DOLLARS.

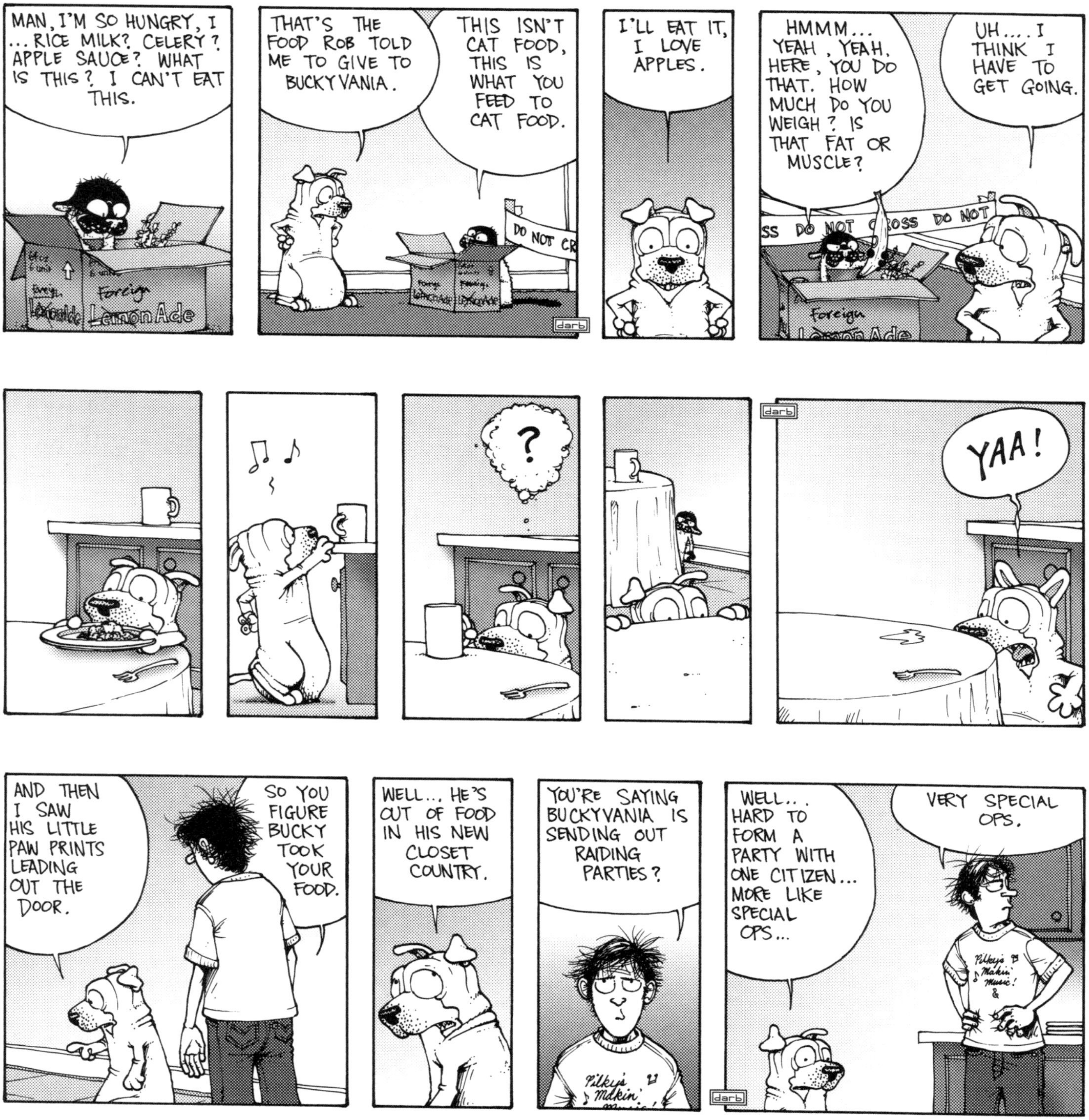
MAN, I'M SO HUNGRY, I ...RICE MILK? CELERY? APPLE SAUCE? WHAT IS THIS? I CAN'T EAT THIS.
THAT'S THE FOOD ROB TOLD ME TO GIVE TO BUCKYVANIA.
THIS ISN'T CAT FOOD, THIS IS WHAT YOU FEED TO CAT FOOD.
I'LL EAT IT, I LOVE APPLES.
HMMM... YEAH, YEAH. HERE, YOU DO THAT. HOW MUCH DO YOU WEIGH? IS THAT FAT OR MUSCLE?
UH.... I THINK I HAVE TO GET GOING.
?
YAA!
AND THEN I SAW HIS LITTLE PAW PRINTS LEADING OUT THE DOOR.
SO YOU FIGURE BUCKY TOOK YOUR FOOD.
WELL... HE'S OUT OF FOOD IN HIS NEW CLOSET COUNTRY.
YOU'RE SAYING BUCKYVANIA IS SENDING OUT RAIDING PARTIES?
WELL... HARD TO FORM A PARTY WITH ONE CITIZEN... MORE LIKE SPECIAL OPS...
VERY SPECIAL OPS.

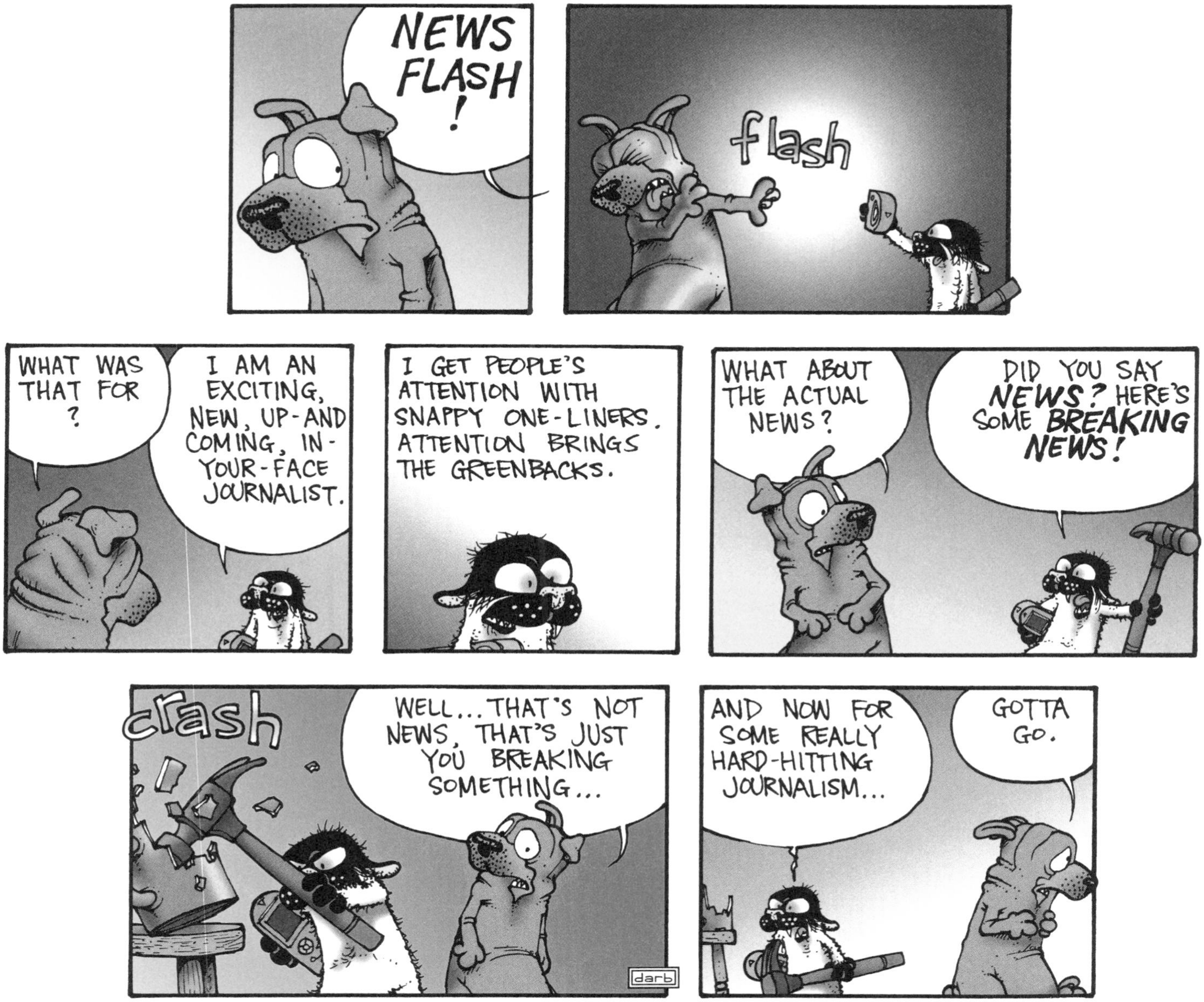
NEWS FLASH !
flash
WHAT WAS THAT FOR ?
I AM AN EXCITING, NEW, UP-AND COMING, IN-YOUR-FACE JOURNALIST.
I GET PEOPLE'S ATTENTION WITH SNAPPY ONE-LINERS. ATTENTION BRINGS THE GREENBACKS.
WHAT ABOUT THE ACTUAL NEWS?
DID YOU SAY NEWS? HERE'S SOME BREAKING NEWS!
crash
WELL... THAT'S NOT NEWS, THAT'S JUST YOU BREAKING SOMETHING...
darb
AND NOW FOR SOME REALLY HARD-HITTING JOURNALISM...
GOTTA GO.

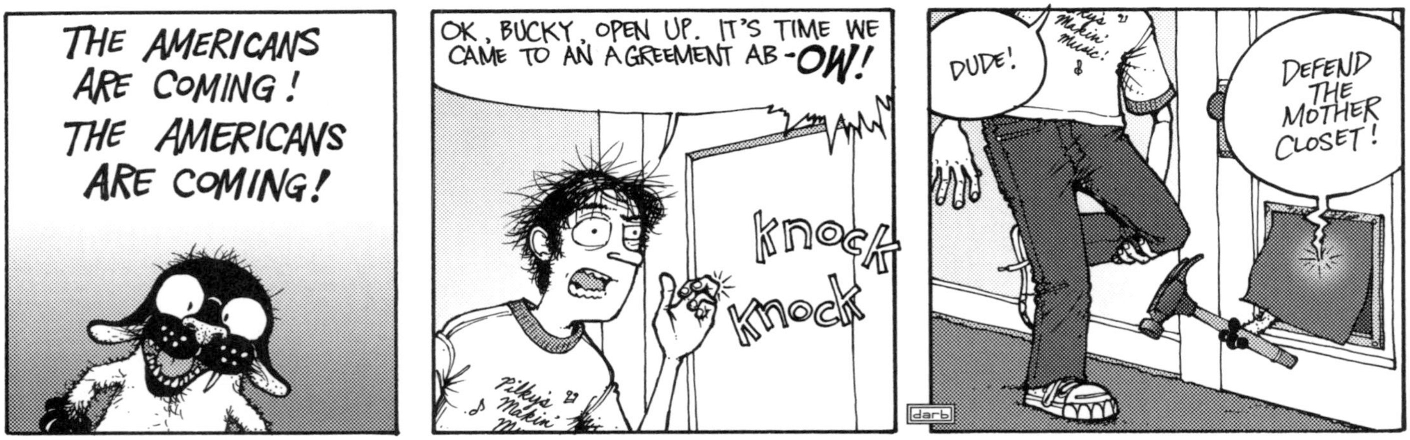
THE AMERICANS ARE COMING! THE AMERICANS ARE COMING!
OK, BUCKY, OPEN UP. IT'S TIME WE CAME TO AN AGREEMENT AB-OW!
knock knock
DUDE!
DEFEND THE MOTHER CLOSET!
darb

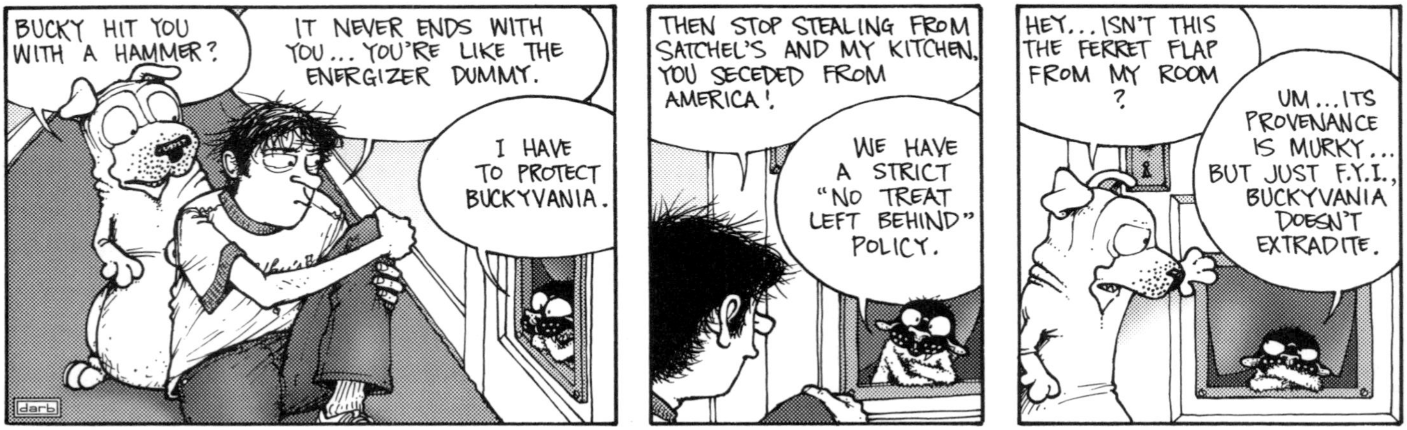
BUCKY HIT YOU WITH A HAMMER?
IT NEVER ENDS WITH YOU... YOU'RE LIKE THE ENERGIZER DUMMY.
I HAVE TO PROTECT BUCKYVANIA.
darb
THEN STOP STEALING FROM SATCHEL'S AND MY KITCHEN. YOU SECEDED FROM AMERICA!
WE HAVE A STRICT "NO TREAT LEFT BEHIND" POLICY.
HEY... ISN'T THIS THE FERRET FLAP FROM MY ROOM?
UM... ITS PROVENANCE IS MURKY... BUT JUST F.Y.I., BUCKYVANIA DOESN'T EXTRADITE.

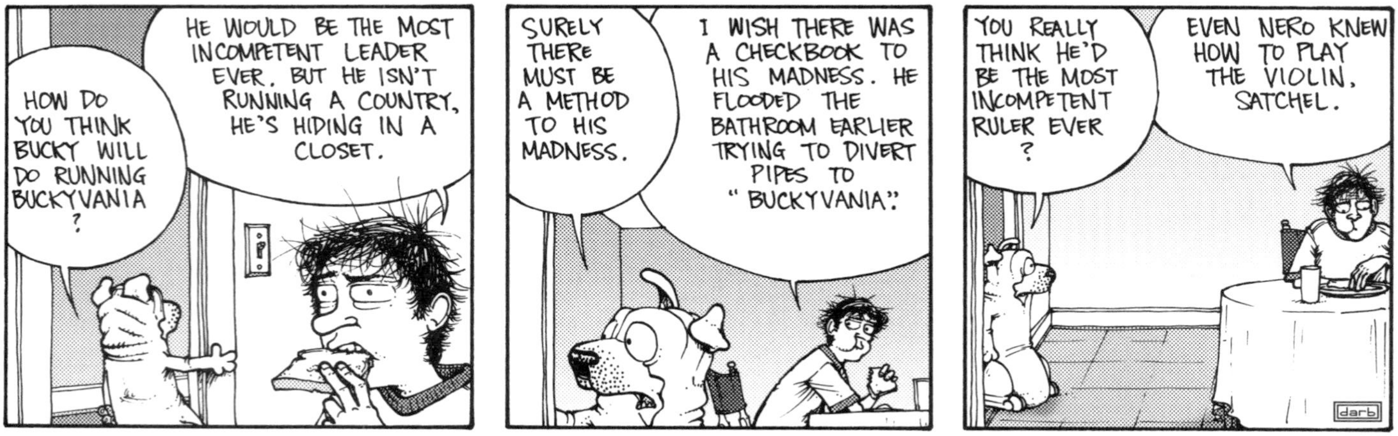
HOW DO YOU THINK BUCKY WILL DO RUNNING BUCKYVANIA?
HE WOULD BE THE MOST INCOMPETENT LEADER EVER. BUT HE ISN'T RUNNING A COUNTRY, HE'S HIDING IN A CLOSET.
SURELY THERE MUST BE A METHOD TO HIS MADNESS.
I WISH THERE WAS A CHECKBOOK TO HIS MADNESS. HE FLOODED THE BATHROOM EARLIER TRYING TO DIVERT PIPES TO "BUCKYVANIA".
YOU REALLY THINK HE'D BE THE MOST INCOMPETENT RULER EVER?
EVEN NERO KNEW HOW TO PLAY THE VIOLIN, SATCHEL.
darb

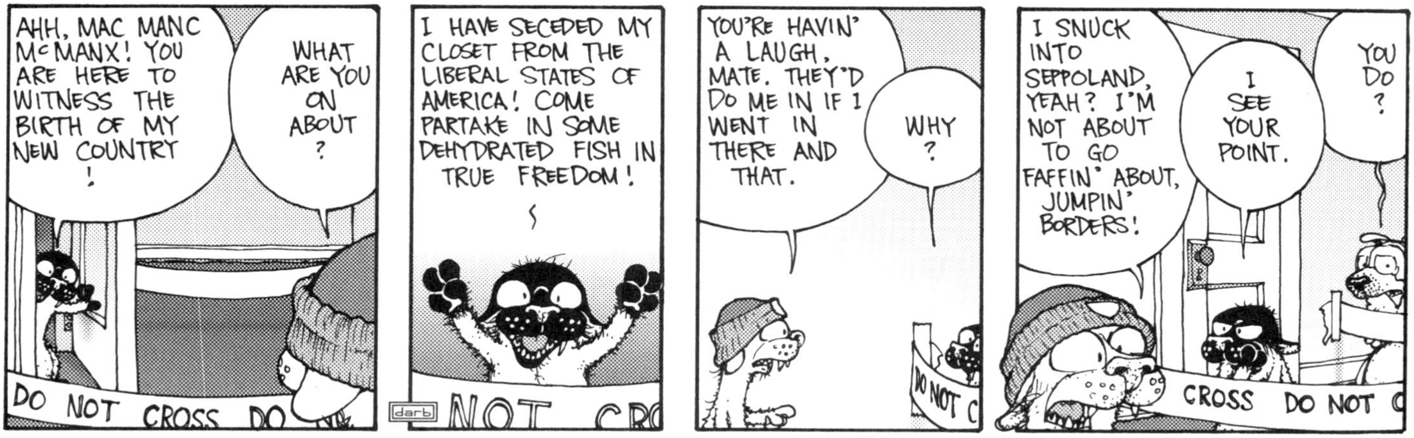
AHH, MAC MANC McMANX! YOU ARE HERE TO WITNESS THE BIRTH OF MY NEW COUNTRY!
WHAT ARE YOU ON ABOUT?
DO NOT CROSS DO
darb
I HAVE SECEDED MY CLOSET FROM THE LIBERAL STATES OF AMERICA! COME PARTAKE IN SOME DEHYDRATED FISH IN TRUE FREEDOM!
NOT CRO
YOU'RE HAVIN' A LAUGH, MATE. THEY'D DO ME IN IF I WENT IN THERE AND THAT.
WHY?
DO NOT C
I SNUCK INTO SEPPOLAND, YEAH? I'M NOT ABOUT TO GO FAFFIN' ABOUT, JUMPIN' BORDERS!
I SEE YOUR POINT.
YOU DO?
CROSS DO NOT

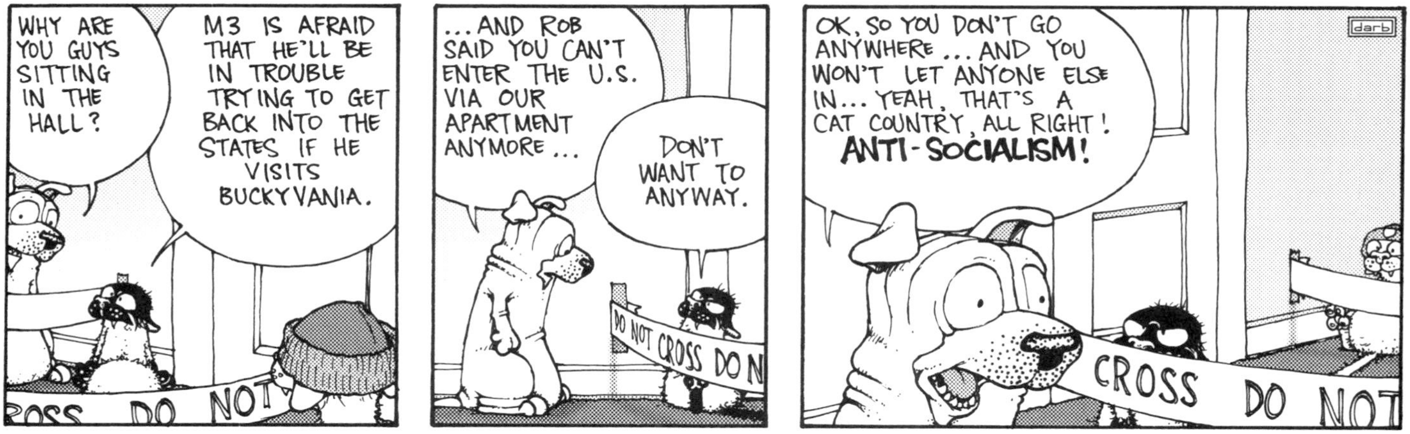
WHY ARE YOU GUYS SITTING IN THE HALL?
M3 IS AFRAID THAT HE'LL BE IN TROUBLE TRYING TO GET BACK INTO THE STATES IF HE VISITS BUCKYVANIA.
ROSS DO NOT
...AND ROB SAID YOU CAN'T ENTER THE U.S. VIA OUR APARTMENT ANYMORE...
DON'T WANT TO ANYWAY.
DO NOT CROSS DO N
darb
OK, SO YOU DON'T GO ANYWHERE... AND YOU WON'T LET ANYONE ELSE IN... YEAH, THAT'S A CAT COUNTRY, ALL RIGHT! ANTI-SOCIALISM!
CROSS DO NOT

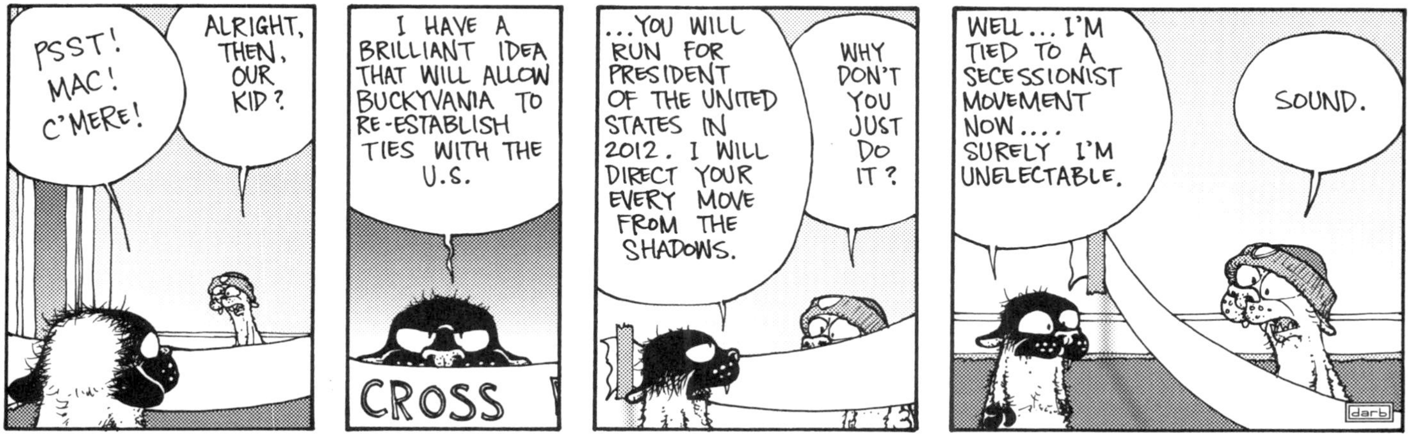
PSST! MAC! C'MERE!
ALRIGHT, THEN, OUR KID?
I HAVE A BRILLIANT IDEA THAT WILL ALLOW BUCKYVANIA TO RE-ESTABLISH TIES WITH THE U.S.
CROSS
...YOU WILL RUN FOR PRESIDENT OF THE UNITED STATES IN 2012. I WILL DIRECT YOUR EVERY MOVE FROM THE SHADOWS.
WHY DON'T YOU JUST DO IT?
WELL... I'M TIED TO A SECESSIONIST MOVEMENT NOW.... SURELY I'M UNELECTABLE.
SOUND.
darb

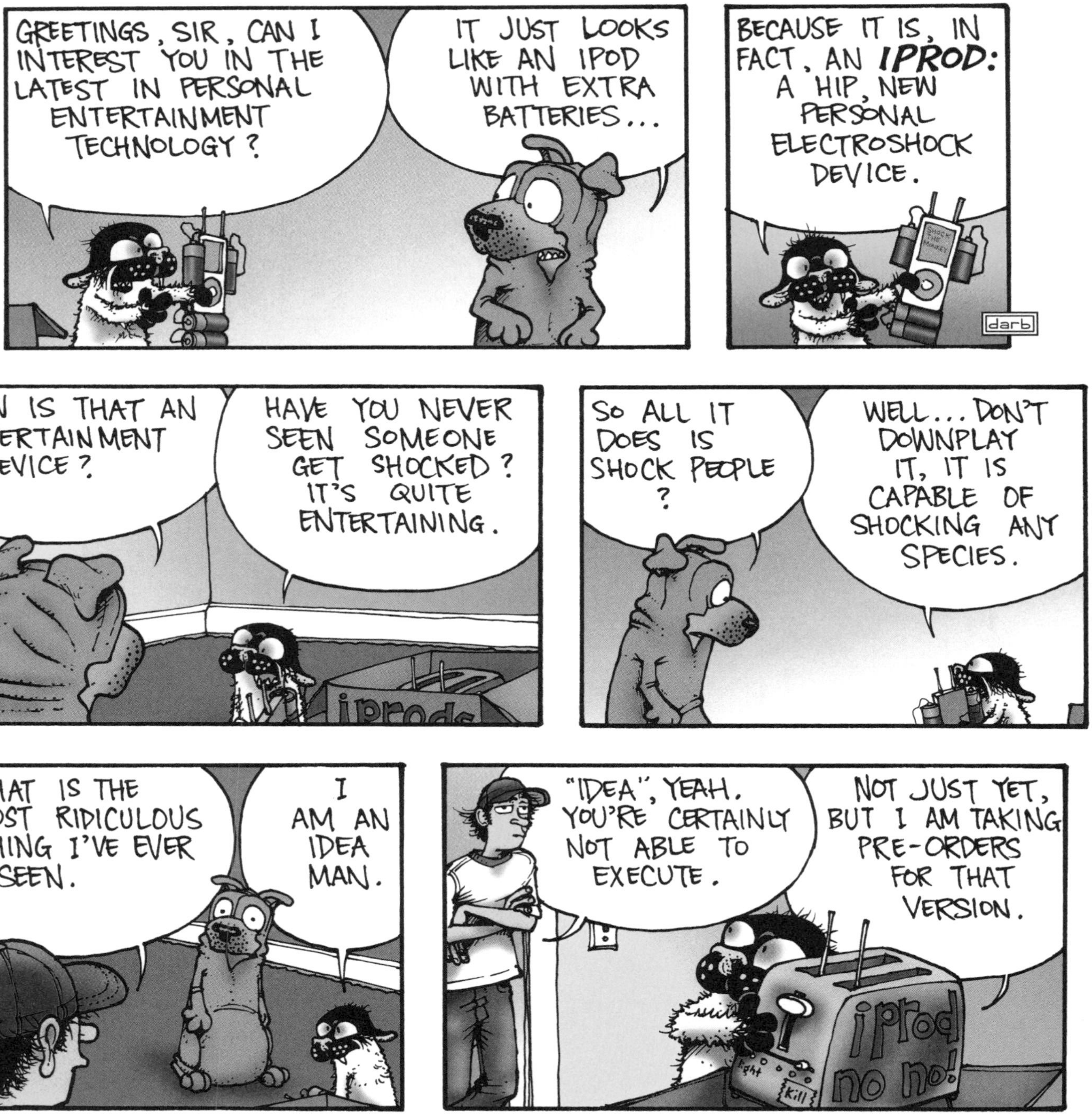
GREETINGS, SIR, CAN I INTEREST YOU IN THE LATEST IN PERSONAL ENTERTAINMENT TECHNOLOGY?
IT JUST LOOKS LIKE AN IPOD WITH EXTRA BATTERIES...
BECAUSE IT IS, IN FACT, AN IPROD: A HIP, NEW PERSONAL ELECTROSHOCK DEVICE.
darb
HOW IS THAT AN ENTERTAINMENT DEVICE?
HAVE YOU NEVER SEEN SOMEONE GET SHOCKED? IT'S QUITE ENTERTAINING.
iprods
SO ALL IT DOES IS SHOCK PEOPLE?
WELL... DON'T DOWNPLAY IT, IT IS CAPABLE OF SHOCKING ANY SPECIES.
THAT IS THE MOST RIDICULOUS THING I'VE EVER SEEN.
I AM AN IDEA MAN.
"IDEA", YEAH. YOU'RE CERTAINLY NOT ABLE TO EXECUTE.
NOT JUST YET, BUT I AM TAKING PRE-ORDERS FOR THAT VERSION.
iprod no no!
kill

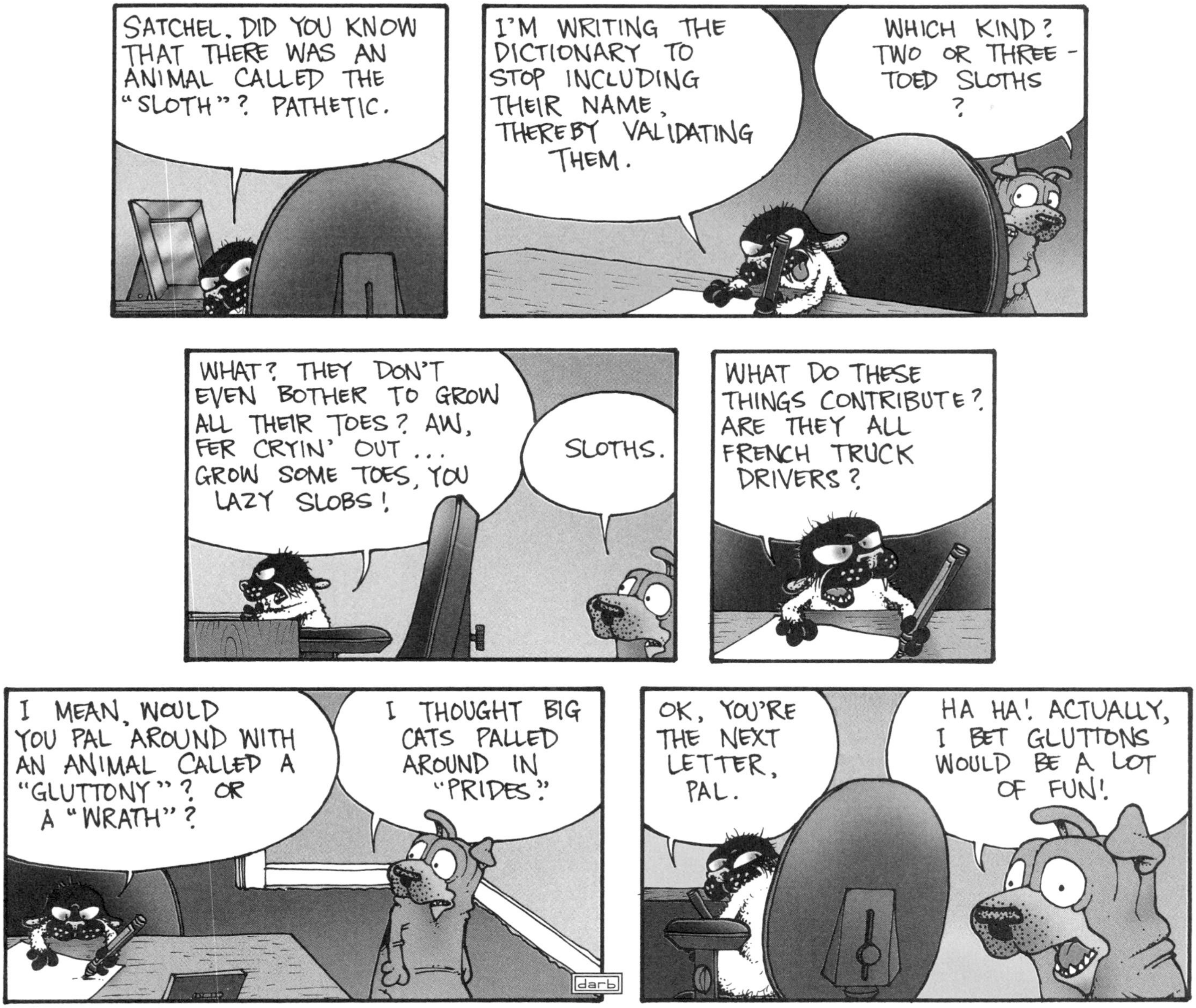
SATCHEL. DID YOU KNOW THAT THERE WAS AN ANIMAL CALLED THE "SLOTH"? PATHETIC.
I'M WRITING THE DICTIONARY TO STOP INCLUDING THEIR NAME, THEREBY VALIDATING THEM.
WHICH KIND? TWO OR THREE-TOED SLOTHS?
WHAT? THEY DON'T EVEN BOTHER TO GROW ALL THEIR TOES? AW, FER CRYIN' OUT... GROW SOME TOES, YOU LAZY SLOBS!
SLOTHS.
WHAT DO THESE THINGS CONTRIBUTE? ARE THEY ALL FRENCH TRUCK DRIVERS?
I MEAN, WOULD YOU PAL AROUND WITH AN ANIMAL CALLED A "GLUTTONY"? OR A "WRATH"?
I THOUGHT BIG CATS PALLED AROUND IN "PRIDES."
darb
OK, YOU'RE THE NEXT LETTER, PAL.
HA HA! ACTUALLY, I BET GLUTTONS WOULD BE A LOT OF FUN!

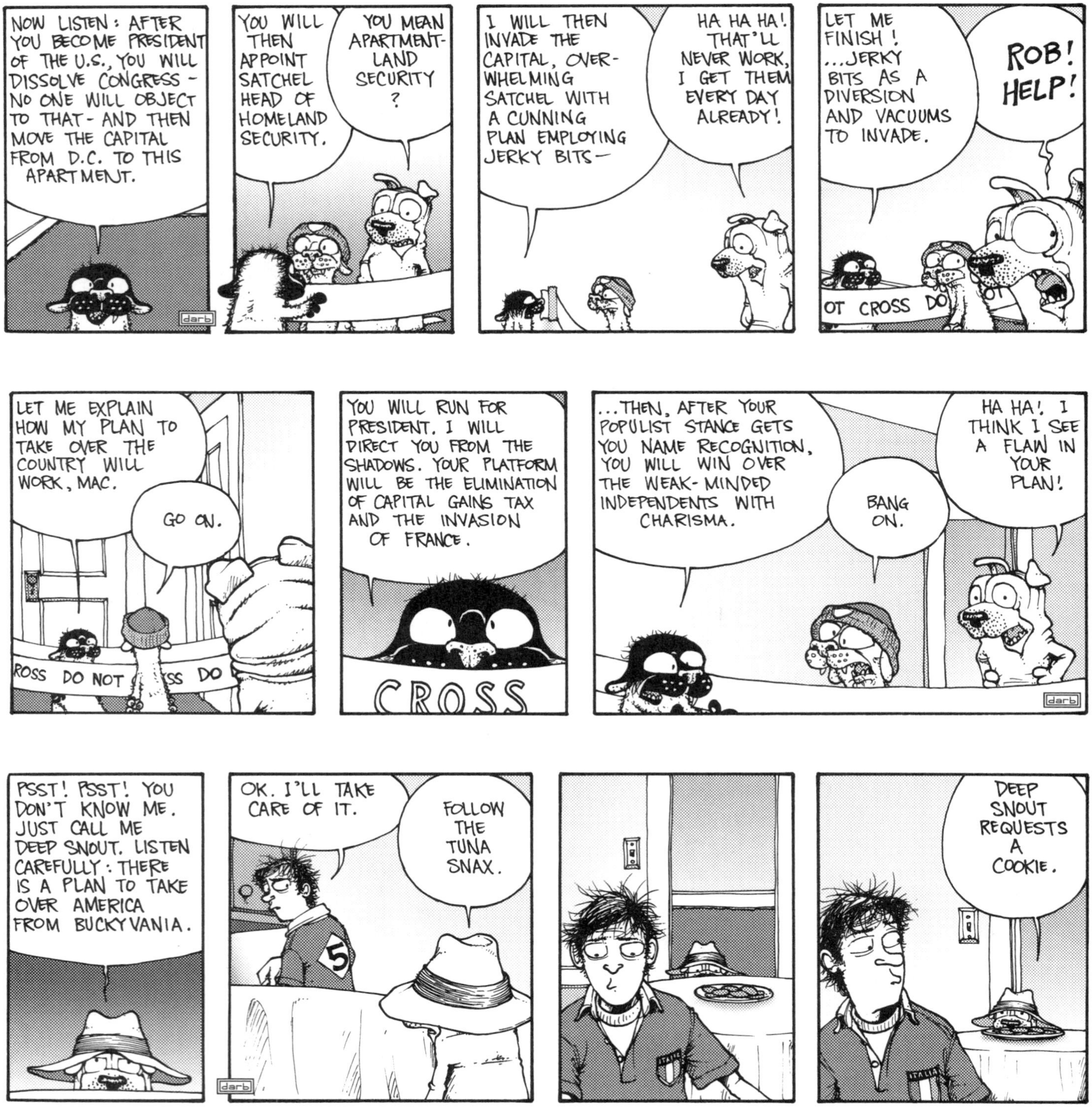
NOW LISTEN: AFTER YOU BECOME PRESIDENT OF THE U.S., YOU WILL DISSOLVE CONGRESS - NO ONE WILL OBJECT TO THAT - AND THEN MOVE THE CAPITAL FROM D.C. TO THIS APARTMENT.
darb
YOU WILL THEN APPOINT SATCHEL HEAD OF HOMELAND SECURITY.
YOU MEAN APARTMENT-LAND SECURITY ?
I WILL THEN INVADE THE CAPITAL, OVER-WHELMING SATCHEL WITH A CUNNING PLAN EMPLOYING JERKY BITS—
HA HA HA! THAT'LL NEVER WORK, I GET THEM EVERY DAY ALREADY!
LET ME FINISH! ...JERKY BITS AS A DIVERSION AND VACUUMS TO INVADE.
ROB! HELP!
OT CROSS DO
LET ME EXPLAIN HOW MY PLAN TO TAKE OVER THE COUNTRY WILL WORK, MAC.
GO ON.
ROSS DO NOT
SS DO
YOU WILL RUN FOR PRESIDENT. I WILL DIRECT YOU FROM THE SHADOWS. YOUR PLATFORM WILL BE THE ELIMINATION OF CAPITAL GAINS TAX AND THE INVASION OF FRANCE.
CROSS
...THEN, AFTER YOUR POPULIST STANCE GETS YOU NAME RECOGNITION, YOU WILL WIN OVER THE WEAK-MINDED INDEPENDENTS WITH CHARISMA.
BANG ON.
HA HA! I THINK I SEE A FLAW IN YOUR PLAN!
darb
PSST! PSST! YOU DON'T KNOW ME. JUST CALL ME DEEP SNOUT. LISTEN CAREFULLY: THERE IS A PLAN TO TAKE OVER AMERICA FROM BUCKYVANIA.
darb
OK. I'LL TAKE CARE OF IT.
FOLLOW THE TUNA SNAX.
5
DEEP SNOUT REQUESTS A COOKIE.

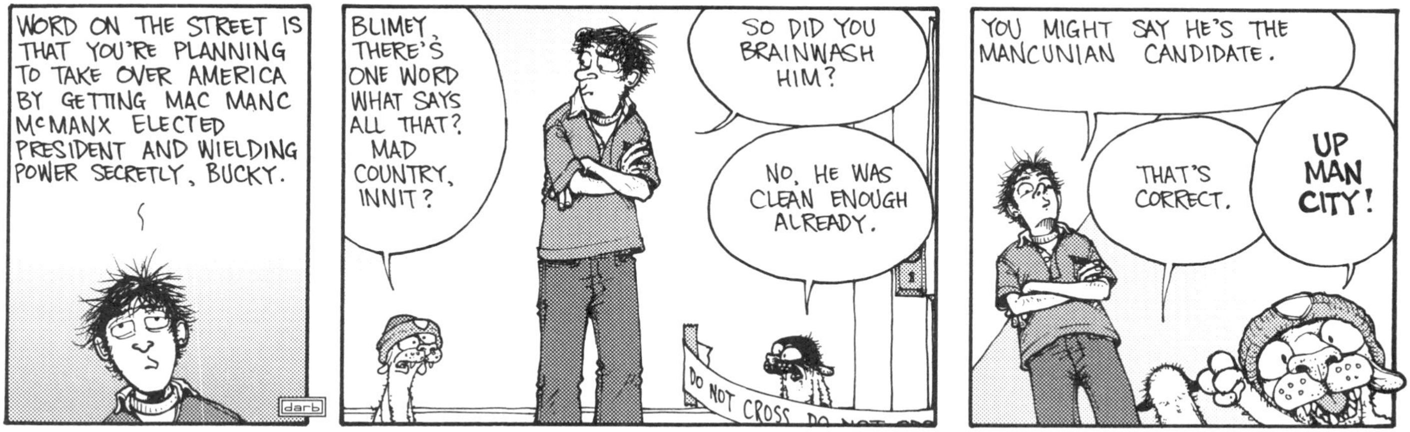
WORD ON THE STREET IS THAT YOU'RE PLANNING TO TAKE OVER AMERICA BY GETTING MAC MANC McMANX ELECTED PRESIDENT AND WIELDING POWER SECRETLY, BUCKY.
BLIMEY, THERE'S ONE WORD WHAT SAYS ALL THAT? MAD COUNTRY, INNIT?
SO DID YOU BRAINWASH HIM?
NO, HE WAS CLEAN ENOUGH ALREADY.
DO NOT CROSS
YOU MIGHT SAY HE'S THE MANCUNIAN CANDIDATE.
THAT'S CORRECT.
UP MAN CITY!

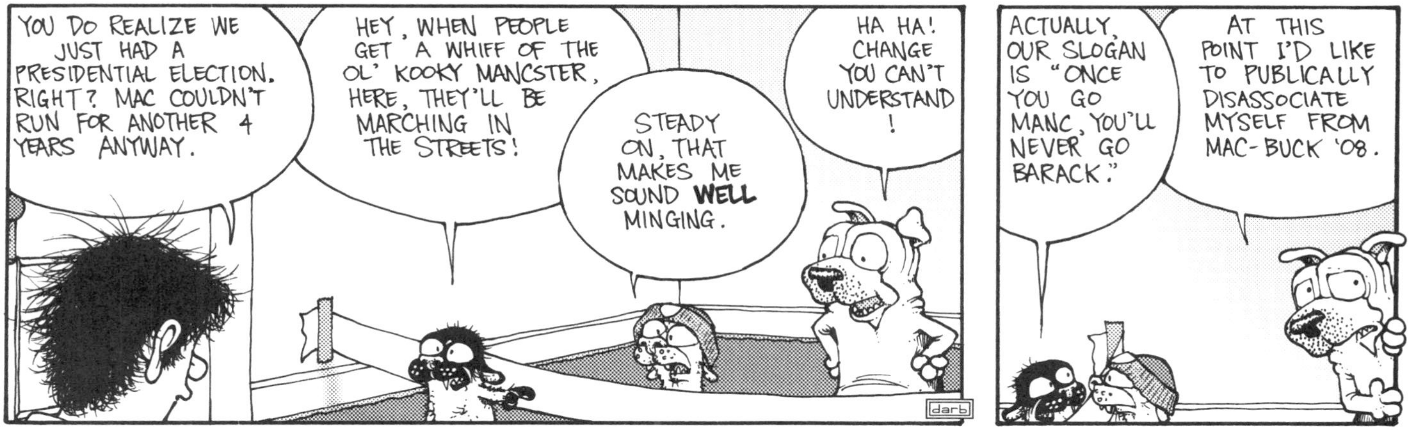
YOU DO REALIZE WE JUST HAD A PRESIDENTIAL ELECTION, RIGHT? MAC COULDN'T RUN FOR ANOTHER 4 YEARS ANYWAY.
HEY, WHEN PEOPLE GET A WHIFF OF THE OL' KOOKY MANCSTER, HERE, THEY'LL BE MARCHING IN THE STREETS!
STEADY ON, THAT MAKES ME SOUND WELL MINGING.
HA HA! CHANGE YOU CAN'T UNDERSTAND!
ACTUALLY, OUR SLOGAN IS "ONCE YOU GO MANC, YOU'LL NEVER GO BARACK."
AT THIS POINT I'D LIKE TO PUBLICALLY DISASSOCIATE MYSELF FROM MAC-BUCK '08.

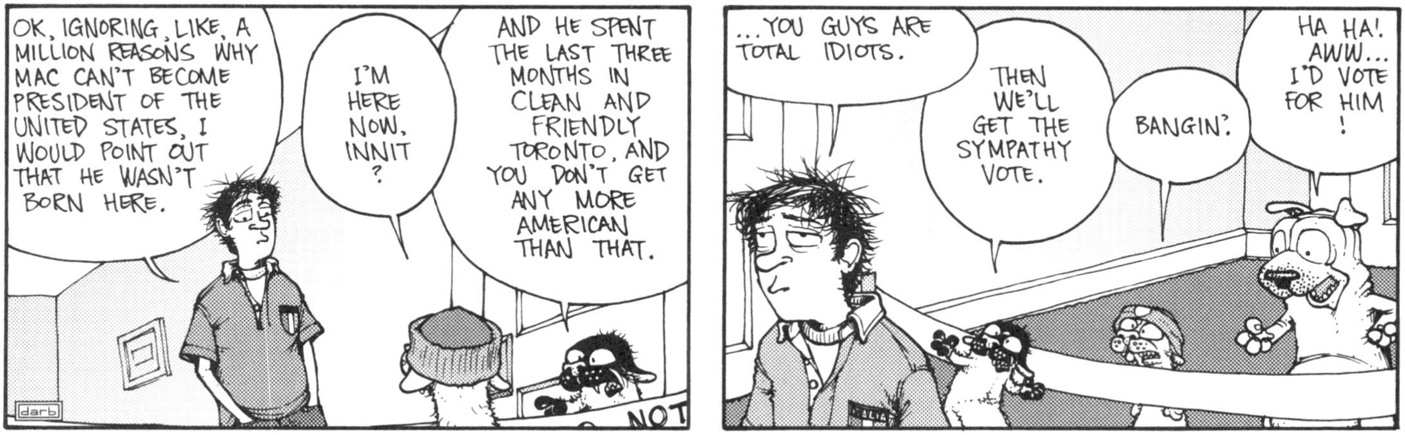
OK, IGNORING, LIKE, A MILLION REASONS WHY MAC CAN'T BECOME PRESIDENT OF THE UNITED STATES, I WOULD POINT OUT THAT HE WASN'T BORN HERE.
I'M HERE NOW, INNIT?
AND HE SPENT THE LAST THREE MONTHS IN CLEAN AND FRIENDLY TORONTO, AND YOU DON'T GET ANY MORE AMERICAN THAN THAT.
...YOU GUYS ARE TOTAL IDIOTS.
THEN WE'LL GET THE SYMPATHY VOTE.
BANGIN'.
HA HA! AWW... I'D VOTE FOR HIM!

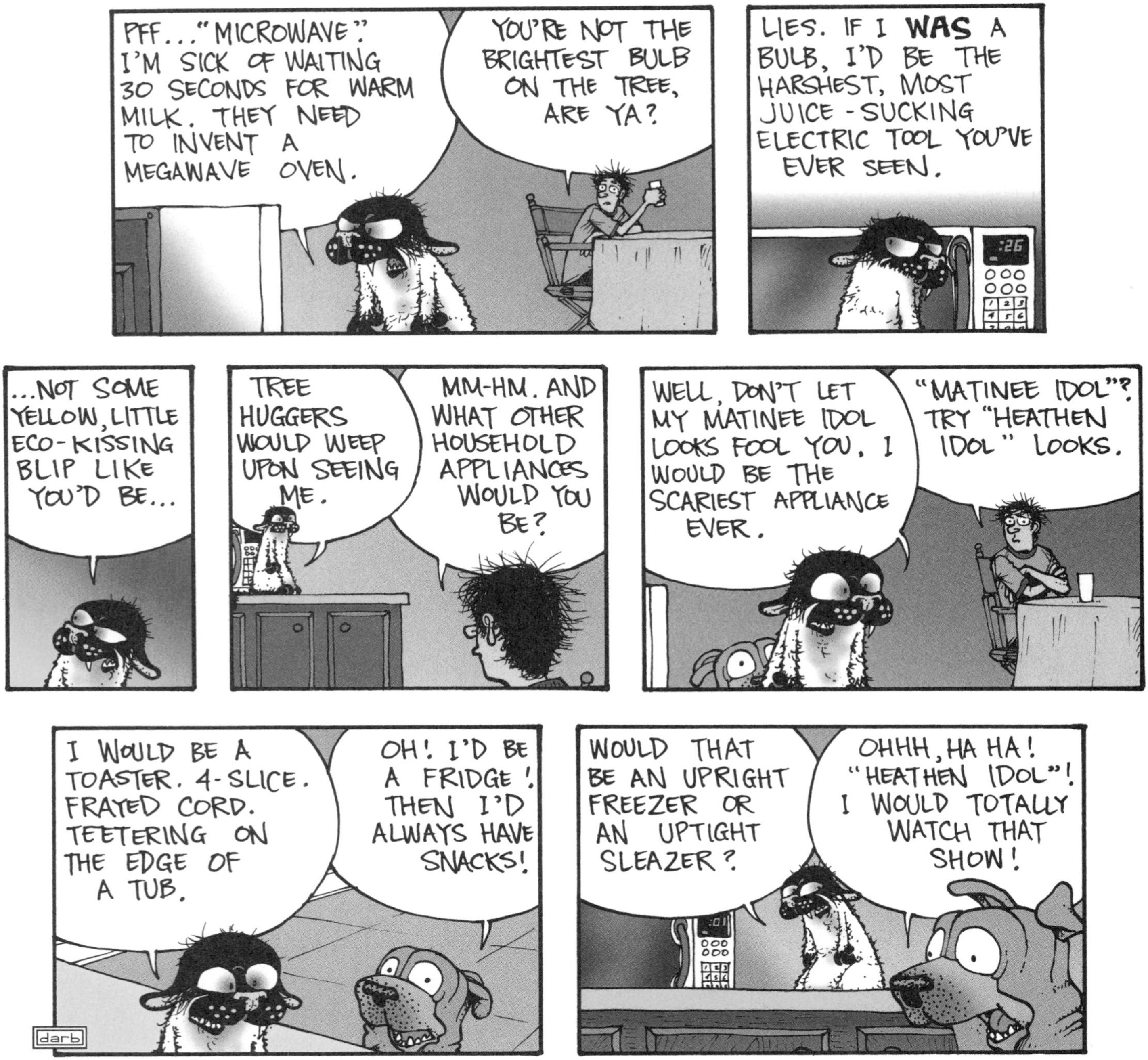
PFF..."MICROWAVE." I'M SICK OF WAITING 30 SECONDS FOR WARM MILK. THEY NEED TO INVENT A MEGAWAVE OVEN.
YOU'RE NOT THE BRIGHTEST BULB ON THE TREE, ARE YA?
LIES. IF I WAS A BULB, I'D BE THE HARSHEST, MOST JUICE-SUCKING ELECTRIC TOOL YOU'VE EVER SEEN.
...NOT SOME YELLOW, LITTLE ECO-KISSING BLIP LIKE YOU'D BE...
TREE HUGGERS WOULD WEEP UPON SEEING ME.
MM-HM. AND WHAT OTHER HOUSEHOLD APPLIANCES WOULD YOU BE?
WELL, DON'T LET MY MATINEE IDOL LOOKS FOOL YOU. I WOULD BE THE SCARIEST APPLIANCE EVER.
"MATINEE IDOL"? TRY "HEATHEN IDOL" LOOKS.
I WOULD BE A TOASTER. 4-SLICE. FRAYED CORD. TEETERING ON THE EDGE OF A TUB.
OH! I'D BE A FRIDGE! THEN I'D ALWAYS HAVE SNACKS!
darb
WOULD THAT BE AN UPRIGHT FREEZER OR AN UPTIGHT SLEAZER?
OHHH, HA HA! "HEATHEN IDOL"! I WOULD TOTALLY WATCH THAT SHOW!

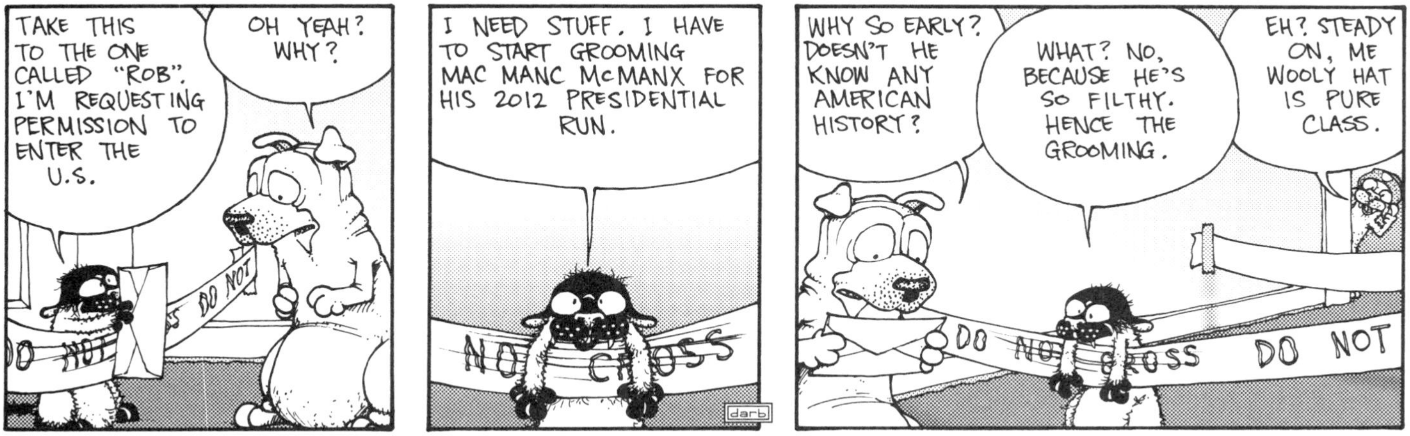
TAKE THIS TO THE ONE CALLED "ROB". I'M REQUESTING PERMISSION TO ENTER THE U.S.
OH YEAH? WHY?
I NEED STUFF. I HAVE TO START GROOMING MAC MANC McMANX FOR HIS 2012 PRESIDENTIAL RUN.
WHY SO EARLY? DOESN'T HE KNOW ANY AMERICAN HISTORY?
WHAT? NO, BECAUSE HE'S SO FILTHY. HENCE THE GROOMING.
EH? STEADY ON, ME WOOLY HAT IS PURE CLASS.

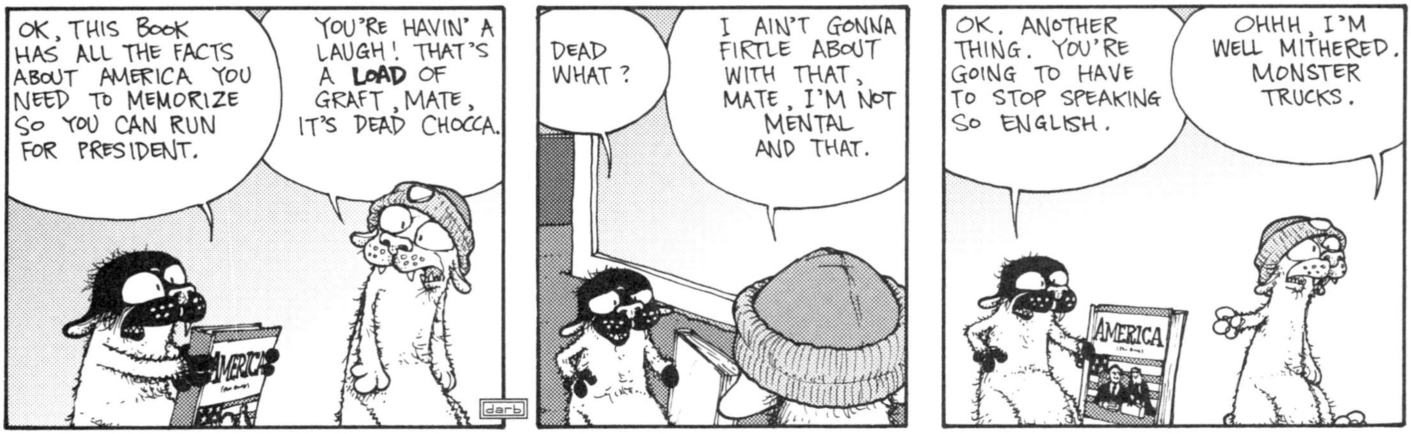
OK, THIS BOOK HAS ALL THE FACTS ABOUT AMERICA YOU NEED TO MEMORIZE SO YOU CAN RUN FOR PRESIDENT.
YOU'RE HAVIN' A LAUGH! THAT'S A **LOAD** OF GRAFT, MATE, IT'S DEAD CHOCCA.
DEAD WHAT?
I AIN'T GONNA FIRTLE ABOUT WITH THAT, MATE, I'M NOT MENTAL AND THAT.
OK. ANOTHER THING. YOU'RE GOING TO HAVE TO STOP SPEAKING SO ENGLISH.
OHHH, I'M WELL MITHERED. MONSTER TRUCKS.
AMERICA

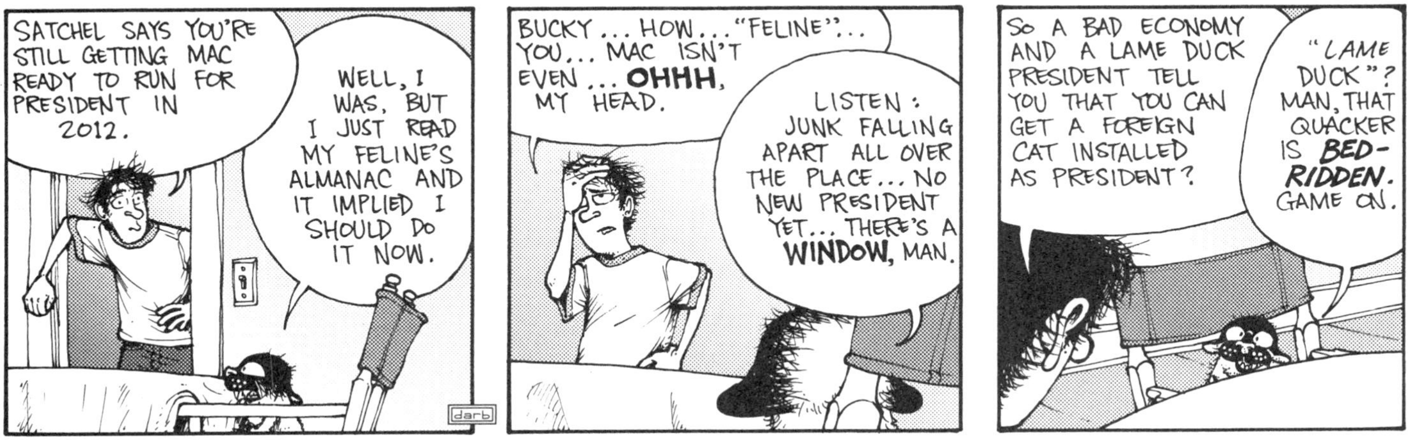
SATCHEL SAYS YOU'RE STILL GETTING MAC READY TO RUN FOR PRESIDENT IN 2012.
WELL, I WAS, BUT I JUST READ MY FELINE'S ALMANAC AND IT IMPLIED I SHOULD DO IT NOW.
BUCKY... HOW... "FELINE"... YOU... MAC ISN'T EVEN... **OHHH**, MY HEAD.
LISTEN: JUNK FALLING APART ALL OVER THE PLACE... NO NEW PRESIDENT YET... THERE'S A **WINDOW**, MAN.
SO A BAD ECONOMY AND A LAME DUCK PRESIDENT TELL YOU THAT YOU CAN GET A FOREIGN CAT INSTALLED AS PRESIDENT?
"*LAME DUCK*"? MAN, THAT QUACKER IS ***BED-RIDDEN***. GAME ON.

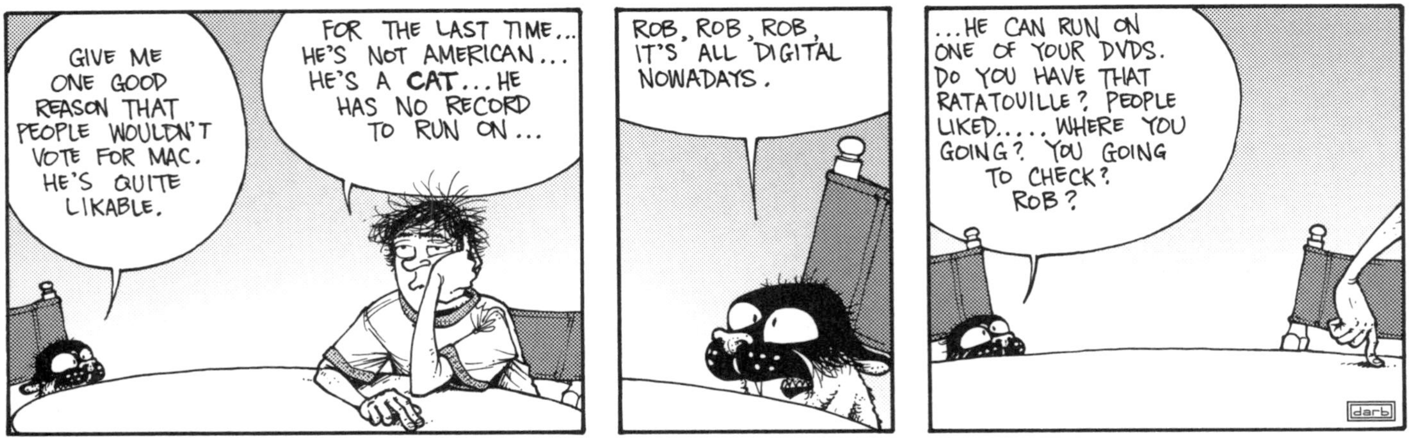
GIVE ME ONE GOOD REASON THAT PEOPLE WOULDN'T VOTE FOR MAC. HE'S QUITE LIKABLE.
FOR THE LAST TIME... HE'S NOT AMERICAN... HE'S A **CAT**... HE HAS NO RECORD TO RUN ON...
ROB, ROB, ROB, IT'S ALL DIGITAL NOWADAYS.
...HE CAN RUN ON ONE OF YOUR DVDS. DO YOU HAVE THAT RATATOUILLE? PEOPLE LIKED..... WHERE YOU GOING? YOU GOING TO CHECK? ROB?
darb

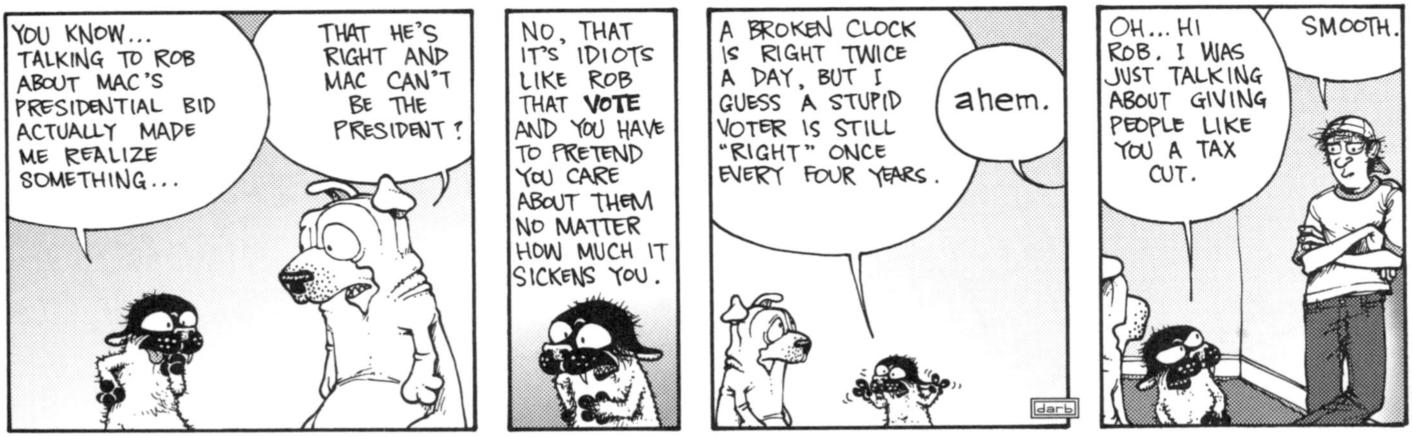
YOU KNOW... TALKING TO ROB ABOUT MAC'S PRESIDENTIAL BID ACTUALLY MADE ME REALIZE SOMETHING...
THAT HE'S RIGHT AND MAC CAN'T BE THE PRESIDENT?
NO, THAT IT'S IDIOTS LIKE ROB THAT **VOTE** AND YOU HAVE TO PRETEND YOU CARE ABOUT THEM NO MATTER HOW MUCH IT SICKENS YOU.
A BROKEN CLOCK IS RIGHT TWICE A DAY, BUT I GUESS A STUPID VOTER IS STILL "RIGHT" ONCE EVERY FOUR YEARS.
ahem.
darb
OH... HI ROB. I WAS JUST TALKING ABOUT GIVING PEOPLE LIKE YOU A TAX CUT.
SMOOTH.

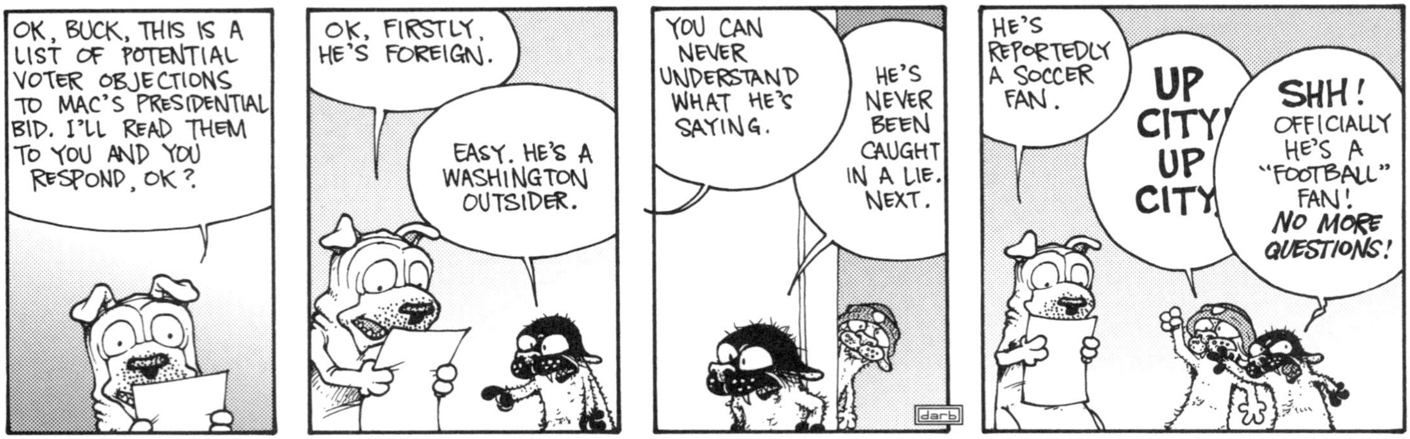
OK, BUCK, THIS IS A LIST OF POTENTIAL VOTER OBJECTIONS TO MAC'S PRESIDENTIAL BID. I'LL READ THEM TO YOU AND YOU RESPOND, OK?
OK, FIRSTLY, HE'S FOREIGN.
EASY. HE'S A WASHINGTON OUTSIDER.
YOU CAN NEVER UNDERSTAND WHAT HE'S SAYING.
HE'S NEVER BEEN CAUGHT IN A LIE. NEXT.
darb
HE'S REPORTEDLY A SOCCER FAN.
UP CITY! UP CITY!
SHH! OFFICIALLY HE'S A "FOOTBALL" FAN! ***NO MORE QUESTIONS!***

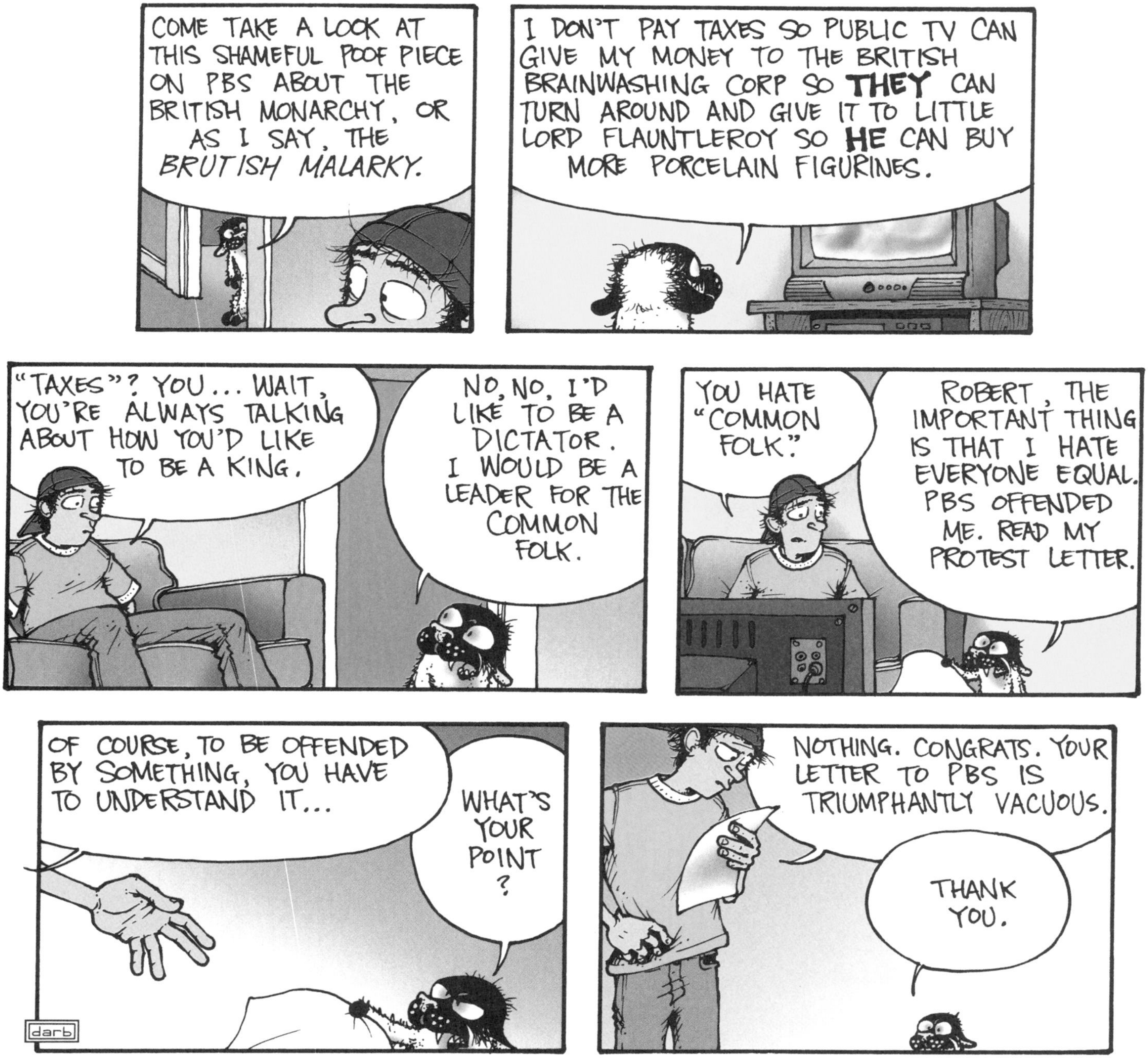
COME TAKE A LOOK AT THIS SHAMEFUL POOF PIECE ON PBS ABOUT THE BRITISH MONARCHY, OR AS I SAY, THE *BRUTISH MALARKY.*
I DON'T PAY TAXES SO PUBLIC TV CAN GIVE MY MONEY TO THE BRITISH BRAINWASHING CORP SO **THEY** CAN TURN AROUND AND GIVE IT TO LITTLE LORD FLAUNTLEROY SO **HE** CAN BUY MORE PORCELAIN FIGURINES.
"TAXES"? YOU... WAIT, YOU'RE ALWAYS TALKING ABOUT HOW YOU'D LIKE TO BE A KING.
NO, NO, I'D LIKE TO BE A DICTATOR. I WOULD BE A LEADER FOR THE COMMON FOLK.
YOU HATE "COMMON FOLK."
ROBERT, THE IMPORTANT THING IS THAT I HATE EVERYONE EQUAL. PBS OFFENDED ME. READ MY PROTEST LETTER.
OF COURSE, TO BE OFFENDED BY SOMETHING, YOU HAVE TO UNDERSTAND IT...
WHAT'S YOUR POINT?
darb
NOTHING. CONGRATS. YOUR LETTER TO PBS IS TRIUMPHANTLY VACUOUS.
THANK YOU.

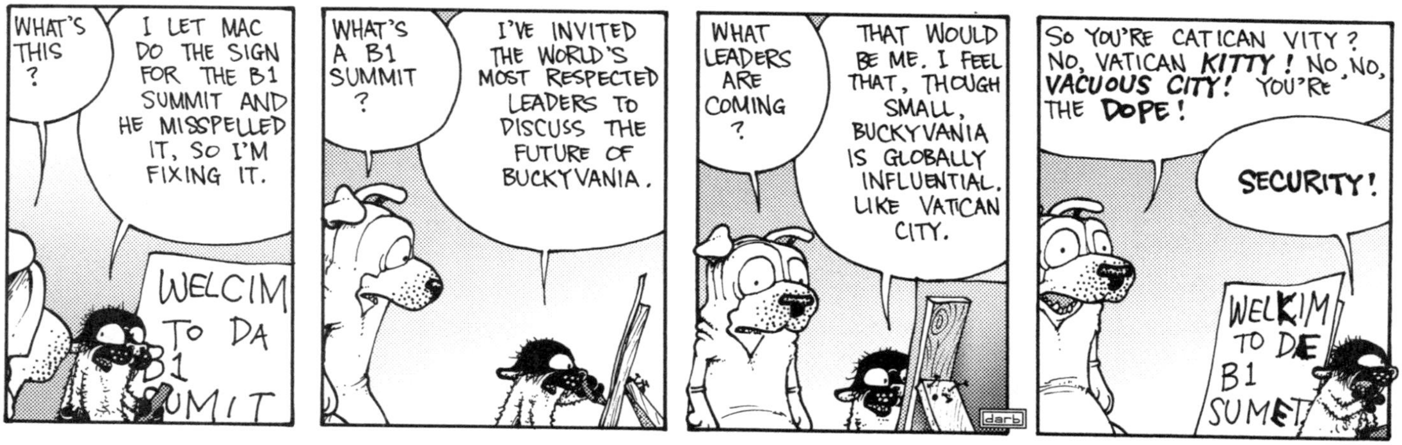
WHAT'S THIS ?
I LET MAC DO THE SIGN FOR THE B1 SUMMIT AND HE MISSPELLED IT, SO I'M FIXING IT.
WELCIM TO DA B1 SUMIT
WHAT'S A B1 SUMMIT ?
I'VE INVITED THE WORLD'S MOST RESPECTED LEADERS TO DISCUSS THE FUTURE OF BUCKYVANIA.
WHAT LEADERS ARE COMING ?
THAT WOULD BE ME. I FEEL THAT, THOUGH SMALL, BUCKYVANIA IS GLOBALLY INFLUENTIAL. LIKE VATICAN CITY.
SO YOU'RE CATICAN VITY? NO, VATICAN **KITTY!** NO, NO, **VACUOUS CITY!** YOU'RE THE **DOPE!**
SECURITY!
WELKIM TO DE B1 SUMET

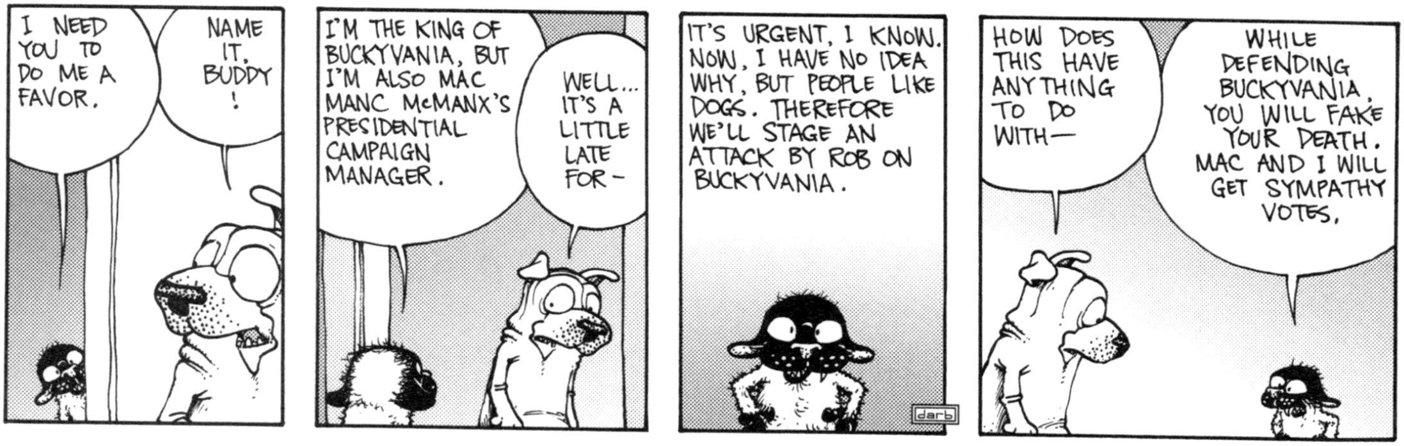
I NEED YOU TO DO ME A FAVOR.
NAME IT, BUDDY !
I'M THE KING OF BUCKYVANIA, BUT I'M ALSO MAC MANC McMANX'S PRESIDENTIAL CAMPAIGN MANAGER.
WELL... IT'S A LITTLE LATE FOR-
IT'S URGENT, I KNOW. NOW, I HAVE NO IDEA WHY, BUT PEOPLE LIKE DOGS. THEREFORE WE'LL STAGE AN ATTACK BY ROB ON BUCKYVANIA.
HOW DOES THIS HAVE ANYTHING TO DO WITH—
WHILE DEFENDING BUCKYVANIA, YOU WILL FAKE YOUR DEATH. MAC AND I WILL GET SYMPATHY VOTES.

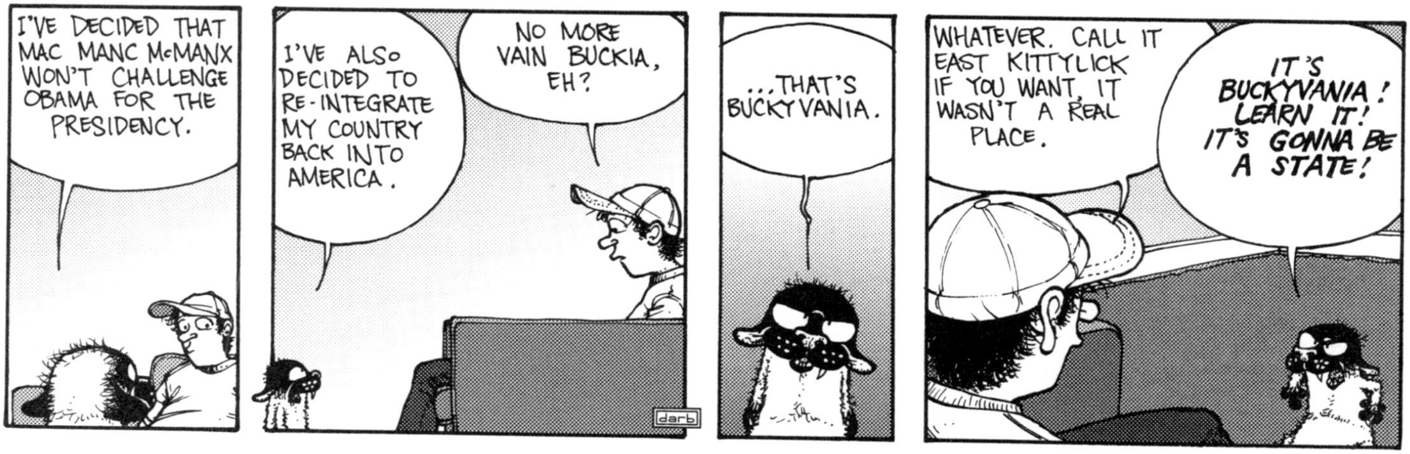
I'VE DECIDED THAT MAC MANC McMANX WON'T CHALLENGE OBAMA FOR THE PRESIDENCY.
I'VE ALSO DECIDED TO RE-INTEGRATE MY COUNTRY BACK INTO AMERICA.
NO MORE VAIN BUCKIA, EH?
...THAT'S BUCKYVANIA.
WHATEVER. CALL IT EAST KITTYLICK IF YOU WANT, IT WASN'T A REAL PLACE.
IT'S BUCKYVANIA! LEARN IT! IT'S GONNA BE A STATE!

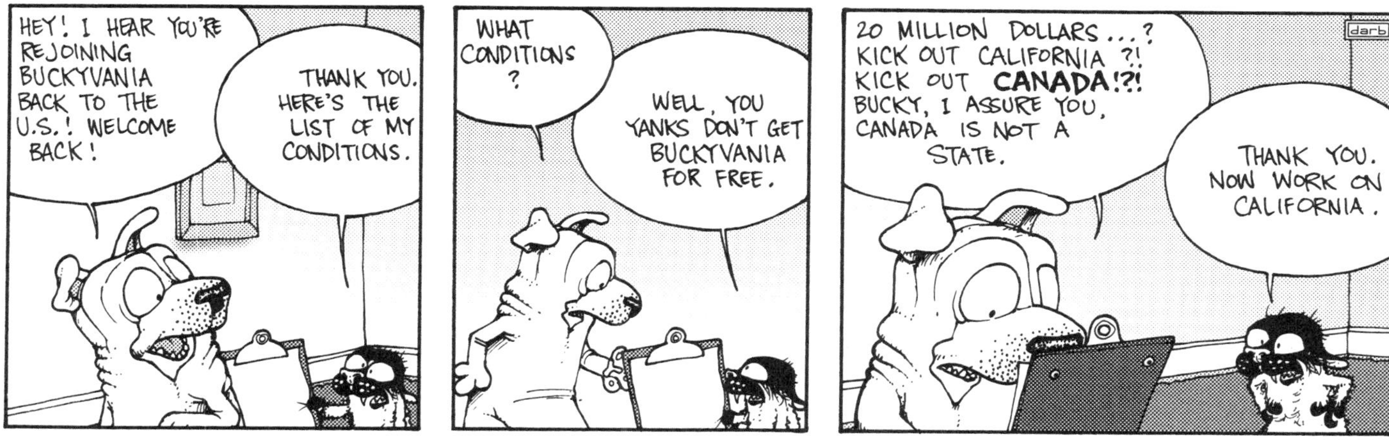
HEY! I HEAR YOU'RE REJOINING BUCKYVANIA BACK TO THE U.S.! WELCOME BACK!
THANK YOU. HERE'S THE LIST OF MY CONDITIONS.
WHAT CONDITIONS ?
WELL, YOU YANKS DON'T GET BUCKYVANIA FOR FREE.
20 MILLION DOLLARS...? KICK OUT CALIFORNIA ?! KICK OUT CANADA!?! BUCKY, I ASSURE YOU, CANADA IS NOT A STATE.
THANK YOU. NOW WORK ON CALIFORNIA.
darb

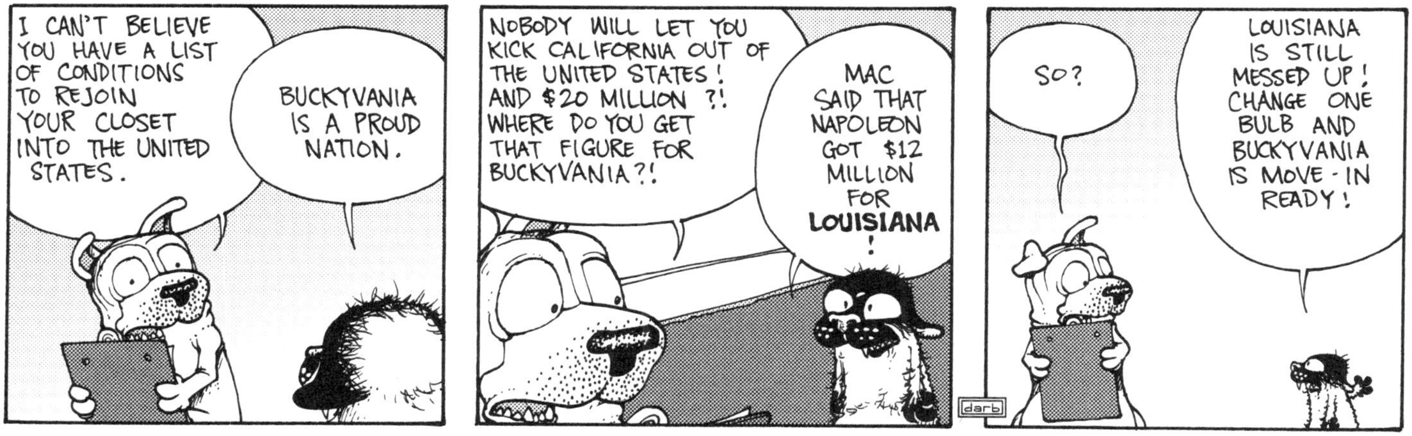
I CAN'T BELIEVE YOU HAVE A LIST OF CONDITIONS TO REJOIN YOUR CLOSET INTO THE UNITED STATES.
BUCKYVANIA IS A PROUD NATION.
NOBODY WILL LET YOU KICK CALIFORNIA OUT OF THE UNITED STATES! AND $20 MILLION ?! WHERE DO YOU GET THAT FIGURE FOR BUCKYVANIA?!
MAC SAID THAT NAPOLEON GOT $12 MILLION FOR LOUISIANA !
SO?
LOUISIANA IS STILL MESSED UP! CHANGE ONE BULB AND BUCKYVANIA IS MOVE-IN READY!
darb

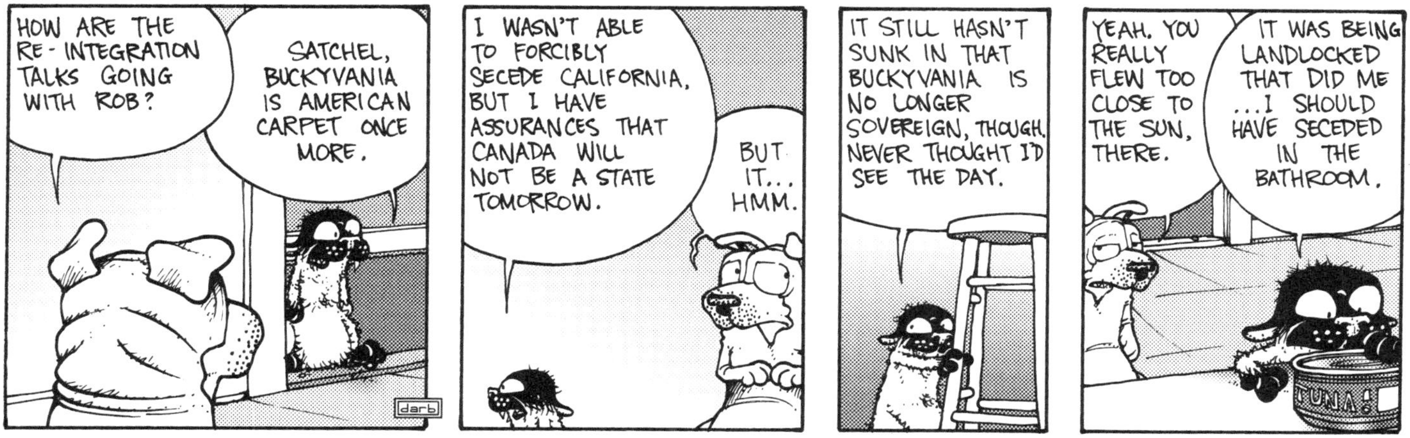
HOW ARE THE RE-INTEGRATION TALKS GOING WITH ROB?
SATCHEL, BUCKYVANIA IS AMERICAN CARPET ONCE MORE.
I WASN'T ABLE TO FORCIBLY SECEDE CALIFORNIA, BUT I HAVE ASSURANCES THAT CANADA WILL NOT BE A STATE TOMORROW.
BUT IT... HMM.
IT STILL HASN'T SUNK IN THAT BUCKYVANIA IS NO LONGER SOVEREIGN, THOUGH. NEVER THOUGHT I'D SEE THE DAY.
YEAH. YOU REALLY FLEW TOO CLOSE TO THE SUN, THERE.
IT WAS BEING LANDLOCKED THAT DID ME ...I SHOULD HAVE SECEDED IN THE BATHROOM.
TUNA!
darb

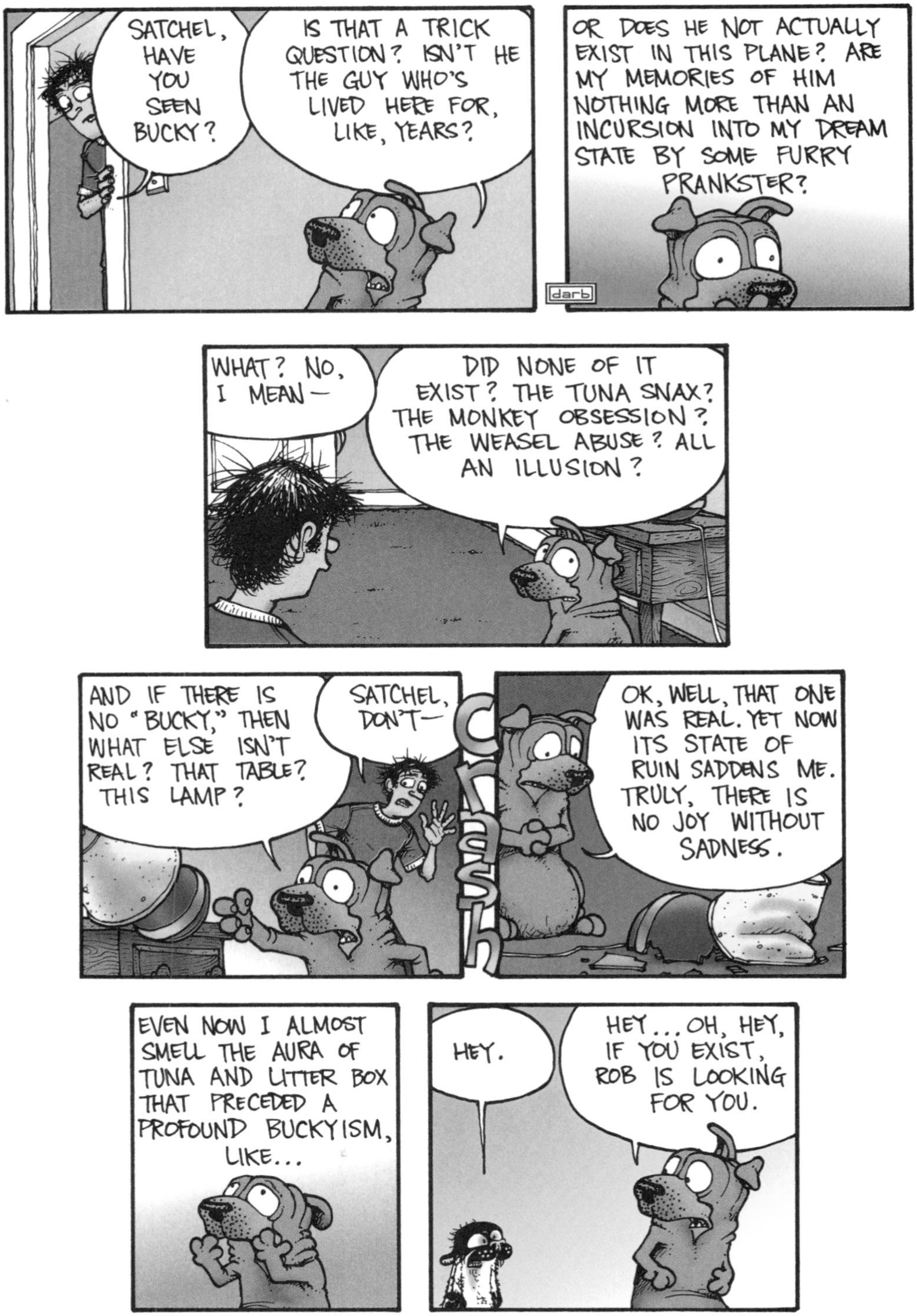
SATCHEL, HAVE YOU SEEN BUCKY?
IS THAT A TRICK QUESTION? ISN'T HE THE GUY WHO'S LIVED HERE FOR, LIKE, YEARS?
OR DOES HE NOT ACTUALLY EXIST IN THIS PLANE? ARE MY MEMORIES OF HIM NOTHING MORE THAN AN INCURSION INTO MY DREAM STATE BY SOME FURRY PRANKSTER?
darb
WHAT? NO, I MEAN—
DID NONE OF IT EXIST? THE TUNA SNAX? THE MONKEY OBSESSION? THE WEASEL ABUSE? ALL AN ILLUSION?
AND IF THERE IS NO "BUCKY," THEN WHAT ELSE ISN'T REAL? THAT TABLE? THIS LAMP?
SATCHEL, DON'T—
Crash
OK, WELL, THAT ONE WAS REAL. YET NOW ITS STATE OF RUIN SADDENS ME. TRULY, THERE IS NO JOY WITHOUT SADNESS.
EVEN NOW I ALMOST SMELL THE AURA OF TUNA AND LITTER BOX THAT PRECEDED A PROFOUND BUCKYISM, LIKE...
HEY.
HEY... OH, HEY, IF YOU EXIST, ROB IS LOOKING FOR YOU.

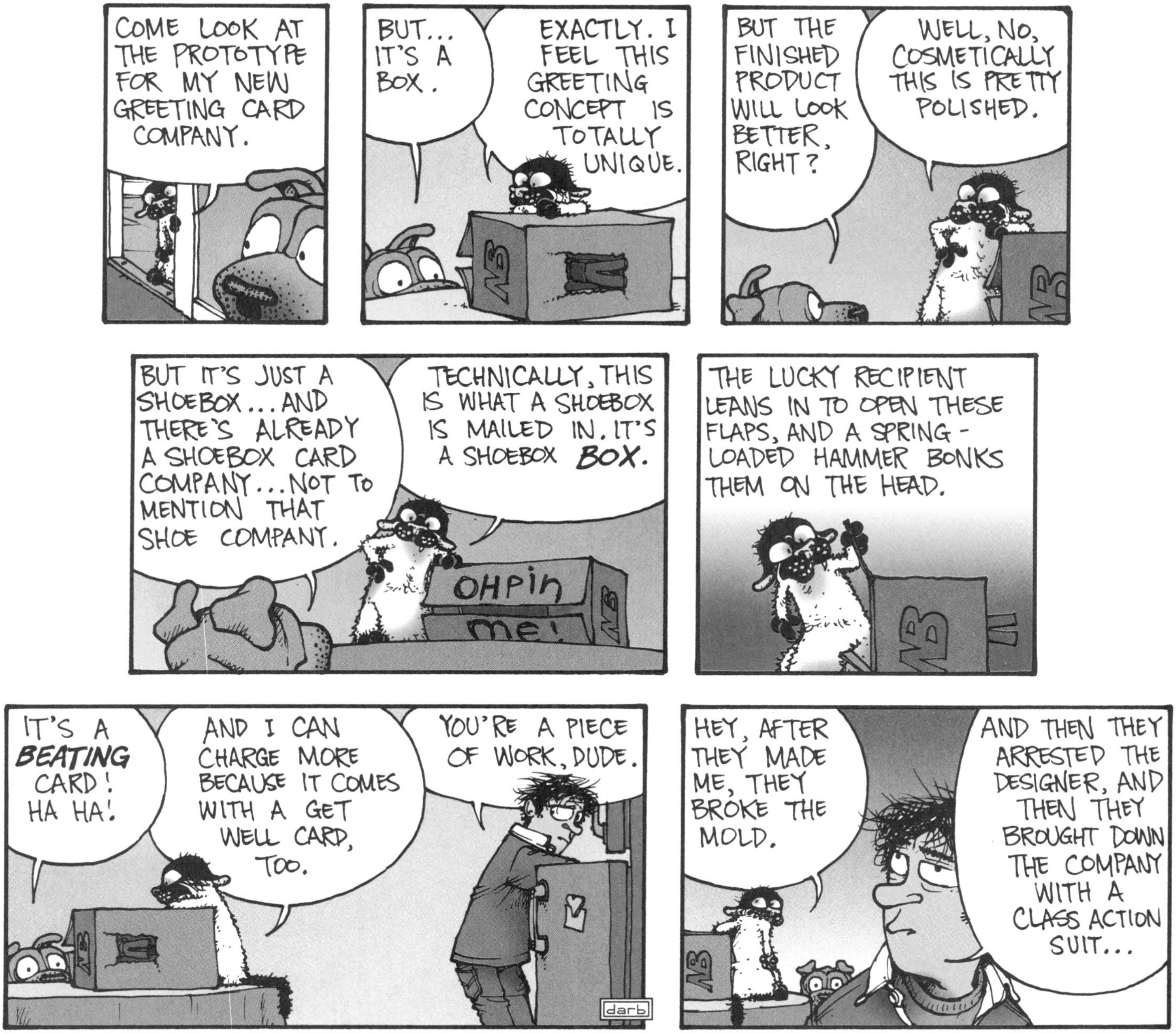
COME LOOK AT THE PROTOTYPE FOR MY NEW GREETING CARD COMPANY.
BUT... IT'S A BOX.
EXACTLY. I FEEL THIS GREETING CONCEPT IS TOTALLY UNIQUE.
BUT THE FINISHED PRODUCT WILL LOOK BETTER, RIGHT?
WELL, NO, COSMETICALLY THIS IS PRETTY POLISHED.
BUT IT'S JUST A SHOEBOX... AND THERE'S ALREADY A SHOEBOX CARD COMPANY... NOT TO MENTION THAT SHOE COMPANY.
TECHNICALLY, THIS IS WHAT A SHOEBOX IS MAILED IN. IT'S A SHOEBOX **BOX**.
OHPin
me!
THE LUCKY RECIPIENT LEANS IN TO OPEN THESE FLAPS, AND A SPRING-LOADED HAMMER BONKS THEM ON THE HEAD.
IT'S A **BEATING** CARD! HA HA!
AND I CAN CHARGE MORE BECAUSE IT COMES WITH A GET WELL CARD, TOO.
YOU'RE A PIECE OF WORK, DUDE.
darb
HEY, AFTER THEY MADE ME, THEY BROKE THE MOLD.
AND THEN THEY ARRESTED THE DESIGNER, AND THEN THEY BROUGHT DOWN THE COMPANY WITH A CLASS ACTION SUIT...

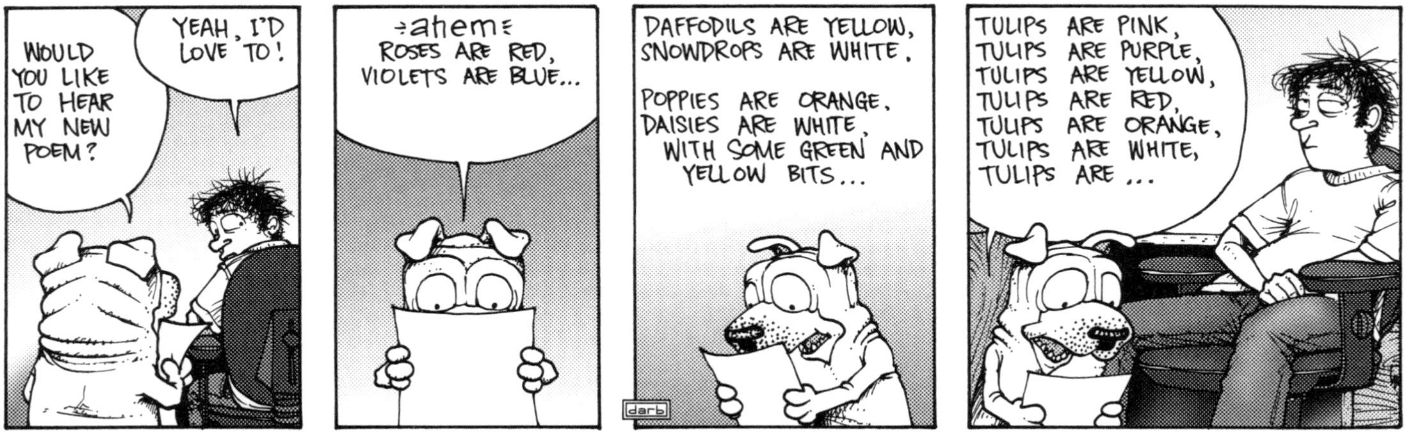
WOULD YOU LIKE TO HEAR MY NEW POEM?
YEAH, I'D LOVE TO!
ahem
ROSES ARE RED, VIOLETS ARE BLUE...
DAFFODILS ARE YELLOW, SNOWDROPS ARE WHITE.
POPPIES ARE ORANGE. DAISIES ARE WHITE, WITH SOME GREEN AND YELLOW BITS...
darb
TULIPS ARE PINK, TULIPS ARE PURPLE, TULIPS ARE YELLOW, TULIPS ARE RED, TULIPS ARE ORANGE, TULIPS ARE WHITE, TULIPS ARE...

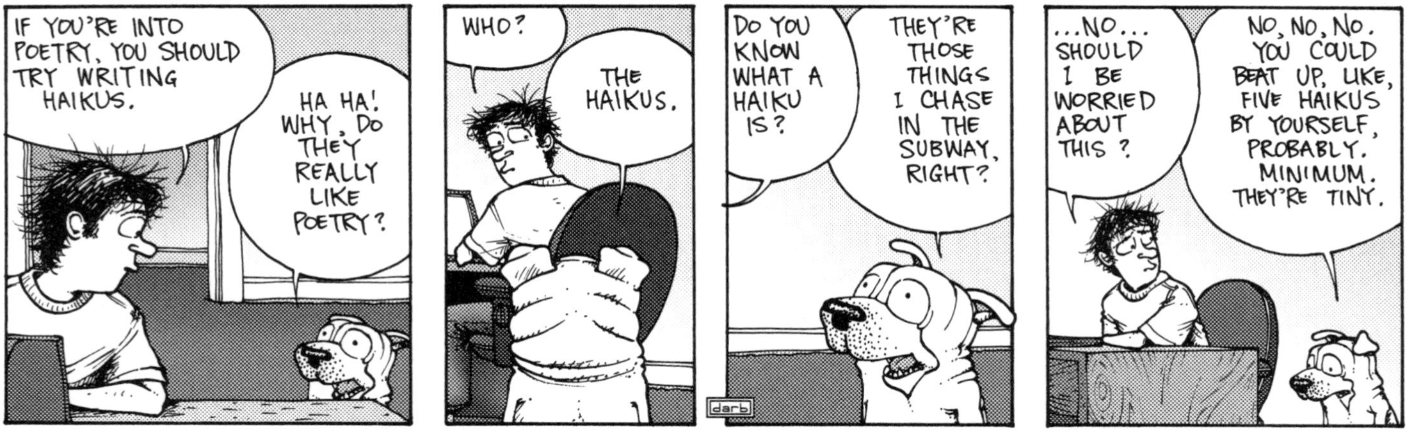
IF YOU'RE INTO POETRY, YOU SHOULD TRY WRITING HAIKUS.
HA HA! WHY, DO THEY REALLY LIKE POETRY?
WHO?
THE HAIKUS.
darb
DO YOU KNOW WHAT A HAIKU IS?
THEY'RE THOSE THINGS I CHASE IN THE SUBWAY, RIGHT?
...NO... SHOULD I BE WORRIED ABOUT THIS?
NO, NO, NO. YOU COULD BEAT UP, LIKE, FIVE HAIKUS BY YOURSELF, PROBABLY. MINIMUM. THEY'RE TINY.

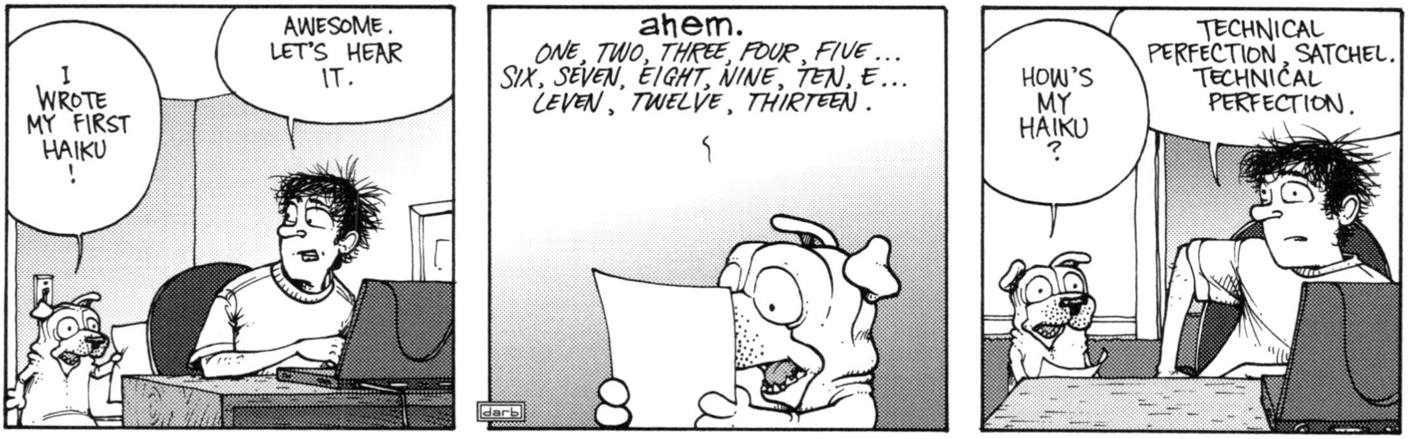
I WROTE MY FIRST HAIKU!
AWESOME. LET'S HEAR IT.
darb
ahem.
ONE, TWO, THREE, FOUR, FIVE... SIX, SEVEN, EIGHT, NINE, TEN, E... LEVEN, TWELVE, THIRTEEN.
HOW'S MY HAIKU?
TECHNICAL PERFECTION, SATCHEL. TECHNICAL PERFECTION.

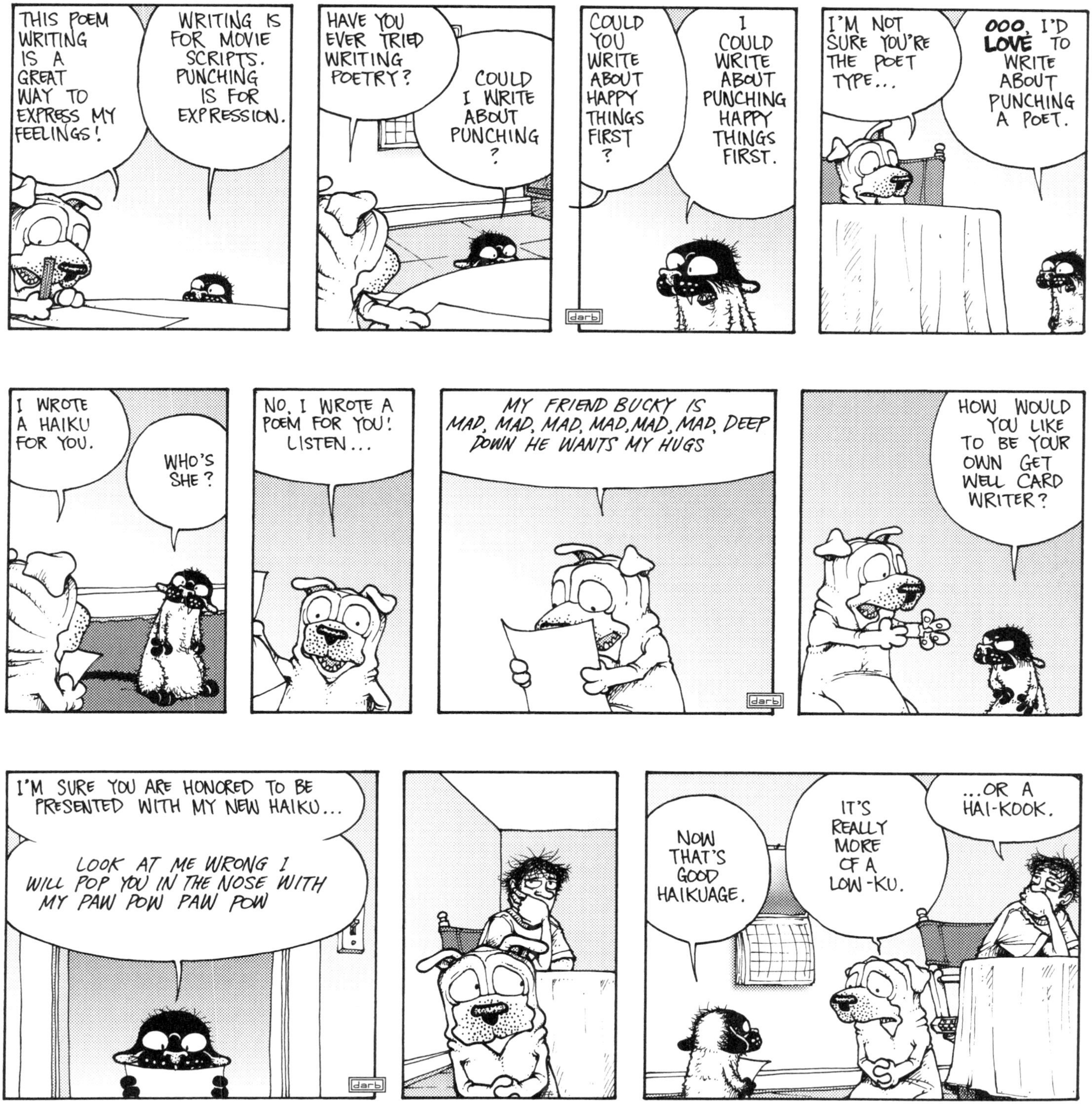
THIS POEM WRITING IS A GREAT WAY TO EXPRESS MY FEELINGS!
WRITING IS FOR MOVIE SCRIPTS. PUNCHING IS FOR EXPRESSION.
HAVE YOU EVER TRIED WRITING POETRY?
COULD I WRITE ABOUT PUNCHING?
COULD YOU WRITE ABOUT HAPPY THINGS FIRST?
I COULD WRITE ABOUT PUNCHING HAPPY THINGS FIRST.
I'M NOT SURE YOU'RE THE POET TYPE...
OOO, I'D LOVE TO WRITE ABOUT PUNCHING A POET.
I WROTE A HAIKU FOR YOU.
WHO'S SHE?
NO, I WROTE A POEM FOR YOU! LISTEN...
MY FRIEND BUCKY IS MAD, MAD, MAD, MAD, MAD, MAD, DEEP DOWN HE WANTS MY HUGS
HOW WOULD YOU LIKE TO BE YOUR OWN GET WELL CARD WRITER?
I'M SURE YOU ARE HONORED TO BE PRESENTED WITH MY NEW HAIKU...
LOOK AT ME WRONG I WILL POP YOU IN THE NOSE WITH MY PAW POW PAW POW
NOW THAT'S GOOD HAIKUAGE.
IT'S REALLY MORE OF A LOW-KU.
...OR A HAI-KOOK.

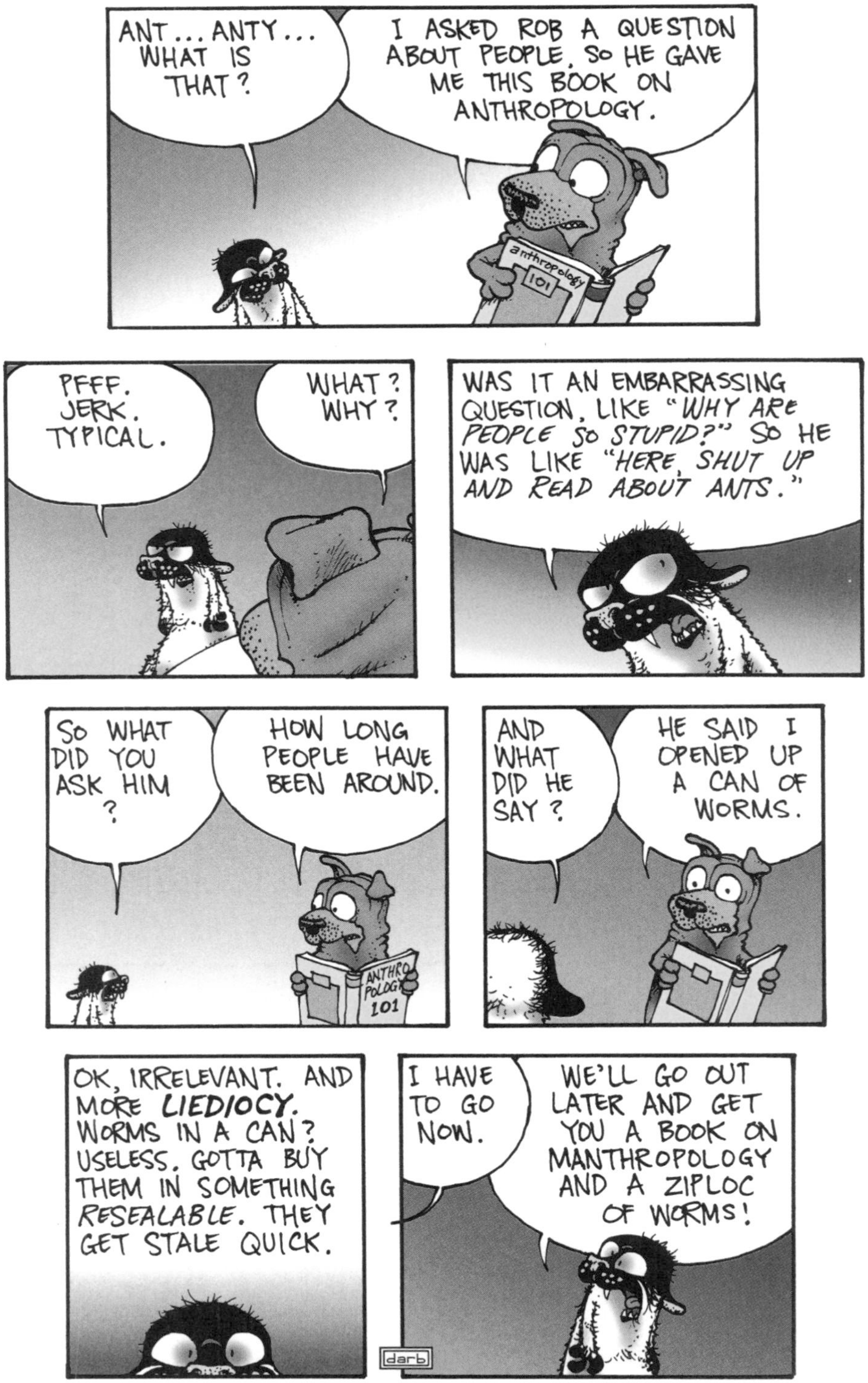
ANT... ANTY... WHAT IS THAT?
I ASKED ROB A QUESTION ABOUT PEOPLE, SO HE GAVE ME THIS BOOK ON ANTHROPOLOGY.
anthropology 101
PFFF. JERK. TYPICAL.
WHAT? WHY?
WAS IT AN EMBARRASSING QUESTION, LIKE "*WHY ARE PEOPLE SO STUPID?*" SO HE WAS LIKE "*HERE, SHUT UP AND READ ABOUT ANTS.*"
SO WHAT DID YOU ASK HIM?
HOW LONG PEOPLE HAVE BEEN AROUND.
ANTHROPOLOGY 101
AND WHAT DID HE SAY?
HE SAID I OPENED UP A CAN OF WORMS.
OK, IRRELEVANT. AND MORE **LIEDIOCY**. WORMS IN A CAN? USELESS. GOTTA BUY THEM IN SOMETHING *RESEALABLE*. THEY GET STALE QUICK.
darb
I HAVE TO GO NOW.
WE'LL GO OUT LATER AND GET YOU A BOOK ON MANTHROPOLOGY AND A ZIPLOC OF WORMS!

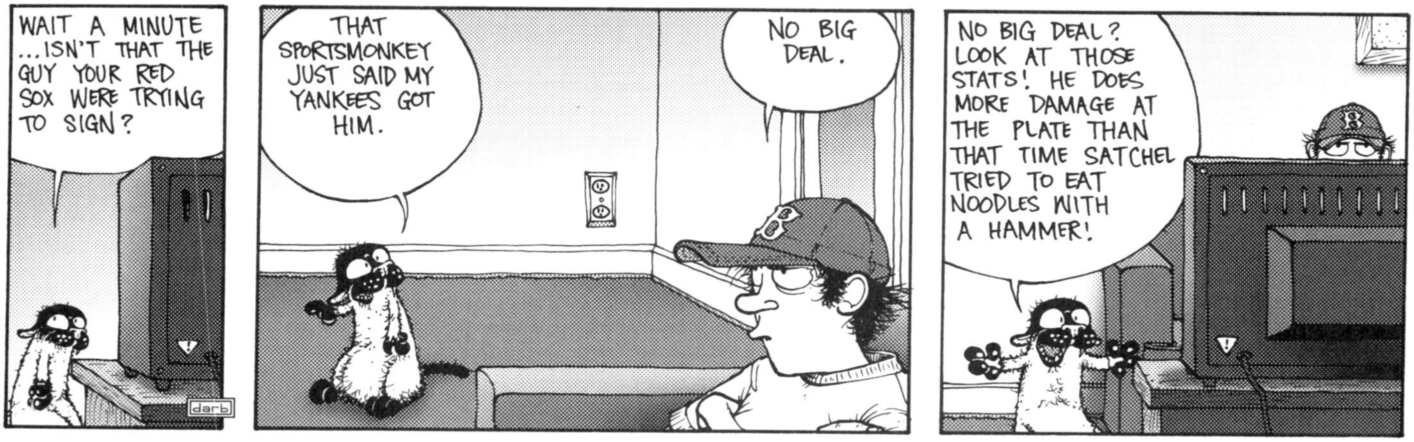
WAIT A MINUTE ...ISN'T THAT THE GUY YOUR RED SOX WERE TRYING TO SIGN?
THAT SPORTSMONKEY JUST SAID MY YANKEES GOT HIM.
NO BIG DEAL.
NO BIG DEAL? LOOK AT THOSE STATS! HE DOES MORE DAMAGE AT THE PLATE THAN THAT TIME SATCHEL TRIED TO EAT NOODLES WITH A HAMMER!
darb

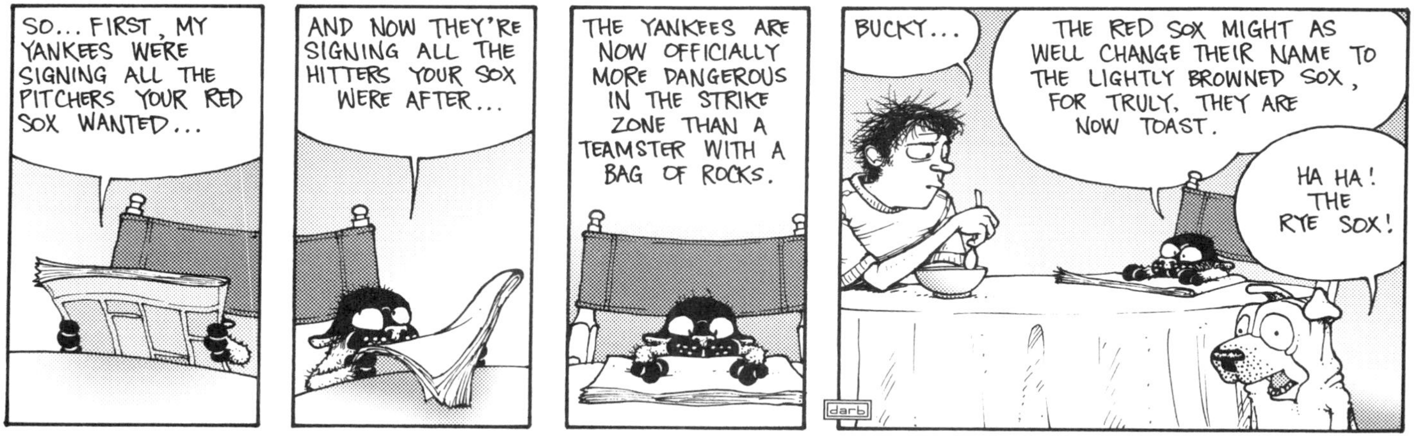
SO... FIRST, MY YANKEES WERE SIGNING ALL THE PITCHERS YOUR RED SOX WANTED...
AND NOW THEY'RE SIGNING ALL THE HITTERS YOUR SOX WERE AFTER...
THE YANKEES ARE NOW OFFICIALLY MORE DANGEROUS IN THE STRIKE ZONE THAN A TEAMSTER WITH A BAG OF ROCKS.
BUCKY...
THE RED SOX MIGHT AS WELL CHANGE THEIR NAME TO THE LIGHTLY BROWNED SOX, FOR TRULY, THEY ARE NOW TOAST.
HA HA! THE RYE SOX!
darb

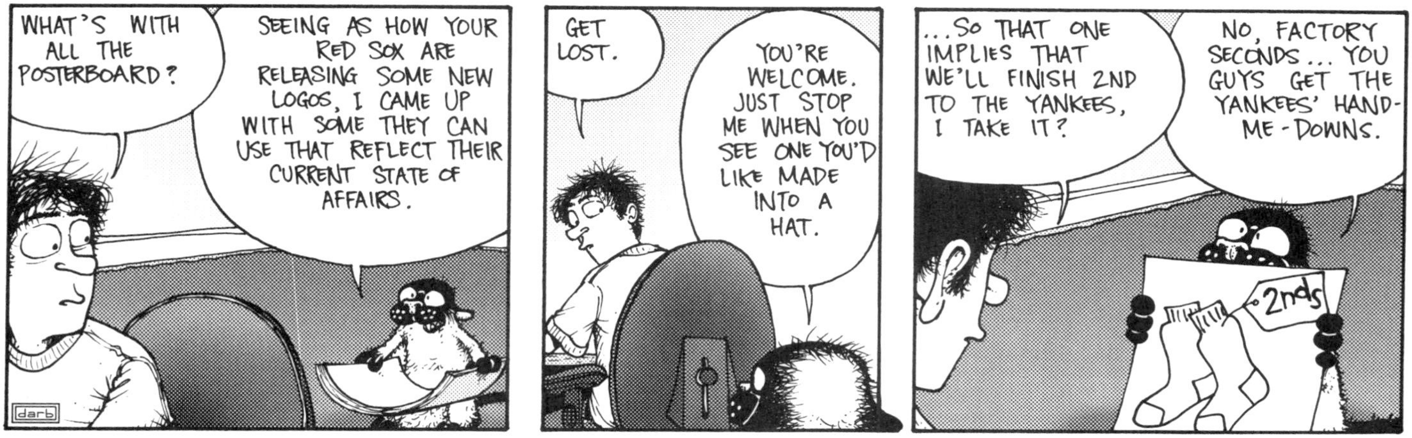
WHAT'S WITH ALL THE POSTERBOARD?
SEEING AS HOW YOUR RED SOX ARE RELEASING SOME NEW LOGOS, I CAME UP WITH SOME THEY CAN USE THAT REFLECT THEIR CURRENT STATE OF AFFAIRS.
GET LOST.
YOU'RE WELCOME. JUST STOP ME WHEN YOU SEE ONE YOU'D LIKE MADE INTO A HAT.
...SO THAT ONE IMPLIES THAT WE'LL FINISH 2ND TO THE YANKEES, I TAKE IT?
NO, FACTORY SECONDS... YOU GUYS GET THE YANKEES' HAND-ME-DOWNS.
2nds
darb

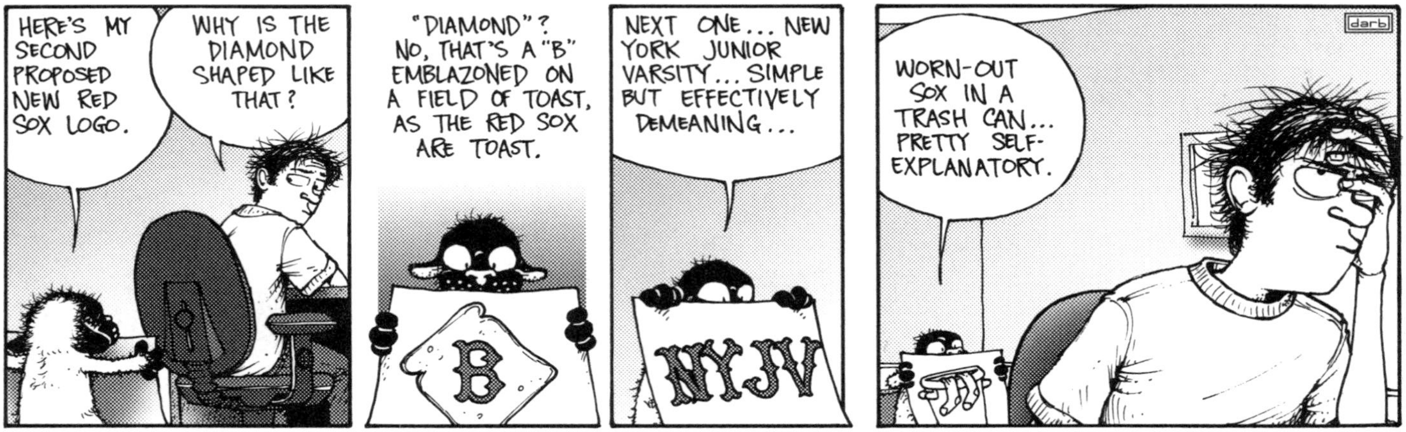
HERE'S MY SECOND PROPOSED NEW RED SOX LOGO.
WHY IS THE DIAMOND SHAPED LIKE THAT?
"DIAMOND"? NO, THAT'S A "B" EMBLAZONED ON A FIELD OF TOAST, AS THE RED SOX ARE TOAST.
B
NEXT ONE... NEW YORK JUNIOR VARSITY... SIMPLE BUT EFFECTIVELY DEMEANING...
NYJV
WORN-OUT SOX IN A TRASH CAN... PRETTY SELF-EXPLANATORY.
darb

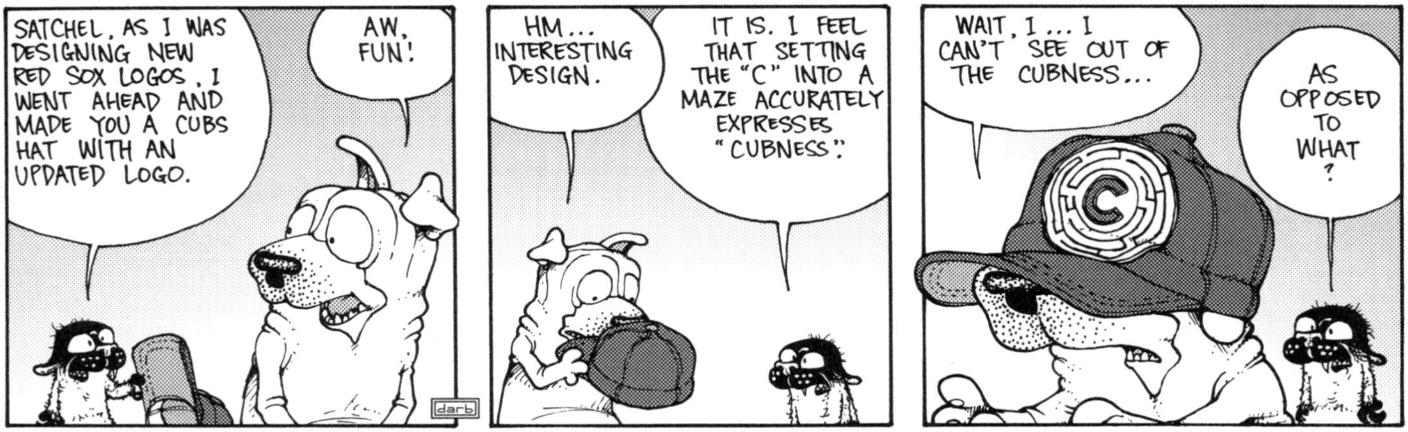
SATCHEL, AS I WAS DESIGNING NEW RED SOX LOGOS, I WENT AHEAD AND MADE YOU A CUBS HAT WITH AN UPDATED LOGO.
AW, FUN!
darb
HM... INTERESTING DESIGN.
IT IS. I FEEL THAT SETTING THE "C" INTO A MAZE ACCURATELY EXPRESSES "CUBNESS."
WAIT, I... I CAN'T SEE OUT OF THE CUBNESS...
AS OPPOSED TO WHAT?
C

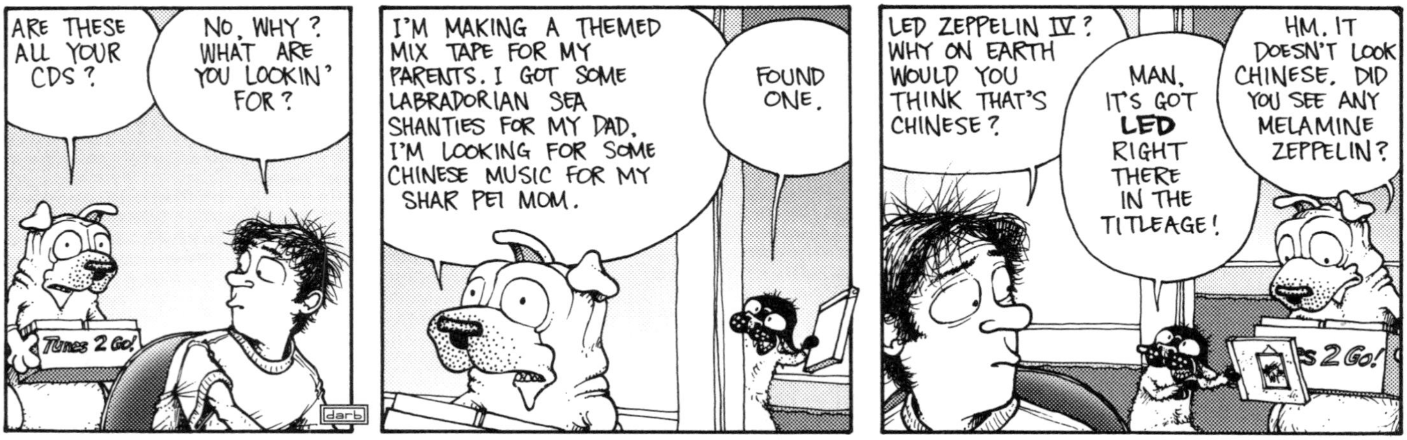
ARE THESE ALL YOUR CDS?
NO, WHY? WHAT ARE YOU LOOKIN' FOR?
Tunes 2 Go!
darb
I'M MAKING A THEMED MIX TAPE FOR MY PARENTS. I GOT SOME LABRADORIAN SEA SHANTIES FOR MY DAD. I'M LOOKING FOR SOME CHINESE MUSIC FOR MY SHAR PEI MOM.
FOUND ONE.
LED ZEPPELIN IV? WHY ON EARTH WOULD YOU THINK THAT'S CHINESE?
MAN, IT'S GOT **LED** RIGHT THERE IN THE TITLEAGE!
HM. IT DOESN'T LOOK CHINESE. DID YOU SEE ANY MELAMINE ZEPPELIN?
s 2 Go!

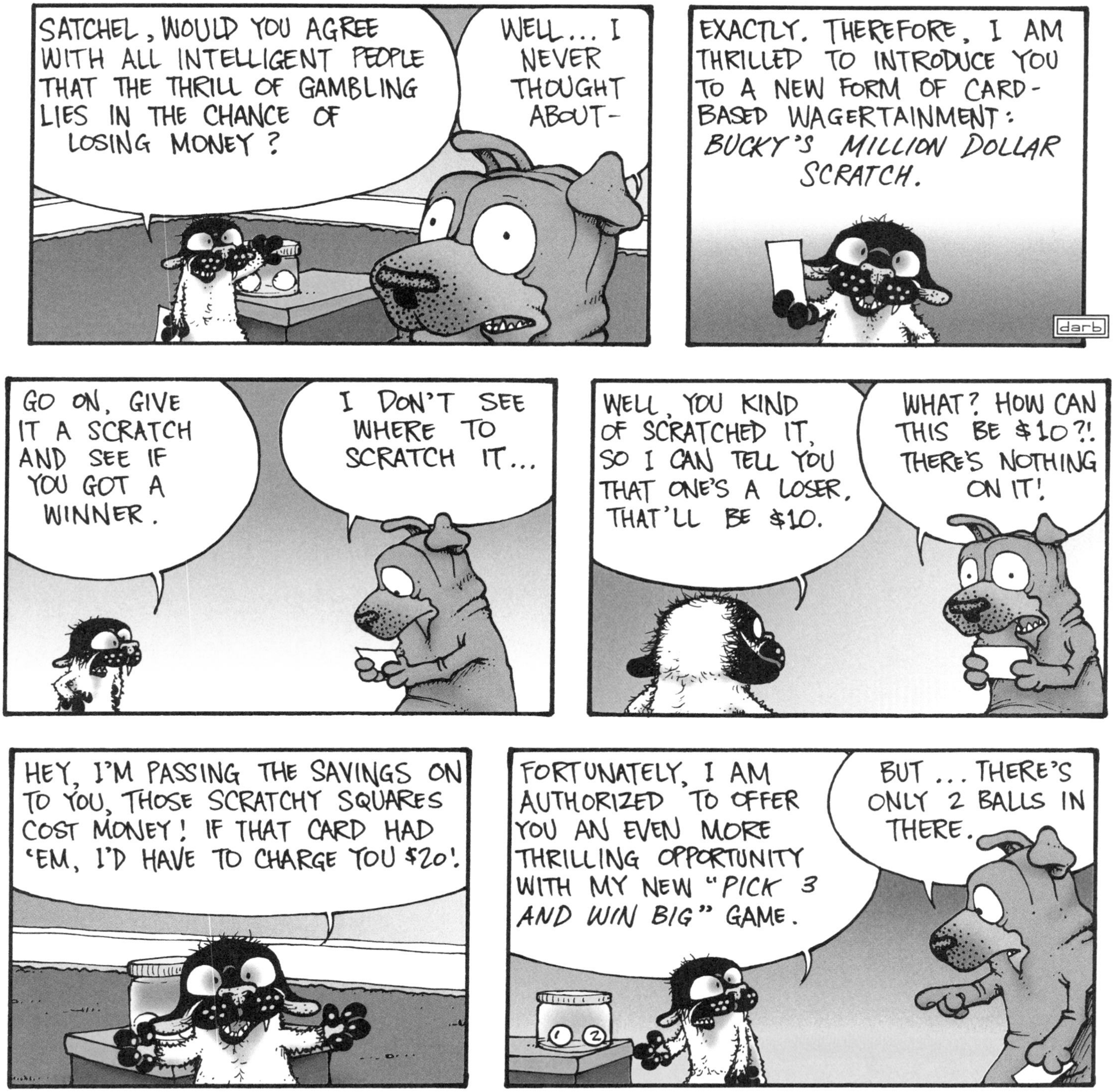
SATCHEL, WOULD YOU AGREE WITH ALL INTELLIGENT PEOPLE THAT THE THRILL OF GAMBLING LIES IN THE CHANCE OF LOSING MONEY?
WELL... I NEVER THOUGHT ABOUT-
EXACTLY. THEREFORE, I AM THRILLED TO INTRODUCE YOU TO A NEW FORM OF CARD-BASED WAGERTAINMENT: *BUCKY'S MILLION DOLLAR SCRATCH.*
darb
GO ON, GIVE IT A SCRATCH AND SEE IF YOU GOT A WINNER.
I DON'T SEE WHERE TO SCRATCH IT...
WELL, YOU KIND OF SCRATCHED IT, SO I CAN TELL YOU THAT ONE'S A LOSER. THAT'LL BE $10.
WHAT? HOW CAN THIS BE $10?! THERE'S NOTHING ON IT!
HEY, I'M PASSING THE SAVINGS ON TO YOU, THOSE SCRATCHY SQUARES COST MONEY! IF THAT CARD HAD 'EM, I'D HAVE TO CHARGE YOU $20!
FORTUNATELY, I AM AUTHORIZED TO OFFER YOU AN EVEN MORE THRILLING OPPORTUNITY WITH MY NEW "*PICK 3 AND WIN BIG*" GAME.
BUT... THERE'S ONLY 2 BALLS IN THERE.
1
2

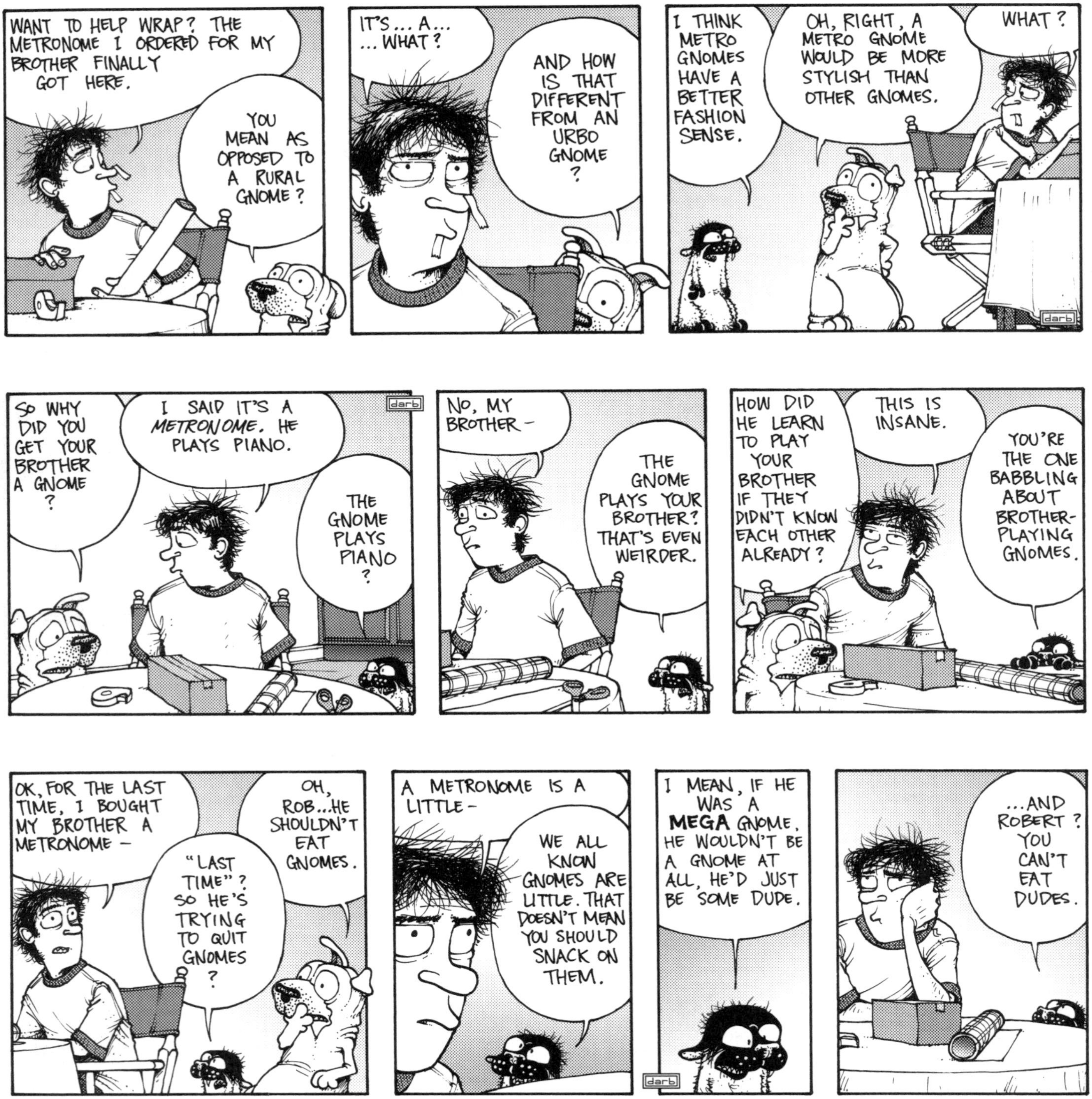
WANT TO HELP WRAP? THE METRONOME I ORDERED FOR MY BROTHER FINALLY GOT HERE.
YOU MEAN AS OPPOSED TO A RURAL GNOME?
IT'S... A... ...WHAT?
AND HOW IS THAT DIFFERENT FROM AN URBO GNOME?
I THINK METRO GNOMES HAVE A BETTER FASHION SENSE.
OH, RIGHT, A METRO GNOME WOULD BE MORE STYLISH THAN OTHER GNOMES.
WHAT?
SO WHY DID YOU GET YOUR BROTHER A GNOME?
I SAID IT'S A *METRONOME*. HE PLAYS PIANO.
THE GNOME PLAYS PIANO?
NO, MY BROTHER–
THE GNOME PLAYS YOUR BROTHER? THAT'S EVEN WEIRDER.
HOW DID HE LEARN TO PLAY YOUR BROTHER IF THEY DIDN'T KNOW EACH OTHER ALREADY?
THIS IS INSANE.
YOU'RE THE ONE BABBLING ABOUT BROTHER-PLAYING GNOMES.
OK, FOR THE LAST TIME, I BOUGHT MY BROTHER A METRONOME–
"LAST TIME"? SO HE'S TRYING TO QUIT GNOMES?
OH, ROB...HE SHOULDN'T EAT GNOMES.
A METRONOME IS A LITTLE–
WE ALL KNOW GNOMES ARE LITTLE. THAT DOESN'T MEAN YOU SHOULD SNACK ON THEM.
I MEAN, IF HE WAS A **MEGA** GNOME, HE WOULDN'T BE A GNOME AT ALL, HE'D JUST BE SOME DUDE.
...AND ROBERT? YOU CAN'T EAT DUDES.

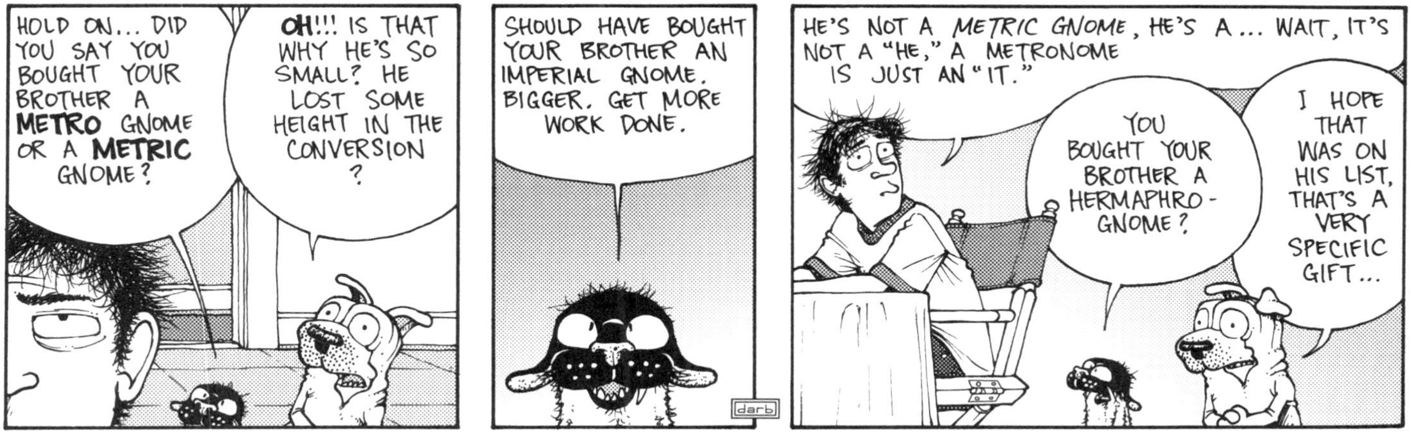
HOLD ON... DID YOU SAY YOU BOUGHT YOUR BROTHER A **METRO** GNOME OR A **METRIC** GNOME?
OH!!! IS THAT WHY HE'S SO SMALL? HE LOST SOME HEIGHT IN THE CONVERSION?
SHOULD HAVE BOUGHT YOUR BROTHER AN IMPERIAL GNOME. BIGGER. GET MORE WORK DONE.
darb
HE'S NOT A *METRIC GNOME*, HE'S A... WAIT, IT'S NOT A "HE," A METRONOME IS JUST AN "IT."
YOU BOUGHT YOUR BROTHER A HERMAPHRO-GNOME?
I HOPE THAT WAS ON HIS LIST, THAT'S A VERY SPECIFIC GIFT...

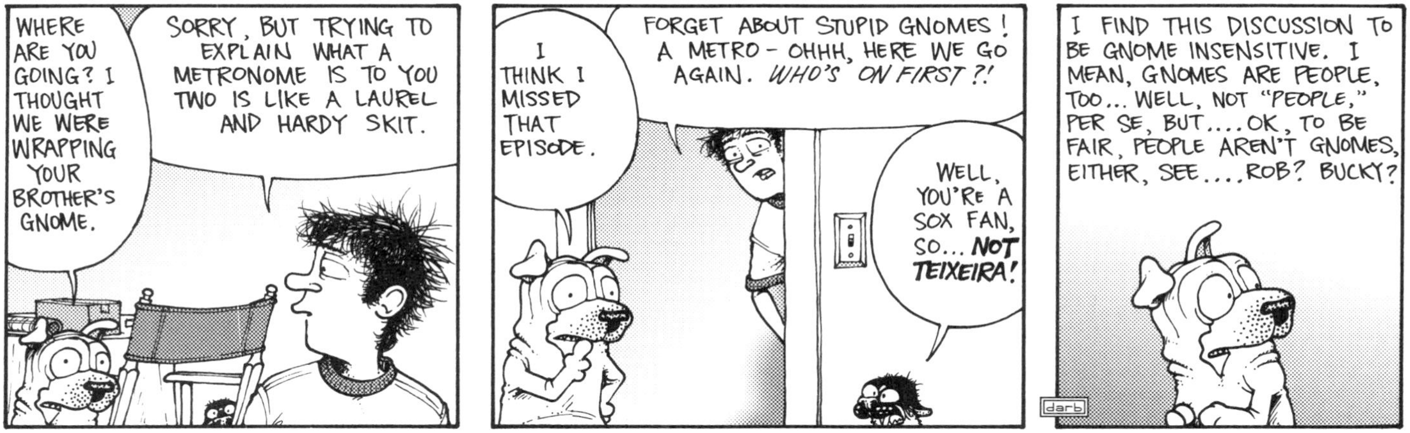
WHERE ARE YOU GOING? I THOUGHT WE WERE WRAPPING YOUR BROTHER'S GNOME.
SORRY, BUT TRYING TO EXPLAIN WHAT A METRONOME IS TO YOU TWO IS LIKE A LAUREL AND HARDY SKIT.
I THINK I MISSED THAT EPISODE.
FORGET ABOUT STUPID GNOMES! A METRO - OHHH, HERE WE GO AGAIN. *WHO'S ON FIRST?!*
WELL, YOU'RE A SOX FAN, SO... ***NOT TEIXEIRA!***
darb
I FIND THIS DISCUSSION TO BE GNOME INSENSITIVE. I MEAN, GNOMES ARE PEOPLE, TOO... WELL, NOT "PEOPLE," PER SE, BUT.... OK, TO BE FAIR, PEOPLE AREN'T GNOMES, EITHER, SEE.... ROB? BUCKY?

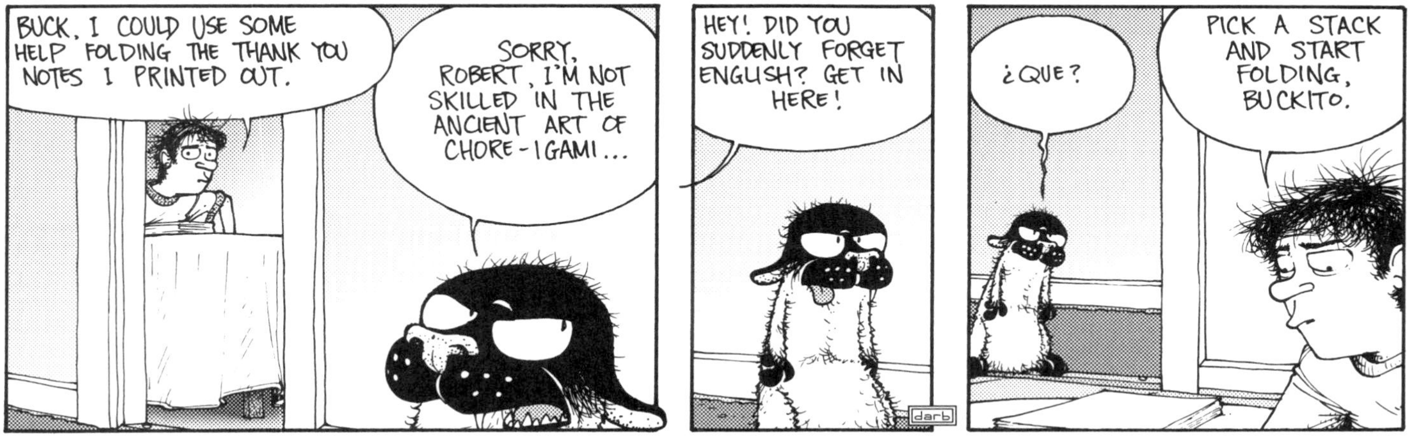
BUCK, I COULD USE SOME HELP FOLDING THE THANK YOU NOTES I PRINTED OUT.
SORRY, ROBERT, I'M NOT SKILLED IN THE ANCIENT ART OF CHORE-IGAMI...
HEY! DID YOU SUDDENLY FORGET ENGLISH? GET IN HERE!
darb
¿QUE?
PICK A STACK AND START FOLDING, BUCKITO.

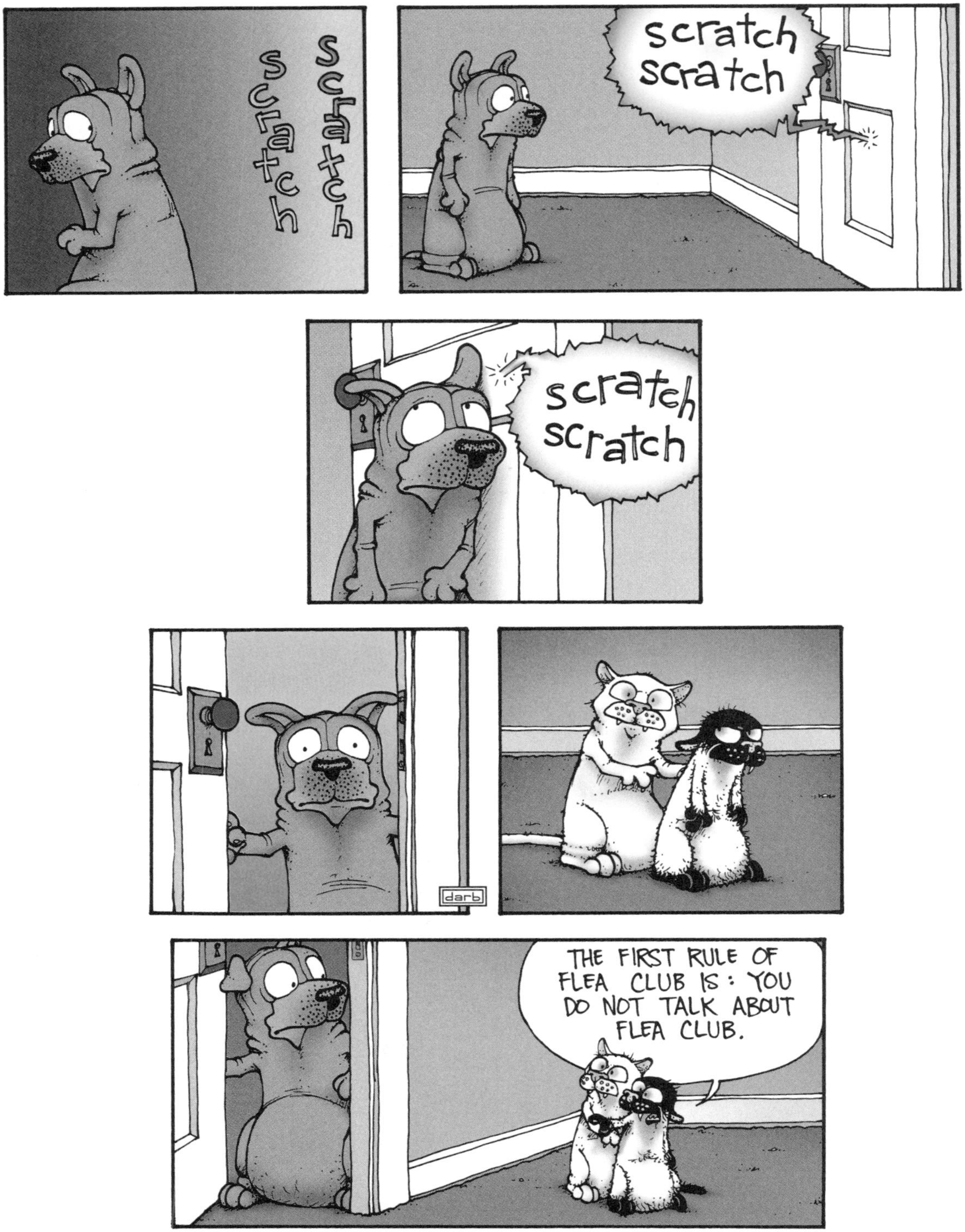
scratch
scratch
scratch scratch
scratch scratch
darb
THE FIRST RULE OF FLEA CLUB IS: YOU DO NOT TALK ABOUT FLEA CLUB.

OOO, A VIDEO!

THAT ONE'S FOR BUCKY.

ANGER MANAGEMENT

OHHH, I WOULDN'T GIVE HIM THIS JOB...

WHAT JOB?

I JUST DON'T THINK IT'S RIGHT TO GO TO A BUNCH OF ANGRY PEOPLE AND SAY, "ANGRY PEOPLE, THIS IS BUCKY. HE'S YOUR NEW BOSS."

SATCHEL, THAT'S A VIDEO TO HELP BUCKY LEARN HOW TO DEAL WITH HIS ANGER.

OK, GOOD, GOOD. I THOUGHT IT WAS A JOB DESCRIPTION. LIKE FRENCH BAKER. OR JERK CHICKEN.

I GOT YOU A VIDEO, TOO.

DOGS 101

WELL, I'VE ALREADY SEEN DALMATIANS 101, AND THIS SOUNDS LESS IN DEPTH, SO...

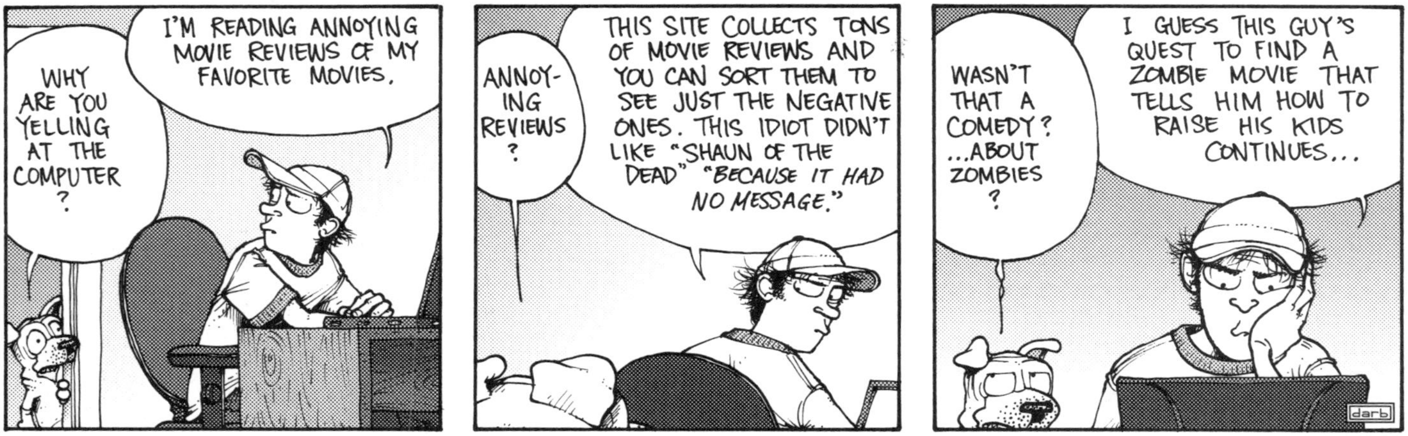
I'M READING ANNOYING MOVIE REVIEWS OF MY FAVORITE MOVIES.
WHY ARE YOU YELLING AT THE COMPUTER ?
THIS SITE COLLECTS TONS OF MOVIE REVIEWS AND YOU CAN SORT THEM TO SEE JUST THE NEGATIVE ONES. THIS IDIOT DIDN'T LIKE "SHAUN OF THE DEAD" *"BECAUSE IT HAD NO MESSAGE."*
ANNOY-ING REVIEWS ?
I GUESS THIS GUY'S QUEST TO FIND A ZOMBIE MOVIE THAT TELLS HIM HOW TO RAISE HIS KIDS CONTINUES...
WASN'T THAT A COMEDY? ...ABOUT ZOMBIES ?
darb

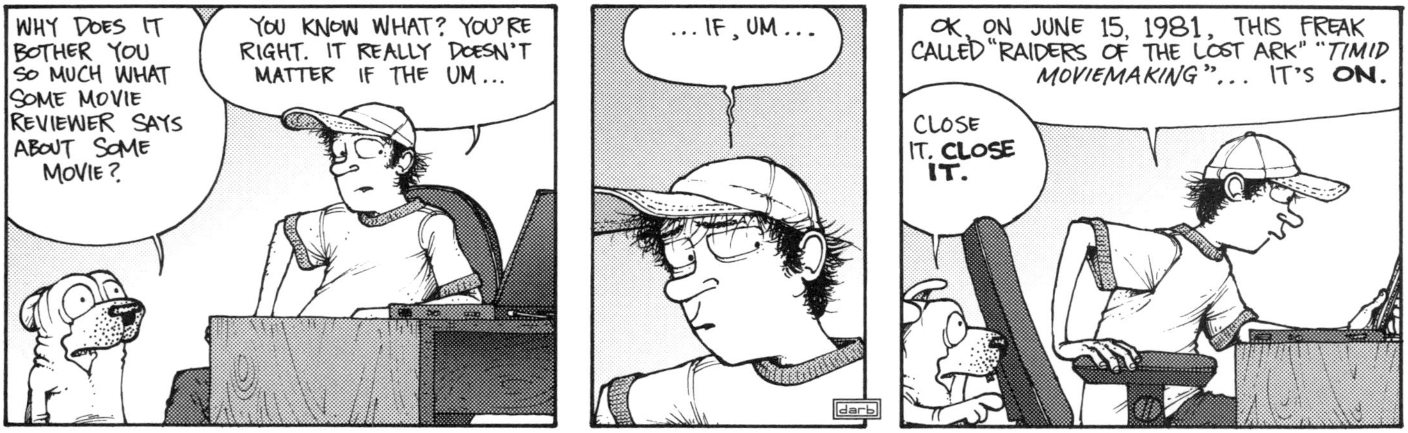
WHY DOES IT BOTHER YOU SO MUCH WHAT SOME MOVIE REVIEWER SAYS ABOUT SOME MOVIE?
YOU KNOW WHAT? YOU'RE RIGHT. IT REALLY DOESN'T MATTER IF THE UM...
...IF, UM...
darb
OK, ON JUNE 15, 1981, THIS FREAK CALLED "RAIDERS OF THE LOST ARK" *"TIMID MOVIEMAKING"*... IT'S **ON.**
CLOSE IT. **CLOSE IT.**

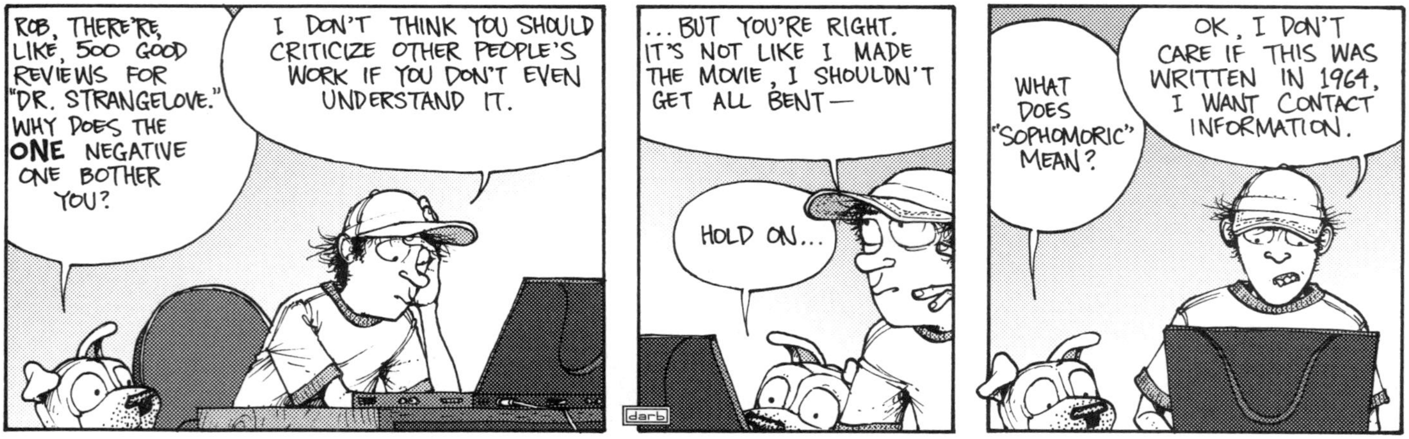
ROB, THERE'RE, LIKE, 500 GOOD REVIEWS FOR "DR. STRANGELOVE." WHY DOES THE **ONE** NEGATIVE ONE BOTHER YOU?
I DON'T THINK YOU SHOULD CRITICIZE OTHER PEOPLE'S WORK IF YOU DON'T EVEN UNDERSTAND IT.
darb
...BUT YOU'RE RIGHT. IT'S NOT LIKE I MADE THE MOVIE, I SHOULDN'T GET ALL BENT—
HOLD ON...
OK, I DON'T CARE IF THIS WAS WRITTEN IN 1964, I WANT CONTACT INFORMATION.
WHAT DOES "SOPHOMORIC" MEAN?

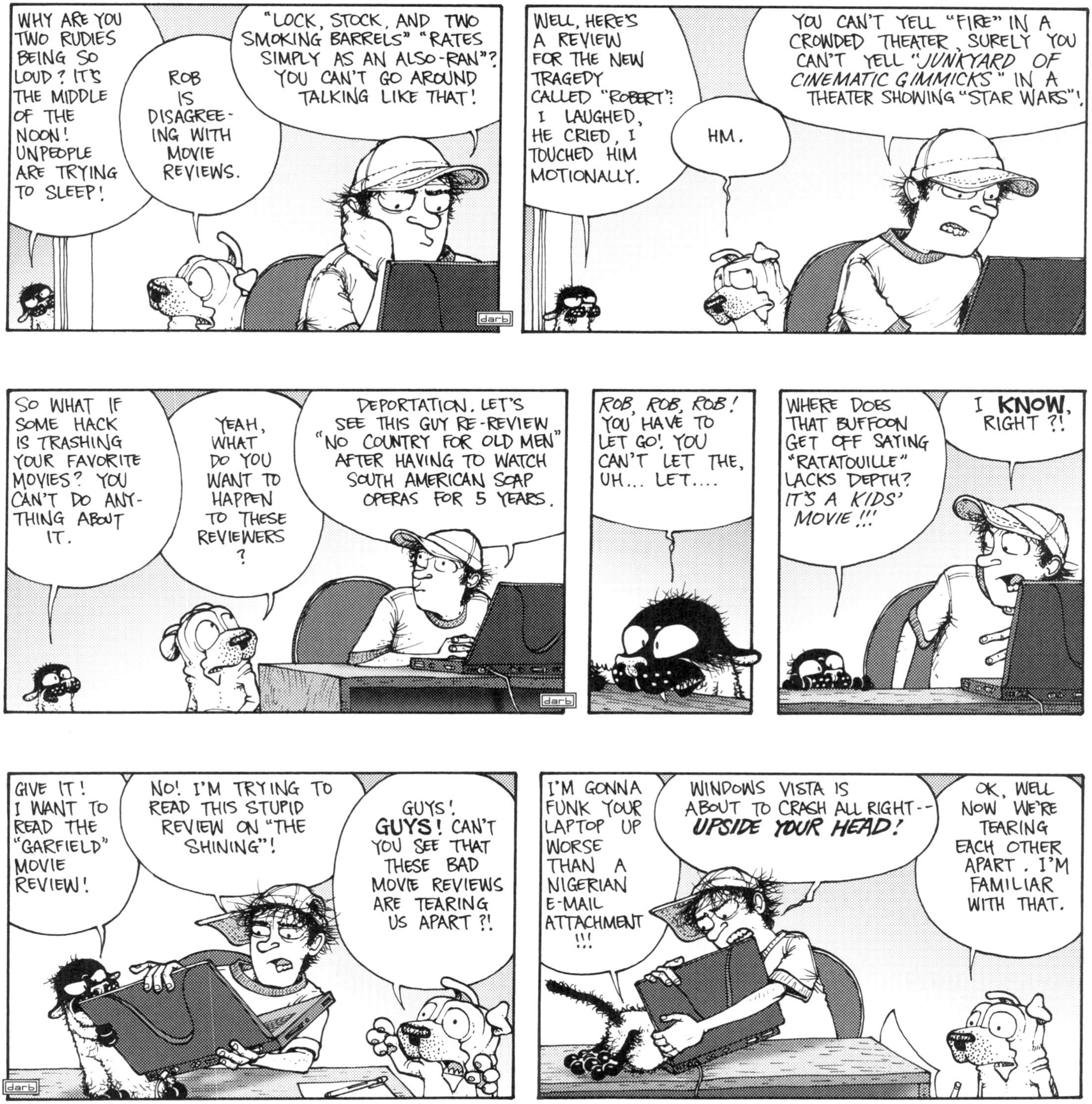
WHY ARE YOU TWO RUDIES BEING SO LOUD? IT'S THE MIDDLE OF THE NOON! UNPEOPLE ARE TRYING TO SLEEP!
ROB IS DISAGREEING WITH MOVIE REVIEWS.
"LOCK, STOCK, AND TWO SMOKING BARRELS" "RATES SIMPLY AS AN ALSO-RAN"?! YOU CAN'T GO AROUND TALKING LIKE THAT!
darb
WELL, HERE'S A REVIEW FOR THE NEW TRAGEDY CALLED "ROBERT": I LAUGHED, HE CRIED, I TOUCHED HIM MOTIONALLY.
HM.
YOU CAN'T YELL "FIRE" IN A CROWDED THEATER, SURELY YOU CAN'T YELL "JUNKYARD OF CINEMATIC GIMMICKS" IN A THEATER SHOWING "STAR WARS"!
SO WHAT IF SOME HACK IS TRASHING YOUR FAVORITE MOVIES? YOU CAN'T DO ANYTHING ABOUT IT.
YEAH, WHAT DO YOU WANT TO HAPPEN TO THESE REVIEWERS?
DEPORTATION. LET'S SEE THIS GUY RE-REVIEW "NO COUNTRY FOR OLD MEN" AFTER HAVING TO WATCH SOUTH AMERICAN SOAP OPERAS FOR 5 YEARS.
darb
ROB, ROB, ROB! YOU HAVE TO LET GO! YOU CAN'T LET THE, UH... LET....
WHERE DOES THAT BUFFOON GET OFF SAYING "RATATOUILLE" LACKS DEPTH? IT'S A KIDS' MOVIE!!!
I KNOW, RIGHT?!
GIVE IT! I WANT TO READ THE "GARFIELD" MOVIE REVIEW!
NO! I'M TRYING TO READ THIS STUPID REVIEW ON "THE SHINING"!
GUYS! GUYS! CAN'T YOU SEE THAT THESE BAD MOVIE REVIEWS ARE TEARING US APART?!
darb
I'M GONNA FUNK YOUR LAPTOP UP WORSE THAN A NIGERIAN E-MAIL ATTACHMENT!!!
WINDOWS VISTA IS ABOUT TO CRASH ALL RIGHT-- UPSIDE YOUR HEAD!
OK, WELL NOW WE'RE TEARING EACH OTHER APART. I'M FAMILIAR WITH THAT.

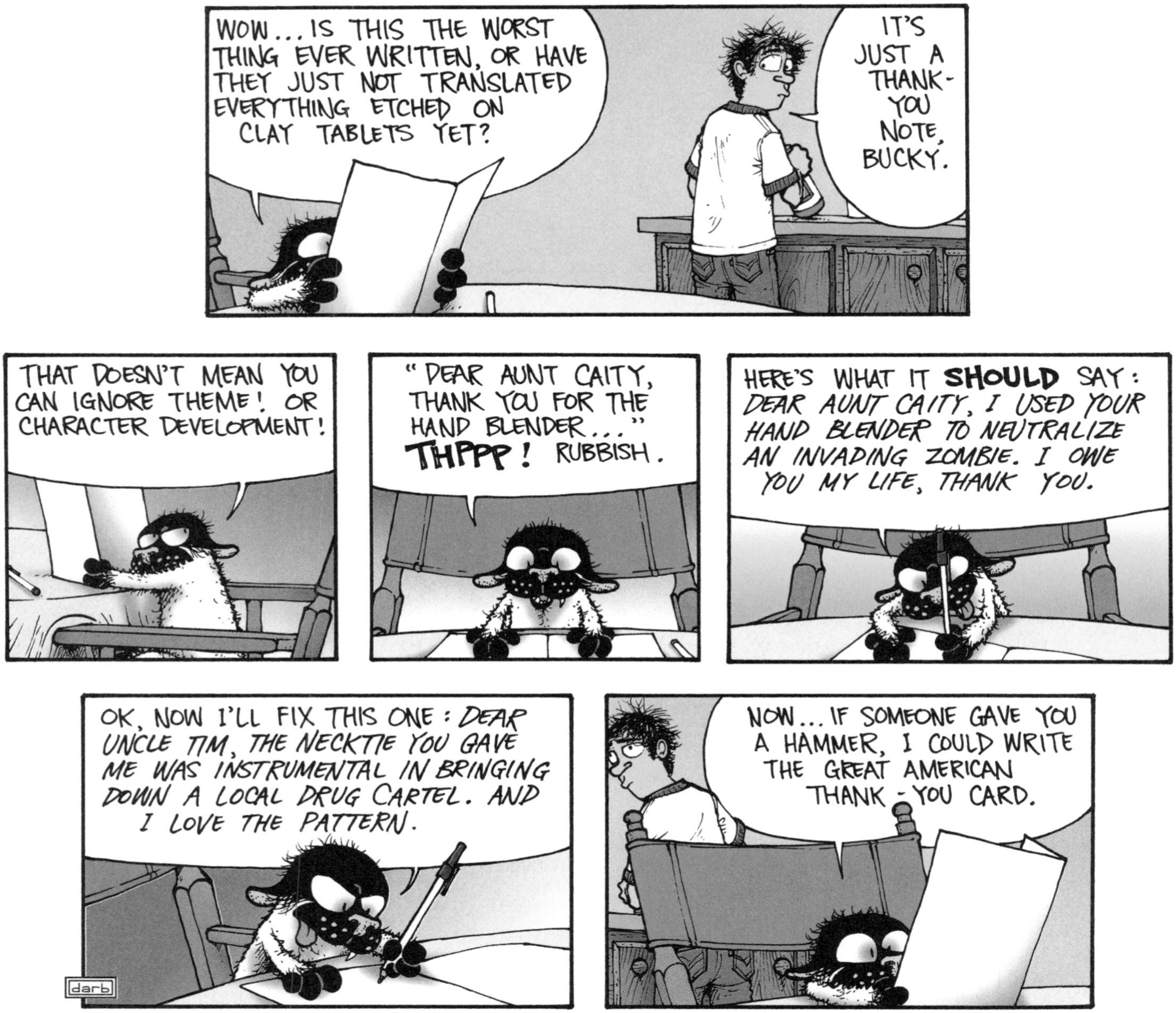
WOW... IS THIS THE WORST THING EVER WRITTEN, OR HAVE THEY JUST NOT TRANSLATED EVERYTHING ETCHED ON CLAY TABLETS YET?
IT'S JUST A THANK-YOU NOTE, BUCKY.
THAT DOESN'T MEAN YOU CAN IGNORE THEME! OR CHARACTER DEVELOPMENT!
"DEAR AUNT CAITY, THANK YOU FOR THE HAND BLENDER..." THPPP! RUBBISH.
HERE'S WHAT IT SHOULD SAY: DEAR AUNT CAITY, I USED YOUR HAND BLENDER TO NEUTRALIZE AN INVADING ZOMBIE. I OWE YOU MY LIFE, THANK YOU.
OK, NOW I'LL FIX THIS ONE: DEAR UNCLE TIM, THE NECKTIE YOU GAVE ME WAS INSTRUMENTAL IN BRINGING DOWN A LOCAL DRUG CARTEL. AND I LOVE THE PATTERN.
darb
NOW... IF SOMEONE GAVE YOU A HAMMER, I COULD WRITE THE GREAT AMERICAN THANK-YOU CARD.

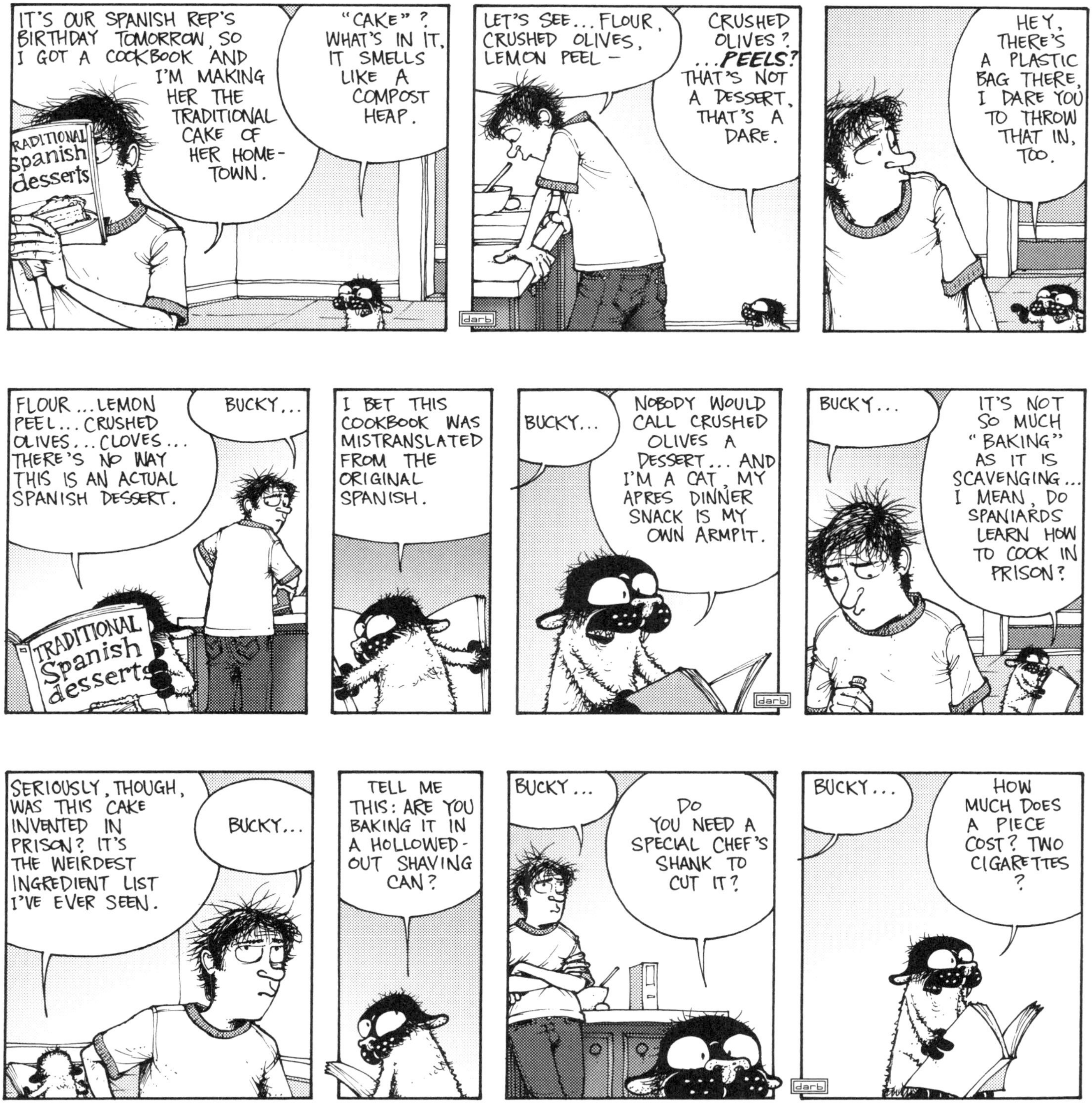
IT'S OUR SPANISH REP'S BIRTHDAY TOMORROW, SO I GOT A COOKBOOK AND I'M MAKING HER THE TRADITIONAL CAKE OF HER HOMETOWN.
TRADITIONAL Spanish desserts
"CAKE"? WHAT'S IN IT, IT SMELLS LIKE A COMPOST HEAP.
LET'S SEE... FLOUR, CRUSHED OLIVES, LEMON PEEL –
CRUSHED OLIVES? ...PEELS? THAT'S NOT A DESSERT, THAT'S A DARE.
darb
HEY, THERE'S A PLASTIC BAG THERE, I DARE YOU TO THROW THAT IN, TOO.
FLOUR... LEMON PEEL... CRUSHED OLIVES... CLOVES... THERE'S NO WAY THIS IS AN ACTUAL SPANISH DESSERT.
BUCKY...
TRADITIONAL Spanish desserts
I BET THIS COOKBOOK WAS MISTRANSLATED FROM THE ORIGINAL SPANISH.
BUCKY...
NOBODY WOULD CALL CRUSHED OLIVES A DESSERT... AND I'M A CAT, MY APRES DINNER SNACK IS MY OWN ARMPIT.
darb
BUCKY...
IT'S NOT SO MUCH "BAKING" AS IT IS SCAVENGING... I MEAN, DO SPANIARDS LEARN HOW TO COOK IN PRISON?
SERIOUSLY, THOUGH, WAS THIS CAKE INVENTED IN PRISON? IT'S THE WEIRDEST INGREDIENT LIST I'VE EVER SEEN.
BUCKY...
TELL ME THIS: ARE YOU BAKING IT IN A HOLLOWED-OUT SHAVING CAN?
BUCKY...
DO YOU NEED A SPECIAL CHEF'S SHANK TO CUT IT?
darb
BUCKY...
HOW MUCH DOES A PIECE COST? TWO CIGARETTES?

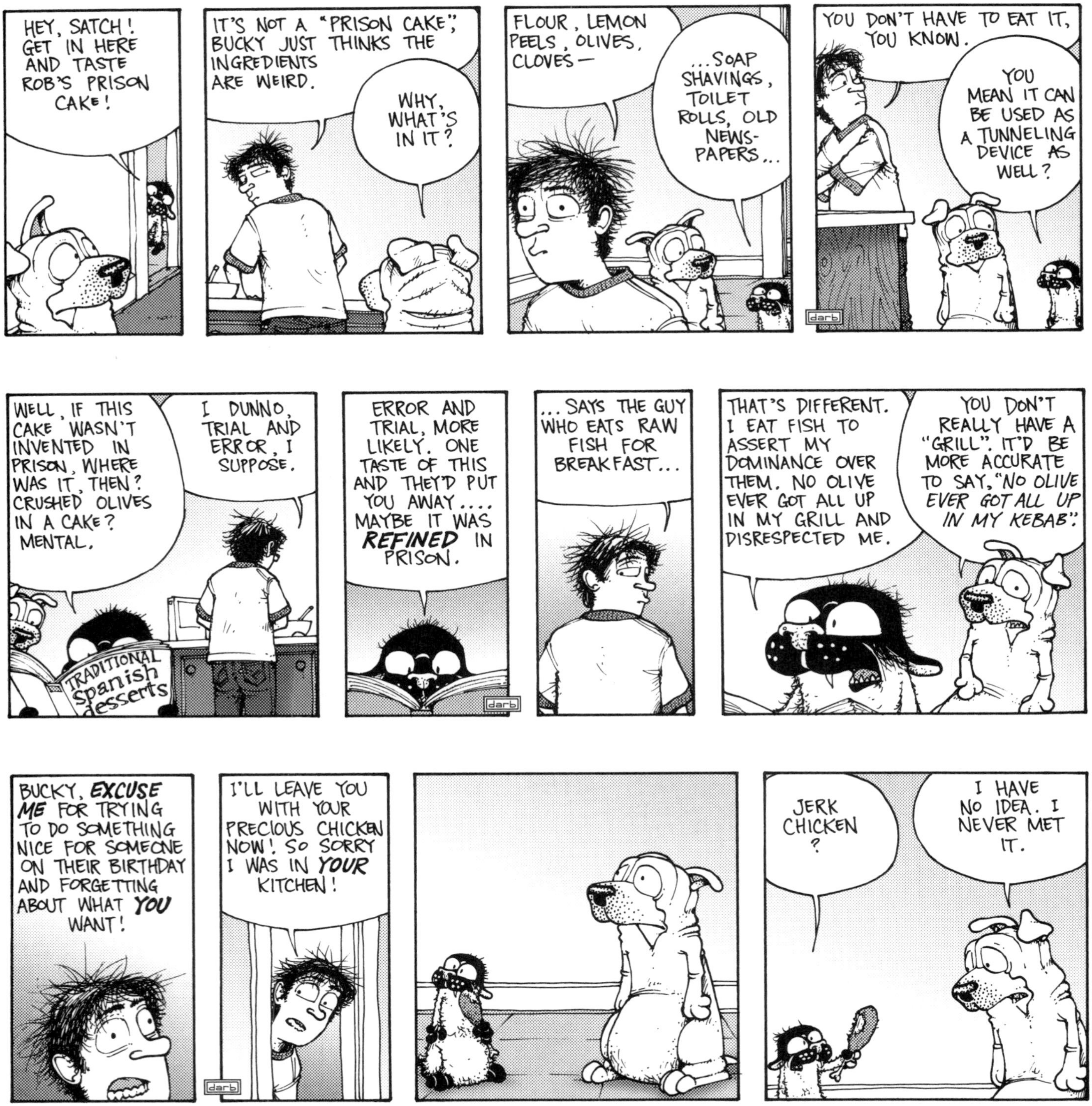
HEY, SATCH! GET IN HERE AND TASTE ROB'S PRISON CAKE!
IT'S NOT A "PRISON CAKE"; BUCKY JUST THINKS THE INGREDIENTS ARE WEIRD.
WHY, WHAT'S IN IT?
FLOUR, LEMON PEELS, OLIVES, CLOVES—
...SOAP SHAVINGS, TOILET ROLLS, OLD NEWS-PAPERS...
YOU DON'T HAVE TO EAT IT, YOU KNOW.
YOU MEAN IT CAN BE USED AS A TUNNELING DEVICE AS WELL?
darb
WELL, IF THIS CAKE WASN'T INVENTED IN PRISON, WHERE WAS IT, THEN? CRUSHED OLIVES IN A CAKE? MENTAL.
I DUNNO. TRIAL AND ERROR, I SUPPOSE.
TRADITIONAL Spanish desserts
ERROR AND TRIAL, MORE LIKELY. ONE TASTE OF THIS AND THEY'D PUT YOU AWAY.... MAYBE IT WAS **REFINED** IN PRISON.
darb
...SAYS THE GUY WHO EATS RAW FISH FOR BREAKFAST...
THAT'S DIFFERENT. I EAT FISH TO ASSERT MY DOMINANCE OVER THEM. NO OLIVE EVER GOT ALL UP IN MY GRILL AND DISRESPECTED ME.
YOU DON'T REALLY HAVE A "GRILL". IT'D BE MORE ACCURATE TO SAY, "*NO OLIVE EVER GOT ALL UP IN MY KEBAB*".
BUCKY, ***EXCUSE ME*** FOR TRYING TO DO SOMETHING NICE FOR SOMEONE ON THEIR BIRTHDAY AND FORGETTING ABOUT WHAT ***YOU*** WANT!
darb
I'LL LEAVE YOU WITH YOUR PRECIOUS CHICKEN NOW! SO SORRY I WAS IN ***YOUR*** KITCHEN!
JERK CHICKEN?
I HAVE NO IDEA. I NEVER MET IT.

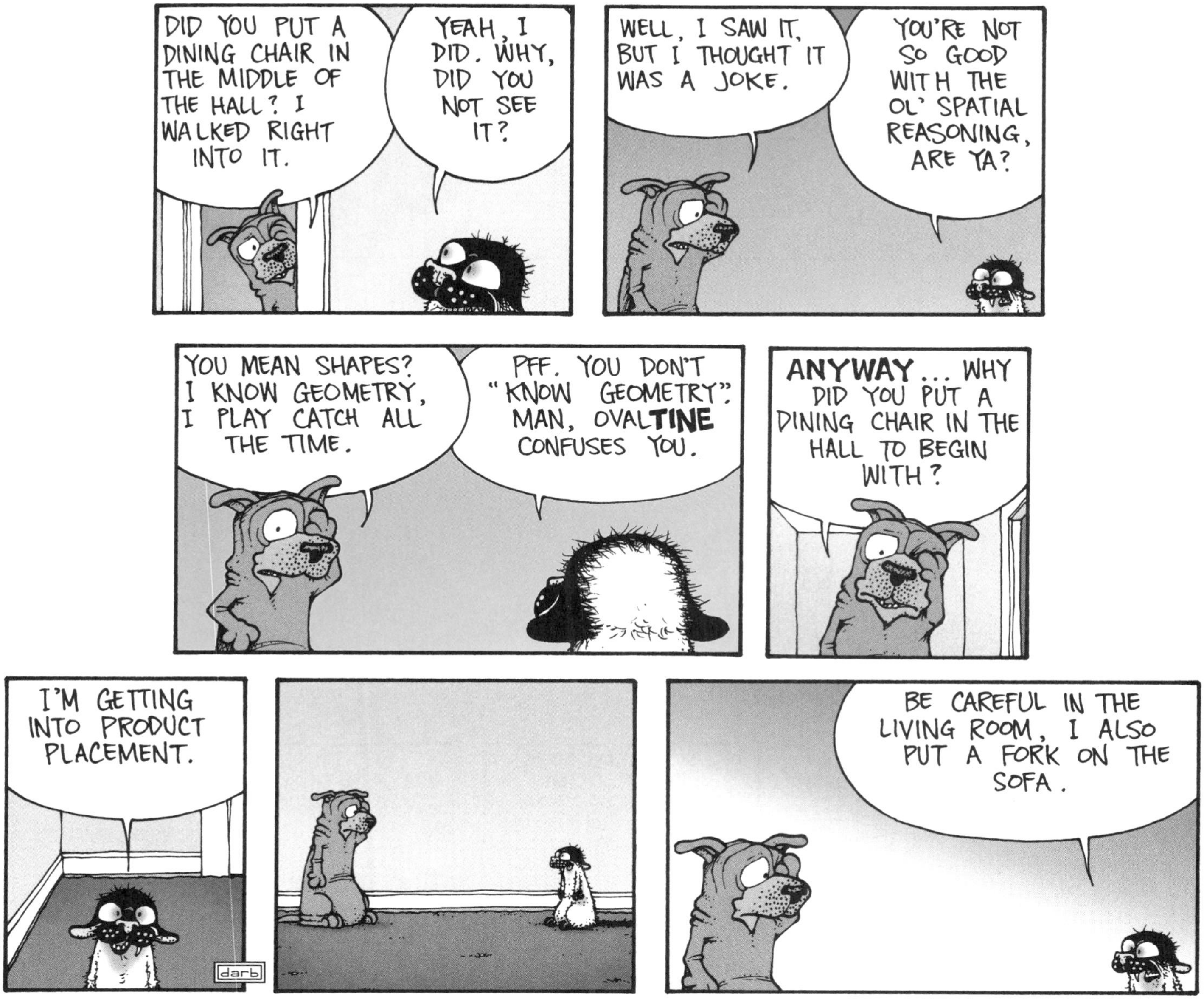
DID YOU PUT A DINING CHAIR IN THE MIDDLE OF THE HALL? I WALKED RIGHT INTO IT.
YEAH, I DID. WHY, DID YOU NOT SEE IT?
WELL, I SAW IT, BUT I THOUGHT IT WAS A JOKE.
YOU'RE NOT SO GOOD WITH THE OL' SPATIAL REASONING, ARE YA?
YOU MEAN SHAPES? I KNOW GEOMETRY, I PLAY CATCH ALL THE TIME.
PFF. YOU DON'T "KNOW GEOMETRY." MAN, OVALTINE CONFUSES YOU.
ANYWAY... WHY DID YOU PUT A DINING CHAIR IN THE HALL TO BEGIN WITH?
I'M GETTING INTO PRODUCT PLACEMENT.
darb
BE CAREFUL IN THE LIVING ROOM, I ALSO PUT A FORK ON THE SOFA.

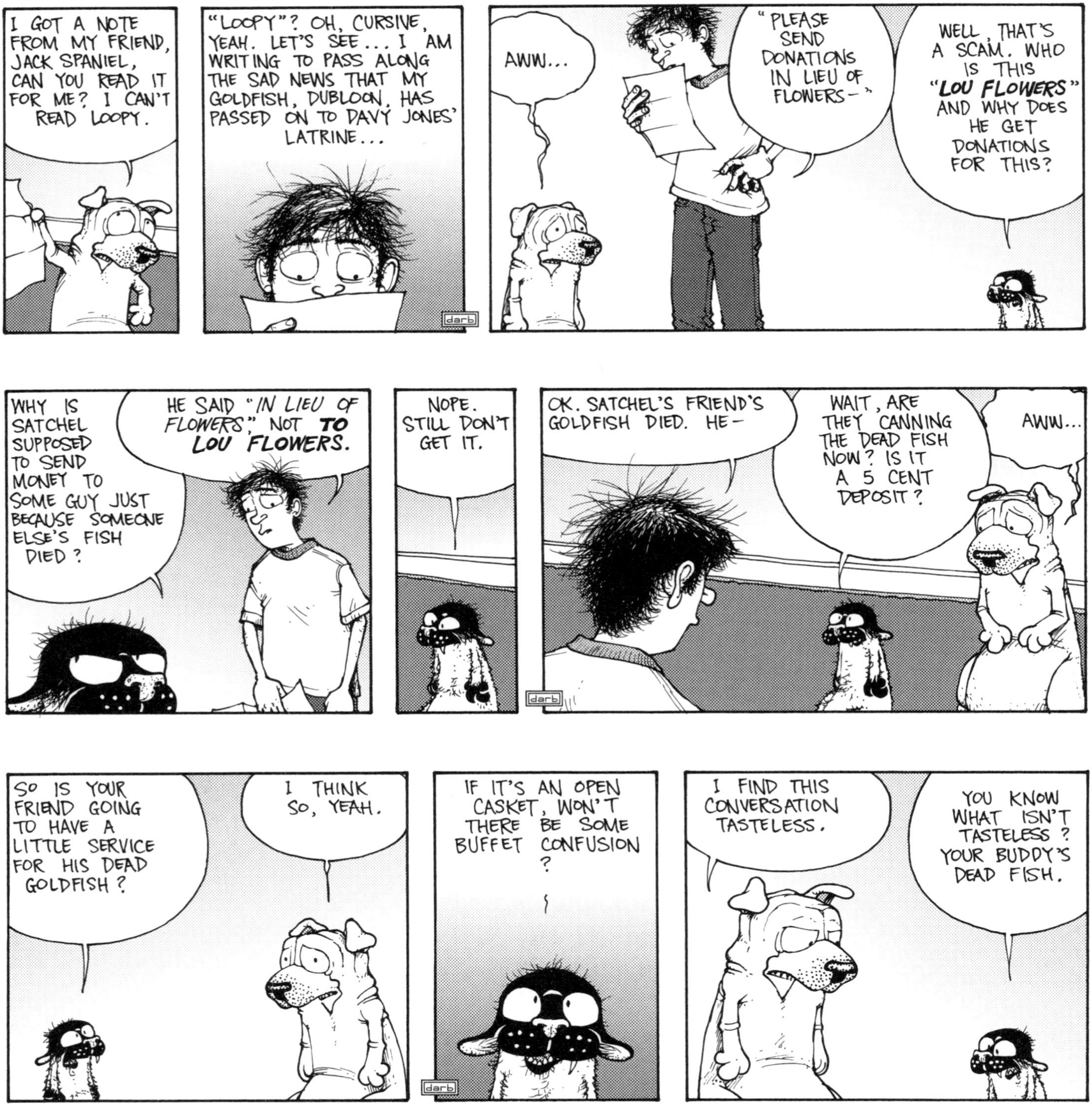
I GOT A NOTE FROM MY FRIEND, JACK SPANIEL, CAN YOU READ IT FOR ME? I CAN'T READ LOOPY.
"LOOPY"? OH, CURSIVE, YEAH. LET'S SEE... I AM WRITING TO PASS ALONG THE SAD NEWS THAT MY GOLDFISH, DUBLOON, HAS PASSED ON TO DAVY JONES' LATRINE...
darb
AWW...
"PLEASE SEND DONATIONS IN LIEU OF FLOWERS-"
WELL, THAT'S A SCAM. WHO IS THIS "**LOU FLOWERS**" AND WHY DOES HE GET DONATIONS FOR THIS?
WHY IS SATCHEL SUPPOSED TO SEND MONEY TO SOME GUY JUST BECAUSE SOMEONE ELSE'S FISH DIED?
HE SAID "*IN LIEU OF FLOWERS*," NOT ***TO LOU FLOWERS.***
NOPE. STILL DON'T GET IT.
darb
OK. SATCHEL'S FRIEND'S GOLDFISH DIED. HE-
WAIT, ARE THEY CANNING THE DEAD FISH NOW? IS IT A 5 CENT DEPOSIT?
AWW...
SO IS YOUR FRIEND GOING TO HAVE A LITTLE SERVICE FOR HIS DEAD GOLDFISH?
I THINK SO, YEAH.
darb
IF IT'S AN OPEN CASKET, WON'T THERE BE SOME BUFFET CONFUSION?
I FIND THIS CONVERSATION TASTELESS.
YOU KNOW WHAT ISN'T TASTELESS? YOUR BUDDY'S DEAD FISH.

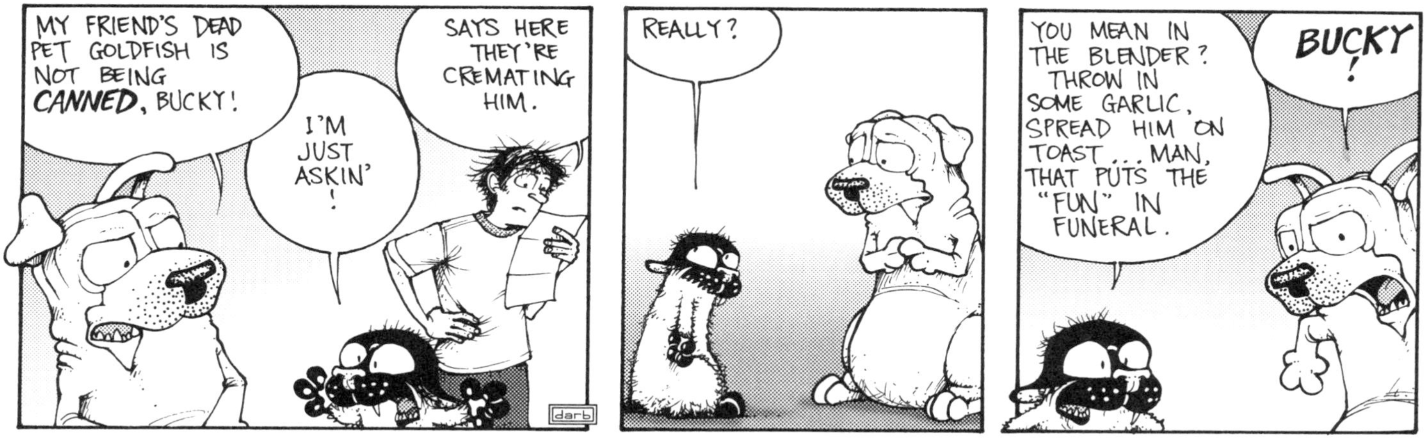
MY FRIEND'S DEAD PET GOLDFISH IS NOT BEING **CANNED**, BUCKY!
I'M JUST ASKIN'!
SAYS HERE THEY'RE CREMATING HIM.
darb
REALLY?
YOU MEAN IN THE BLENDER? THROW IN SOME GARLIC, SPREAD HIM ON TOAST ... MAN, THAT PUTS THE "FUN" IN FUNERAL.
BUCKY!

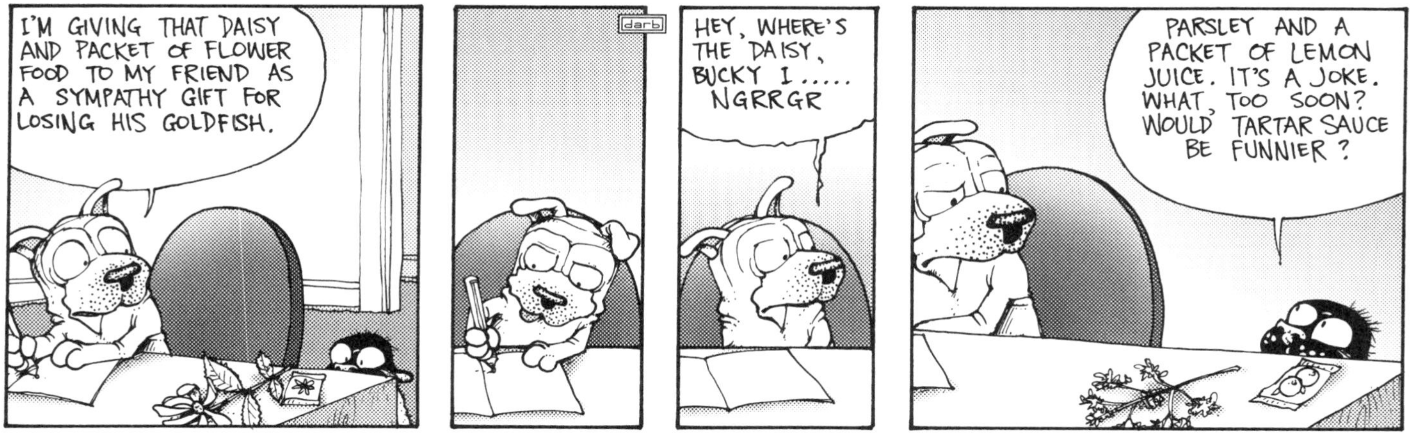
I'M GIVING THAT DAISY AND PACKET OF FLOWER FOOD TO MY FRIEND AS A SYMPATHY GIFT FOR LOSING HIS GOLDFISH.
darb
HEY, WHERE'S THE DAISY, BUCKY I..... NGRRGR
PARSLEY AND A PACKET OF LEMON JUICE. IT'S A JOKE. WHAT, TOO SOON? WOULD TARTAR SAUCE BE FUNNIER?

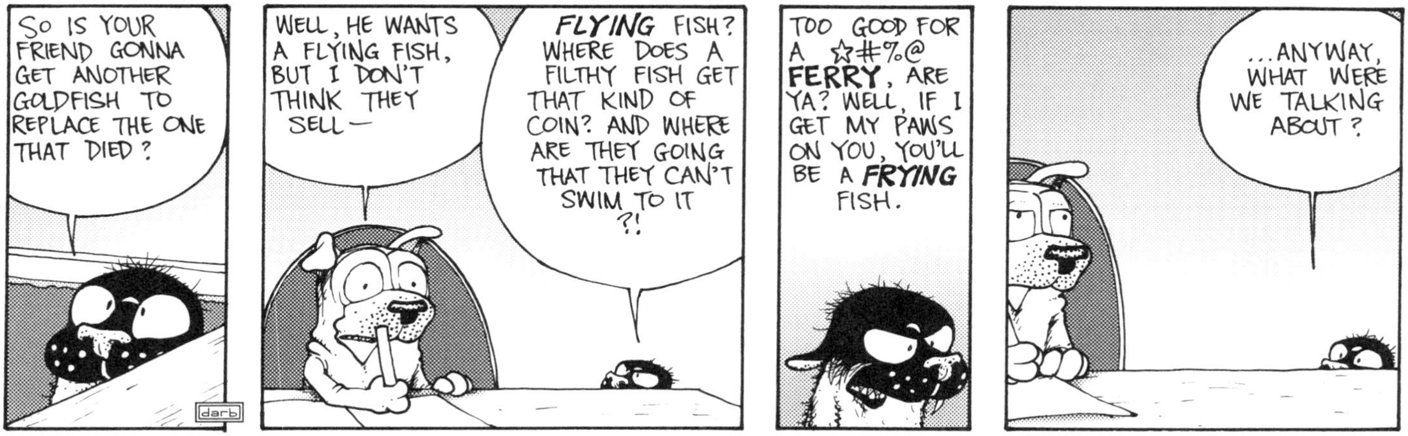
SO IS YOUR FRIEND GONNA GET ANOTHER GOLDFISH TO REPLACE THE ONE THAT DIED?
darb
WELL, HE WANTS A FLYING FISH, BUT I DON'T THINK THEY SELL—
FLYING FISH? WHERE DOES A FILTHY FISH GET THAT KIND OF COIN? AND WHERE ARE THEY GOING THAT THEY CAN'T SWIM TO IT ?!
TOO GOOD FOR A ☆#%@ **FERRY**, ARE YA? WELL, IF I GET MY PAWS ON YOU, YOU'LL BE A ***FRYING*** FISH.
...ANYWAY, WHAT WERE WE TALKING ABOUT?

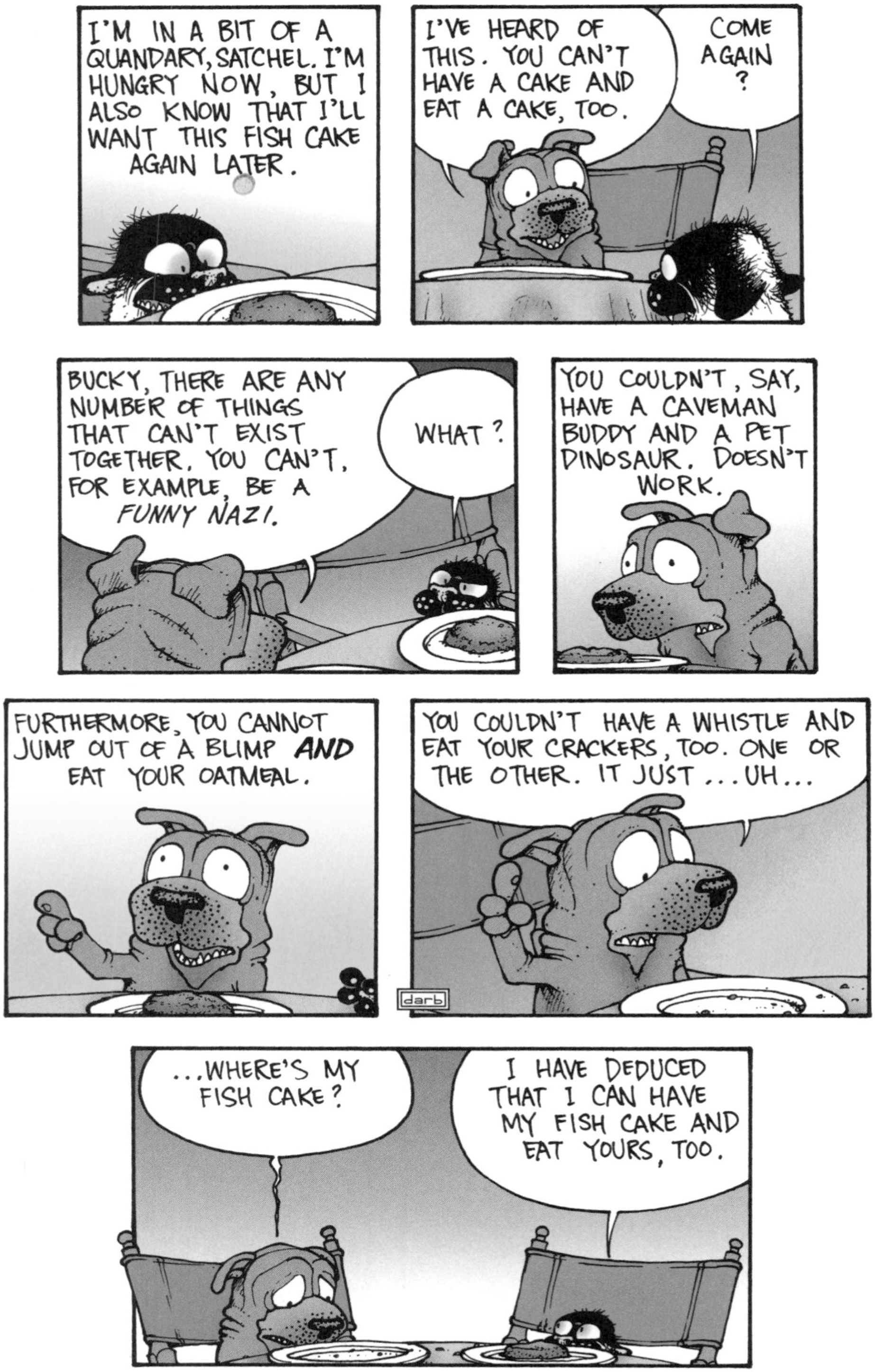
I'M IN A BIT OF A QUANDARY, SATCHEL. I'M HUNGRY NOW, BUT I ALSO KNOW THAT I'LL WANT THIS FISH CAKE AGAIN LATER.
I'VE HEARD OF THIS. YOU CAN'T HAVE A CAKE AND EAT A CAKE, TOO.
COME AGAIN?
BUCKY, THERE ARE ANY NUMBER OF THINGS THAT CAN'T EXIST TOGETHER. YOU CAN'T, FOR EXAMPLE, BE A *FUNNY NAZI*.
WHAT?
YOU COULDN'T, SAY, HAVE A CAVEMAN BUDDY AND A PET DINOSAUR. DOESN'T WORK.
FURTHERMORE, YOU CANNOT JUMP OUT OF A BLIMP **AND** EAT YOUR OATMEAL.
YOU COULDN'T HAVE A WHISTLE AND EAT YOUR CRACKERS, TOO. ONE OR THE OTHER. IT JUST . . . UH . . .
darb
. . . WHERE'S MY FISH CAKE?
I HAVE DEDUCED THAT I CAN HAVE MY FISH CAKE AND EAT YOURS, TOO.

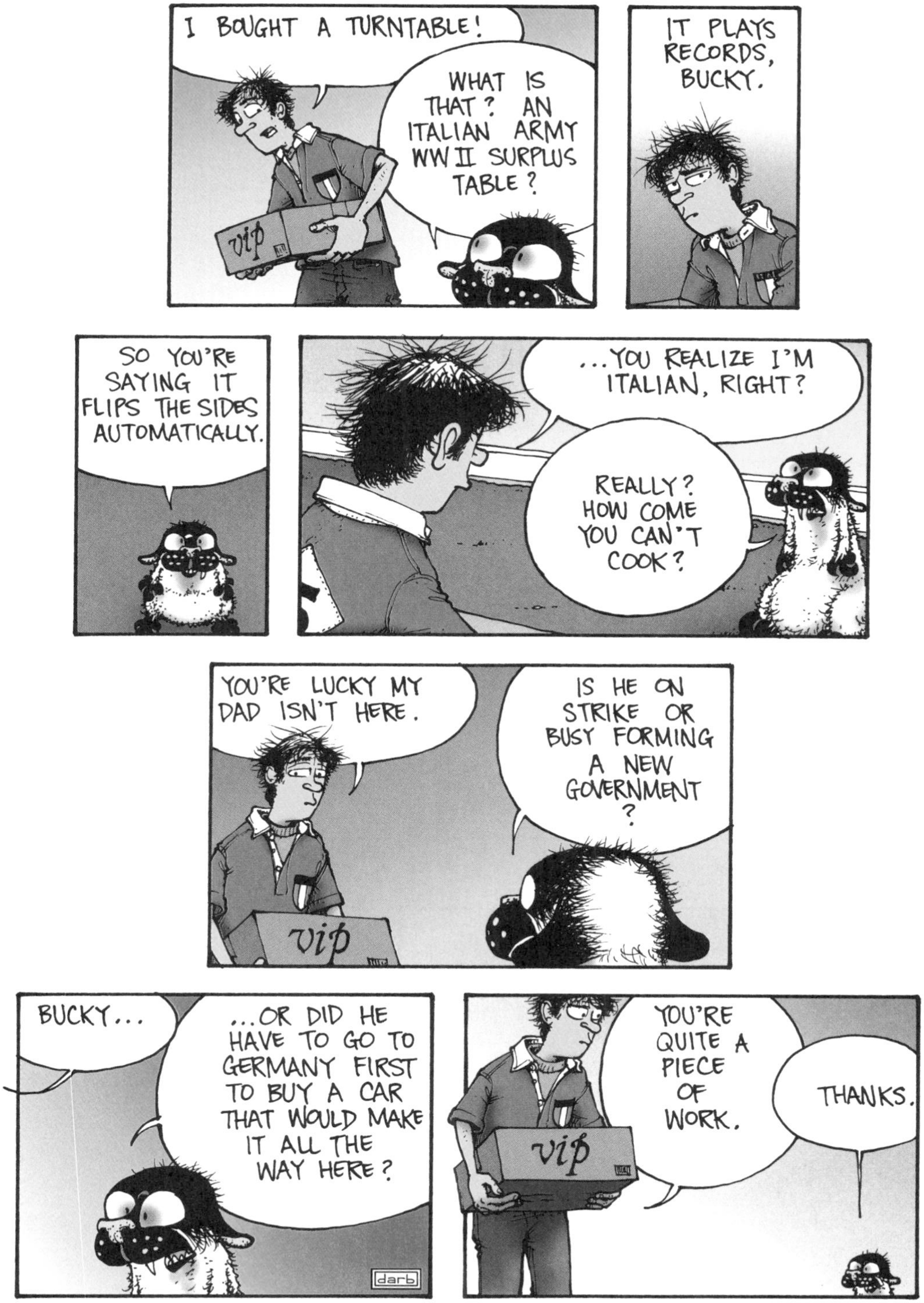
I BOUGHT A TURNTABLE!
WHAT IS THAT? AN ITALIAN ARMY WW II SURPLUS TABLE?
IT PLAYS RECORDS, BUCKY.
SO YOU'RE SAYING IT FLIPS THE SIDES AUTOMATICALLY.
...YOU REALIZE I'M ITALIAN, RIGHT?
REALLY? HOW COME YOU CAN'T COOK?
YOU'RE LUCKY MY DAD ISN'T HERE.
IS HE ON STRIKE OR BUSY FORMING A NEW GOVERNMENT?
BUCKY...
...OR DID HE HAVE TO GO TO GERMANY FIRST TO BUY A CAR THAT WOULD MAKE IT ALL THE WAY HERE?
darb
YOU'RE QUITE A PIECE OF WORK.
THANKS.

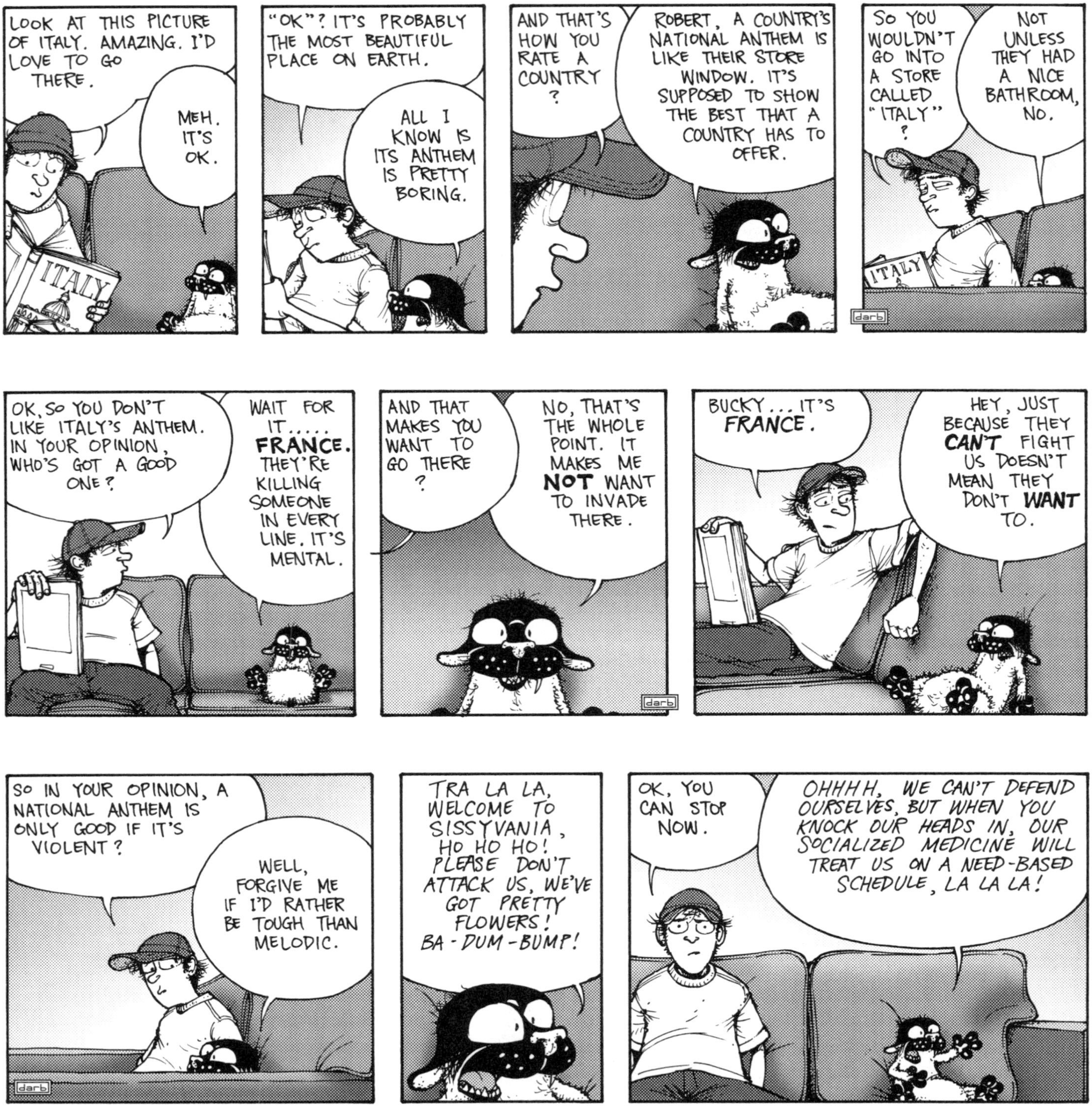
LOOK AT THIS PICTURE OF ITALY. AMAZING. I'D LOVE TO GO THERE.
MEH. IT'S OK.
ITALY
"OK"? IT'S PROBABLY THE MOST BEAUTIFUL PLACE ON EARTH.
ALL I KNOW IS ITS ANTHEM IS PRETTY BORING.
AND THAT'S HOW YOU RATE A COUNTRY?
ROBERT, A COUNTRY'S NATIONAL ANTHEM IS LIKE THEIR STORE WINDOW. IT'S SUPPOSED TO SHOW THE BEST THAT A COUNTRY HAS TO OFFER.
SO YOU WOULDN'T GO INTO A STORE CALLED "ITALY"?
NOT UNLESS THEY HAD A NICE BATHROOM, NO.
ITALY
darb
OK, SO YOU DON'T LIKE ITALY'S ANTHEM. IN YOUR OPINION, WHO'S GOT A GOOD ONE?
WAIT FOR IT..... **FRANCE.** THEY'RE KILLING SOMEONE IN EVERY LINE. IT'S MENTAL.
AND THAT MAKES YOU WANT TO GO THERE?
NO, THAT'S THE WHOLE POINT. IT MAKES ME **NOT** WANT TO INVADE THERE.
darb
BUCKY... IT'S **FRANCE**.
HEY, JUST BECAUSE THEY **CAN'T** FIGHT US DOESN'T MEAN THEY DON'T **WANT** TO.
SO IN YOUR OPINION, A NATIONAL ANTHEM IS ONLY GOOD IF IT'S VIOLENT?
WELL, FORGIVE ME IF I'D RATHER BE TOUGH THAN MELODIC.
darb
TRA LA LA, WELCOME TO SISSYVANIA, HO HO HO! PLEASE DON'T ATTACK US, WE'VE GOT PRETTY FLOWERS! BA-DUM-BUMP!
OK, YOU CAN STOP NOW.
OHHHH, WE CAN'T DEFEND OURSELVES, BUT WHEN YOU KNOCK OUR HEADS IN, OUR SOCIALIZED MEDICINE WILL TREAT US ON A NEED-BASED SCHEDULE, LA LA LA!

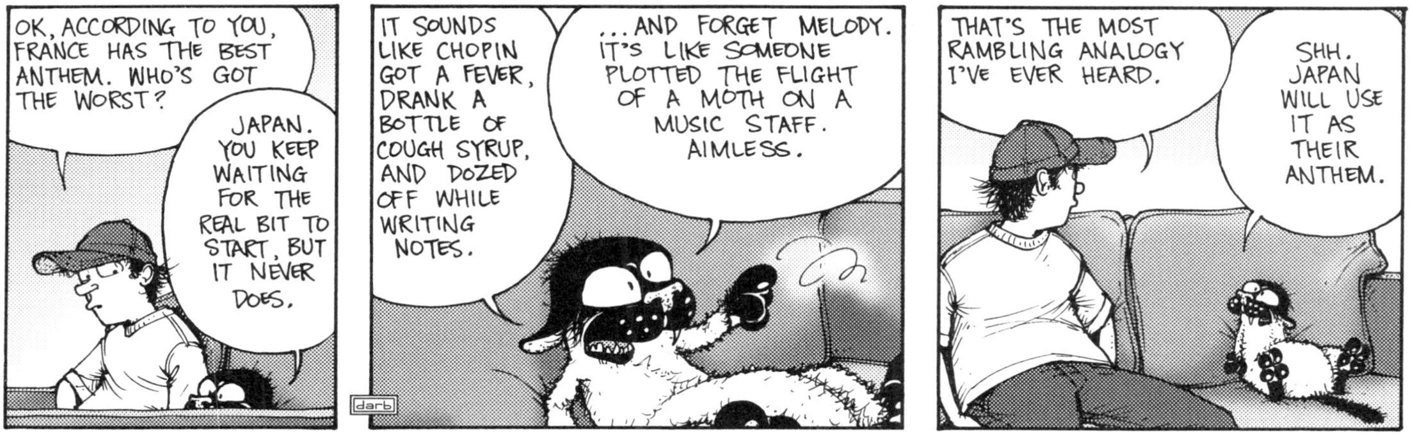
OK, ACCORDING TO YOU, FRANCE HAS THE BEST ANTHEM. WHO'S GOT THE WORST?
JAPAN. YOU KEEP WAITING FOR THE REAL BIT TO START, BUT IT NEVER DOES.
IT SOUNDS LIKE CHOPIN GOT A FEVER, DRANK A BOTTLE OF COUGH SYRUP, AND DOZED OFF WHILE WRITING NOTES.
...AND FORGET MELODY. IT'S LIKE SOMEONE PLOTTED THE FLIGHT OF A MOTH ON A MUSIC STAFF. AIMLESS.
THAT'S THE MOST RAMBLING ANALOGY I'VE EVER HEARD.
SHH. JAPAN WILL USE IT AS THEIR ANTHEM.

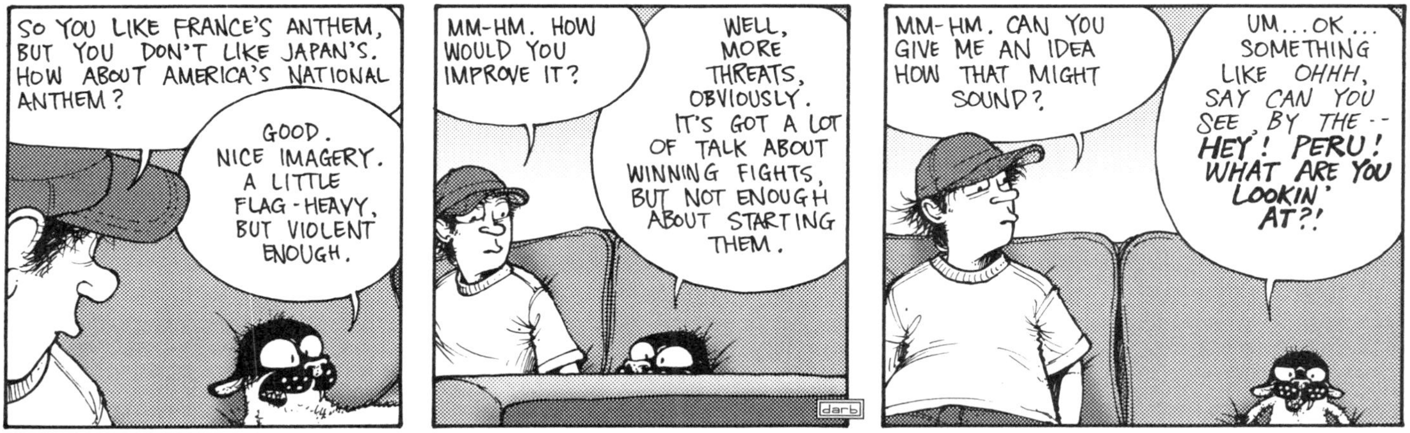
SO YOU LIKE FRANCE'S ANTHEM, BUT YOU DON'T LIKE JAPAN'S. HOW ABOUT AMERICA'S NATIONAL ANTHEM?
GOOD. NICE IMAGERY. A LITTLE FLAG-HEAVY, BUT VIOLENT ENOUGH.
MM-HM. HOW WOULD YOU IMPROVE IT?
WELL, MORE THREATS, OBVIOUSLY. IT'S GOT A LOT OF TALK ABOUT WINNING FIGHTS, BUT NOT ENOUGH ABOUT STARTING THEM.
MM-HM. CAN YOU GIVE ME AN IDEA HOW THAT MIGHT SOUND?
UM...OK... SOMETHING LIKE *OHHH, SAY CAN YOU SEE, BY THE--* ***HEY! PERU! WHAT ARE YOU LOOKIN' AT?!***

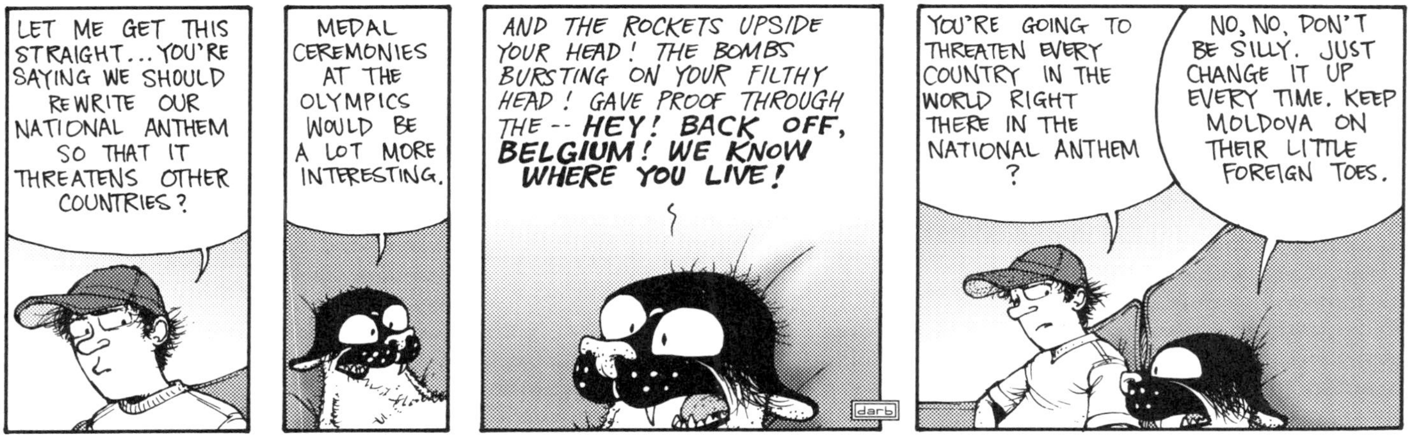
LET ME GET THIS STRAIGHT... YOU'RE SAYING WE SHOULD REWRITE OUR NATIONAL ANTHEM SO THAT IT THREATENS OTHER COUNTRIES?
MEDAL CEREMONIES AT THE OLYMPICS WOULD BE A LOT MORE INTERESTING.
AND THE ROCKETS UPSIDE YOUR HEAD! THE BOMBS BURSTING ON YOUR FILTHY HEAD! GAVE PROOF THROUGH THE-- ***HEY! BACK OFF, BELGIUM! WE KNOW WHERE YOU LIVE!***
YOU'RE GOING TO THREATEN EVERY COUNTRY IN THE WORLD RIGHT THERE IN THE NATIONAL ANTHEM?
NO, NO, DON'T BE SILLY. JUST CHANGE IT UP EVERY TIME. KEEP MOLDOVA ON THEIR LITTLE FOREIGN TOES.

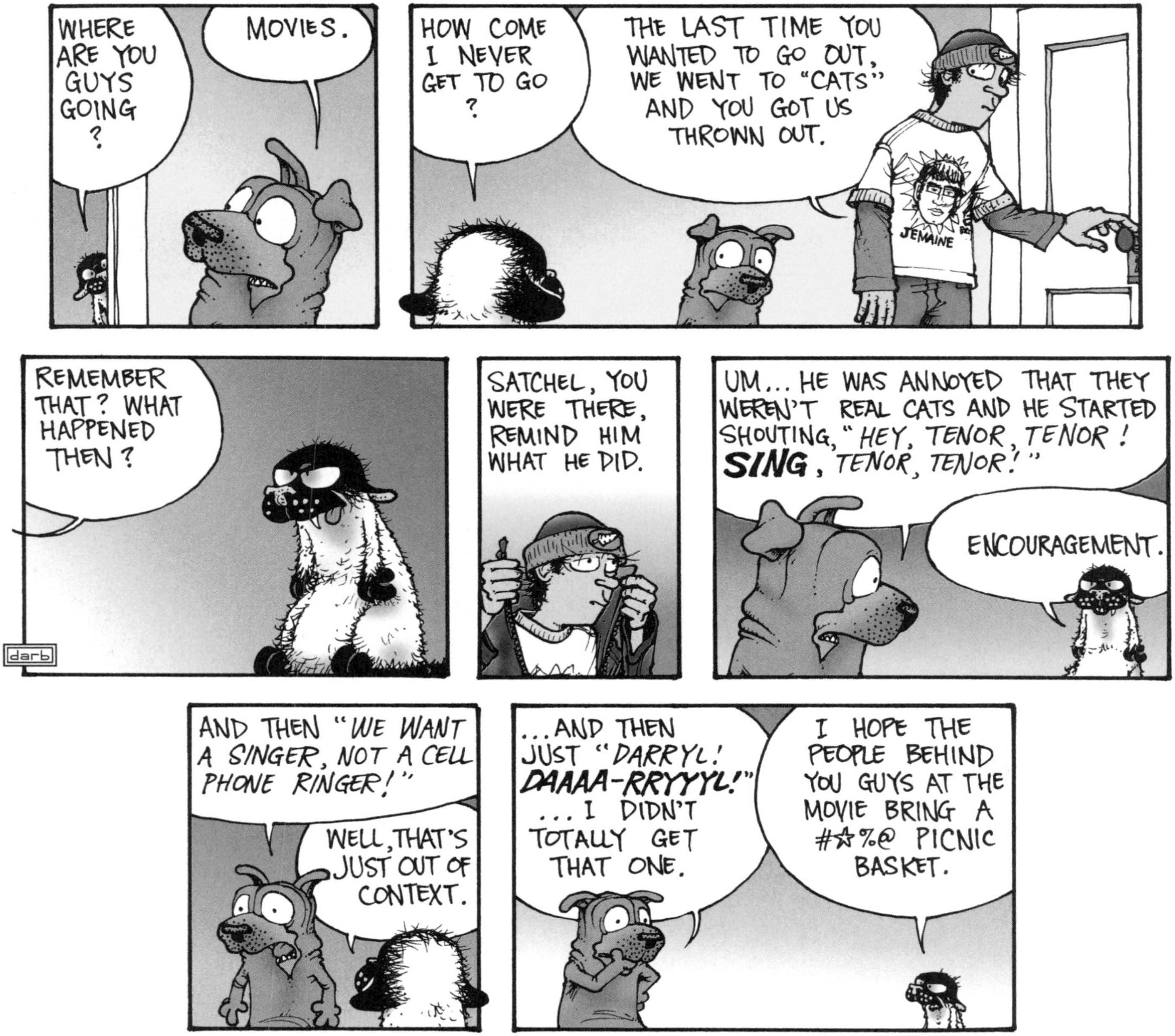
WHERE ARE YOU GUYS GOING ?
MOVIES.
HOW COME I NEVER GET TO GO ?
THE LAST TIME YOU WANTED TO GO OUT, WE WENT TO "CATS" AND YOU GOT US THROWN OUT.
JEMAINE
REMEMBER THAT? WHAT HAPPENED THEN?
darb
SATCHEL, YOU WERE THERE, REMIND HIM WHAT HE DID.
UM... HE WAS ANNOYED THAT THEY WEREN'T REAL CATS AND HE STARTED SHOUTING, "HEY, TENOR, TENOR! SING, TENOR, TENOR!"
ENCOURAGEMENT.
AND THEN "WE WANT A SINGER, NOT A CELL PHONE RINGER!"
WELL, THAT'S JUST OUT OF CONTEXT.
...AND THEN JUST "DARRYL! DAAAA-RRYYYL!" ...I DIDN'T TOTALLY GET THAT ONE.
I HOPE THE PEOPLE BEHIND YOU GUYS AT THE MOVIE BRING A #☆%@ PICNIC BASKET.

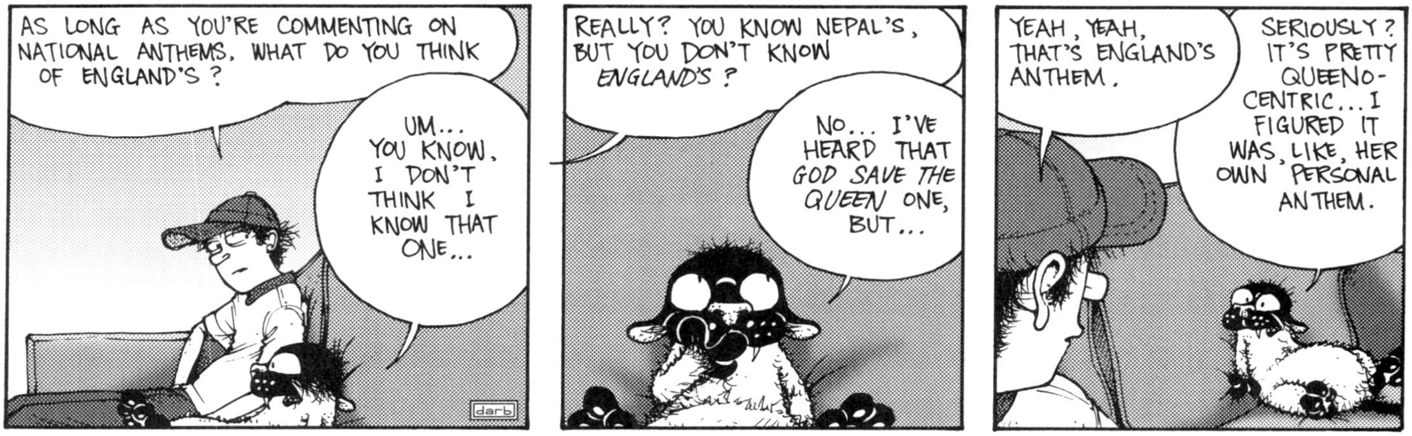
AS LONG AS YOU'RE COMMENTING ON NATIONAL ANTHEMS, WHAT DO YOU THINK OF ENGLAND'S ?
UM... YOU KNOW, I DON'T THINK I KNOW THAT ONE...
darb
REALLY? YOU KNOW NEPAL'S, BUT YOU DON'T KNOW *ENGLAND'S* ?
NO... I'VE HEARD THAT *GOD SAVE THE QUEEN* ONE, BUT...
YEAH, YEAH, THAT'S ENGLAND'S ANTHEM.
SERIOUSLY? IT'S PRETTY QUEENO-CENTRIC... I FIGURED IT WAS, LIKE, HER OWN PERSONAL ANTHEM.

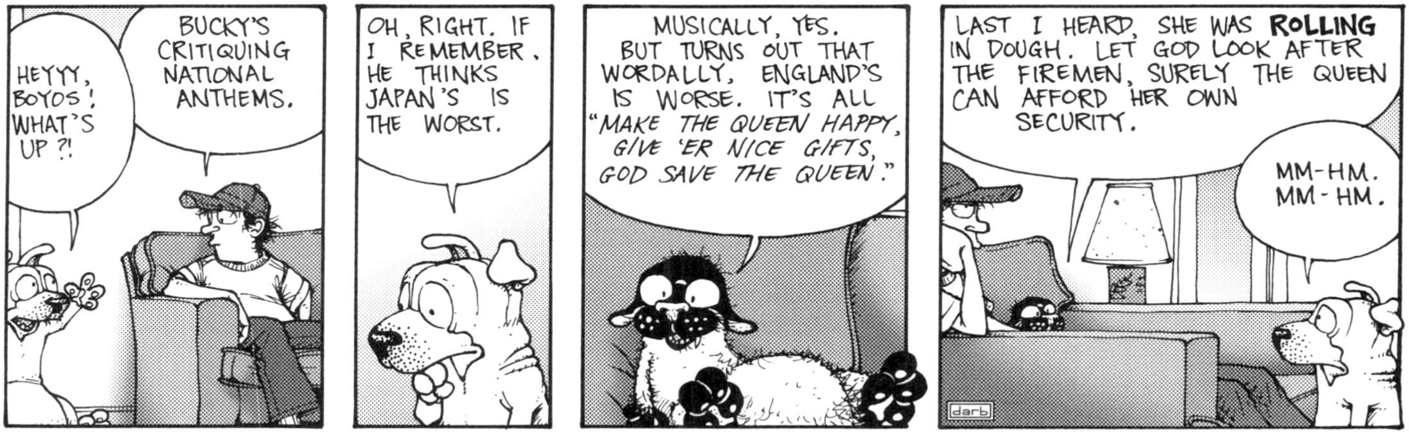
HEYYY, BOYOS! WHAT'S UP ?!
BUCKY'S CRITIQUING NATIONAL ANTHEMS.
OH, RIGHT. IF I REMEMBER, HE THINKS JAPAN'S IS THE WORST.
MUSICALLY, YES. BUT TURNS OUT THAT WORDALLY, ENGLAND'S IS WORSE. IT'S ALL "*MAKE THE QUEEN HAPPY, GIVE 'ER NICE GIFTS, GOD SAVE THE QUEEN*."
LAST I HEARD, SHE WAS **ROLLING** IN DOUGH. LET GOD LOOK AFTER THE FIREMEN, SURELY THE QUEEN CAN AFFORD HER OWN SECURITY.
MM-HM. MM-HM.
darb

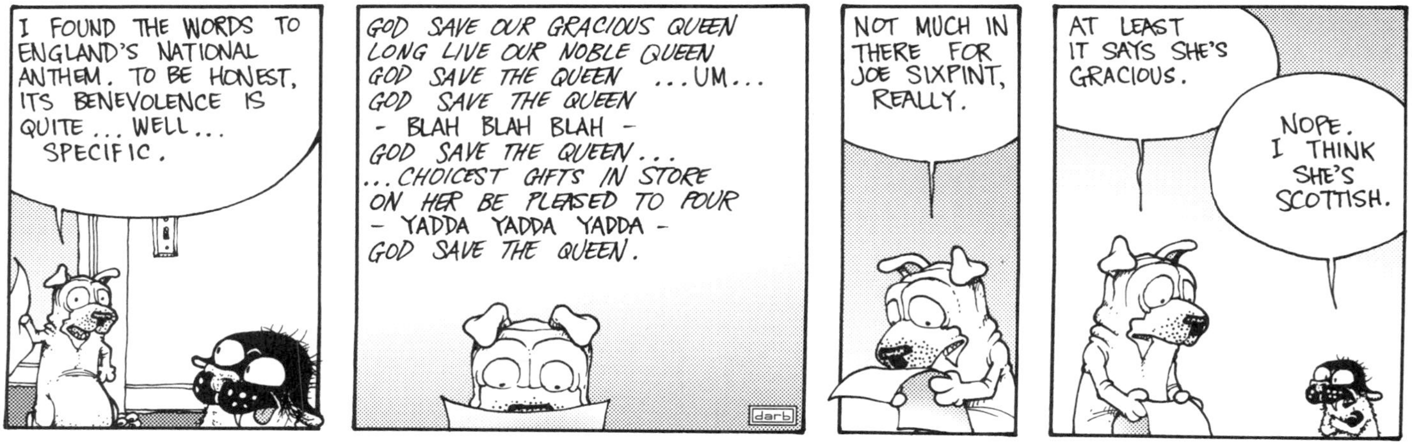
I FOUND THE WORDS TO ENGLAND'S NATIONAL ANTHEM. TO BE HONEST, ITS BENEVOLENCE IS QUITE... WELL... SPECIFIC.
GOD SAVE OUR GRACIOUS QUEEN
LONG LIVE OUR NOBLE QUEEN
GOD SAVE THE QUEEN ...UM...
GOD SAVE THE QUEEN
- BLAH BLAH BLAH -
GOD SAVE THE QUEEN...
...CHOICEST GIFTS IN STORE
ON HER BE PLEASED TO POUR
- YADDA YADDA YADDA -
GOD SAVE THE QUEEN.
darb
NOT MUCH IN THERE FOR JOE SIXPINT, REALLY.
AT LEAST IT SAYS SHE'S GRACIOUS.
NOPE. I THINK SHE'S SCOTTISH.

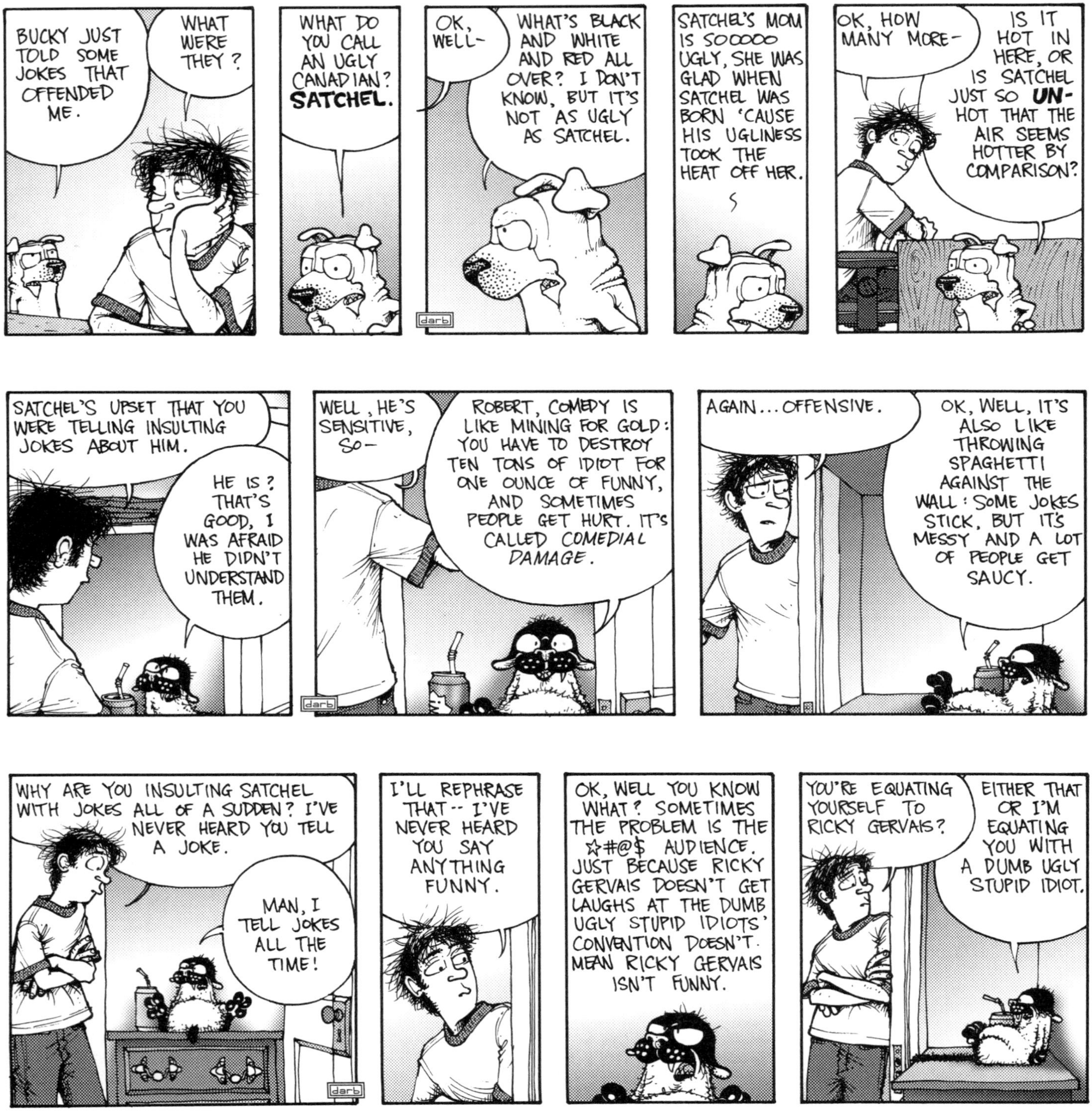
BUCKY JUST TOLD SOME JOKES THAT OFFENDED ME.
WHAT WERE THEY?
WHAT DO YOU CALL AN UGLY CANADIAN? SATCHEL.
OK, WELL-
WHAT'S BLACK AND WHITE AND RED ALL OVER? I DON'T KNOW, BUT IT'S NOT AS UGLY AS SATCHEL.
SATCHEL'S MOM IS SOOOOO UGLY, SHE WAS GLAD WHEN SATCHEL WAS BORN 'CAUSE HIS UGLINESS TOOK THE HEAT OFF HER.
OK, HOW MANY MORE-
IS IT HOT IN HERE, OR IS SATCHEL JUST SO UN-HOT THAT THE AIR SEEMS HOTTER BY COMPARISON?
darb
SATCHEL'S UPSET THAT YOU WERE TELLING INSULTING JOKES ABOUT HIM.
HE IS? THAT'S GOOD, I WAS AFRAID HE DIDN'T UNDERSTAND THEM.
WELL, HE'S SENSITIVE, SO-
ROBERT, COMEDY IS LIKE MINING FOR GOLD: YOU HAVE TO DESTROY TEN TONS OF IDIOT FOR ONE OUNCE OF FUNNY, AND SOMETIMES PEOPLE GET HURT. IT'S CALLED COMEDIAL DAMAGE.
AGAIN... OFFENSIVE.
OK, WELL, IT'S ALSO LIKE THROWING SPAGHETTI AGAINST THE WALL: SOME JOKES STICK, BUT IT'S MESSY AND A LOT OF PEOPLE GET SAUCY.
darb
WHY ARE YOU INSULTING SATCHEL WITH JOKES ALL OF A SUDDEN? I'VE NEVER HEARD YOU TELL A JOKE.
MAN, I TELL JOKES ALL THE TIME!
I'LL REPHRASE THAT-- I'VE NEVER HEARD YOU SAY ANYTHING FUNNY.
OK, WELL YOU KNOW WHAT? SOMETIMES THE PROBLEM IS THE ☆#@$ AUDIENCE. JUST BECAUSE RICKY GERVAIS DOESN'T GET LAUGHS AT THE DUMB UGLY STUPID IDIOTS' CONVENTION DOESN'T MEAN RICKY GERVAIS ISN'T FUNNY.
YOU'RE EQUATING YOURSELF TO RICKY GERVAIS?
EITHER THAT OR I'M EQUATING YOU WITH A DUMB UGLY STUPID IDIOT.
darb

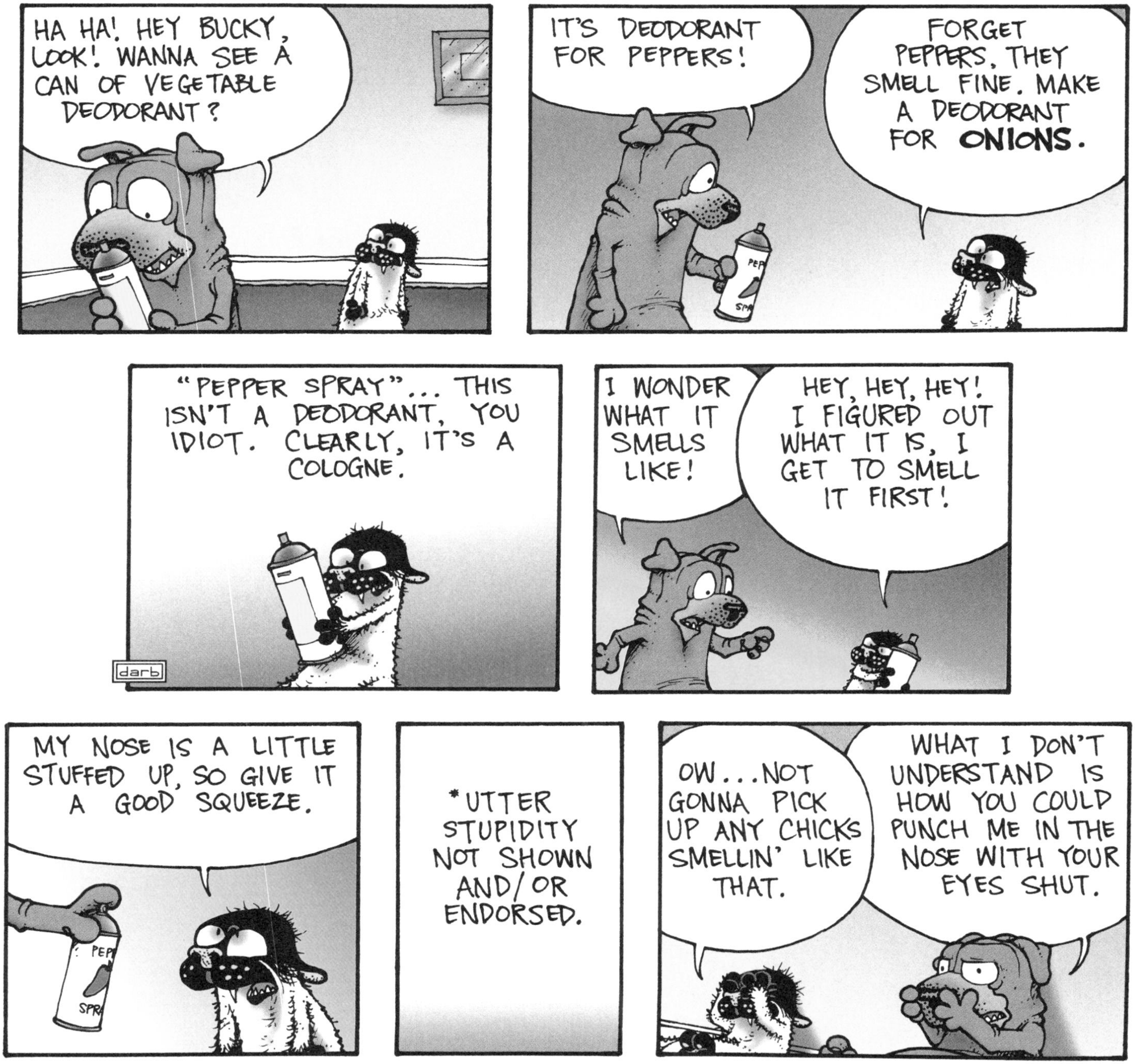
HA HA! HEY BUCKY, LOOK! WANNA SEE A CAN OF VEGETABLE DEODORANT?
IT'S DEODORANT FOR PEPPERS!
FORGET PEPPERS, THEY SMELL FINE. MAKE A DEODORANT FOR **ONIONS**.
"PEPPER SPRAY"... THIS ISN'T A DEODORANT, YOU IDIOT. CLEARLY, IT'S A COLOGNE.
darb
I WONDER WHAT IT SMELLS LIKE!
HEY, HEY, HEY! I FIGURED OUT WHAT IT IS, I GET TO SMELL IT FIRST!
MY NOSE IS A LITTLE STUFFED UP, SO GIVE IT A GOOD SQUEEZE.
*UTTER STUPIDITY NOT SHOWN AND/OR ENDORSED.
OW...NOT GONNA PICK UP ANY CHICKS SMELLIN' LIKE THAT.
WHAT I DON'T UNDERSTAND IS HOW YOU COULD PUNCH ME IN THE NOSE WITH YOUR EYES SHUT.

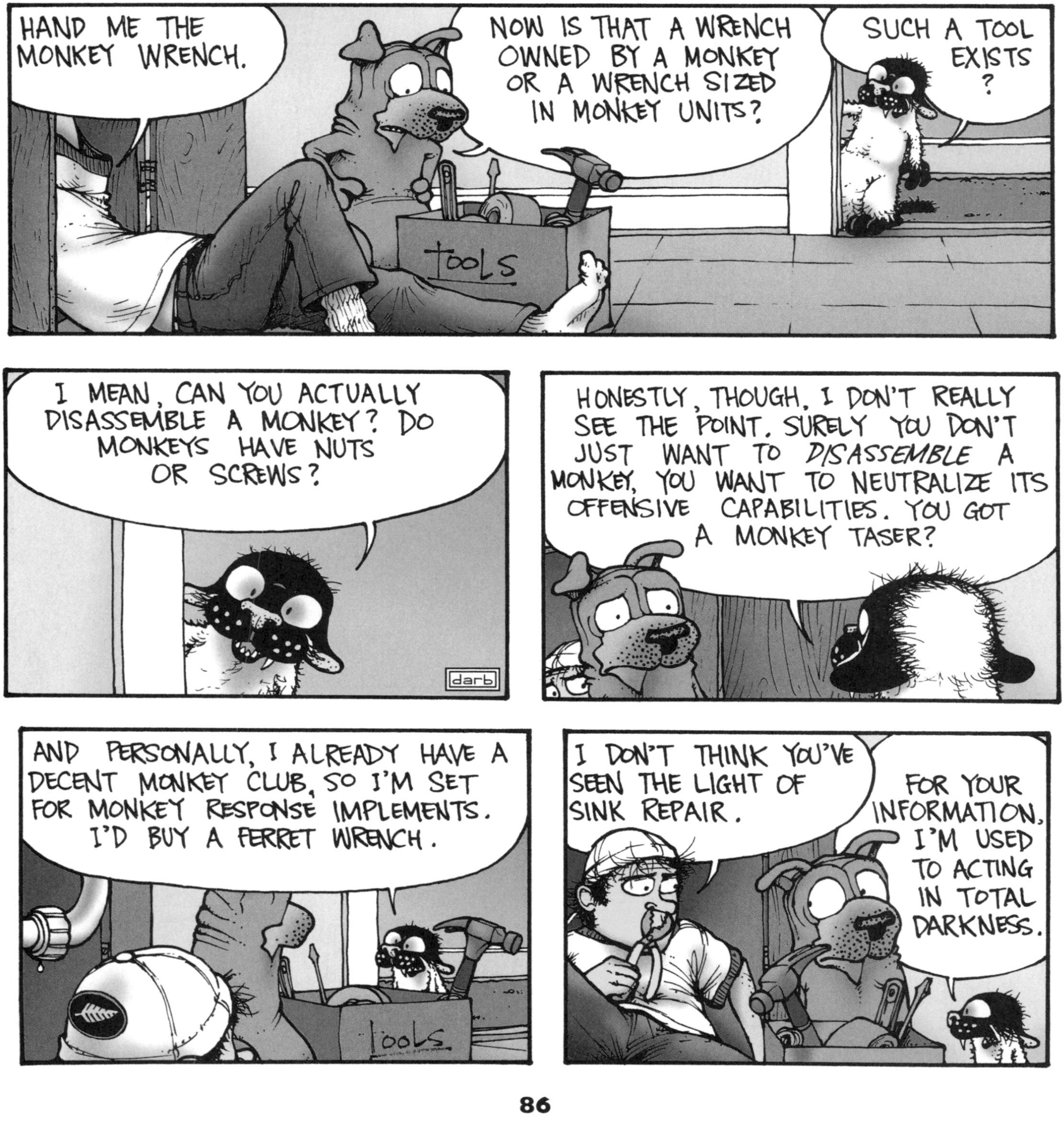

HAND ME THE MONKEY WRENCH.
NOW IS THAT A WRENCH OWNED BY A MONKEY OR A WRENCH SIZED IN MONKEY UNITS?
SUCH A TOOL EXISTS ?
TOOLS
I MEAN, CAN YOU ACTUALLY DISASSEMBLE A MONKEY? DO MONKEYS HAVE NUTS OR SCREWS?
darb
HONESTLY, THOUGH, I DON'T REALLY SEE THE POINT. SURELY YOU DON'T JUST WANT TO *DISASSEMBLE* A MONKEY, YOU WANT TO NEUTRALIZE ITS OFFENSIVE CAPABILITIES. YOU GOT A MONKEY TASER?
AND PERSONALLY, I ALREADY HAVE A DECENT MONKEY CLUB, SO I'M SET FOR MONKEY RESPONSE IMPLEMENTS. I'D BUY A FERRET WRENCH.
TOOLS
I DON'T THINK YOU'VE SEEN THE LIGHT OF SINK REPAIR.
FOR YOUR INFORMATION, I'M USED TO ACTING IN TOTAL DARKNESS.

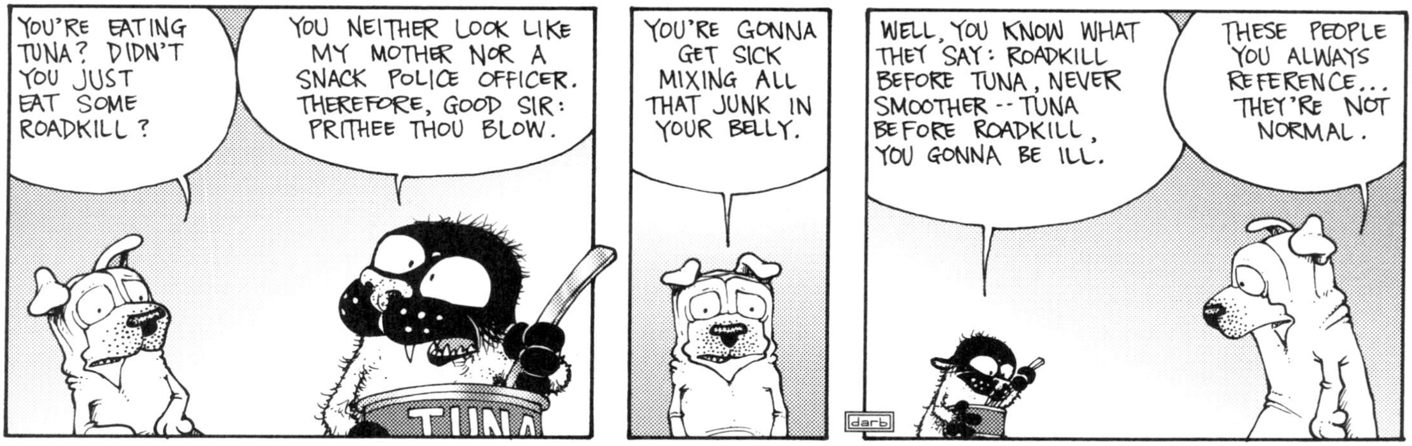
YOU'RE EATING TUNA? DIDN'T YOU JUST EAT SOME ROADKILL?
YOU NEITHER LOOK LIKE MY MOTHER NOR A SNACK POLICE OFFICER. THEREFORE, GOOD SIR: PRITHEE THOU BLOW.
TUNA
YOU'RE GONNA GET SICK MIXING ALL THAT JUNK IN YOUR BELLY.
WELL, YOU KNOW WHAT THEY SAY: ROADKILL BEFORE TUNA, NEVER SMOOTHER -- TUNA BEFORE ROADKILL, YOU GONNA BE ILL.
THESE PEOPLE YOU ALWAYS REFERENCE... THEY'RE NOT NORMAL.
darb

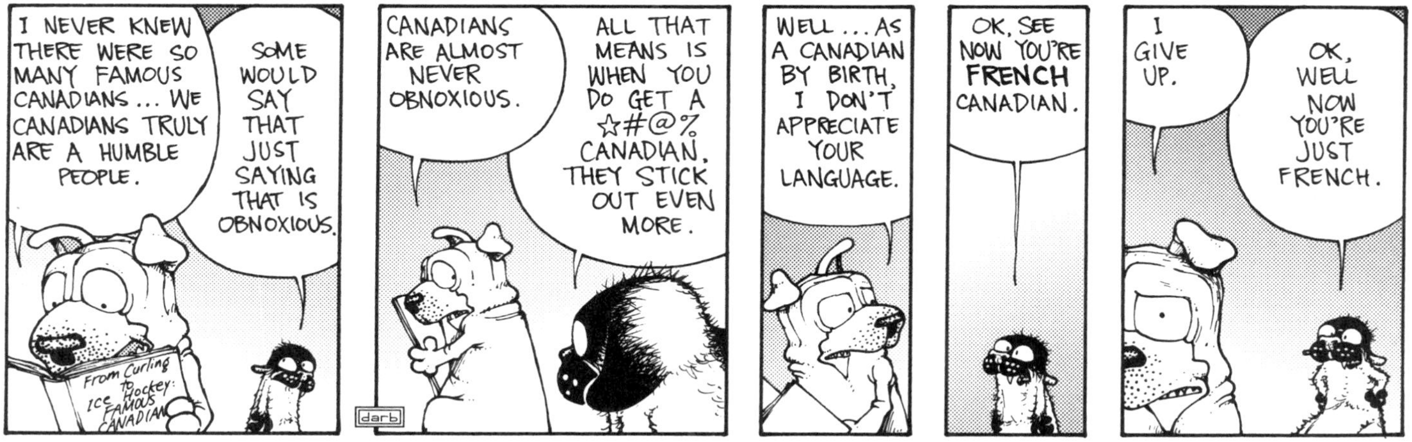
I NEVER KNEW THERE WERE SO MANY FAMOUS CANADIANS... WE CANADIANS TRULY ARE A HUMBLE PEOPLE.
SOME WOULD SAY THAT JUST SAYING THAT IS OBNOXIOUS.
From Curling to Ice Hockey: FAMOUS CANADIANS
darb
CANADIANS ARE ALMOST NEVER OBNOXIOUS.
ALL THAT MEANS IS WHEN YOU DO GET A ☆#@% CANADIAN, THEY STICK OUT EVEN MORE.
WELL... AS A CANADIAN BY BIRTH, I DON'T APPRECIATE YOUR LANGUAGE.
OK, SEE NOW YOU'RE FRENCH CANADIAN.
I GIVE UP.
OK, WELL NOW YOU'RE JUST FRENCH.

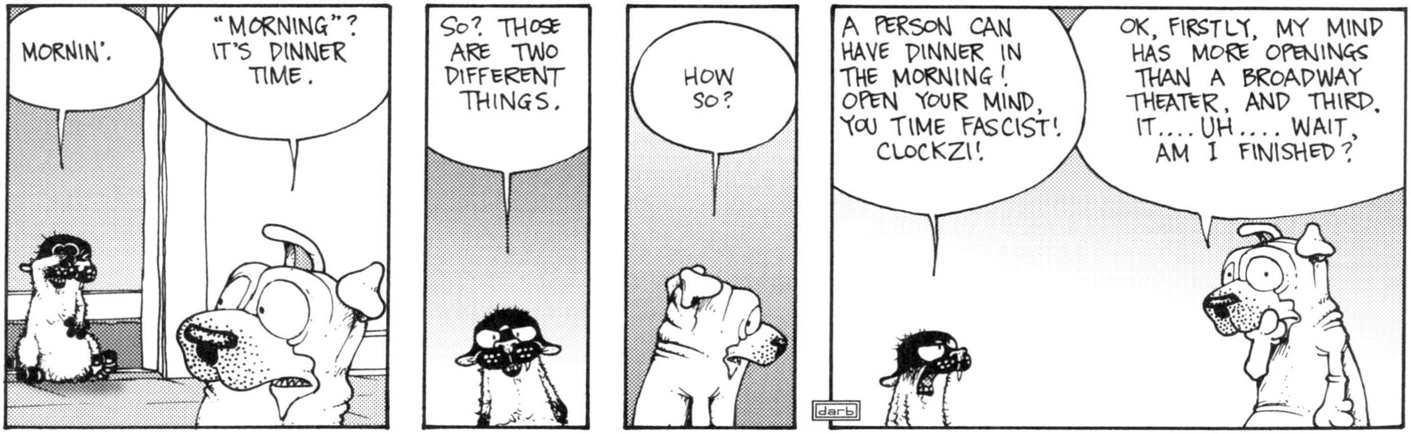
MORNIN'.
"MORNING"? IT'S DINNER TIME.
SO? THOSE ARE TWO DIFFERENT THINGS.
HOW SO?
A PERSON CAN HAVE DINNER IN THE MORNING! OPEN YOUR MIND, YOU TIME FASCIST! CLOCKZI!
OK, FIRSTLY, MY MIND HAS MORE OPENINGS THAN A BROADWAY THEATER, AND THIRD, IT.... UH.... WAIT, AM I FINISHED?
darb

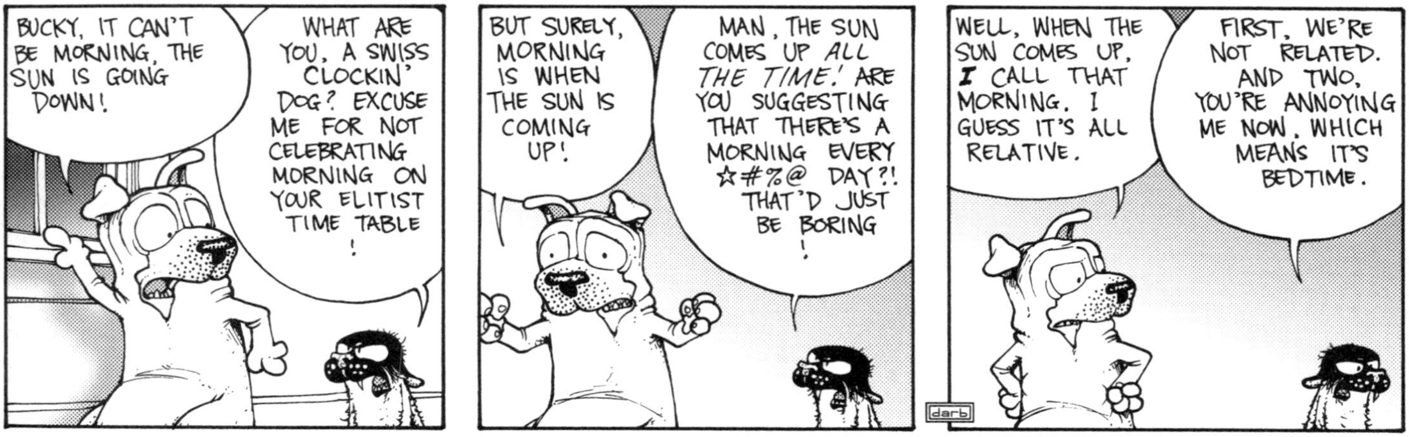
BUCKY, IT CAN'T BE MORNING, THE SUN IS GOING DOWN!
WHAT ARE YOU, A SWISS CLOCKIN' DOG? EXCUSE ME FOR NOT CELEBRATING MORNING ON YOUR ELITIST TIME TABLE!
BUT SURELY, MORNING IS WHEN THE SUN IS COMING UP!
MAN, THE SUN COMES UP *ALL THE TIME!* ARE YOU SUGGESTING THAT THERE'S A MORNING EVERY ☆#%@ DAY?! THAT'D JUST BE BORING!
WELL, WHEN THE SUN COMES UP, ***I*** CALL THAT MORNING. I GUESS IT'S ALL RELATIVE.
FIRST, WE'RE NOT RELATED. AND TWO, YOU'RE ANNOYING ME NOW, WHICH MEANS IT'S BEDTIME.
darb

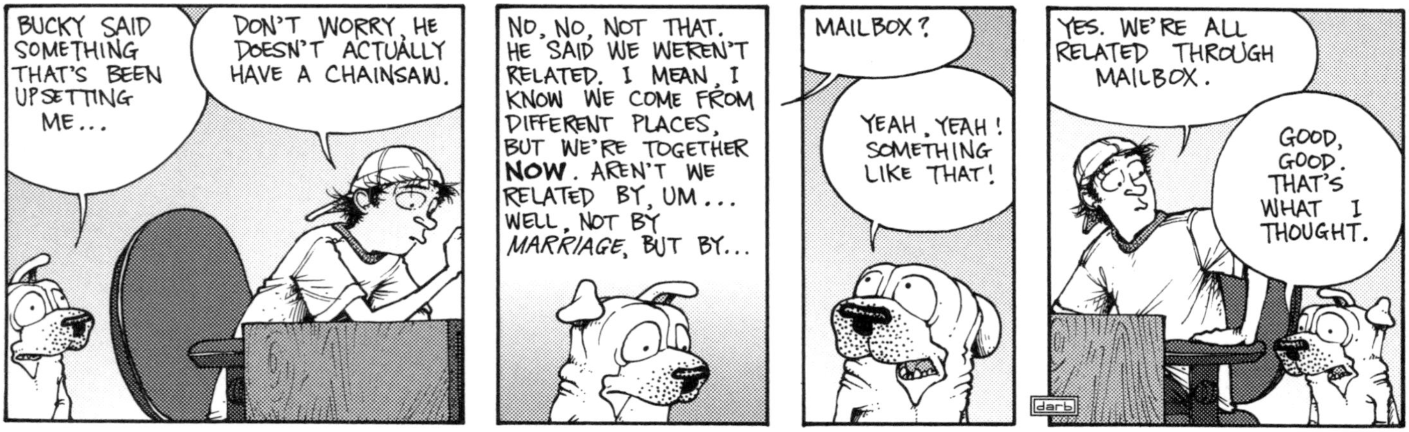
BUCKY SAID SOMETHING THAT'S BEEN UPSETTING ME...
DON'T WORRY, HE DOESN'T ACTUALLY HAVE A CHAINSAW.
NO, NO, NOT THAT. HE SAID WE WEREN'T RELATED. I MEAN, I KNOW WE COME FROM DIFFERENT PLACES, BUT WE'RE TOGETHER **NOW**. AREN'T WE RELATED BY, UM... WELL, NOT BY *MARRIAGE*, BUT BY...
MAILBOX?
YEAH, YEAH! SOMETHING LIKE THAT!
YES. WE'RE ALL RELATED THROUGH MAILBOX.
GOOD, GOOD. THAT'S WHAT I THOUGHT.
darb

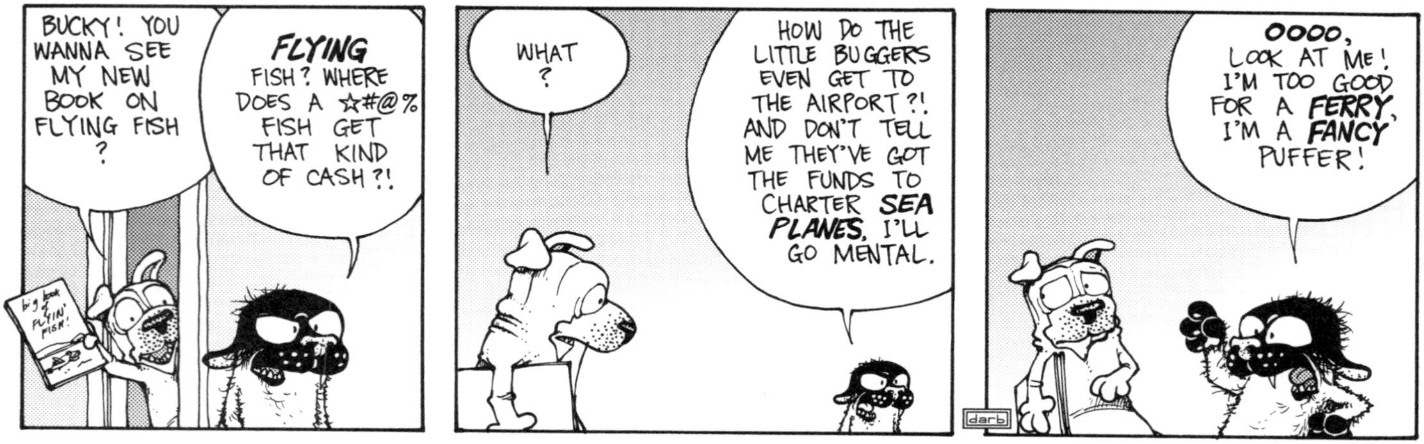
BUCKY! YOU WANNA SEE MY NEW BOOK ON FLYING FISH?
FLYING FISH? WHERE DOES A ☆#@% FISH GET THAT KIND OF CASH?!
big book of FLYIN' FISH!
WHAT?
HOW DO THE LITTLE BUGGERS EVEN GET TO THE AIRPORT?! AND DON'T TELL ME THEY'VE GOT THE FUNDS TO CHARTER ***SEA PLANES***, I'LL GO MENTAL.
OOOO, LOOK AT ME! I'M TOO GOOD FOR A ***FERRY***, I'M A ***FANCY*** PUFFER!
darb

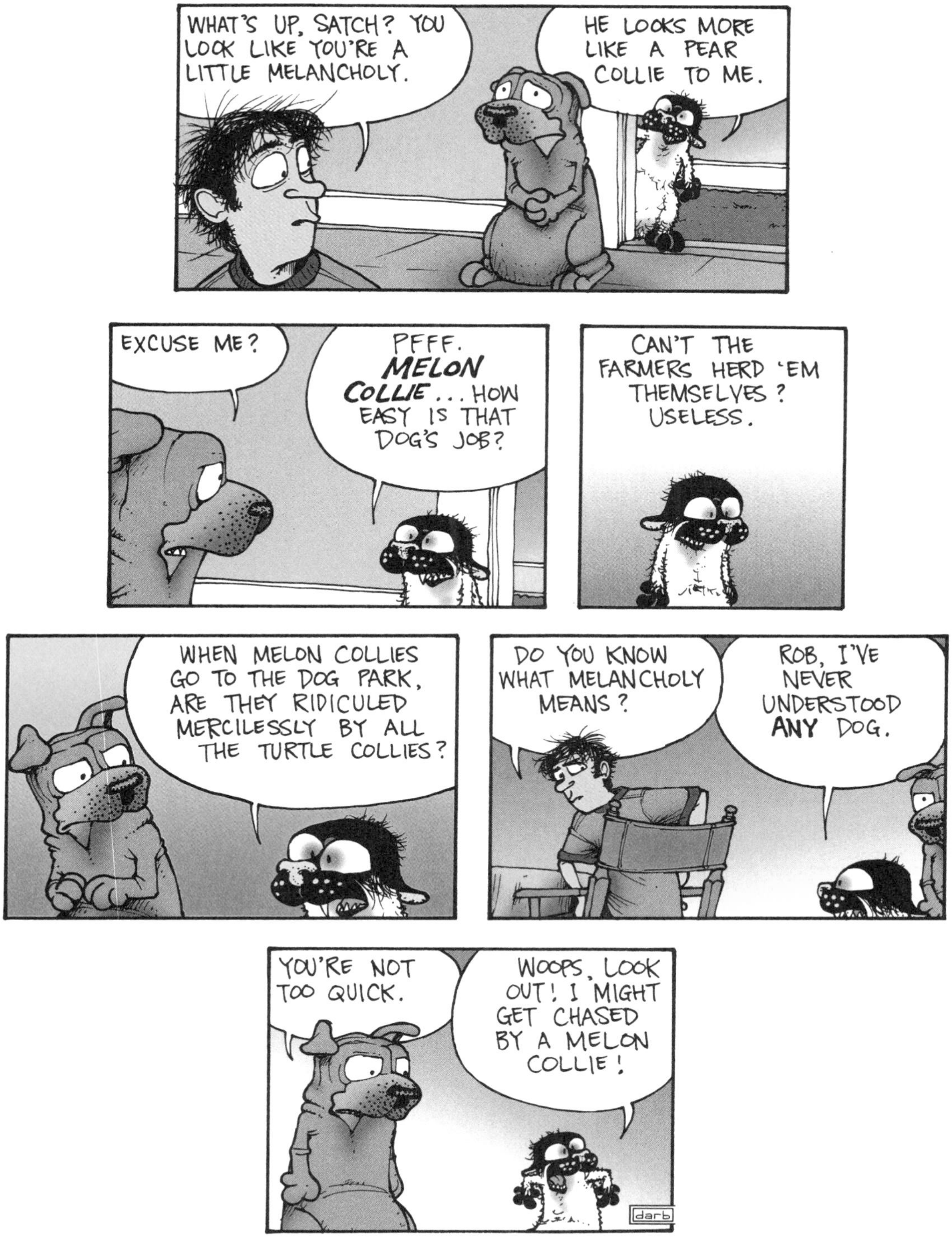
WHAT'S UP, SATCH? YOU LOOK LIKE YOU'RE A LITTLE MELANCHOLY.
HE LOOKS MORE LIKE A PEAR COLLIE TO ME.
EXCUSE ME?
PFFF. MELON COLLIE... HOW EASY IS THAT DOG'S JOB?
CAN'T THE FARMERS HERD 'EM THEMSELVES? USELESS.
WHEN MELON COLLIES GO TO THE DOG PARK, ARE THEY RIDICULED MERCILESSLY BY ALL THE TURTLE COLLIES?
DO YOU KNOW WHAT MELANCHOLY MEANS?
ROB, I'VE NEVER UNDERSTOOD ANY DOG.
YOU'RE NOT TOO QUICK.
WOOPS, LOOK OUT! I MIGHT GET CHASED BY A MELON COLLIE!
darb

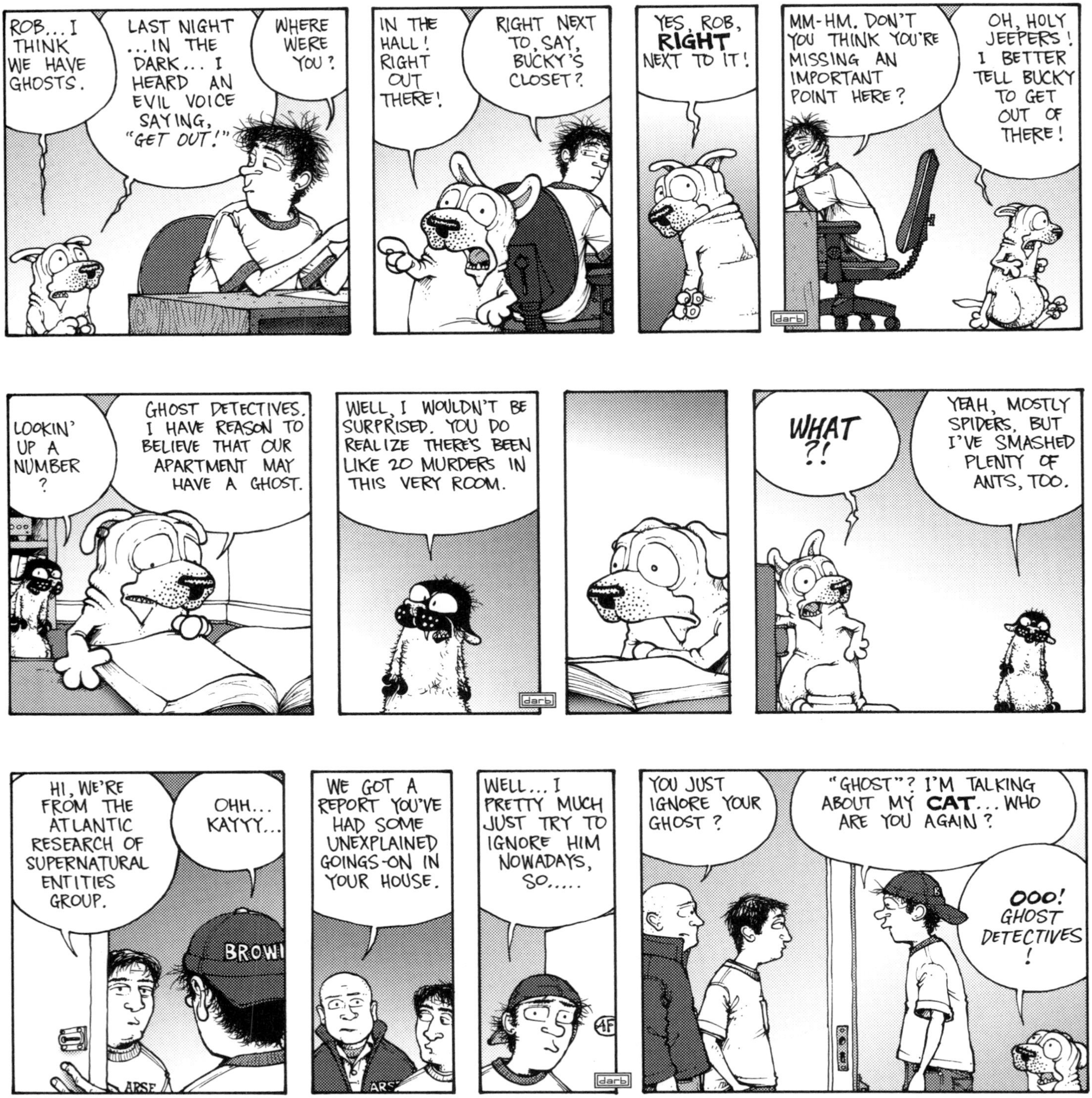
ROB... I THINK WE HAVE GHOSTS.
LAST NIGHT ...IN THE DARK... I HEARD AN EVIL VOICE SAYING, "GET OUT!"
WHERE WERE YOU?
IN THE HALL! RIGHT OUT THERE!
RIGHT NEXT TO, SAY, BUCKY'S CLOSET?
YES, ROB, RIGHT NEXT TO IT!
MM-HM. DON'T YOU THINK YOU'RE MISSING AN IMPORTANT POINT HERE?
OH, HOLY JEEPERS! I BETTER TELL BUCKY TO GET OUT OF THERE!
darb
LOOKIN' UP A NUMBER?
GHOST DETECTIVES. I HAVE REASON TO BELIEVE THAT OUR APARTMENT MAY HAVE A GHOST.
WELL, I WOULDN'T BE SURPRISED. YOU DO REALIZE THERE'S BEEN LIKE 20 MURDERS IN THIS VERY ROOM.
darb
WHAT?!
YEAH, MOSTLY SPIDERS, BUT I'VE SMASHED PLENTY OF ANTS, TOO.
HI, WE'RE FROM THE ATLANTIC RESEARCH OF SUPERNATURAL ENTITIES GROUP.
OHH... KAYYY...
BROWI
ARSE
WE GOT A REPORT YOU'VE HAD SOME UNEXPLAINED GOINGS-ON IN YOUR HOUSE.
WELL... I PRETTY MUCH JUST TRY TO IGNORE HIM NOWADAYS, SO.....
4F
darb
YOU JUST IGNORE YOUR GHOST?
"GHOST"? I'M TALKING ABOUT MY CAT... WHO ARE YOU AGAIN?
OOO! GHOST DETECTIVES!

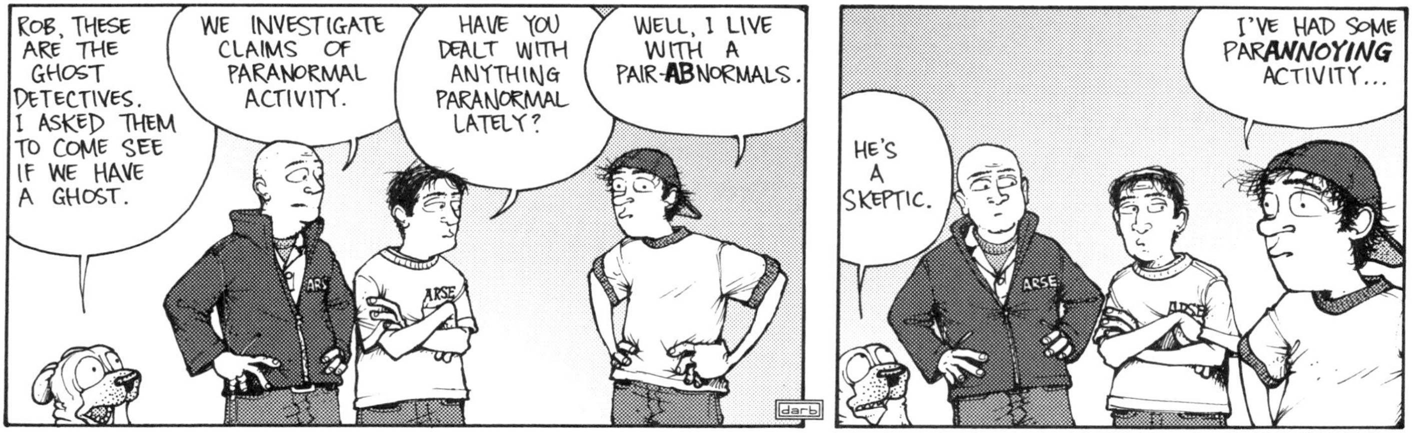
ROB, THESE ARE THE GHOST DETECTIVES. I ASKED THEM TO COME SEE IF WE HAVE A GHOST.
WE INVESTIGATE CLAIMS OF PARANORMAL ACTIVITY.
HAVE YOU DEALT WITH ANYTHING PARANORMAL LATELY?
WELL, I LIVE WITH A PAIR-**AB**NORMALS.
I'VE HAD SOME PAR***ANNOYING*** ACTIVITY...
HE'S A SKEPTIC.
ARSE
ARSE
ARSE
darb

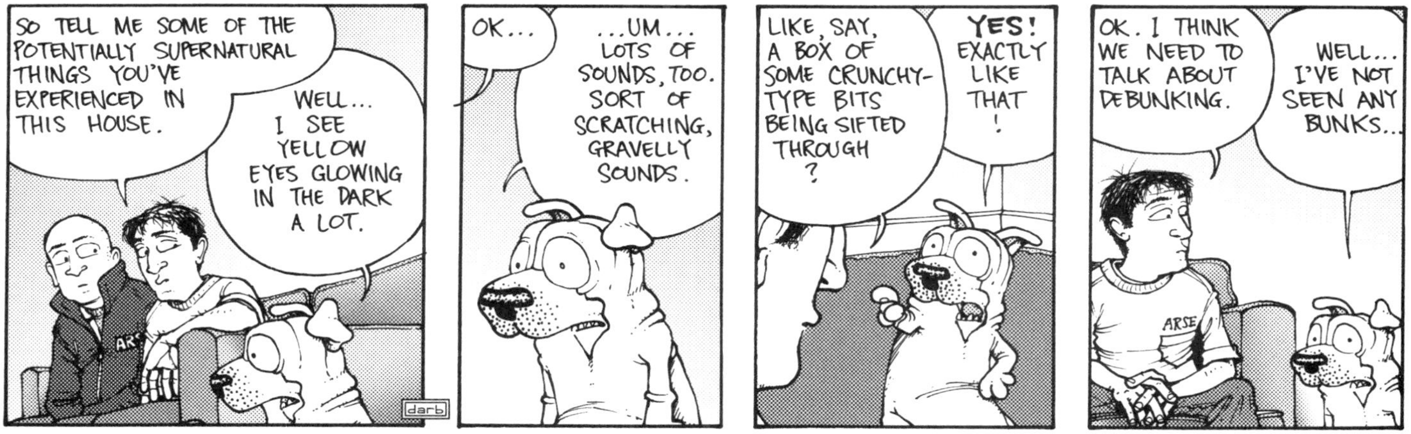
SO TELL ME SOME OF THE POTENTIALLY SUPERNATURAL THINGS YOU'VE EXPERIENCED IN THIS HOUSE.
WELL... I SEE YELLOW EYES GLOWING IN THE DARK A LOT.
ARS
darb
OK...
...UM... LOTS OF SOUNDS, TOO. SORT OF SCRATCHING, GRAVELLY SOUNDS.
LIKE, SAY, A BOX OF SOME CRUNCHY-TYPE BITS BEING SIFTED THROUGH ?
YES! EXACTLY LIKE THAT !
OK. I THINK WE NEED TO TALK ABOUT DEBUNKING.
WELL... I'VE NOT SEEN ANY BUNKS...
ARSE

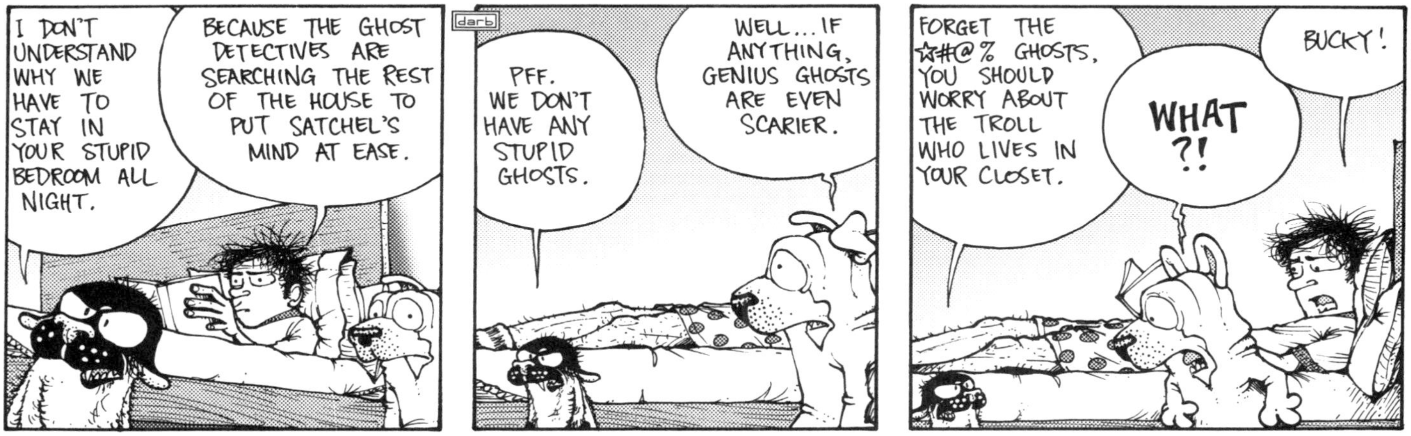
I DON'T UNDERSTAND WHY WE HAVE TO STAY IN YOUR STUPID BEDROOM ALL NIGHT.
BECAUSE THE GHOST DETECTIVES ARE SEARCHING THE REST OF THE HOUSE TO PUT SATCHEL'S MIND AT EASE.
darb
PFF. WE DON'T HAVE ANY STUPID GHOSTS.
WELL... IF ANYTHING, GENIUS GHOSTS ARE EVEN SCARIER.
FORGET THE ☆#@% GHOSTS, YOU SHOULD WORRY ABOUT THE TROLL WHO LIVES IN YOUR CLOSET.
WHAT ?!
BUCKY!

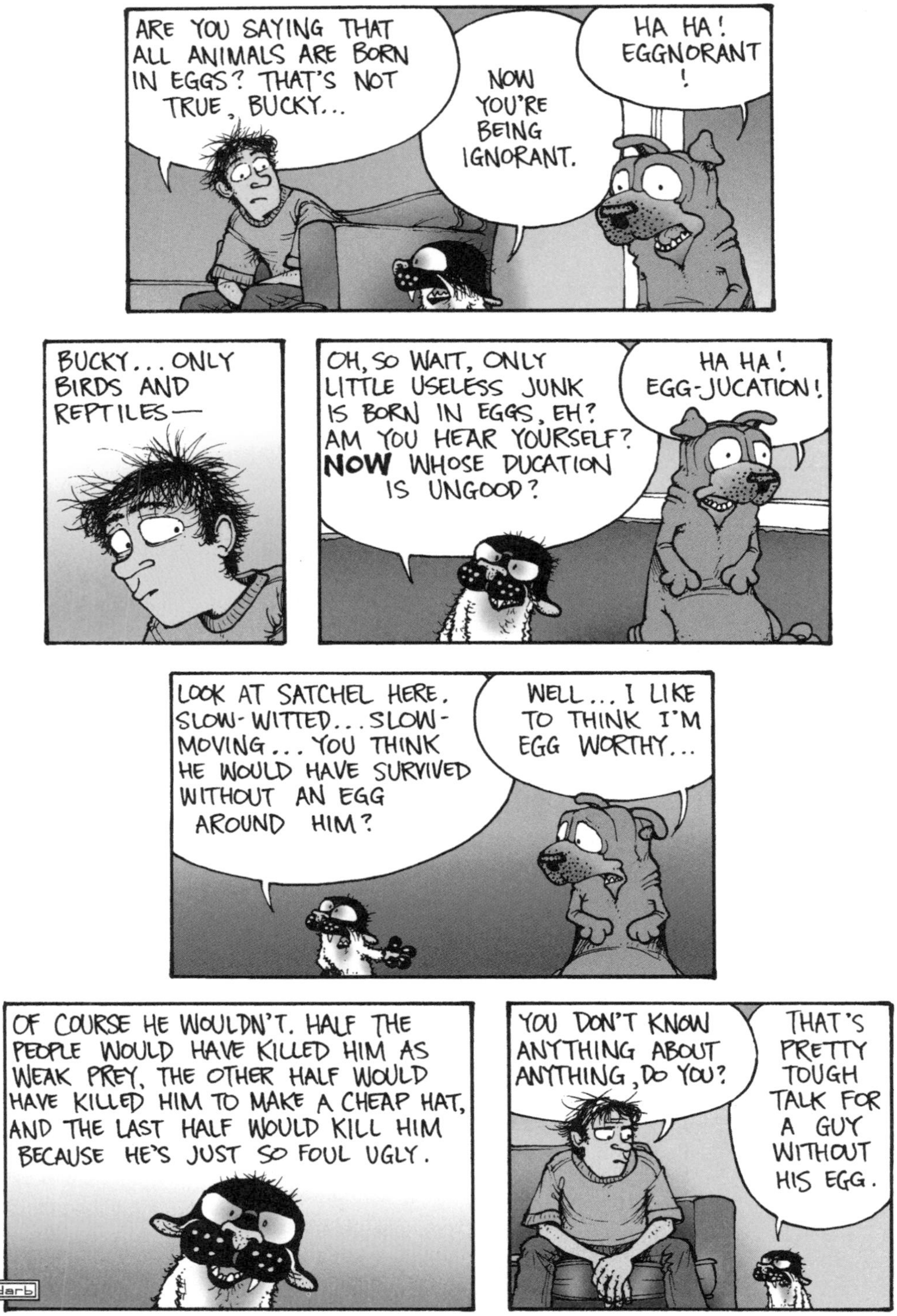
ARE YOU SAYING THAT ALL ANIMALS ARE BORN IN EGGS? THAT'S NOT TRUE, BUCKY...
NOW YOU'RE BEING IGNORANT.
HA HA! EGGNORANT!
BUCKY... ONLY BIRDS AND REPTILES—
OH, SO WAIT, ONLY LITTLE USELESS JUNK IS BORN IN EGGS, EH? AM YOU HEAR YOURSELF? NOW WHOSE DUCATION IS UNGOOD?
HA HA! EGG-JUCATION!
LOOK AT SATCHEL HERE. SLOW-WITTED... SLOW-MOVING... YOU THINK HE WOULD HAVE SURVIVED WITHOUT AN EGG AROUND HIM?
WELL... I LIKE TO THINK I'M EGG WORTHY...
OF COURSE HE WOULDN'T. HALF THE PEOPLE WOULD HAVE KILLED HIM AS WEAK PREY, THE OTHER HALF WOULD HAVE KILLED HIM TO MAKE A CHEAP HAT, AND THE LAST HALF WOULD KILL HIM BECAUSE HE'S JUST SO FOUL UGLY.
darb
YOU DON'T KNOW ANYTHING ABOUT ANYTHING, DO YOU?
THAT'S PRETTY TOUGH TALK FOR A GUY WITHOUT HIS EGG.

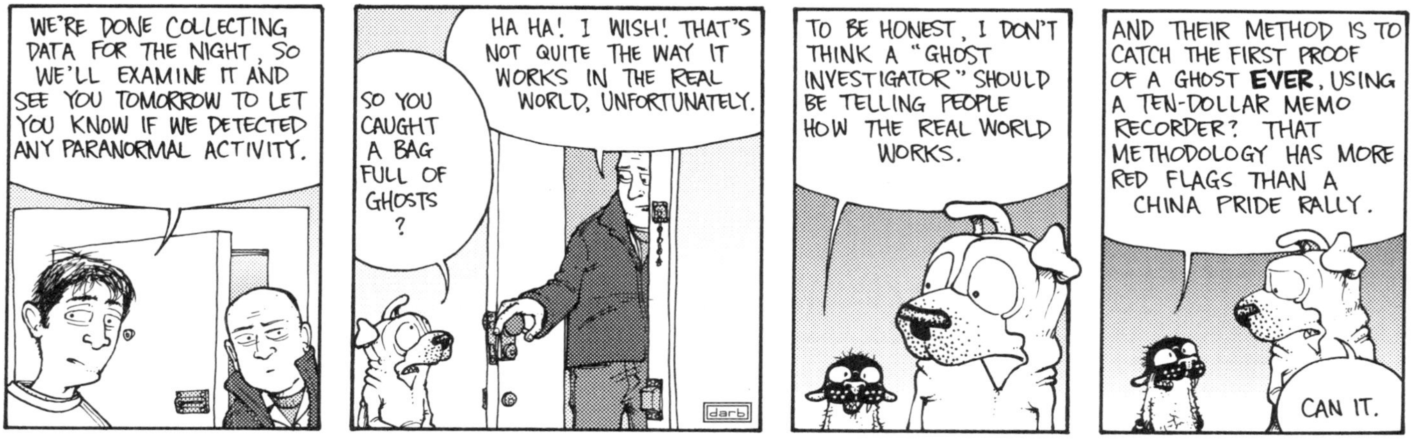
WE'RE DONE COLLECTING DATA FOR THE NIGHT, SO WE'LL EXAMINE IT AND SEE YOU TOMORROW TO LET YOU KNOW IF WE DETECTED ANY PARANORMAL ACTIVITY.
SO YOU CAUGHT A BAG FULL OF GHOSTS?
HA HA! I WISH! THAT'S NOT QUITE THE WAY IT WORKS IN THE REAL WORLD, UNFORTUNATELY.
darb
TO BE HONEST, I DON'T THINK A "GHOST INVESTIGATOR" SHOULD BE TELLING PEOPLE HOW THE REAL WORLD WORKS.
AND THEIR METHOD IS TO CATCH THE FIRST PROOF OF A GHOST **EVER**, USING A TEN-DOLLAR MEMO RECORDER? THAT METHODOLOGY HAS MORE RED FLAGS THAN A CHINA PRIDE RALLY.
CAN IT.

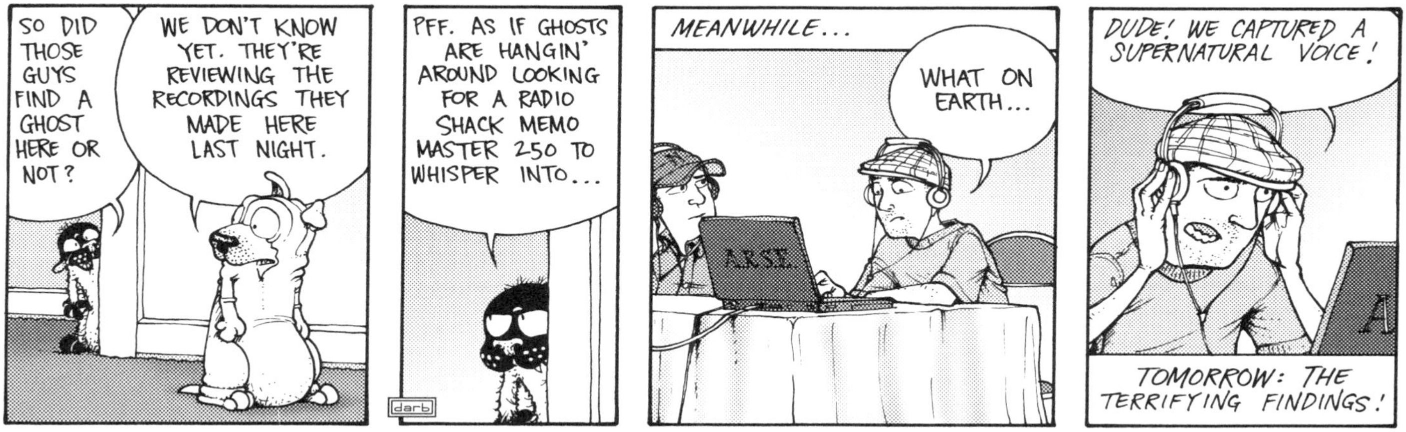
SO DID THOSE GUYS FIND A GHOST HERE OR NOT?
WE DON'T KNOW YET. THEY'RE REVIEWING THE RECORDINGS THEY MADE HERE LAST NIGHT.
PFF. AS IF GHOSTS ARE HANGIN' AROUND LOOKING FOR A RADIO SHACK MEMO MASTER 250 TO WHISPER INTO...
darb
MEANWHILE...
WHAT ON EARTH...
A.R.S.E.
DUDE! WE CAPTURED A SUPERNATURAL VOICE!
TOMORROW: THE TERRIFYING FINDINGS!

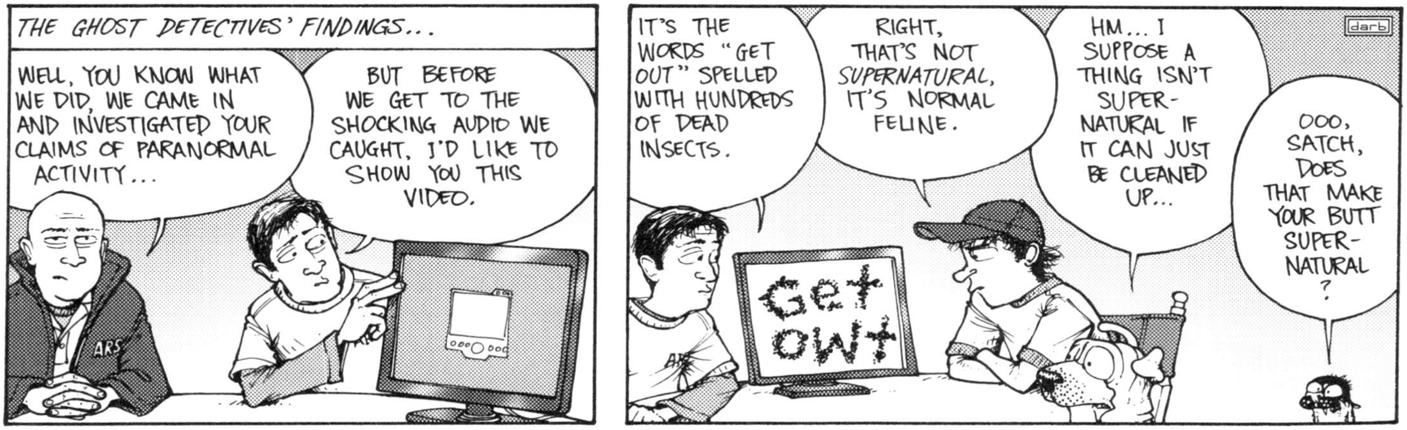
THE GHOST DETECTIVES' FINDINGS...
WELL, YOU KNOW WHAT WE DID, WE CAME IN AND INVESTIGATED YOUR CLAIMS OF PARANORMAL ACTIVITY...
BUT BEFORE WE GET TO THE SHOCKING AUDIO WE CAUGHT, I'D LIKE TO SHOW YOU THIS VIDEO.
ARS
IT'S THE WORDS "GET OUT" SPELLED WITH HUNDREDS OF DEAD INSECTS.
RIGHT, THAT'S NOT *SUPERNATURAL*, IT'S NORMAL FELINE.
HM... I SUPPOSE A THING ISN'T SUPER-NATURAL IF IT CAN JUST BE CLEANED UP...
OOO, SATCH, DOES THAT MAKE YOUR BUTT SUPER-NATURAL?
Get owt
darb

YOU SAID YOU ACTUALLY CAUGHT A DISEMBODIED VOICE ON TAPE DURING YOUR INVESTIGATION?

RIGHT. SO WE DIDN'T GET VIDEO EVIDENCE OF PARANORMAL ACTIVITY, BUT WE DID CATCH THIS CHILLING AUDIO RECORDING...

COR, 'ERE'S A ROPEY WEE YOOFO, INNIT? AND NOWT ELSE AROUND? BIT DICKY MINT...

I DON'T EVEN RECOGNIZE THE LANGUAGE.

NO, I'VE HEARD THAT LANGUAGE BEFORE.

YOU DON'T MEAN OUR GHOST SPEAKS...

MANC.

ARE YOU SAYING THAT A **CAT** MADE THIS VOICE ON MY RECORDER? IT'S ALL GIBBERISH, I FIGURED IT WAS AN ANCIENT SPIRIT...

YOU THINK HE **SOUNDS** FUNNY, YOU SHOULD **SMELL** HIM.

...BUT WHAT LANGUAGE IS HE SPEAKING? IT MAKES NO SENSE.

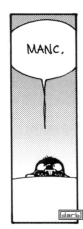

MANC.

"MANC"? WHAT'S MANC?

EE AR, ME NUT FLAPS ARE BURNIN'. MAKE US A KIPPER BUTTY, AR' KID, I'M WELL KNACKERED.

MAC, THE GHOST DETECTIVES HEARD YOUR VOICE ON THE RECORDER AND THOUGHT YOU WERE A SUPERNATURAL BEING BECAUSE OF THE WAY YOU TALK!

MENTAL. TOUCHED.

WELL, WE DIDN'T FIND ANY GHOSTS IN THIS HOUSE, BUT I THINK WE LEARNED A VALUABLE LESSON ALL THE SAME.

DEFO. KNAPPERS ARE FLAPPY. CHUCK 'EM IN THE WHEELIE BIN.

HA HA! YOU CAN SAY THAT AGAIN, MAC!

CHEERS.

NO... I MEAN CAN YOU SAY IT AGAIN? I DIDN'T UNDERSTAND YOU...

94

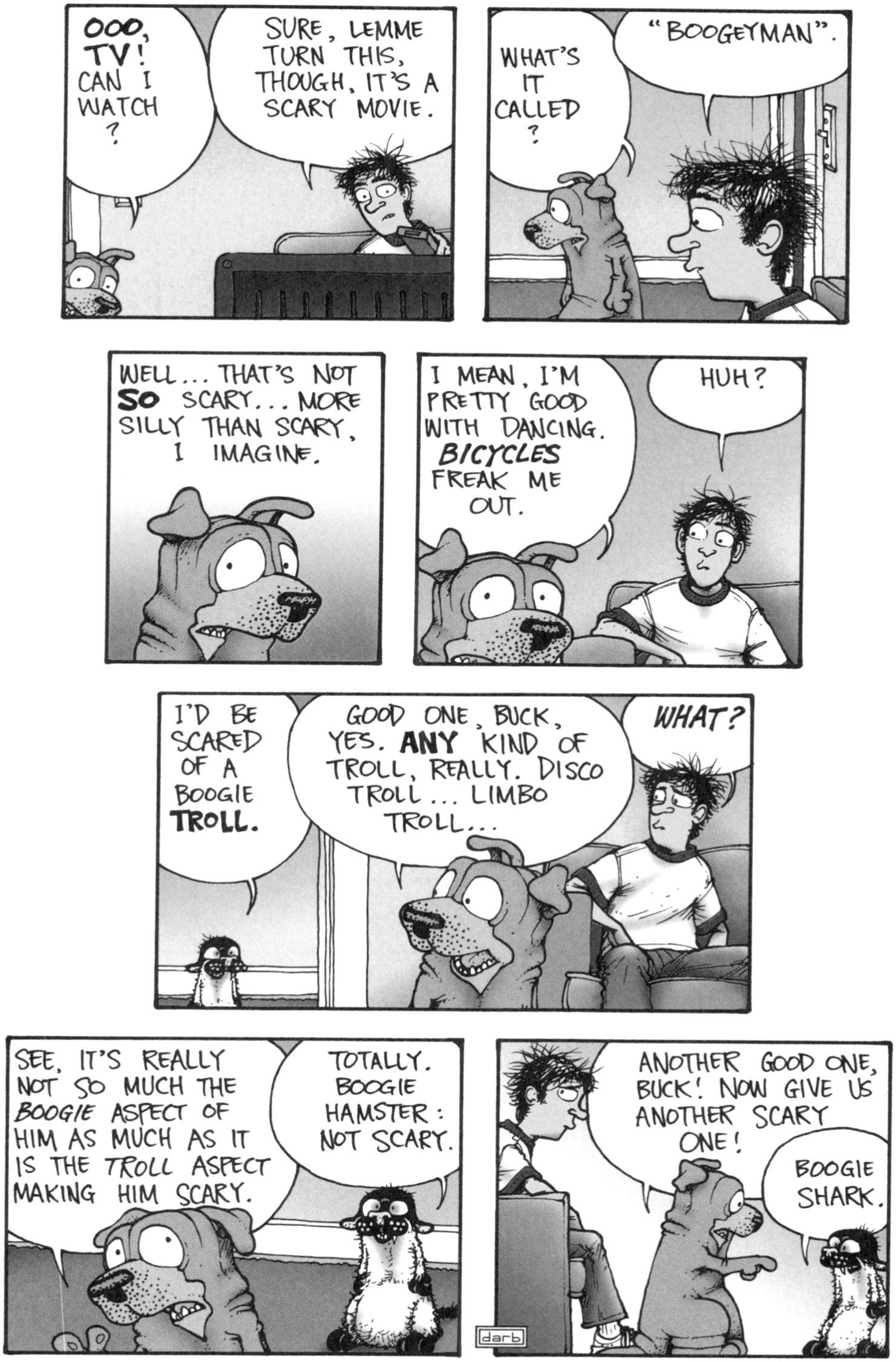
OOO, TV! CAN I WATCH?
SURE, LEMME TURN THIS, THOUGH, IT'S A SCARY MOVIE.
WHAT'S IT CALLED?
"BOOGEYMAN".
WELL... THAT'S NOT SO SCARY... MORE SILLY THAN SCARY, I IMAGINE.
I MEAN, I'M PRETTY GOOD WITH DANCING. BICYCLES FREAK ME OUT.
HUH?
I'D BE SCARED OF A BOOGIE TROLL.
GOOD ONE, BUCK, YES. ANY KIND OF TROLL, REALLY. DISCO TROLL... LIMBO TROLL...
WHAT?
SEE, IT'S REALLY NOT SO MUCH THE BOOGIE ASPECT OF HIM AS MUCH AS IT IS THE TROLL ASPECT MAKING HIM SCARY.
TOTALLY. BOOGIE HAMSTER: NOT SCARY.
darb
ANOTHER GOOD ONE, BUCK! NOW GIVE US ANOTHER SCARY ONE!
BOOGIE SHARK.

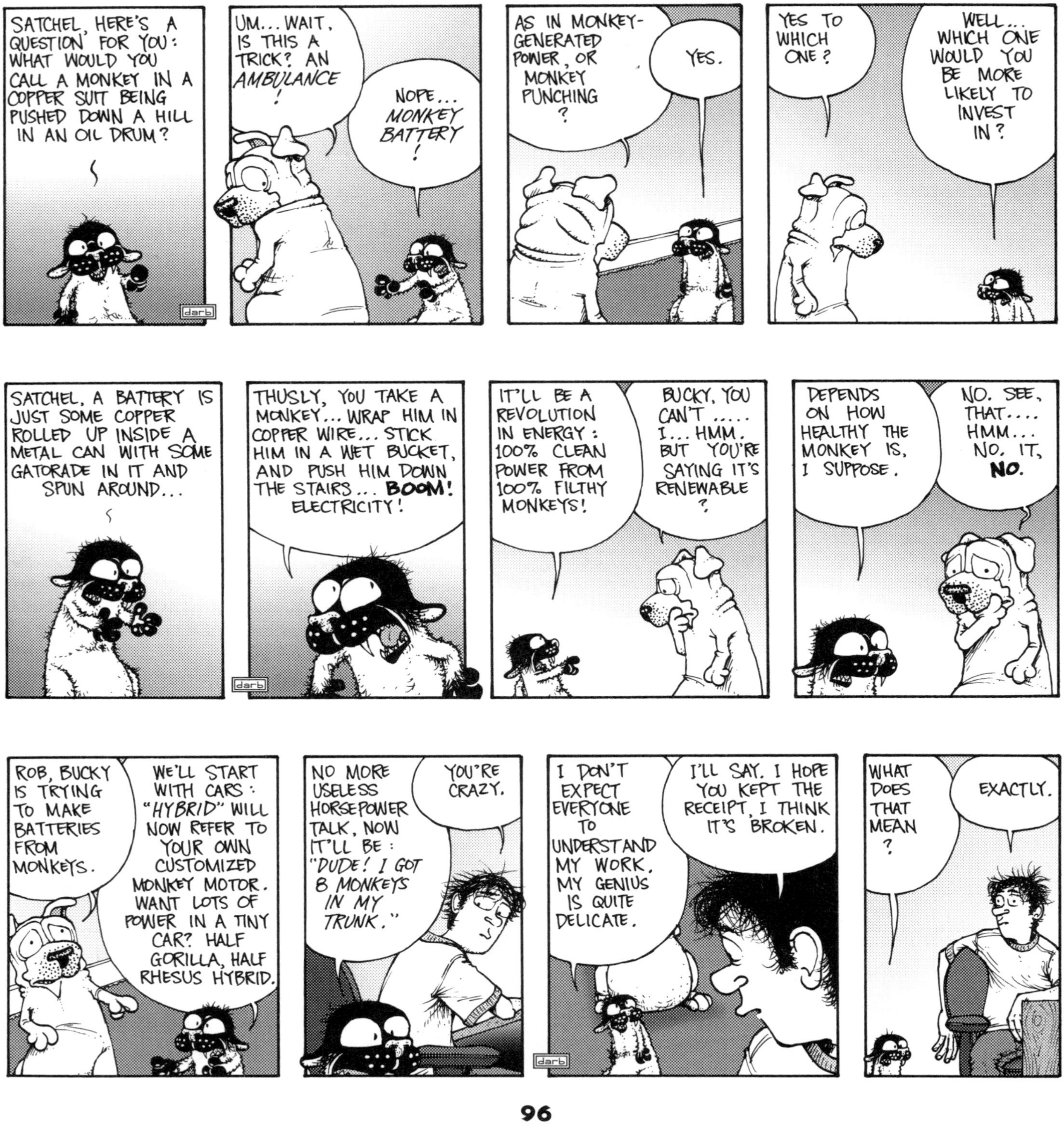
SATCHEL, HERE'S A QUESTION FOR YOU: WHAT WOULD YOU CALL A MONKEY IN A COPPER SUIT BEING PUSHED DOWN A HILL IN AN OIL DRUM?
UM... WAIT, IS THIS A TRICK? AN *AMBULANCE*!
NOPE... *MONKEY BATTERY*!
AS IN MONKEY-GENERATED POWER, OR MONKEY PUNCHING?
YES.
YES TO WHICH ONE?
WELL... WHICH ONE WOULD YOU BE MORE LIKELY TO INVEST IN?
darb
SATCHEL, A BATTERY IS JUST SOME COPPER ROLLED UP INSIDE A METAL CAN WITH SOME GATORADE IN IT AND SPUN AROUND...
THUSLY, YOU TAKE A MONKEY... WRAP HIM IN COPPER WIRE... STICK HIM IN A WET BUCKET, AND PUSH HIM DOWN THE STAIRS... **BOOM!** ELECTRICITY!
IT'LL BE A REVOLUTION IN ENERGY: 100% CLEAN POWER FROM 100% FILTHY MONKEYS!
BUCKY, YOU CAN'T..... I... HMM. BUT YOU'RE SAYING IT'S RENEWABLE?
DEPENDS ON HOW HEALTHY THE MONKEY IS, I SUPPOSE.
NO. SEE, THAT.... HMM... NO, IT, **NO.**
darb
ROB, BUCKY IS TRYING TO MAKE BATTERIES FROM MONKEYS.
WE'LL START WITH CARS: "*HYBRID*" WILL NOW REFER TO YOUR OWN CUSTOMIZED MONKEY MOTOR. WANT LOTS OF POWER IN A TINY CAR? HALF GORILLA, HALF RHESUS HYBRID.
NO MORE USELESS HORSEPOWER TALK, NOW IT'LL BE: "*DUDE! I GOT 8 MONKEYS IN MY TRUNK.*"
YOU'RE CRAZY.
I DON'T EXPECT EVERYONE TO UNDERSTAND MY WORK, MY GENIUS IS QUITE DELICATE.
I'LL SAY. I HOPE YOU KEPT THE RECEIPT, I THINK IT'S BROKEN.
WHAT DOES THAT MEAN?
EXACTLY.
darb

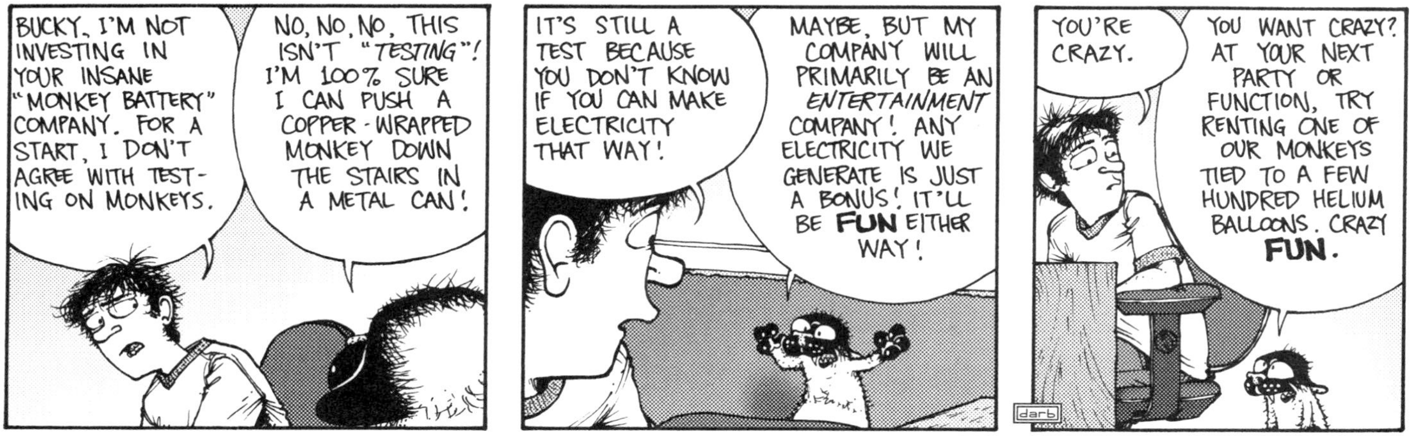
BUCKY, I'M NOT INVESTING IN YOUR INSANE "MONKEY BATTERY" COMPANY. FOR A START, I DON'T AGREE WITH TESTING ON MONKEYS.
NO, NO, NO, THIS ISN'T "*TESTING*"! I'M 100% SURE I CAN PUSH A COPPER-WRAPPED MONKEY DOWN THE STAIRS IN A METAL CAN!
IT'S STILL A TEST BECAUSE YOU DON'T KNOW IF YOU CAN MAKE ELECTRICITY THAT WAY!
MAYBE, BUT MY COMPANY WILL PRIMARILY BE AN *ENTERTAINMENT* COMPANY! ANY ELECTRICITY WE GENERATE IS JUST A BONUS! IT'LL BE **FUN** EITHER WAY!
YOU'RE CRAZY.
YOU WANT CRAZY? AT YOUR NEXT PARTY OR FUNCTION, TRY RENTING ONE OF OUR MONKEYS TIED TO A FEW HUNDRED HELIUM BALLOONS. CRAZY **FUN**.

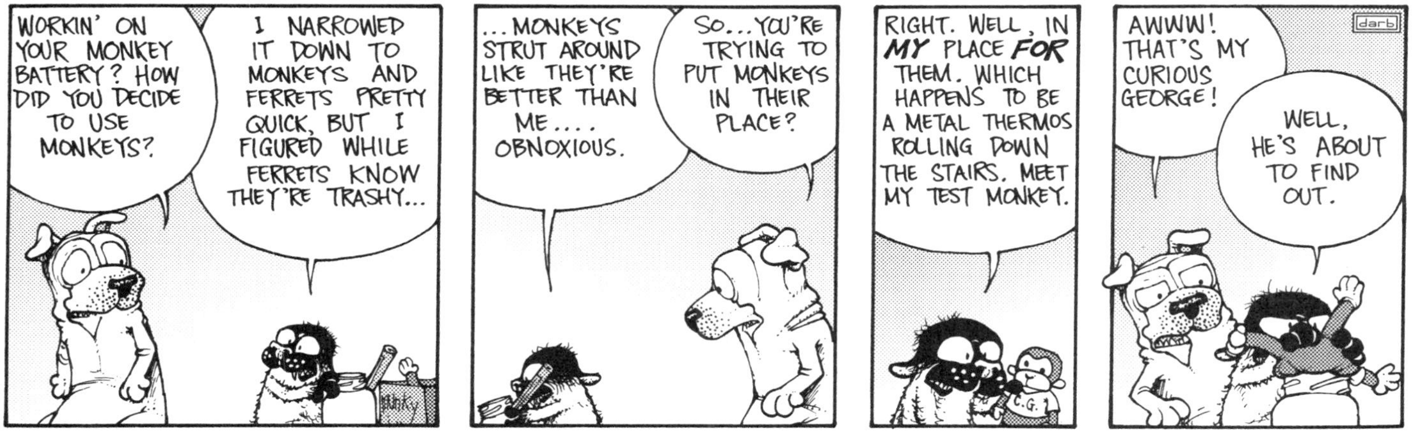
WORKIN' ON YOUR MONKEY BATTERY? HOW DID YOU DECIDE TO USE MONKEYS?
I NARROWED IT DOWN TO MONKEYS AND FERRETS PRETTY QUICK, BUT I FIGURED WHILE FERRETS KNOW THEY'RE TRASHY...
...MONKEYS STRUT AROUND LIKE THEY'RE BETTER THAN ME.... OBNOXIOUS.
SO...YOU'RE TRYING TO PUT MONKEYS IN THEIR PLACE?
RIGHT. WELL, IN ***MY*** PLACE ***FOR*** THEM. WHICH HAPPENS TO BE A METAL THERMOS ROLLING DOWN THE STAIRS. MEET MY TEST MONKEY.
AWWW! THAT'S MY CURIOUS GEORGE!
WELL, HE'S ABOUT TO FIND OUT.

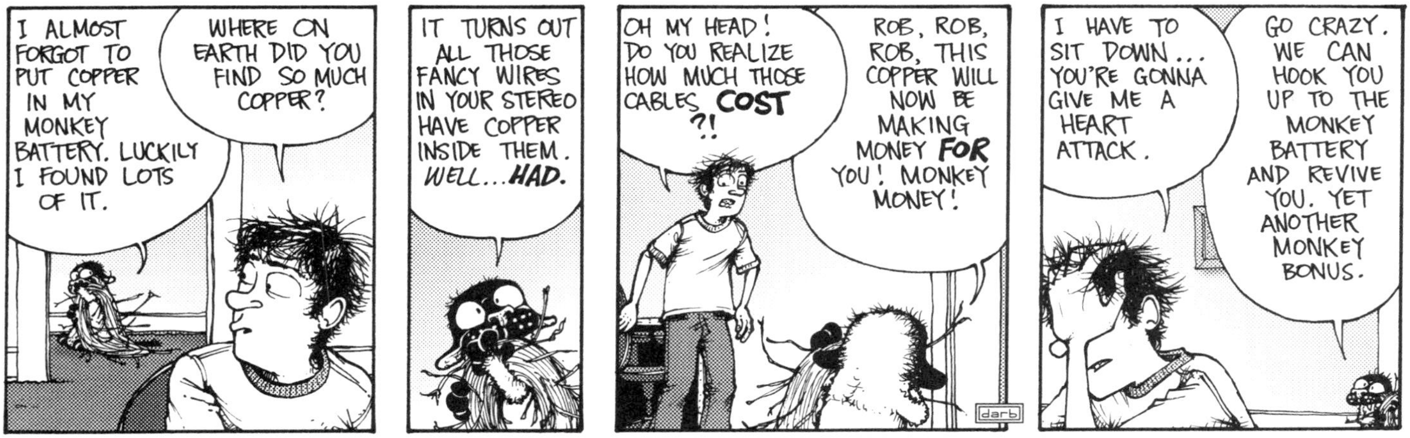
I ALMOST FORGOT TO PUT COPPER IN MY MONKEY BATTERY. LUCKILY I FOUND LOTS OF IT.
WHERE ON EARTH DID YOU FIND SO MUCH COPPER?
IT TURNS OUT ALL THOSE FANCY WIRES IN YOUR STEREO HAVE COPPER INSIDE THEM. *WELL...**HAD**.*
OH MY HEAD! DO YOU REALIZE HOW MUCH THOSE CABLES **COST** ?!
ROB, ROB, ROB, THIS COPPER WILL NOW BE MAKING MONEY ***FOR*** YOU! MONKEY MONEY!
I HAVE TO SIT DOWN... YOU'RE GONNA GIVE ME A HEART ATTACK.
GO CRAZY. WE CAN HOOK YOU UP TO THE MONKEY BATTERY AND REVIVE YOU. YET ANOTHER MONKEY BONUS.

WHERE YA GOIN' ALL DRESSED UP?

MY COLLEGE REUNION IS TONIGHT.

MM-HM. WHAT DO YOU DO AT THAT?

CHAT WITH OLD FRIENDS... HAVE A NICE DINNER... MAYBE EVEN DO A LITTLE DANCING.

YOU'RE GOING DANCING?

PROBLEM?

ONLY FOR **YOU**... MAN, YOU'RE SO OLD YOU'LL BE BODY POPPING WHILE YOU SLOW DANCE.

I'LL HAVE YOU KNOW I COULD BUST QUITE A MOVE IN MY DAY.

WELL, IN **THIS** DAY YOU'LL BE BUSTING QUITE A HIP.

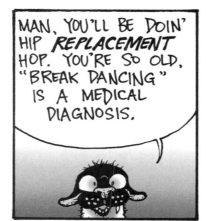

MAN, YOU'LL BE DOIN' HIP **REPLACEMENT** HOP. YOU'RE SO OLD, "BREAK DANCING" IS A MEDICAL DIAGNOSIS.

DON'T WAIT UP.

SLAM!

HOW BAD DO YOU THINK HE'S GONNA HURT HIMSELF?

PUT IT THIS WAY: I GET HIS ROOM.

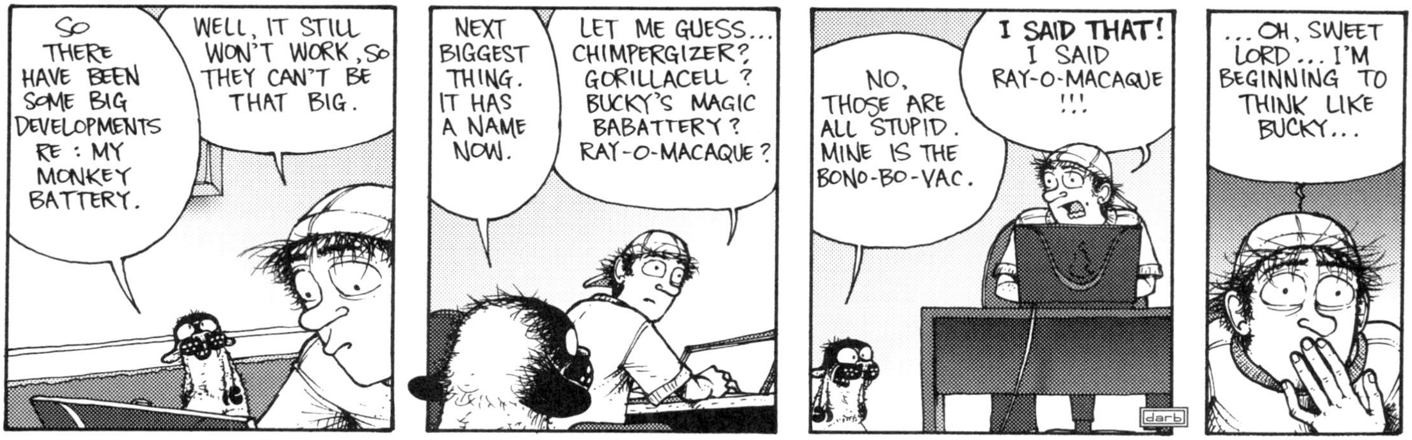
SO THERE HAVE BEEN SOME BIG DEVELOPMENTS RE: MY MONKEY BATTERY.
WELL, IT STILL WON'T WORK, SO THEY CAN'T BE THAT BIG.
NEXT BIGGEST THING. IT HAS A NAME NOW.
LET ME GUESS... CHIMPERGIZER? GORILLACELL? BUCKY'S MAGIC BABATTERY? RAY-O-MACAQUE?
NO, THOSE ARE ALL STUPID. MINE IS THE BONO-BO-VAC.
I SAID THAT! I SAID RAY-O-MACAQUE!!!
...OH, SWEET LORD... I'M BEGINNING TO THINK LIKE BUCKY...
darb

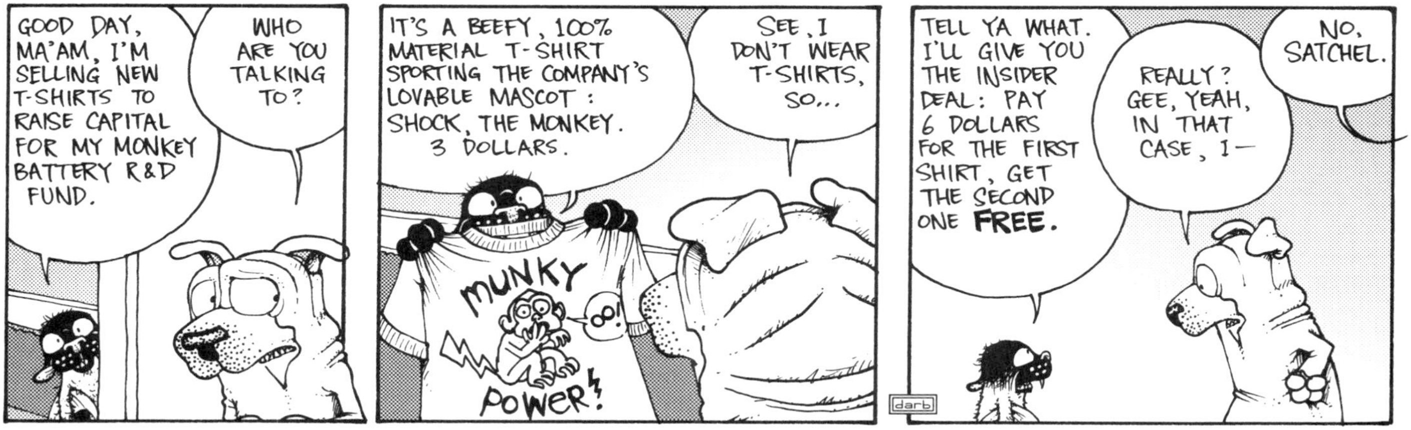
GOOD DAY, MA'AM, I'M SELLING NEW T-SHIRTS TO RAISE CAPITAL FOR MY MONKEY BATTERY R&D FUND.
WHO ARE YOU TALKING TO?
IT'S A BEEFY, 100% MATERIAL T-SHIRT SPORTING THE COMPANY'S LOVABLE MASCOT: SHOCK, THE MONKEY. 3 DOLLARS.
SEE, I DON'T WEAR T-SHIRTS, SO...
MUNKY
OO!
POWER!
darb
TELL YA WHAT. I'LL GIVE YOU THE INSIDER DEAL: PAY 6 DOLLARS FOR THE FIRST SHIRT, GET THE SECOND ONE FREE.
REALLY? GEE, YEAH, IN THAT CASE, I—
NO, SATCHEL.

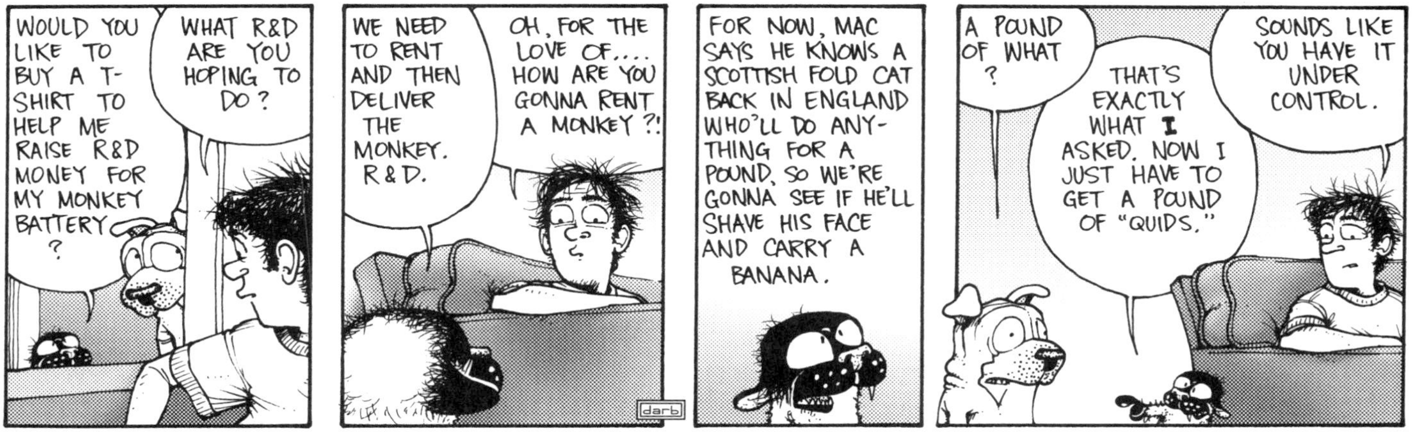
WOULD YOU LIKE TO BUY A T-SHIRT TO HELP ME RAISE R&D MONEY FOR MY MONKEY BATTERY?
WHAT R&D ARE YOU HOPING TO DO?
WE NEED TO RENT AND THEN DELIVER THE MONKEY. R&D.
OH, FOR THE LOVE OF.... HOW ARE YOU GONNA RENT A MONKEY?!
darb
FOR NOW, MAC SAYS HE KNOWS A SCOTTISH FOLD CAT BACK IN ENGLAND WHO'LL DO ANYTHING FOR A POUND, SO WE'RE GONNA SEE IF HE'LL SHAVE HIS FACE AND CARRY A BANANA.
A POUND OF WHAT?
THAT'S EXACTLY WHAT I ASKED. NOW I JUST HAVE TO GET A POUND OF "QUIDS."
SOUNDS LIKE YOU HAVE IT UNDER CONTROL.

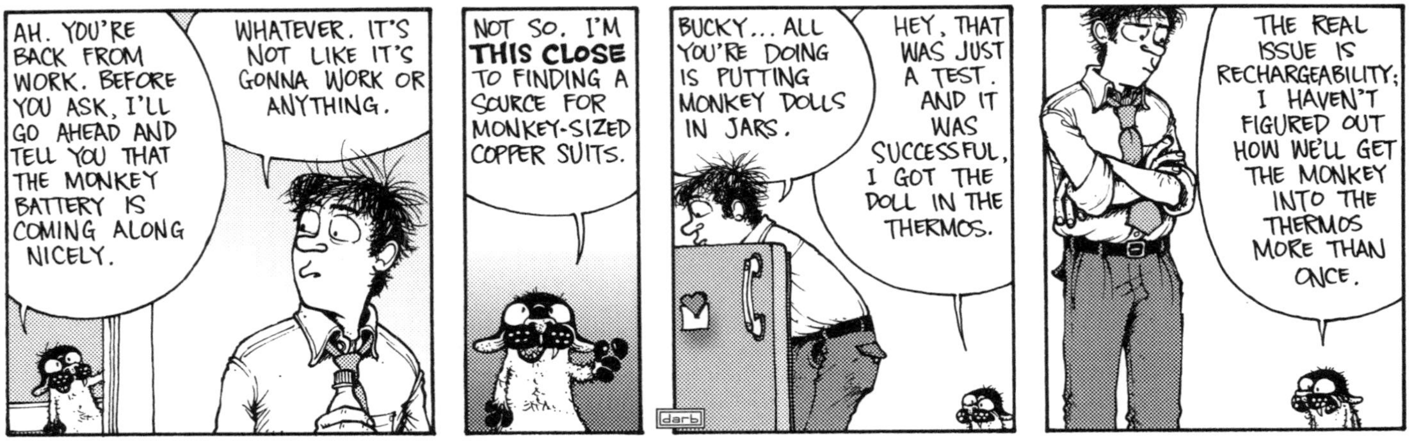
AH. YOU'RE BACK FROM WORK. BEFORE YOU ASK, I'LL GO AHEAD AND TELL YOU THAT THE MONKEY BATTERY IS COMING ALONG NICELY.
WHATEVER. IT'S NOT LIKE IT'S GONNA WORK OR ANYTHING.
NOT SO. I'M **THIS CLOSE** TO FINDING A SOURCE FOR MONKEY-SIZED COPPER SUITS.
BUCKY... ALL YOU'RE DOING IS PUTTING MONKEY DOLLS IN JARS.
HEY, THAT WAS JUST A TEST. AND IT WAS SUCCESSFUL, I GOT THE DOLL IN THE THERMOS.
THE REAL ISSUE IS RECHARGEABILITY; I HAVEN'T FIGURED OUT HOW WE'LL GET THE MONKEY INTO THE THERMOS MORE THAN ONCE.

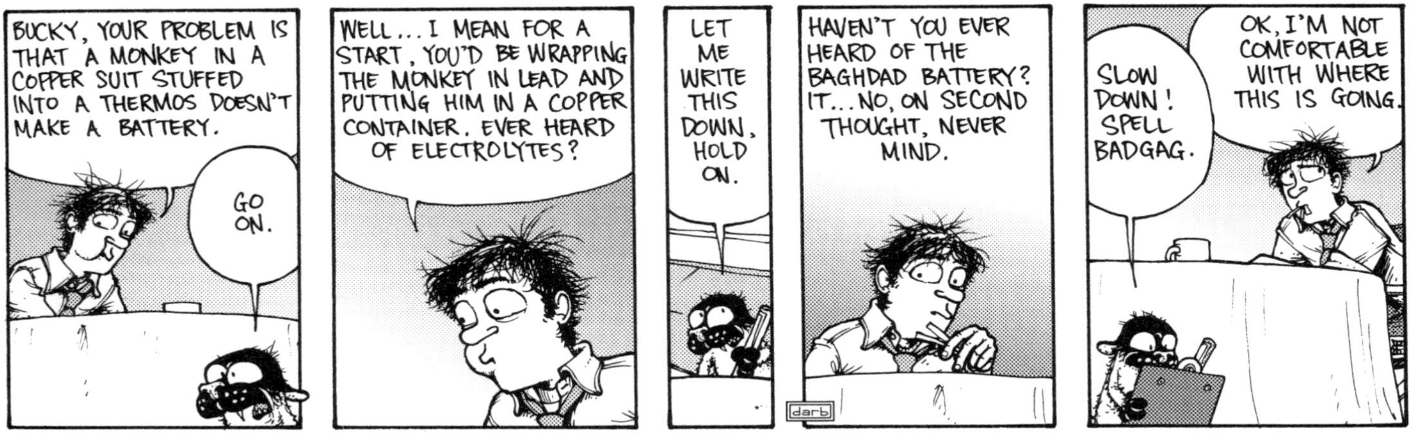
BUCKY, YOUR PROBLEM IS THAT A MONKEY IN A COPPER SUIT STUFFED INTO A THERMOS DOESN'T MAKE A BATTERY.
GO ON.
WELL... I MEAN FOR A START, YOU'D BE WRAPPING THE MONKEY IN LEAD AND PUTTING HIM IN A COPPER CONTAINER. EVER HEARD OF ELECTROLYTES?
LET ME WRITE THIS DOWN, HOLD ON.
HAVEN'T YOU EVER HEARD OF THE BAGHDAD BATTERY? IT... NO, ON SECOND THOUGHT, NEVER MIND.
SLOW DOWN! SPELL BADGAG.
OK, I'M NOT COMFORTABLE WITH WHERE THIS IS GOING.

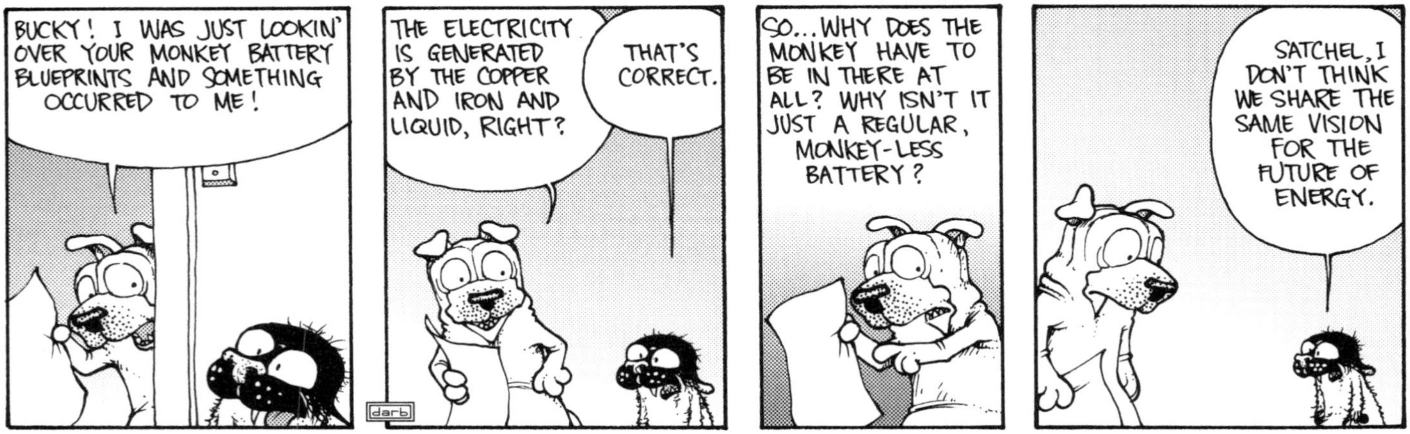
BUCKY! I WAS JUST LOOKIN' OVER YOUR MONKEY BATTERY BLUEPRINTS AND SOMETHING OCCURRED TO ME!
THE ELECTRICITY IS GENERATED BY THE COPPER AND IRON AND LIQUID, RIGHT?
THAT'S CORRECT.
SO... WHY DOES THE MONKEY HAVE TO BE IN THERE AT ALL? WHY ISN'T IT JUST A REGULAR, MONKEY-LESS BATTERY?
SATCHEL, I DON'T THINK WE SHARE THE SAME VISION FOR THE FUTURE OF ENERGY.

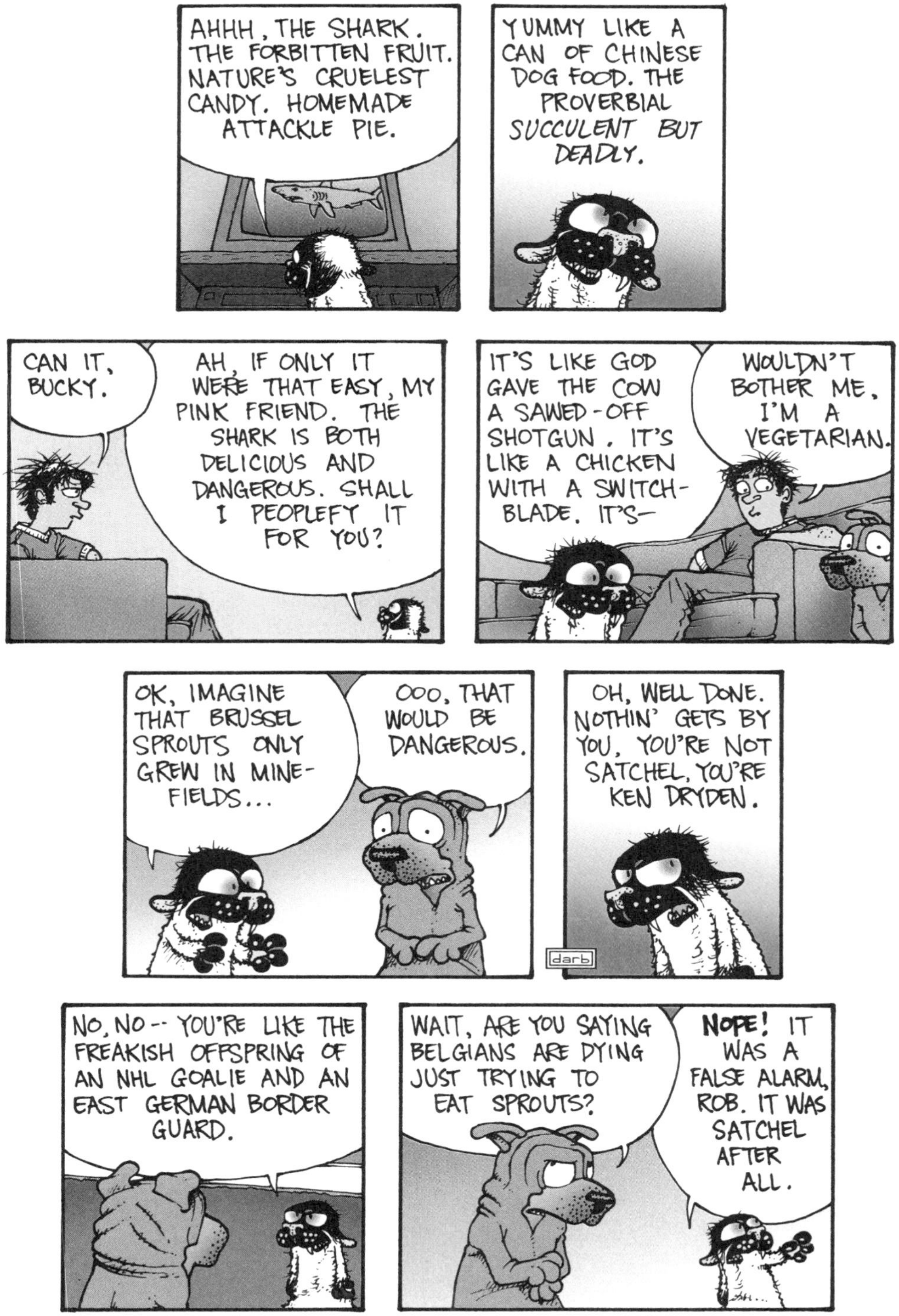
AHHH, THE SHARK. THE FORBITTEN FRUIT. NATURE'S CRUELEST CANDY. HOMEMADE ATTACKLE PIE.
YUMMY LIKE A CAN OF CHINESE DOG FOOD. THE PROVERBIAL *SUCCULENT BUT DEADLY.*
CAN IT, BUCKY.
AH, IF ONLY IT WERE THAT EASY, MY PINK FRIEND. THE SHARK IS BOTH DELICIOUS AND DANGEROUS. SHALL I PEOPLEFY IT FOR YOU?
IT'S LIKE GOD GAVE THE COW A SAWED-OFF SHOTGUN. IT'S LIKE A CHICKEN WITH A SWITCH-BLADE. IT'S—
WOULDN'T BOTHER ME. I'M A VEGETARIAN.
OK, IMAGINE THAT BRUSSEL SPROUTS ONLY GREW IN MINE-FIELDS...
OOO, THAT WOULD BE DANGEROUS.
darb
OH, WELL DONE. NOTHIN' GETS BY YOU. YOU'RE NOT SATCHEL, YOU'RE KEN DRYDEN.
NO, NO-- YOU'RE LIKE THE FREAKISH OFFSPRING OF AN NHL GOALIE AND AN EAST GERMAN BORDER GUARD.
WAIT, ARE YOU SAYING BELGIANS ARE DYING JUST TRYING TO EAT SPROUTS?
NOPE! IT WAS A FALSE ALARM, ROB. IT WAS SATCHEL AFTER ALL.

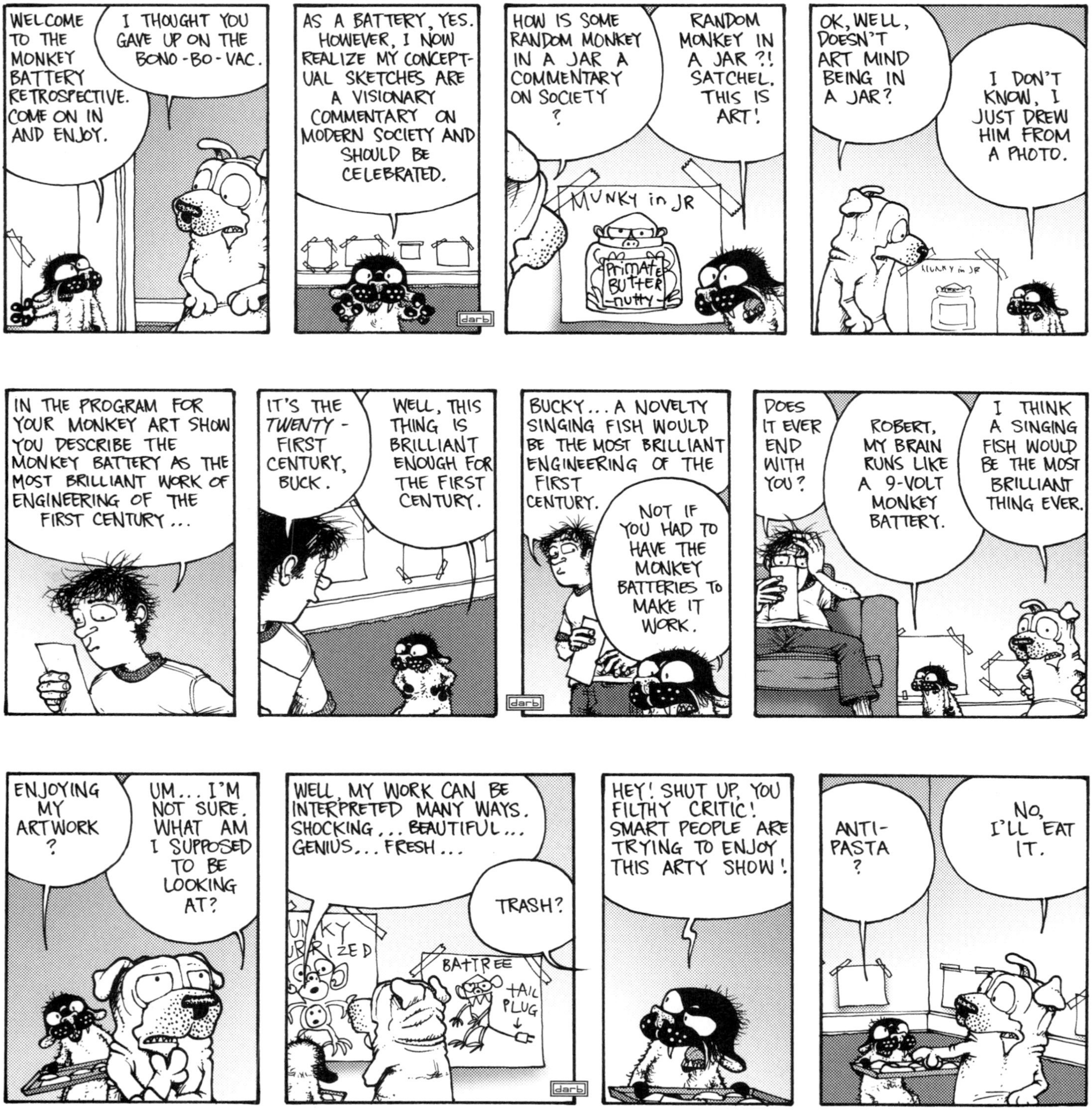
WELCOME TO THE MONKEY BATTERY RETROSPECTIVE. COME ON IN AND ENJOY.
I THOUGHT YOU GAVE UP ON THE BONO-BO-VAC.
AS A BATTERY, YES. HOWEVER, I NOW REALIZE MY CONCEPTUAL SKETCHES ARE A VISIONARY COMMENTARY ON MODERN SOCIETY AND SHOULD BE CELEBRATED.
darb
HOW IS SOME RANDOM MONKEY IN A JAR A COMMENTARY ON SOCIETY ?
RANDOM MONKEY IN A JAR ?! SATCHEL, THIS IS ART!
MUNKY in JR
Primate BUTTER -nutty-
OK, WELL, DOESN'T ART MIND BEING IN A JAR?
I DON'T KNOW, I JUST DREW HIM FROM A PHOTO.
IN THE PROGRAM FOR YOUR MONKEY ART SHOW YOU DESCRIBE THE MONKEY BATTERY AS THE MOST BRILLIANT WORK OF ENGINEERING OF THE FIRST CENTURY...
IT'S THE *TWENTY*-FIRST CENTURY, BUCK.
WELL, THIS THING IS BRILLIANT ENOUGH FOR THE FIRST CENTURY.
darb
BUCKY... A NOVELTY SINGING FISH WOULD BE THE MOST BRILLIANT ENGINEERING OF THE FIRST CENTURY.
NOT IF YOU HAD TO HAVE THE MONKEY BATTERIES TO MAKE IT WORK.
DOES IT EVER END WITH YOU?
ROBERT, MY BRAIN RUNS LIKE A 9-VOLT MONKEY BATTERY.
I THINK A SINGING FISH WOULD BE THE MOST BRILLIANT THING EVER.
ENJOYING MY ARTWORK ?
UM... I'M NOT SURE. WHAT AM I SUPPOSED TO BE LOOKING AT?
WELL, MY WORK CAN BE INTERPRETED MANY WAYS. SHOCKING... BEAUTIFUL... GENIUS... FRESH...
TRASH?
BATTREE
TAIL PLUG
darb
HEY! SHUT UP, YOU FILTHY CRITIC! SMART PEOPLE ARE TRYING TO ENJOY THIS ARTY SHOW!
ANTI-PASTA ?
NO, I'LL EAT IT.

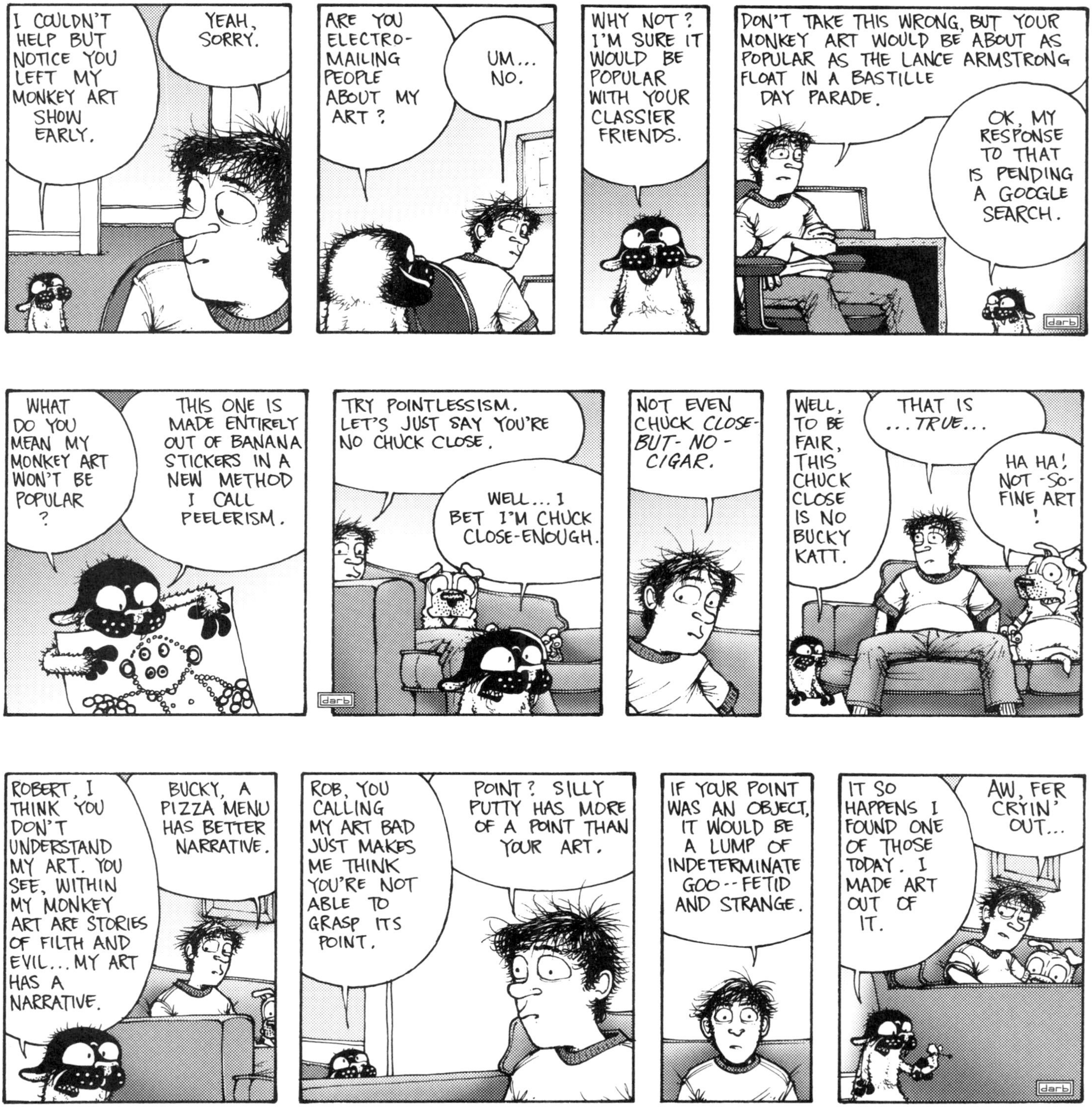
I COULDN'T HELP BUT NOTICE YOU LEFT MY MONKEY ART SHOW EARLY.
YEAH, SORRY.
ARE YOU ELECTRO-MAILING PEOPLE ABOUT MY ART?
UM... NO.
WHY NOT? I'M SURE IT WOULD BE POPULAR WITH YOUR CLASSIER FRIENDS.
DON'T TAKE THIS WRONG, BUT YOUR MONKEY ART WOULD BE ABOUT AS POPULAR AS THE LANCE ARMSTRONG FLOAT IN A BASTILLE DAY PARADE.
OK, MY RESPONSE TO THAT IS PENDING A GOOGLE SEARCH.
darb
WHAT DO YOU MEAN MY MONKEY ART WON'T BE POPULAR?
THIS ONE IS MADE ENTIRELY OUT OF BANANA STICKERS IN A NEW METHOD I CALL PEELERISM.
TRY POINTLESSISM. LET'S JUST SAY YOU'RE NO CHUCK CLOSE.
WELL... I BET I'M CHUCK CLOSE-ENOUGH.
NOT EVEN CHUCK *CLOSE-BUT-NO-CIGAR*.
WELL, TO BE FAIR, THIS CHUCK CLOSE IS NO BUCKY KATT.
THAT IS ...*TRUE*...
HA HA! NOT-SO-FINE ART!
darb
ROBERT, I THINK YOU DON'T UNDERSTAND MY ART. YOU SEE, WITHIN MY MONKEY ART ARE STORIES OF FILTH AND EVIL... MY ART HAS A NARRATIVE.
BUCKY, A PIZZA MENU HAS BETTER NARRATIVE.
ROB, YOU CALLING MY ART BAD JUST MAKES ME THINK YOU'RE NOT ABLE TO GRASP ITS POINT.
POINT? SILLY PUTTY HAS MORE OF A POINT THAN YOUR ART.
IF YOUR POINT WAS AN OBJECT, IT WOULD BE A LUMP OF INDETERMINATE GOO--FETID AND STRANGE.
IT SO HAPPENS I FOUND ONE OF THOSE TODAY. I MADE ART OUT OF IT.
AW, FER CRYIN' OUT...
darb

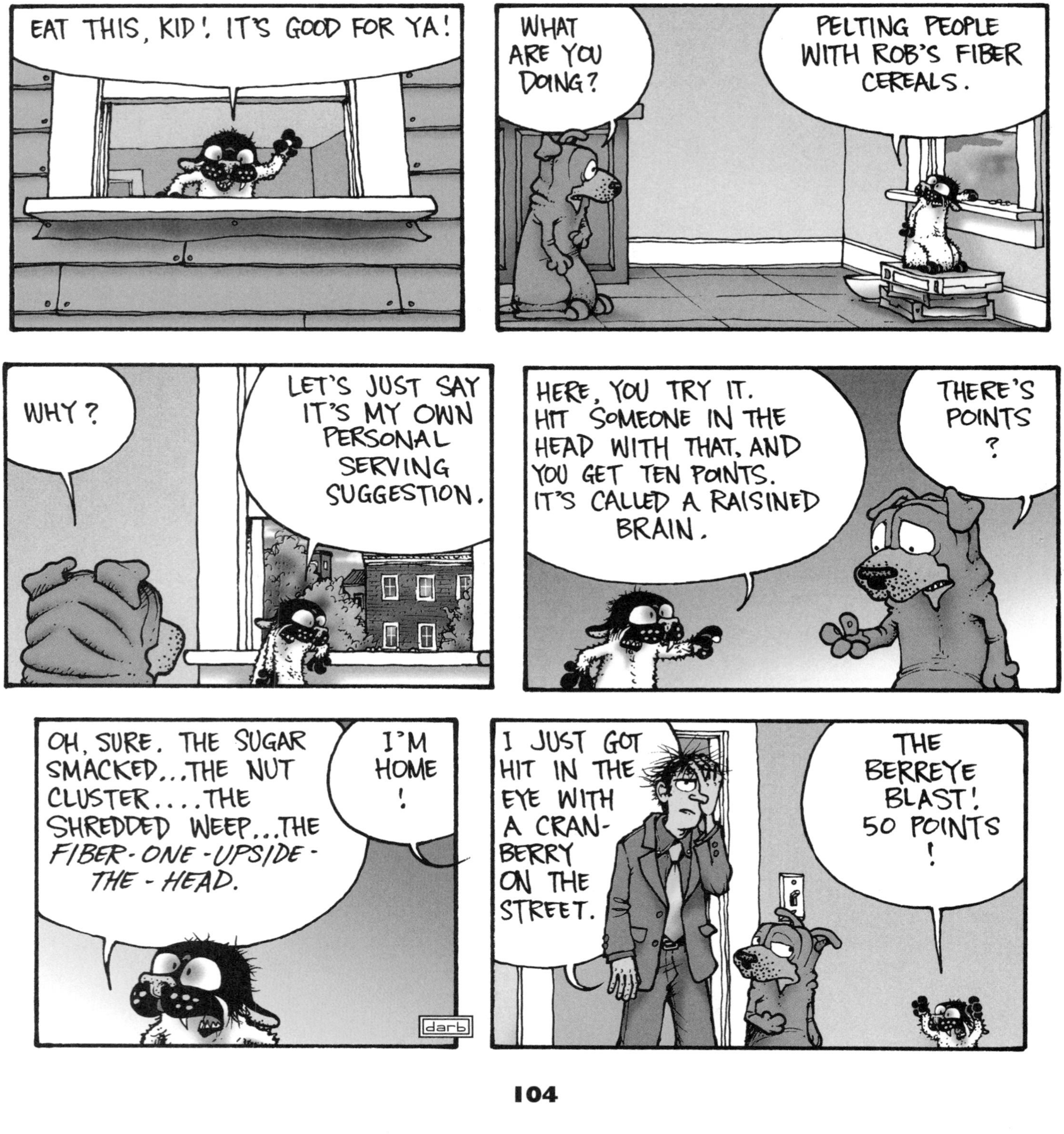
EAT THIS, KID! IT'S GOOD FOR YA!
WHAT ARE YOU DOING?
PELTING PEOPLE WITH ROB'S FIBER CEREALS.
WHY?
LET'S JUST SAY IT'S MY OWN PERSONAL SERVING SUGGESTION.
HERE, YOU TRY IT. HIT SOMEONE IN THE HEAD WITH THAT, AND YOU GET TEN POINTS. IT'S CALLED A RAISINED BRAIN.
THERE'S POINTS?
OH, SURE. THE SUGAR SMACKED...THE NUT CLUSTER....THE SHREDDED WEEP...THE *FIBER-ONE-UPSIDE-THE-HEAD.*
I'M HOME!
darb
I JUST GOT HIT IN THE EYE WITH A CRAN-BERRY ON THE STREET.
THE BERREYE BLAST! 50 POINTS!

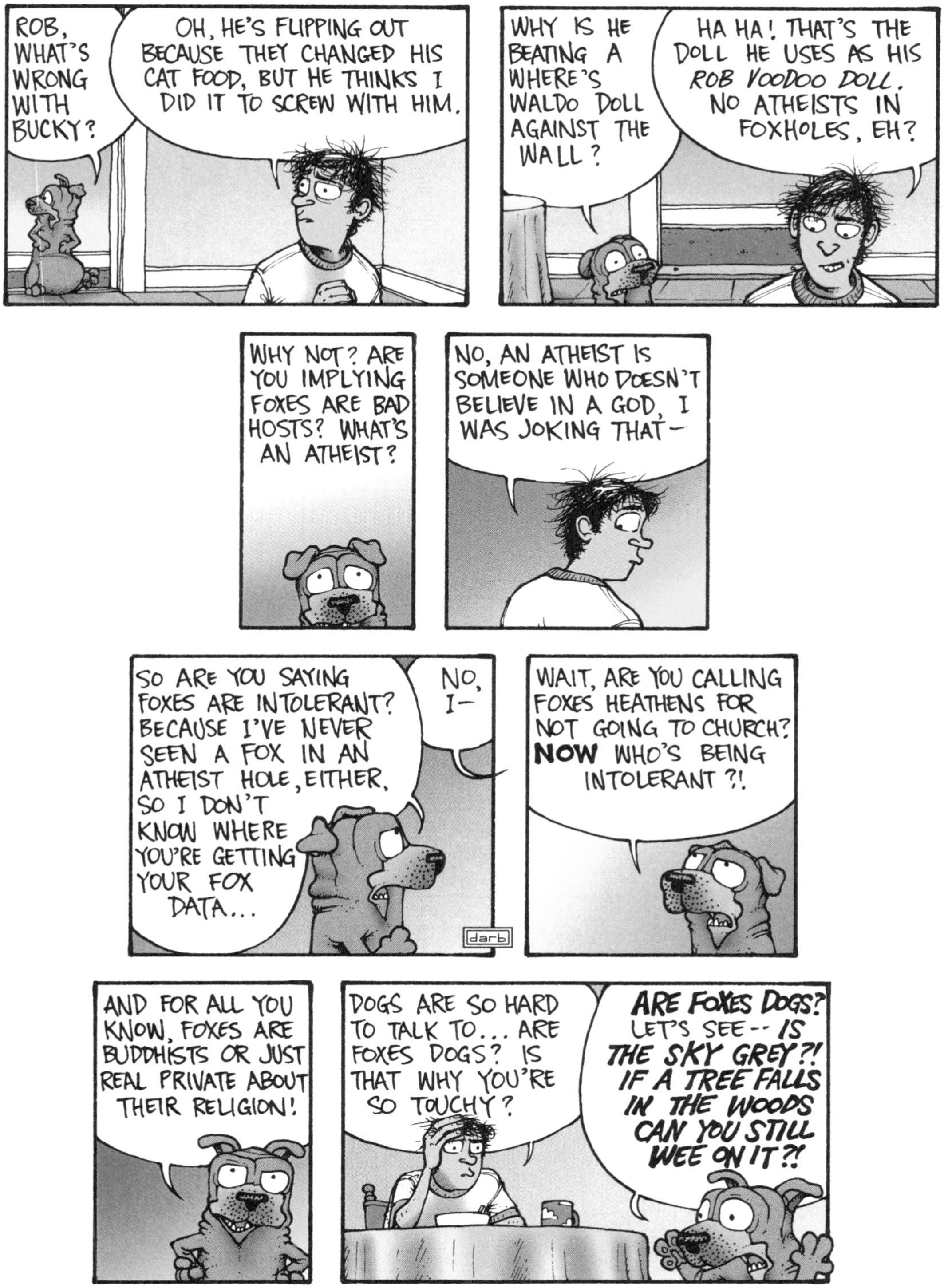
ROB, WHAT'S WRONG WITH BUCKY?
OH, HE'S FLIPPING OUT BECAUSE THEY CHANGED HIS CAT FOOD, BUT HE THINKS I DID IT TO SCREW WITH HIM.
WHY IS HE BEATING A WHERE'S WALDO DOLL AGAINST THE WALL?
HA HA! THAT'S THE DOLL HE USES AS HIS ROB VOODOO DOLL. NO ATHEISTS IN FOXHOLES, EH?
WHY NOT? ARE YOU IMPLYING FOXES ARE BAD HOSTS? WHAT'S AN ATHEIST?
NO, AN ATHEIST IS SOMEONE WHO DOESN'T BELIEVE IN A GOD, I WAS JOKING THAT—
SO ARE YOU SAYING FOXES ARE INTOLERANT? BECAUSE I'VE NEVER SEEN A FOX IN AN ATHEIST HOLE, EITHER, SO I DON'T KNOW WHERE YOU'RE GETTING YOUR FOX DATA...
NO, I—
darb
WAIT, ARE YOU CALLING FOXES HEATHENS FOR NOT GOING TO CHURCH? NOW WHO'S BEING INTOLERANT?!
AND FOR ALL YOU KNOW, FOXES ARE BUDDHISTS OR JUST REAL PRIVATE ABOUT THEIR RELIGION!
DOGS ARE SO HARD TO TALK TO... ARE FOXES DOGS? IS THAT WHY YOU'RE SO TOUCHY?
ARE FOXES DOGS? LET'S SEE-- IS THE SKY GREY?! IF A TREE FALLS IN THE WOODS CAN YOU STILL WEE ON IT?!

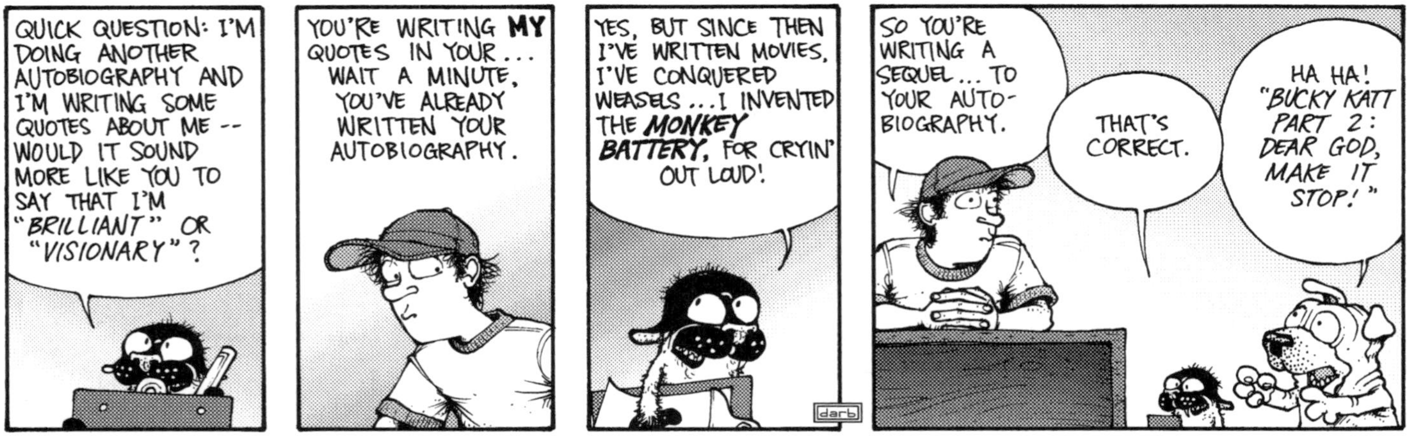
QUICK QUESTION: I'M DOING ANOTHER AUTOBIOGRAPHY AND I'M WRITING SOME QUOTES ABOUT ME -- WOULD IT SOUND MORE LIKE YOU TO SAY THAT I'M "*BRILLIANT*" OR "*VISIONARY*"?
YOU'RE WRITING **MY** QUOTES IN YOUR... WAIT A MINUTE, YOU'VE ALREADY WRITTEN YOUR AUTOBIOGRAPHY.
YES, BUT SINCE THEN I'VE WRITTEN MOVIES, I'VE CONQUERED WEASELS... I INVENTED THE ***MONKEY BATTERY***, FOR CRYIN' OUT LOUD!
darb
SO YOU'RE WRITING A SEQUEL... TO YOUR AUTO-BIOGRAPHY.
THAT'S CORRECT.
HA HA! "*BUCKY KATT PART 2: DEAR GOD, MAKE IT STOP!*"

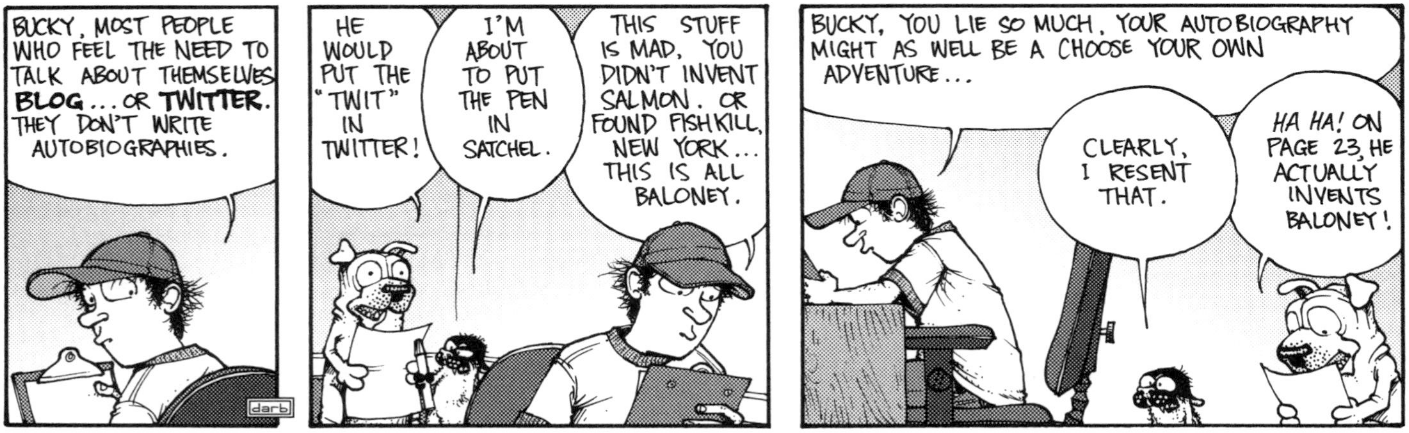
BUCKY, MOST PEOPLE WHO FEEL THE NEED TO TALK ABOUT THEMSELVES **BLOG**... OR **TWITTER**. THEY DON'T WRITE AUTOBIOGRAPHIES.
darb
HE WOULD PUT THE "TWIT" IN TWITTER!
I'M ABOUT TO PUT THE PEN IN SATCHEL.
THIS STUFF IS MAD. YOU DIDN'T INVENT SALMON. OR FOUND FISHKILL, NEW YORK... THIS IS ALL BALONEY.
BUCKY, YOU LIE SO MUCH, YOUR AUTOBIOGRAPHY MIGHT AS WELL BE A CHOOSE YOUR OWN ADVENTURE...
CLEARLY, I RESENT THAT.
HA HA! ON PAGE 23, HE ACTUALLY INVENTS BALONEY!

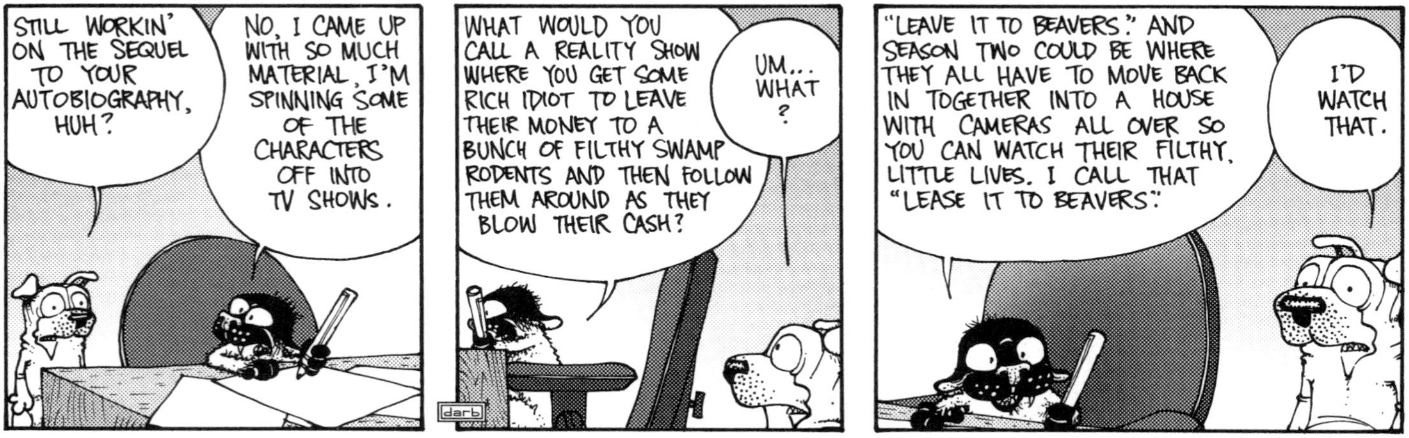
STILL WORKIN' ON THE SEQUEL TO YOUR AUTOBIOGRAPHY, HUH?
NO, I CAME UP WITH SO MUCH MATERIAL, I'M SPINNING SOME OF THE CHARACTERS OFF INTO TV SHOWS.
WHAT WOULD YOU CALL A REALITY SHOW WHERE YOU GET SOME RICH IDIOT TO LEAVE THEIR MONEY TO A BUNCH OF FILTHY SWAMP RODENTS AND THEN FOLLOW THEM AROUND AS THEY BLOW THEIR CASH?
UM... WHAT?
darb
"LEAVE IT TO BEAVERS." AND SEASON TWO COULD BE WHERE THEY ALL HAVE TO MOVE BACK IN TOGETHER INTO A HOUSE WITH CAMERAS ALL OVER SO YOU CAN WATCH THEIR FILTHY, LITTLE LIVES. I CALL THAT "LEASE IT TO BEAVERS."
I'D WATCH THAT.

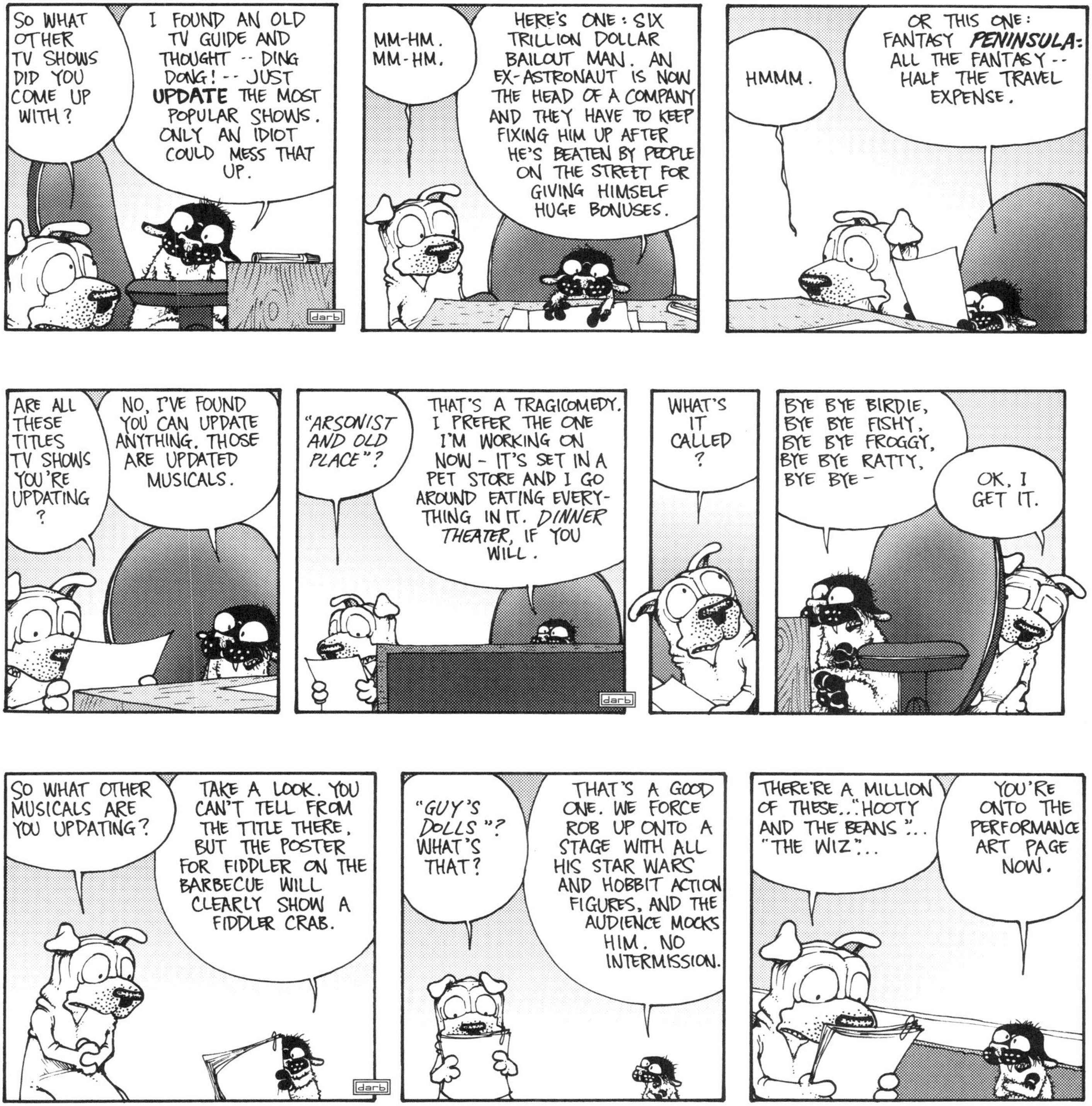
SO WHAT OTHER TV SHOWS DID YOU COME UP WITH?
I FOUND AN OLD TV GUIDE AND THOUGHT -- DING DONG! -- JUST UPDATE THE MOST POPULAR SHOWS. ONLY AN IDIOT COULD MESS THAT UP.
MM-HM. MM-HM.
HERE'S ONE: SIX TRILLION DOLLAR BAILOUT MAN. AN EX-ASTRONAUT IS NOW THE HEAD OF A COMPANY AND THEY HAVE TO KEEP FIXING HIM UP AFTER HE'S BEATEN BY PEOPLE ON THE STREET FOR GIVING HIMSELF HUGE BONUSES.
HMMM.
OR THIS ONE: FANTASY PENINSULA: ALL THE FANTASY -- HALF THE TRAVEL EXPENSE.
ARE ALL THESE TITLES TV SHOWS YOU'RE UPDATING?
NO, I'VE FOUND YOU CAN UPDATE ANYTHING. THOSE ARE UPDATED MUSICALS.
"ARSONIST AND OLD PLACE"?
THAT'S A TRAGICOMEDY. I PREFER THE ONE I'M WORKING ON NOW - IT'S SET IN A PET STORE AND I GO AROUND EATING EVERYTHING IN IT. DINNER THEATER, IF YOU WILL.
WHAT'S IT CALLED?
BYE BYE BIRDIE, BYE BYE FISHY, BYE BYE FROGGY, BYE BYE RATTY, BYE BYE -
OK, I GET IT.
SO WHAT OTHER MUSICALS ARE YOU UPDATING?
TAKE A LOOK. YOU CAN'T TELL FROM THE TITLE THERE, BUT THE POSTER FOR FIDDLER ON THE BARBECUE WILL CLEARLY SHOW A FIDDLER CRAB.
"GUY'S DOLLS"? WHAT'S THAT?
THAT'S A GOOD ONE. WE FORCE ROB UP ONTO A STAGE WITH ALL HIS STAR WARS AND HOBBIT ACTION FIGURES, AND THE AUDIENCE MOCKS HIM. NO INTERMISSION.
THERE'RE A MILLION OF THESE..."HOOTY AND THE BEANS"... "THE WIZ"...
YOU'RE ONTO THE PERFORMANCE ART PAGE NOW.

COULD YOU TELL ME IF MY NEW PICTURE IS STRAIGHT?

WHAT IS THAT?

IT'S A FLEA CIRCUS! HA HA!

A *FLEA* CIRCUS?! WHAT ARE YOU, **MENTAL**?! WHO THE ☆@%# GAVE THOSE THINGS A PLATFORM UPON WHICH TO SPREAD THEIR FILTH?!

UH...

WHO SITS AROUND THINKING "YOU KNOW, IT'S TIRING BRINGING DISEASE *TO* PEOPLE, LET'S BRING PEOPLE TO THE DISEASE!"

"WE'LL TAKE THE FILTHIEST, MOST DISEASE-RIDDEN VERMIN ON EARTH AND INVITE FAMILIES TO COME SEE THEM!"

I DON'T THINK IT—

WHO OWNS IT? THE RINGWORM BROTHERS OR BUBONIC & BAILEY?

THERE'S A BLOOD-SUCKER BORN EVERY MINUTE, EH? YOU OUGHT TO BE ASHAMED.

ROB? CAN YOU HELP ME FOR A MINUTE?

WHAT'S IT CALLED, *CIRQUE DU PLAGUE*? PSH. GOOD DAY.

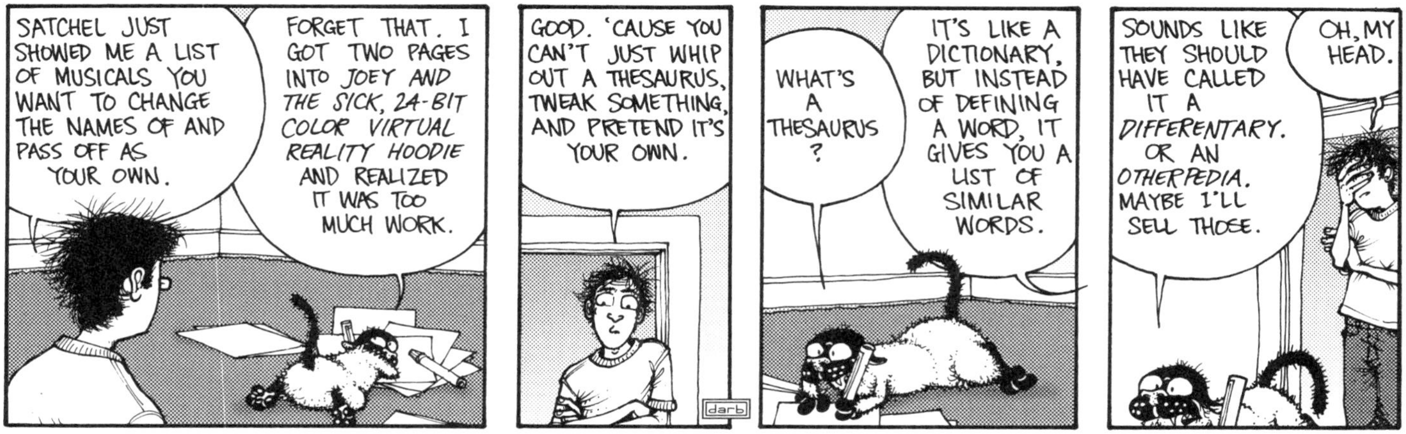
SATCHEL JUST SHOWED ME A LIST OF MUSICALS YOU WANT TO CHANGE THE NAMES OF AND PASS OFF AS YOUR OWN.
FORGET THAT. I GOT TWO PAGES INTO *JOEY AND THE SICK, 24-BIT COLOR VIRTUAL REALITY HOODIE* AND REALIZED IT WAS TOO MUCH WORK.
GOOD. 'CAUSE YOU CAN'T JUST WHIP OUT A THESAURUS, TWEAK SOMETHING, AND PRETEND IT'S YOUR OWN.
darb
WHAT'S A THESAURUS ?
IT'S LIKE A DICTIONARY, BUT INSTEAD OF DEFINING A WORD, IT GIVES YOU A LIST OF SIMILAR WORDS.
SOUNDS LIKE THEY SHOULD HAVE CALLED IT A *DIFFERENTARY*. OR AN *OTHERPEDIA*. MAYBE I'LL SELL THOSE.
OH, MY HEAD.

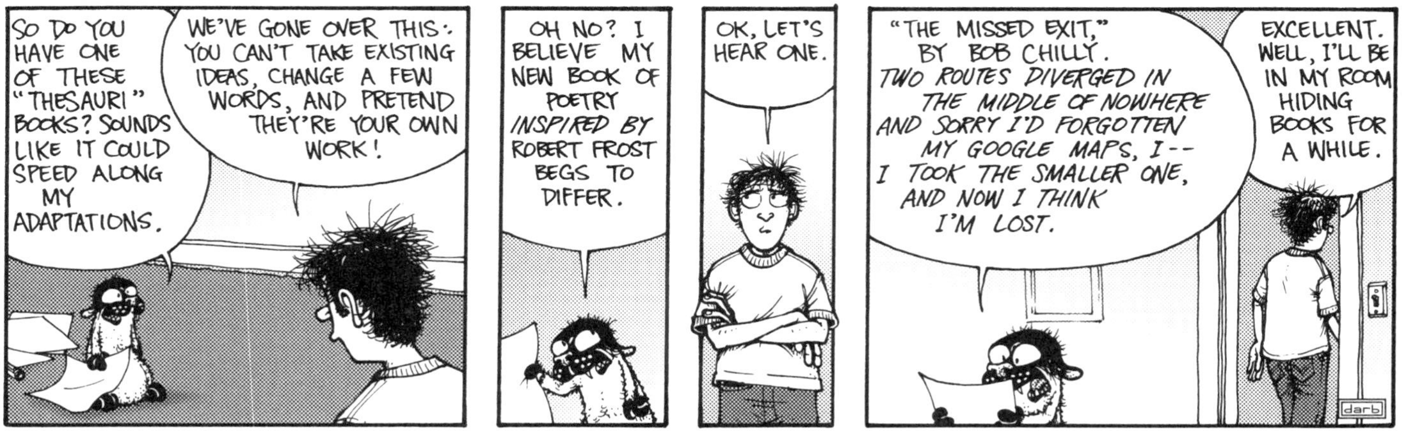
SO DO YOU HAVE ONE OF THESE "THESAURI" BOOKS? SOUNDS LIKE IT COULD SPEED ALONG MY ADAPTATIONS.
WE'VE GONE OVER THIS: YOU CAN'T TAKE EXISTING IDEAS, CHANGE A FEW WORDS, AND PRETEND THEY'RE YOUR OWN WORK!
OH NO? I BELIEVE MY NEW BOOK OF POETRY *INSPIRED BY* ROBERT FROST BEGS TO DIFFER.
OK, LET'S HEAR ONE.
"THE MISSED EXIT," BY BOB CHILLY. *TWO ROUTES DIVERGED IN THE MIDDLE OF NOWHERE AND SORRY I'D FORGOTTEN MY GOOGLE MAPS, I-- I TOOK THE SMALLER ONE, AND NOW I THINK I'M LOST.*
EXCELLENT. WELL, I'LL BE IN MY ROOM HIDING BOOKS FOR A WHILE.
darb

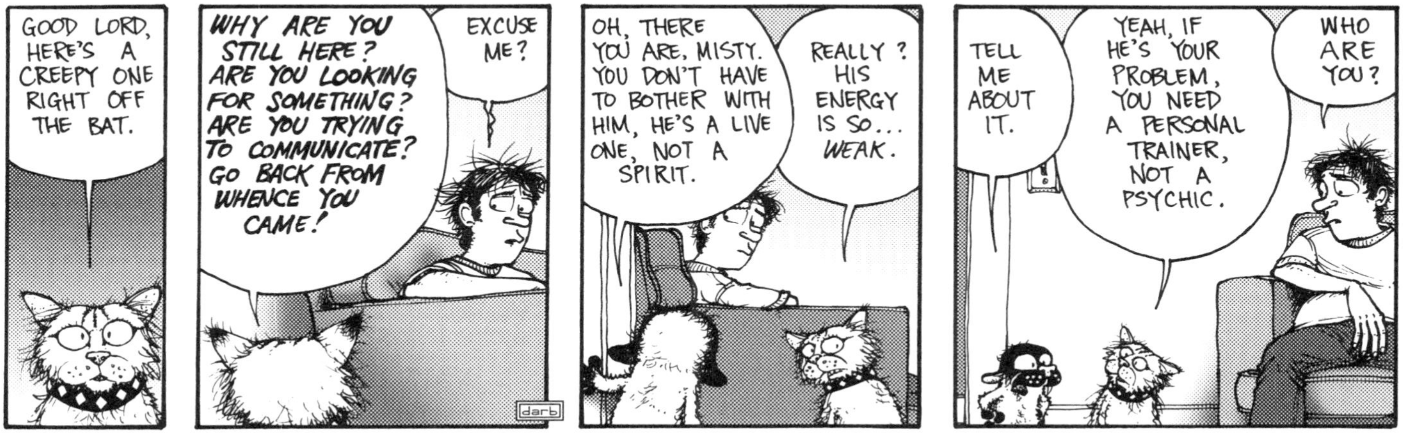
GOOD LORD, HERE'S A CREEPY ONE RIGHT OFF THE BAT.
WHY ARE YOU STILL HERE? ARE YOU LOOKING FOR SOMETHING? ARE YOU TRYING TO COMMUNICATE? GO BACK FROM WHENCE YOU CAME!
EXCUSE ME?
darb
OH, THERE YOU ARE, MISTY. YOU DON'T HAVE TO BOTHER WITH HIM, HE'S A LIVE ONE, NOT A SPIRIT.
REALLY ? HIS ENERGY IS SO... *WEAK*.
TELL ME ABOUT IT.
YEAH, IF HE'S YOUR PROBLEM, YOU NEED A PERSONAL TRAINER, NOT A PSYCHIC.
WHO ARE YOU?

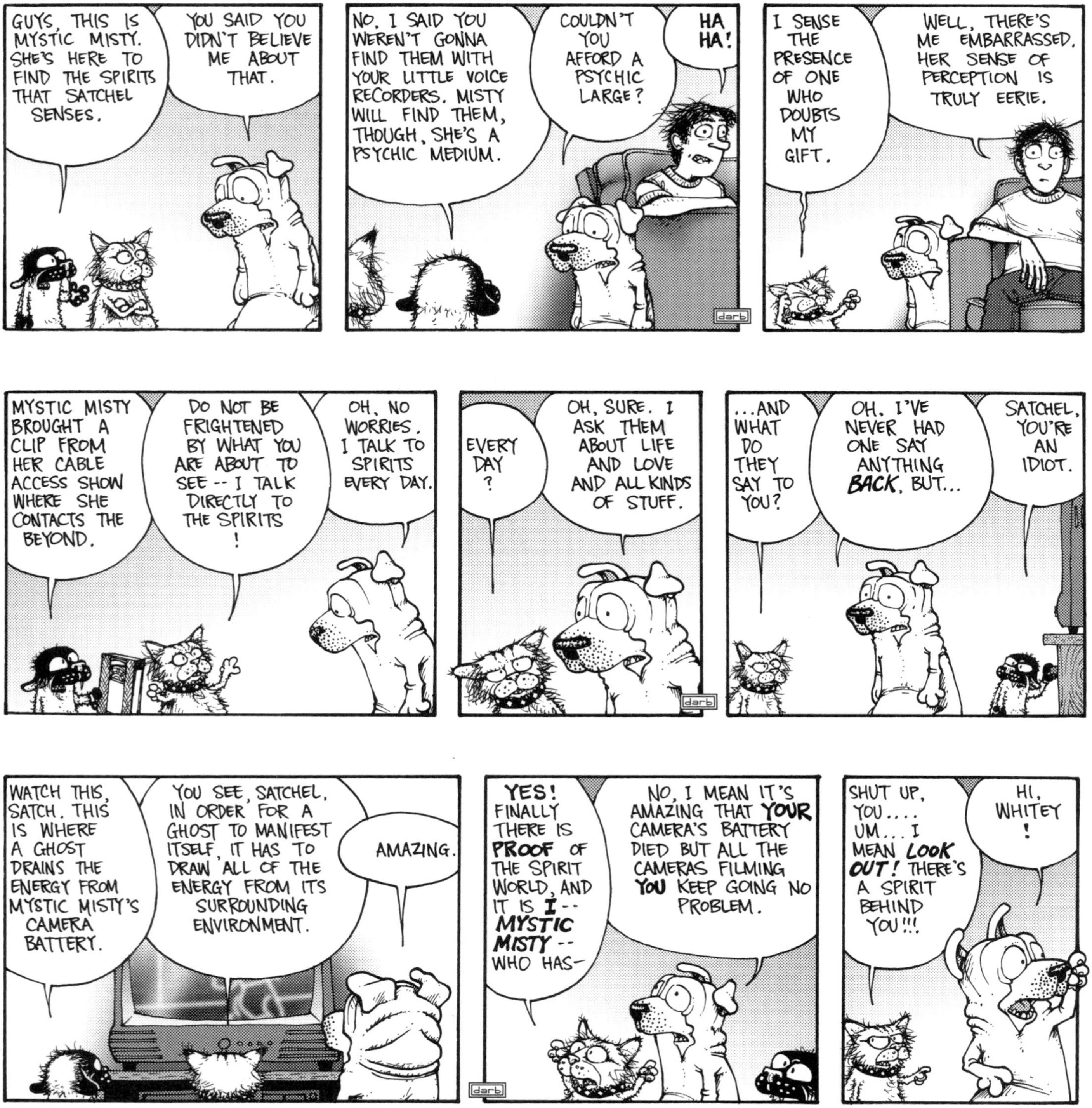
GUYS, THIS IS MYSTIC MISTY. SHE'S HERE TO FIND THE SPIRITS THAT SATCHEL SENSES.
YOU SAID YOU DIDN'T BELIEVE ME ABOUT THAT.
NO. I SAID YOU WEREN'T GONNA FIND THEM WITH YOUR LITTLE VOICE RECORDERS. MISTY WILL FIND THEM, THOUGH, SHE'S A PSYCHIC MEDIUM.
COULDN'T YOU AFFORD A PSYCHIC LARGE?
HA HA!
I SENSE THE PRESENCE OF ONE WHO DOUBTS MY GIFT.
WELL, THERE'S ME EMBARRASSED. HER SENSE OF PERCEPTION IS TRULY EERIE.
darb
MYSTIC MISTY BROUGHT A CLIP FROM HER CABLE ACCESS SHOW WHERE SHE CONTACTS THE BEYOND.
DO NOT BE FRIGHTENED BY WHAT YOU ARE ABOUT TO SEE -- I TALK DIRECTLY TO THE SPIRITS!
OH, NO WORRIES. I TALK TO SPIRITS EVERY DAY.
EVERY DAY?
OH, SURE. I ASK THEM ABOUT LIFE AND LOVE AND ALL KINDS OF STUFF.
...AND WHAT DO THEY SAY TO YOU?
OH. I'VE NEVER HAD ONE SAY ANYTHING **BACK**, BUT...
SATCHEL, YOU'RE AN IDIOT.
darb
WATCH THIS, SATCH. THIS IS WHERE A GHOST DRAINS THE ENERGY FROM MYSTIC MISTY'S CAMERA BATTERY.
YOU SEE, SATCHEL, IN ORDER FOR A GHOST TO MANIFEST ITSELF, IT HAS TO DRAW ALL OF THE ENERGY FROM ITS SURROUNDING ENVIRONMENT.
AMAZING.
YES! FINALLY THERE IS **PROOF** OF THE SPIRIT WORLD, AND IT IS **I** -- ***MYSTIC MISTY*** -- WHO HAS-
NO, I MEAN IT'S AMAZING THAT **YOUR** CAMERA'S BATTERY DIED BUT ALL THE CAMERAS FILMING **YOU** KEEP GOING NO PROBLEM.
SHUT UP, YOU.... UM... I MEAN ***LOOK OUT!*** THERE'S A SPIRIT BEHIND YOU!!!
HI, WHITEY!
darb

ROB. ROB. ROB. ROB. ROB. ROB. ROB. ROB. ROB. ROB. ROB. ROB. ROB. ROB. ROB. ROB. ROB. ROB. ROB.
darb
ROB. ROB. ROB. ROB. ROB. ROB. ROB. ROBERT. ROB. ROB. ROB. ROB. R–
WHAT?
EMERGENCY. GET UP. WE'RE OUT OF WET FOOD.
OH, FOR... ...WHAT TIME IS IT?
IT'S FOOD O'CLOCK.
TWO WAYS WE CAN GO ABOUT THIS, ONE: YOU CAN GET UP FOR 5 MINUTES AND FEED ME, OR...
B: I CAN EAT CARPET FIBERS UNTIL I THROW UP ON YOUR COMPUTER.
JUST GO HAVE SOME DRY FOOD FOR ONCE!
I'M GOING TO PRETEND YOU DIDN'T SAY THAT.
BEAT IT.
I PREFER NOT TO BRING VIOLENCE INTO THIS EQUATION, BUT IF I DON'T GET MY WAY, I'LL DO THINGS TO SATCHEL THAT HE WON'T UNDERSTAND.
WHAT'D I DO ?!

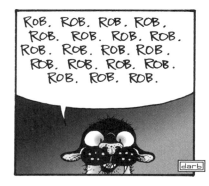

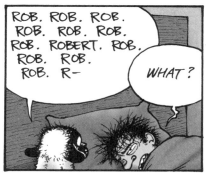

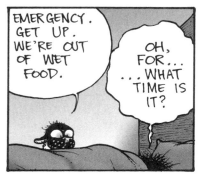

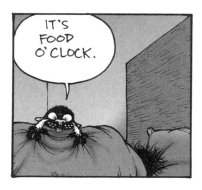

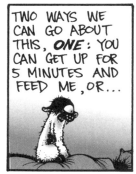

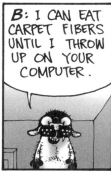

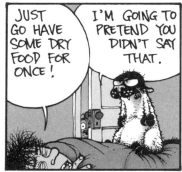

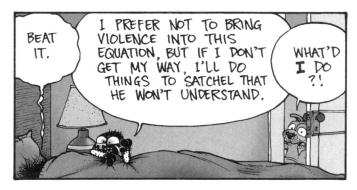

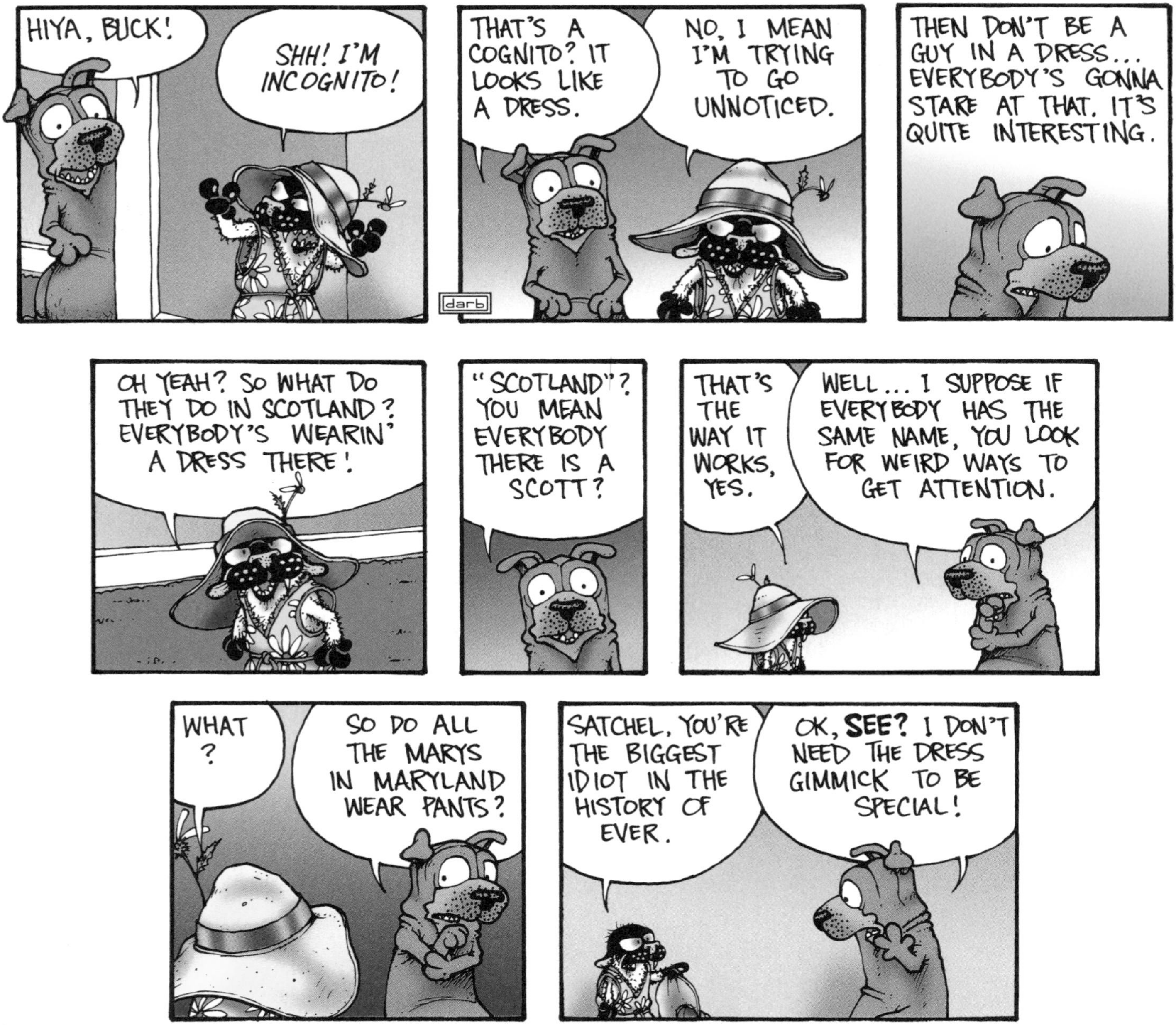
HIYA, BUCK!
SHH! I'M INCOGNITO!
darb
THAT'S A COGNITO? IT LOOKS LIKE A DRESS.
NO, I MEAN I'M TRYING TO GO UNNOTICED.
THEN DON'T BE A GUY IN A DRESS... EVERYBODY'S GONNA STARE AT THAT. IT'S QUITE INTERESTING.
OH YEAH? SO WHAT DO THEY DO IN SCOTLAND? EVERYBODY'S WEARIN' A DRESS THERE!
"SCOTLAND"? YOU MEAN EVERYBODY THERE IS A SCOTT?
THAT'S THE WAY IT WORKS, YES.
WELL... I SUPPOSE IF EVERYBODY HAS THE SAME NAME, YOU LOOK FOR WEIRD WAYS TO GET ATTENTION.
WHAT?
SO DO ALL THE MARYS IN MARYLAND WEAR PANTS?
SATCHEL, YOU'RE THE BIGGEST IDIOT IN THE HISTORY OF EVER.
OK, SEE? I DON'T NEED THE DRESS GIMMICK TO BE SPECIAL!

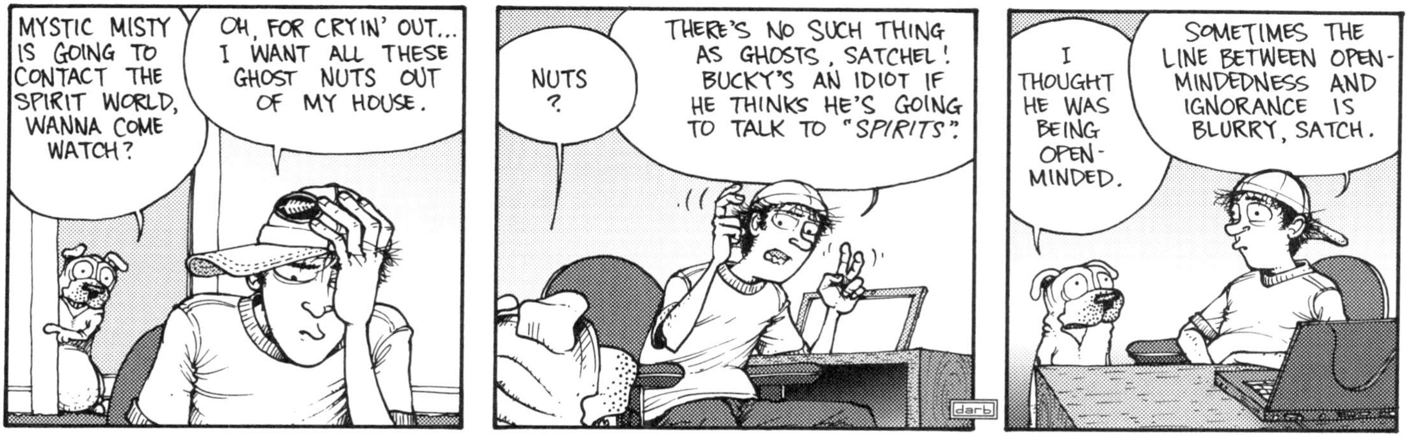
MYSTIC MISTY IS GOING TO CONTACT THE SPIRIT WORLD, WANNA COME WATCH?
OH, FOR CRYIN' OUT... I WANT ALL THESE GHOST NUTS OUT OF MY HOUSE.
NUTS?
THERE'S NO SUCH THING AS GHOSTS, SATCHEL! BUCKY'S AN IDIOT IF HE THINKS HE'S GOING TO TALK TO "SPIRITS".
I THOUGHT HE WAS BEING OPEN-MINDED.
SOMETIMES THE LINE BETWEEN OPEN-MINDEDNESS AND IGNORANCE IS BLURRY, SATCH.
darb

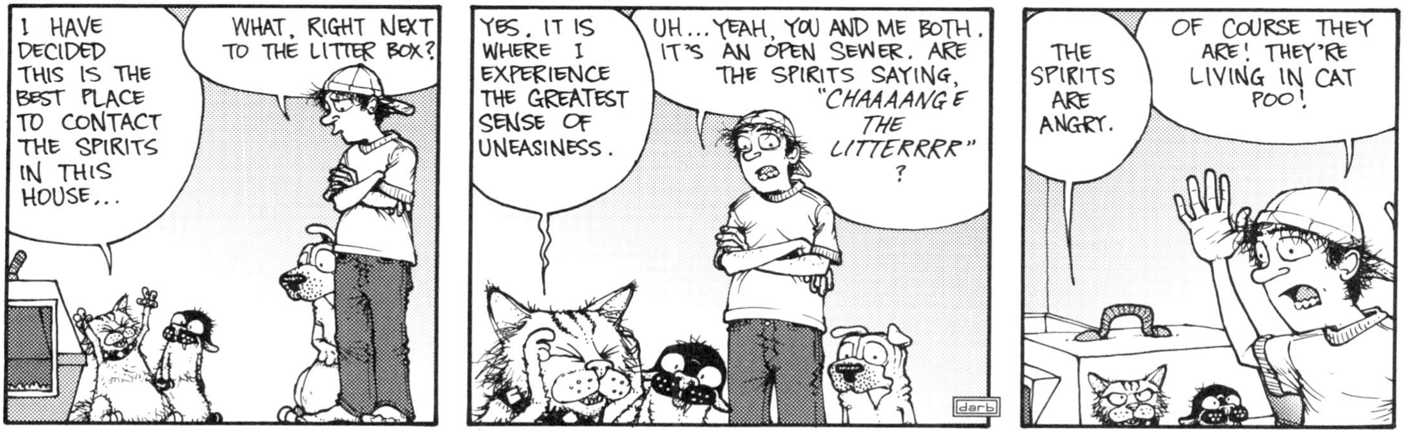
I HAVE DECIDED THIS IS THE BEST PLACE TO CONTACT THE SPIRITS IN THIS HOUSE...
WHAT, RIGHT NEXT TO THE LITTER BOX?
YES. IT IS WHERE I EXPERIENCE THE GREATEST SENSE OF UNEASINESS.
UH... YEAH, YOU AND ME BOTH. IT'S AN OPEN SEWER. ARE THE SPIRITS SAYING, "CHAAAANGE THE LITTERRRR"?
THE SPIRITS ARE ANGRY.
OF COURSE THEY ARE! THEY'RE LIVING IN CAT POO!
darb

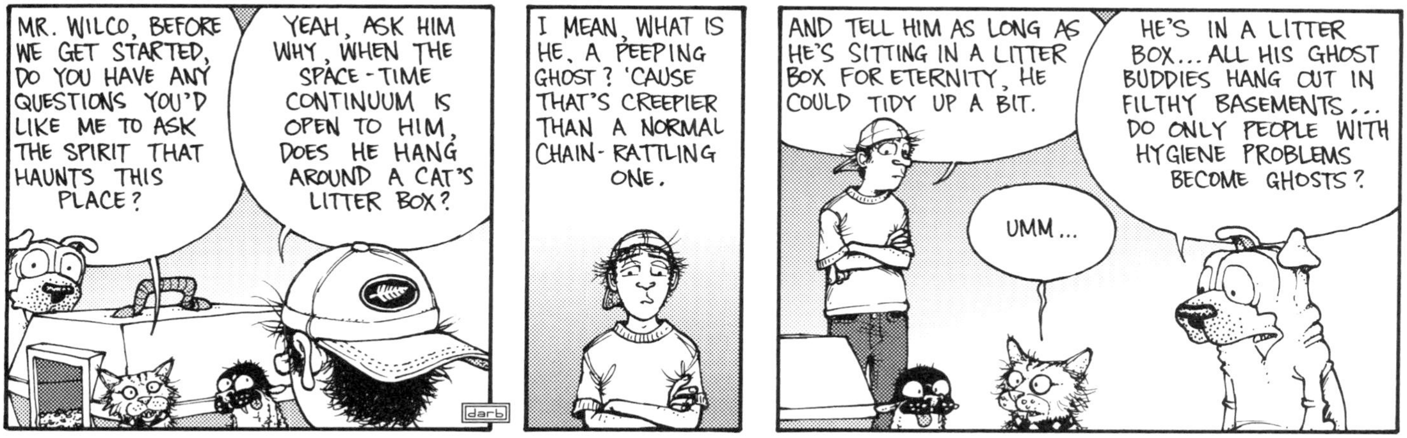
MR. WILCO, BEFORE WE GET STARTED, DO YOU HAVE ANY QUESTIONS YOU'D LIKE ME TO ASK THE SPIRIT THAT HAUNTS THIS PLACE?
YEAH, ASK HIM WHY, WHEN THE SPACE-TIME CONTINUUM IS OPEN TO HIM, DOES HE HANG AROUND A CAT'S LITTER BOX?
I MEAN, WHAT IS HE, A PEEPING GHOST? 'CAUSE THAT'S CREEPIER THAN A NORMAL CHAIN-RATTLING ONE.
AND TELL HIM AS LONG AS HE'S SITTING IN A LITTER BOX FOR ETERNITY, HE COULD TIDY UP A BIT.
UMM...
HE'S IN A LITTER BOX... ALL HIS GHOST BUDDIES HANG OUT IN FILTHY BASEMENTS... DO ONLY PEOPLE WITH HYGIENE PROBLEMS BECOME GHOSTS?
darb

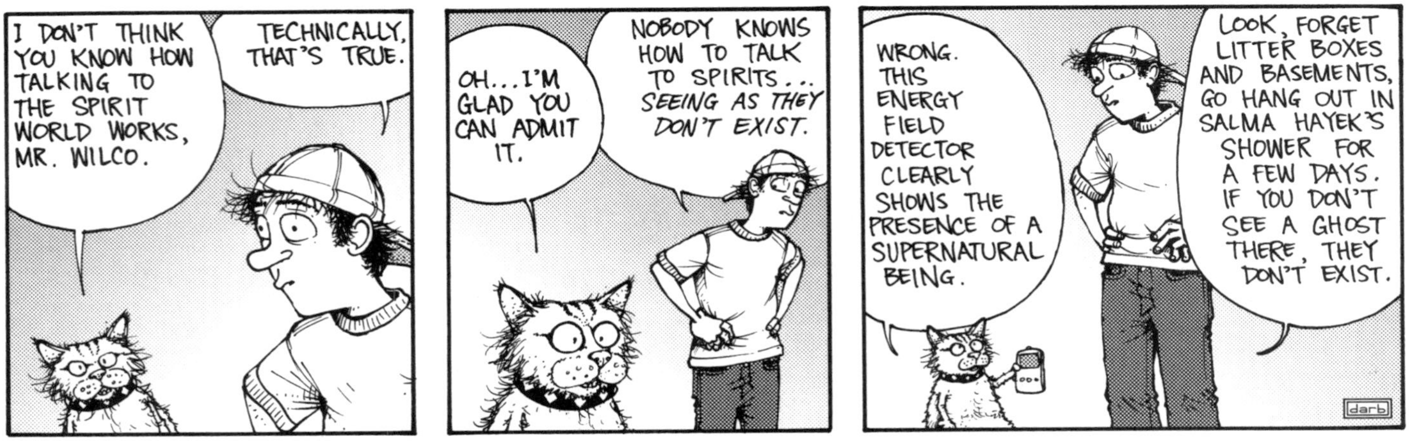
I DON'T THINK YOU KNOW HOW TALKING TO THE SPIRIT WORLD WORKS, MR. WILCO.
TECHNICALLY, THAT'S TRUE.
OH... I'M GLAD YOU CAN ADMIT IT.
NOBODY KNOWS HOW TO TALK TO SPIRITS... *SEEING AS THEY DON'T EXIST.*
WRONG. THIS ENERGY FIELD DETECTOR CLEARLY SHOWS THE PRESENCE OF A SUPERNATURAL BEING.
LOOK, FORGET LITTER BOXES AND BASEMENTS, GO HANG OUT IN SALMA HAYEK'S SHOWER FOR A FEW DAYS. IF YOU DON'T SEE A GHOST THERE, THEY DON'T EXIST.
darb

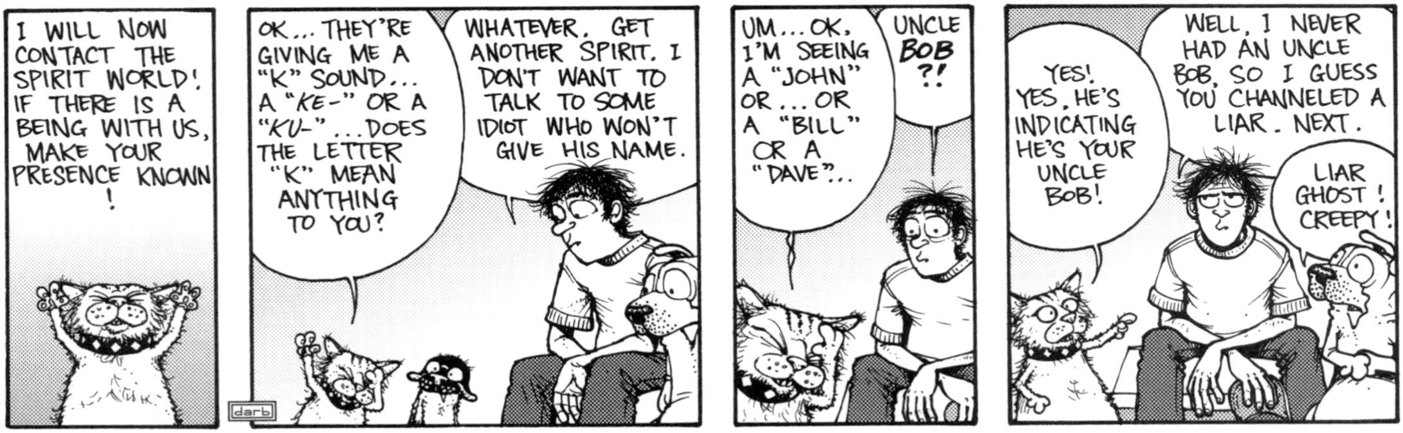
I WILL NOW CONTACT THE SPIRIT WORLD! IF THERE IS A BEING WITH US, MAKE YOUR PRESENCE KNOWN!
darb
OK... THEY'RE GIVING ME A "K" SOUND... A "*KE-*" OR A "*KU-*"... DOES THE LETTER "K" MEAN ANYTHING TO YOU?
WHATEVER. GET ANOTHER SPIRIT. I DON'T WANT TO TALK TO SOME IDIOT WHO WON'T GIVE HIS NAME.
UM... OK. I'M SEEING A "JOHN" OR... OR A "BILL" OR A "DAVE"...
UNCLE ***BOB*** ?!
YES! YES, HE'S INDICATING HE'S YOUR UNCLE BOB!
WELL, I NEVER HAD AN UNCLE BOB, SO I GUESS YOU CHANNELED A LIAR. NEXT.
LIAR GHOST! CREEPY!

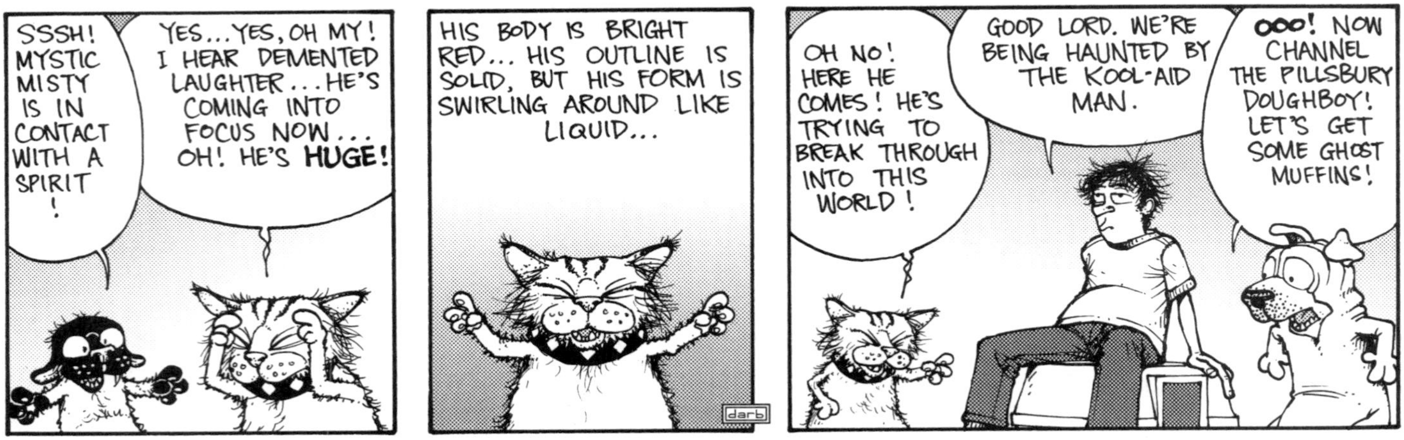
SSSH! MYSTIC MISTY IS IN CONTACT WITH A SPIRIT!
YES... YES, OH MY! I HEAR DEMENTED LAUGHTER... HE'S COMING INTO FOCUS NOW... OH! HE'S **HUGE!**
HIS BODY IS BRIGHT RED... HIS OUTLINE IS SOLID, BUT HIS FORM IS SWIRLING AROUND LIKE LIQUID...
darb
OH NO! HERE HE COMES! HE'S TRYING TO BREAK THROUGH INTO THIS WORLD!
GOOD LORD. WE'RE BEING HAUNTED BY THE KOOL-AID MAN.
OOO! NOW CHANNEL THE PILLSBURY DOUGHBOY! LET'S GET SOME GHOST MUFFINS!

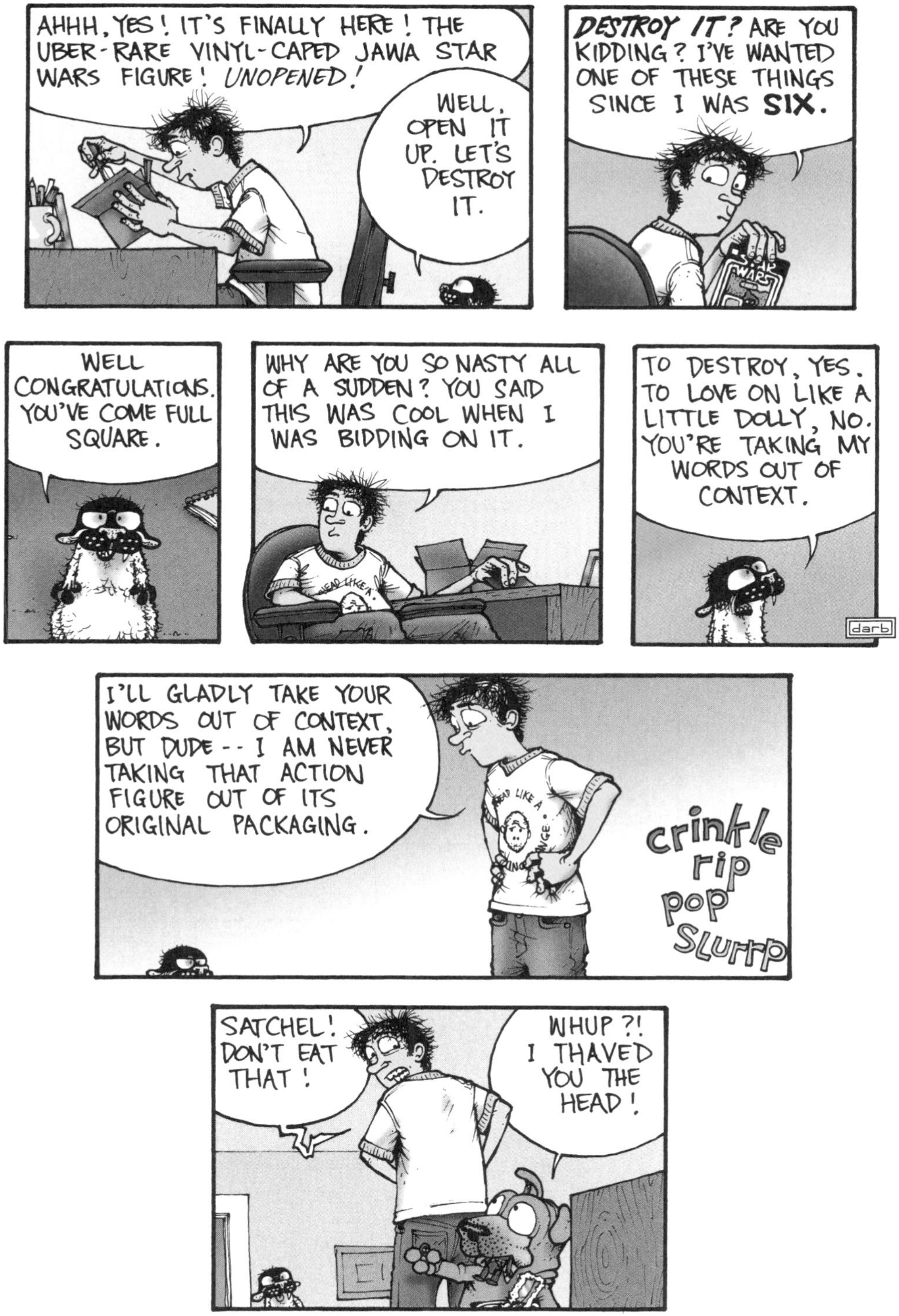
AHHH, YES! IT'S FINALLY HERE! THE UBER-RARE VINYL-CAPED JAWA STAR WARS FIGURE! *UNOPENED!*
WELL, OPEN IT UP. LET'S DESTROY IT.
DESTROY IT? ARE YOU KIDDING? I'VE WANTED ONE OF THESE THINGS SINCE I WAS **SIX.**
WARS
WELL CONGRATULATIONS. YOU'VE COME FULL SQUARE.
WHY ARE YOU SO NASTY ALL OF A SUDDEN? YOU SAID THIS WAS COOL WHEN I WAS BIDDING ON IT.
HEAD LIKE A
TO DESTROY, YES. TO LOVE ON LIKE A LITTLE DOLLY, NO. YOU'RE TAKING MY WORDS OUT OF CONTEXT.
darb
I'LL GLADLY TAKE YOUR WORDS OUT OF CONTEXT, BUT DUDE -- I AM NEVER TAKING THAT ACTION FIGURE OUT OF ITS ORIGINAL PACKAGING.
HEAD LIKE A
crinkle
rip
pop
SLurrp
SATCHEL! DON'T EAT THAT!
WHUP?! I THAVED YOU THE HEAD!

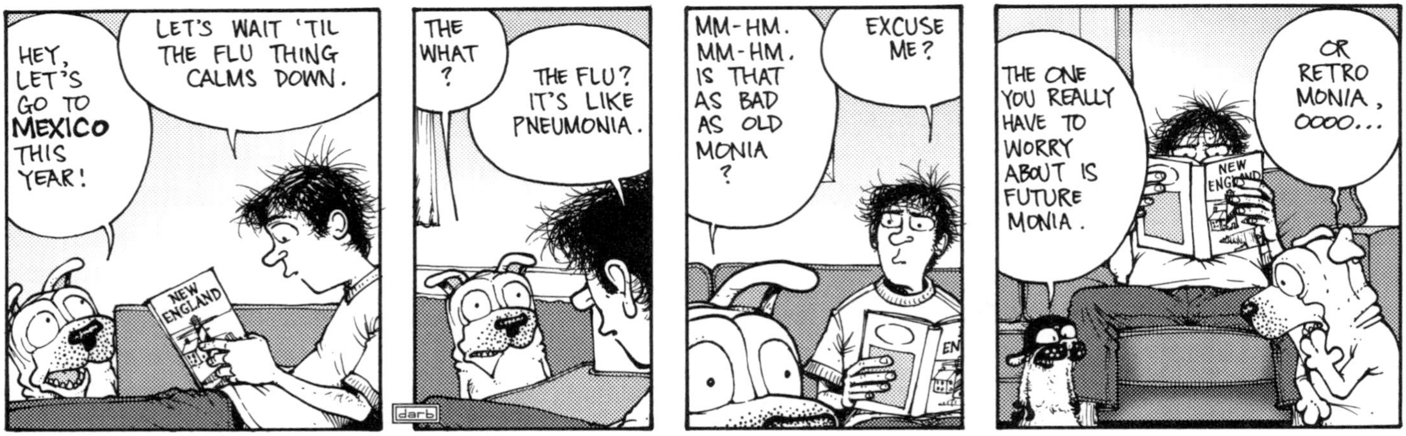
HEY, LET'S GO TO **MEXICO** THIS YEAR!
LET'S WAIT 'TIL THE FLU THING CALMS DOWN.
NEW ENGLAND
THE WHAT ?
THE FLU? IT'S LIKE PNEUMONIA.
MM-HM. MM-HM. IS THAT AS BAD AS OLD MONIA ?
EXCUSE ME?
THE ONE YOU REALLY HAVE TO WORRY ABOUT IS FUTURE MONIA.
OR RETRO MONIA, OOOO...
darb

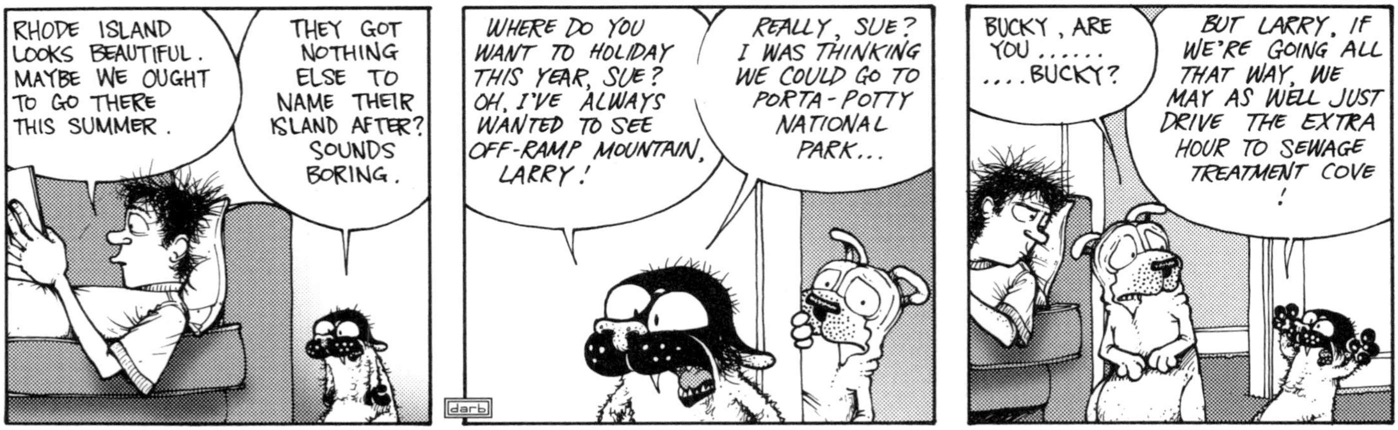
RHODE ISLAND LOOKS BEAUTIFUL. MAYBE WE OUGHT TO GO THERE THIS SUMMER.
THEY GOT NOTHING ELSE TO NAME THEIR ISLAND AFTER? SOUNDS BORING.
WHERE DO YOU WANT TO HOLIDAY THIS YEAR, SUE? OH, I'VE ALWAYS WANTED TO SEE OFF-RAMP MOUNTAIN, LARRY!
REALLY, SUE? I WAS THINKING WE COULD GO TO PORTA-POTTY NATIONAL PARK...
BUCKY, ARE YOU...... ....BUCKY?
BUT LARRY, IF WE'RE GOING ALL THAT WAY, WE MAY AS WELL JUST DRIVE THE EXTRA HOUR TO SEWAGE TREATMENT COVE !
darb

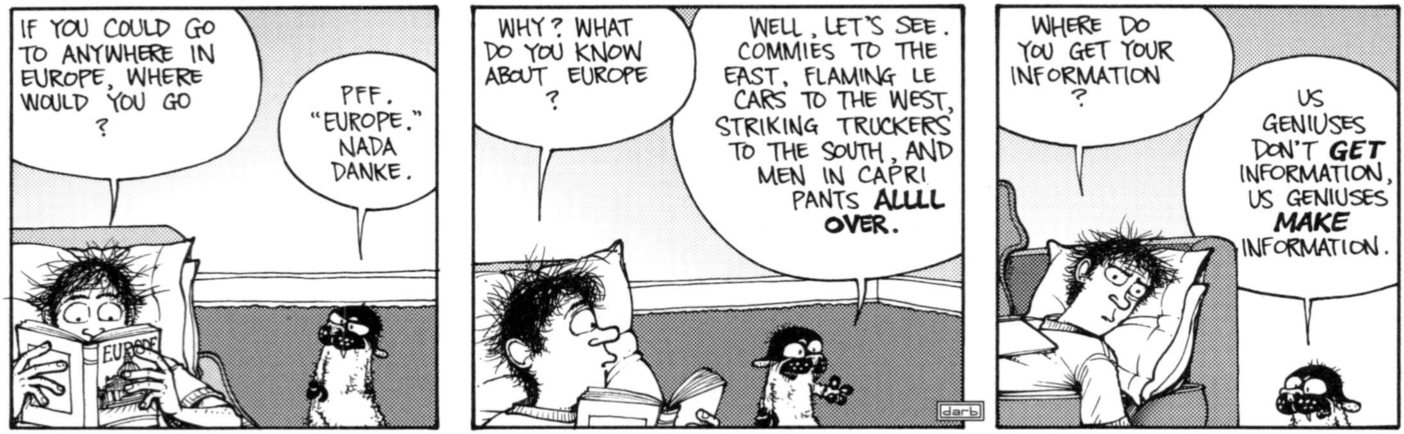
IF YOU COULD GO TO ANYWHERE IN EUROPE, WHERE WOULD YOU GO ?
PFF. "EUROPE." NADA DANKE.
EUROPE
WHY? WHAT DO YOU KNOW ABOUT EUROPE ?
WELL, LET'S SEE. COMMIES TO THE EAST, FLAMING LE CARS TO THE WEST, STRIKING TRUCKERS TO THE SOUTH, AND MEN IN CAPRI PANTS **ALLLL OVER.**
WHERE DO YOU GET YOUR INFORMATION ?
US GENIUSES DON'T **GET** INFORMATION, US GENIUSES **MAKE** INFORMATION.
darb

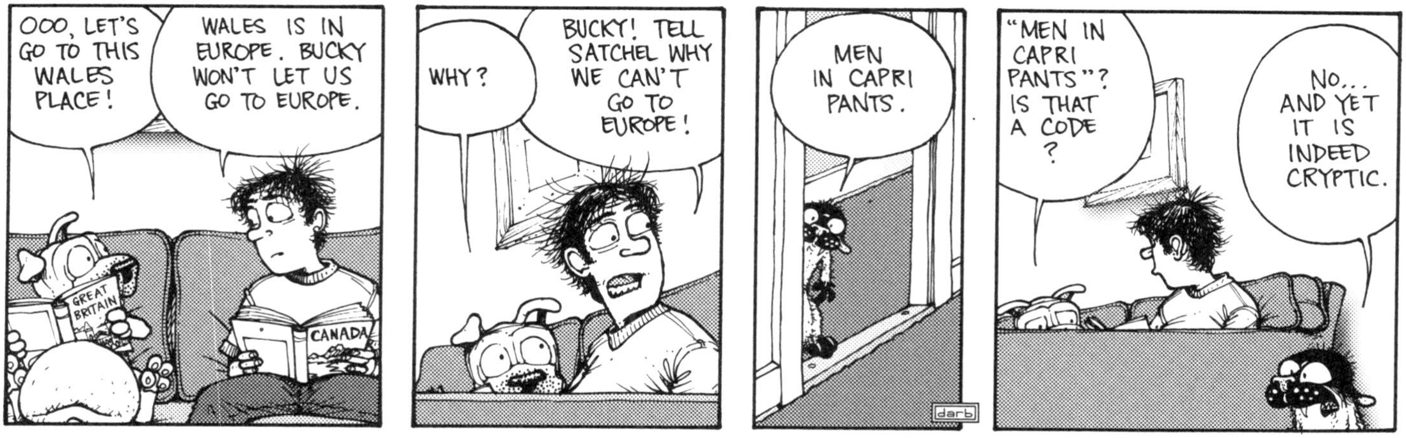
OOO, LET'S GO TO THIS WALES PLACE!
WALES IS IN EUROPE. BUCKY WON'T LET US GO TO EUROPE.
GREAT BRITAIN
CANADA
WHY?
BUCKY! TELL SATCHEL WHY WE CAN'T GO TO EUROPE!
MEN IN CAPRI PANTS.
"MEN IN CAPRI PANTS"? IS THAT A CODE?
NO... AND YET IT IS INDEED CRYPTIC.
darb

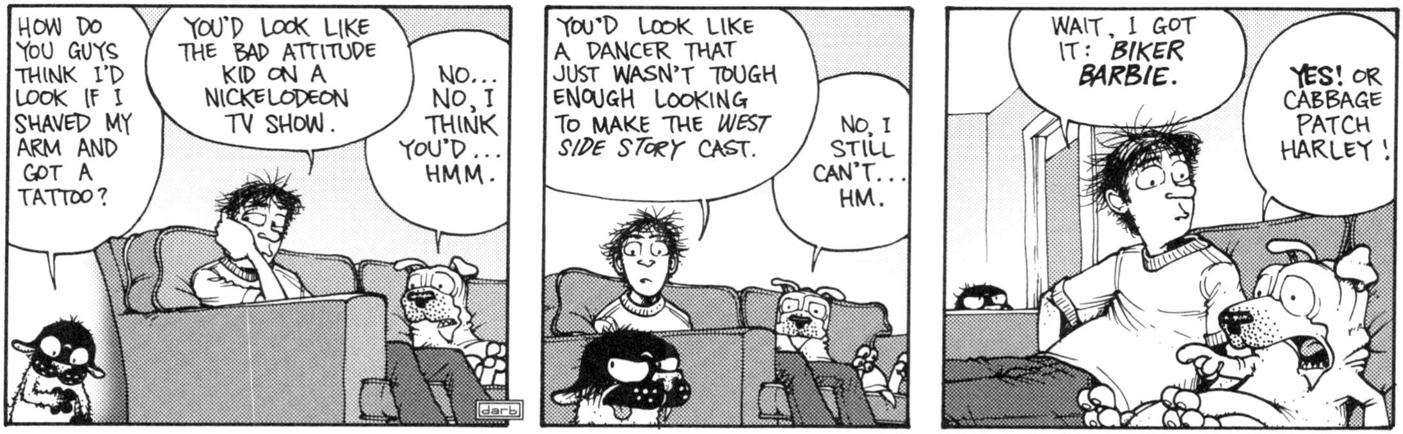
HOW DO YOU GUYS THINK I'D LOOK IF I SHAVED MY ARM AND GOT A TATTOO?
YOU'D LOOK LIKE THE BAD ATTITUDE KID ON A NICKELODEON TV SHOW.
NO... NO, I THINK YOU'D... HMM.
darb
YOU'D LOOK LIKE A DANCER THAT JUST WASN'T TOUGH ENOUGH LOOKING TO MAKE THE *WEST SIDE STORY* CAST.
NO, I STILL CAN'T... HM.
WAIT, I GOT IT: ***BIKER BARBIE.***
YES! OR CABBAGE PATCH HARLEY!

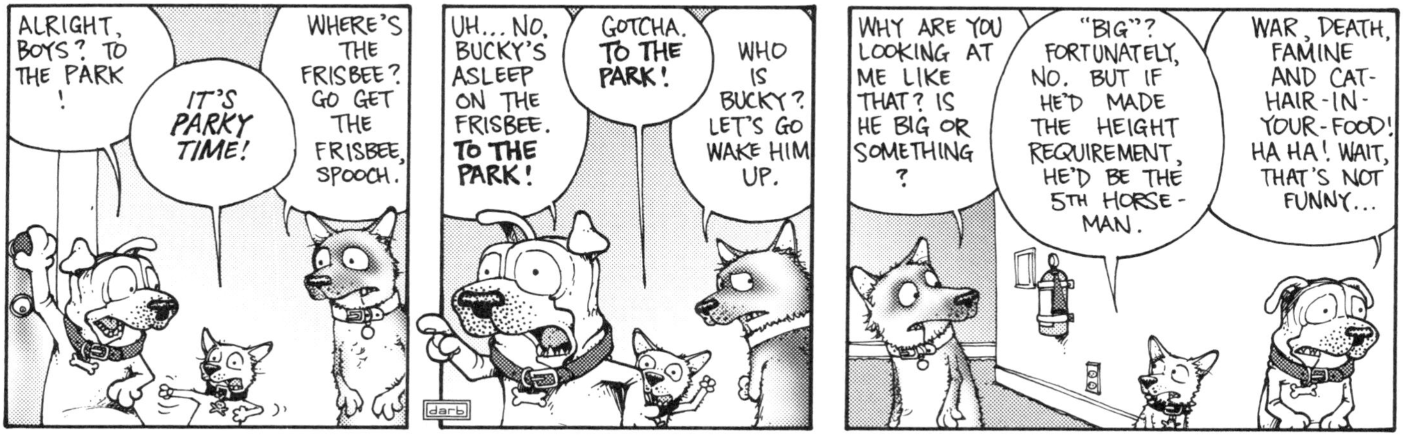
ALRIGHT, BOYS? TO THE PARK!
IT'S PARKY TIME!
WHERE'S THE FRISBEE? GO GET THE FRISBEE, SPOOCH.
UH... NO, BUCKY'S ASLEEP ON THE FRISBEE. **TO THE PARK!**
GOTCHA. **TO THE PARK!**
WHO IS BUCKY? LET'S GO WAKE HIM UP.
darb
WHY ARE YOU LOOKING AT ME LIKE THAT? IS HE BIG OR SOMETHING?
"BIG"? FORTUNATELY, NO. BUT IF HE'D MADE THE HEIGHT REQUIREMENT, HE'D BE THE 5TH HORSE-MAN.
WAR, DEATH, FAMINE AND CAT-HAIR-IN-YOUR-FOOD! HA HA! WAIT, THAT'S NOT FUNNY...

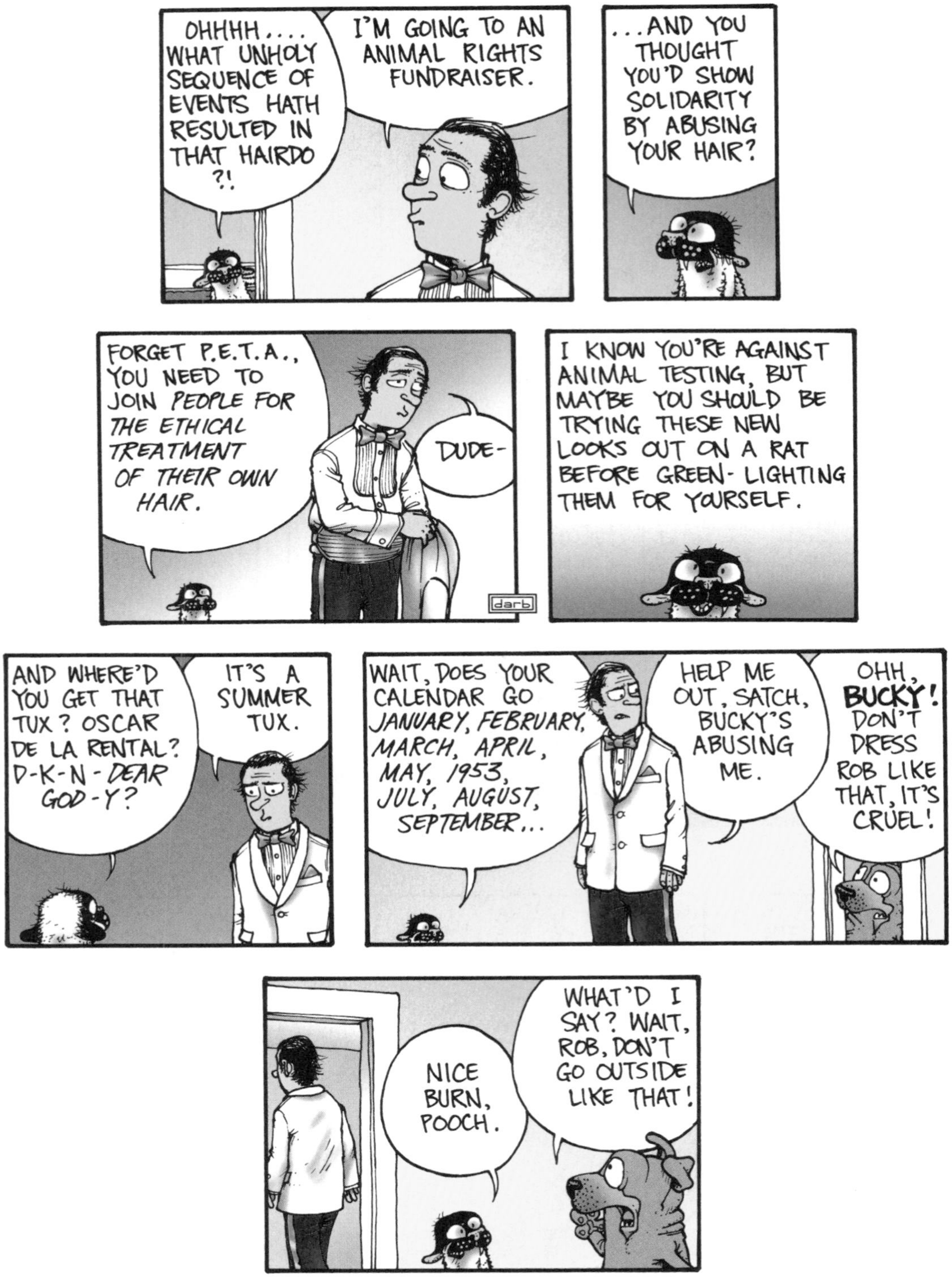
OHHHH.... WHAT UNHOLY SEQUENCE OF EVENTS HATH RESULTED IN THAT HAIRDO ?!
I'M GOING TO AN ANIMAL RIGHTS FUNDRAISER.
...AND YOU THOUGHT YOU'D SHOW SOLIDARITY BY ABUSING YOUR HAIR?
FORGET P.E.T.A., YOU NEED TO JOIN *PEOPLE FOR THE ETHICAL TREATMENT OF THEIR OWN HAIR.*
DUDE-
darb
I KNOW YOU'RE AGAINST ANIMAL TESTING, BUT MAYBE YOU SHOULD BE TRYING THESE NEW LOOKS OUT ON A RAT BEFORE GREEN-LIGHTING THEM FOR YOURSELF.
AND WHERE'D YOU GET THAT TUX? OSCAR DE LA RENTAL? D-K-N-*DEAR GOD*-Y?
IT'S A SUMMER TUX.
WAIT, DOES YOUR CALENDAR GO *JANUARY, FEBRUARY, MARCH, APRIL, MAY, 1953, JULY, AUGUST, SEPTEMBER...*
HELP ME OUT, SATCH, BUCKY'S ABUSING ME.
OHH, **BUCKY!** DON'T DRESS ROB LIKE THAT, IT'S CRUEL!
NICE BURN, POOCH.
WHAT'D I SAY? WAIT, ROB, DON'T GO OUTSIDE LIKE THAT!

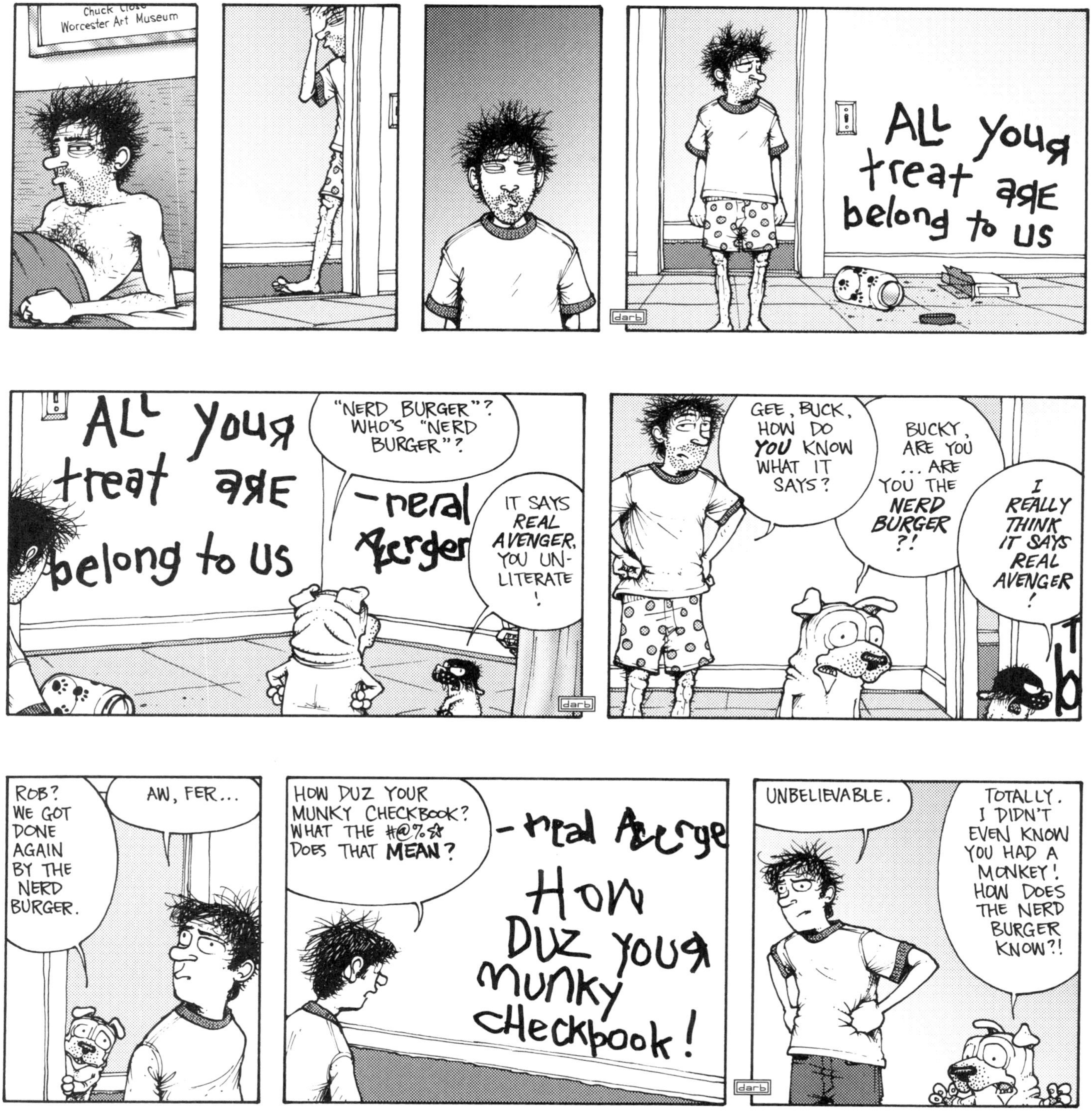
Worcester Art Museum
All your treat are belong to us
"NERD BURGER"? WHO'S "NERD BURGER"?
IT SAYS REAL AVENGER, YOU UN-LITERATE!
GEE, BUCK, HOW DO YOU KNOW WHAT IT SAYS?
BUCKY, ARE YOU ... ARE YOU THE NERD BURGER?!
I REALLY THINK IT SAYS REAL AVENGER!
ROB? WE GOT DONE AGAIN BY THE NERD BURGER.
AW, FER...
HOW DUZ YOUR MUNKY CHECKBOOK? WHAT THE #@%☆ DOES THAT MEAN?
How Duz your munky checkbook!
UNBELIEVABLE.
TOTALLY. I DIDN'T EVEN KNOW YOU HAD A MONKEY! HOW DOES THE NERD BURGER KNOW?!

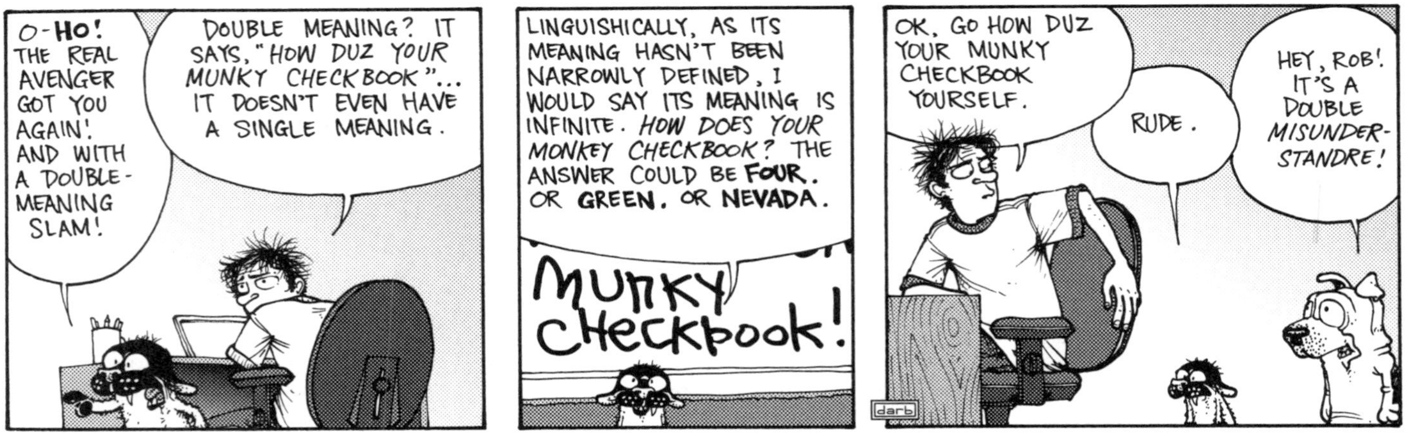
O-HO! THE REAL AVENGER GOT YOU AGAIN! AND WITH A DOUBLE-MEANING SLAM!
DOUBLE MEANING? IT SAYS, "HOW DUZ YOUR MUNKY CHECKBOOK"... IT DOESN'T EVEN HAVE A SINGLE MEANING.
LINGUISHICALLY, AS ITS MEANING HASN'T BEEN NARROWLY DEFINED, I WOULD SAY ITS MEANING IS INFINITE. HOW DOES YOUR MONKEY CHECKBOOK? THE ANSWER COULD BE FOUR. OR GREEN. OR NEVADA.
munky checkbook!
OK. GO HOW DUZ YOUR MUNKY CHECKBOOK YOURSELF.
RUDE.
HEY, ROB! IT'S A DOUBLE MISUNDERSTANDRE!
darb

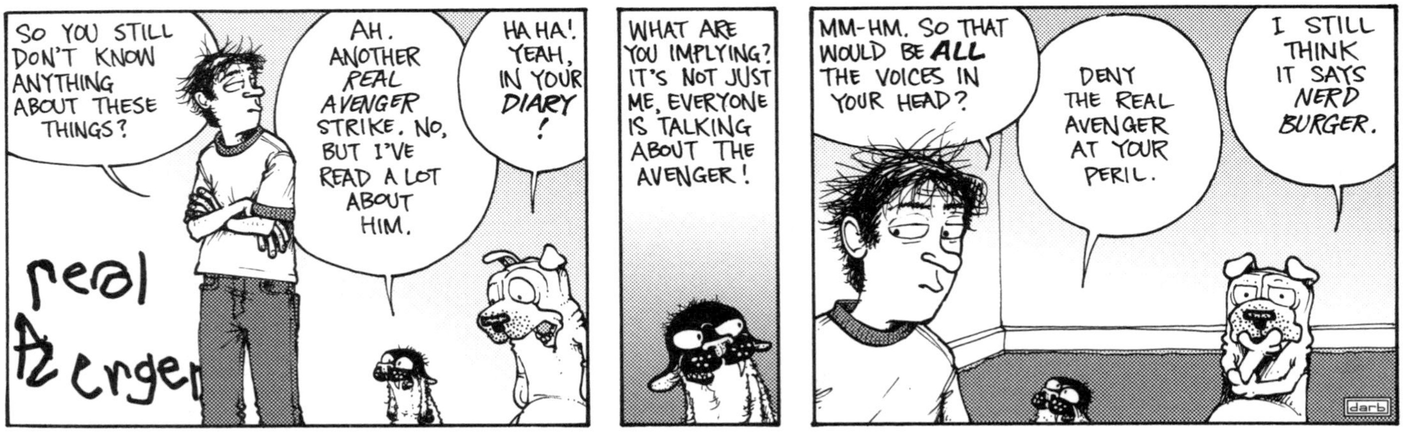
SO YOU STILL DON'T KNOW ANYTHING ABOUT THESE THINGS?
AH. ANOTHER REAL AVENGER STRIKE. NO, BUT I'VE READ A LOT ABOUT HIM.
HA HA! YEAH, IN YOUR DIARY!
real Avenger
WHAT ARE YOU IMPLYING? IT'S NOT JUST ME, EVERYONE IS TALKING ABOUT THE AVENGER!
MM-HM. SO THAT WOULD BE ALL THE VOICES IN YOUR HEAD?
DENY THE REAL AVENGER AT YOUR PERIL.
I STILL THINK IT SAYS NERD BURGER.
darb

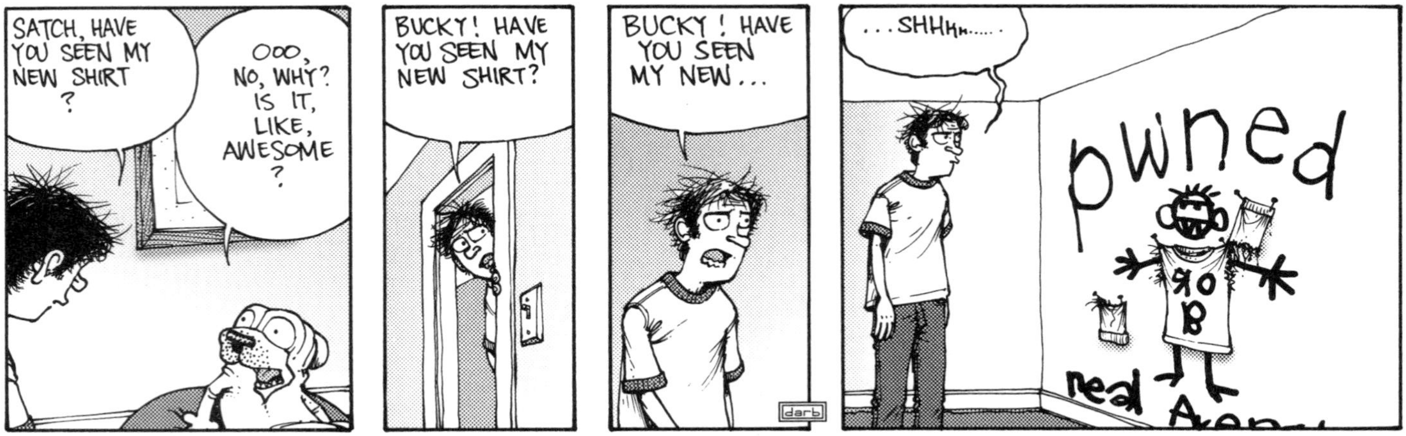
SATCH, HAVE YOU SEEN MY NEW SHIRT?
OOO, NO, WHY? IS IT, LIKE, AWESOME?
BUCKY! HAVE YOU SEEN MY NEW SHIRT?
BUCKY! HAVE YOU SEEN MY NEW...
darb
...SHHhh......
pwned
real

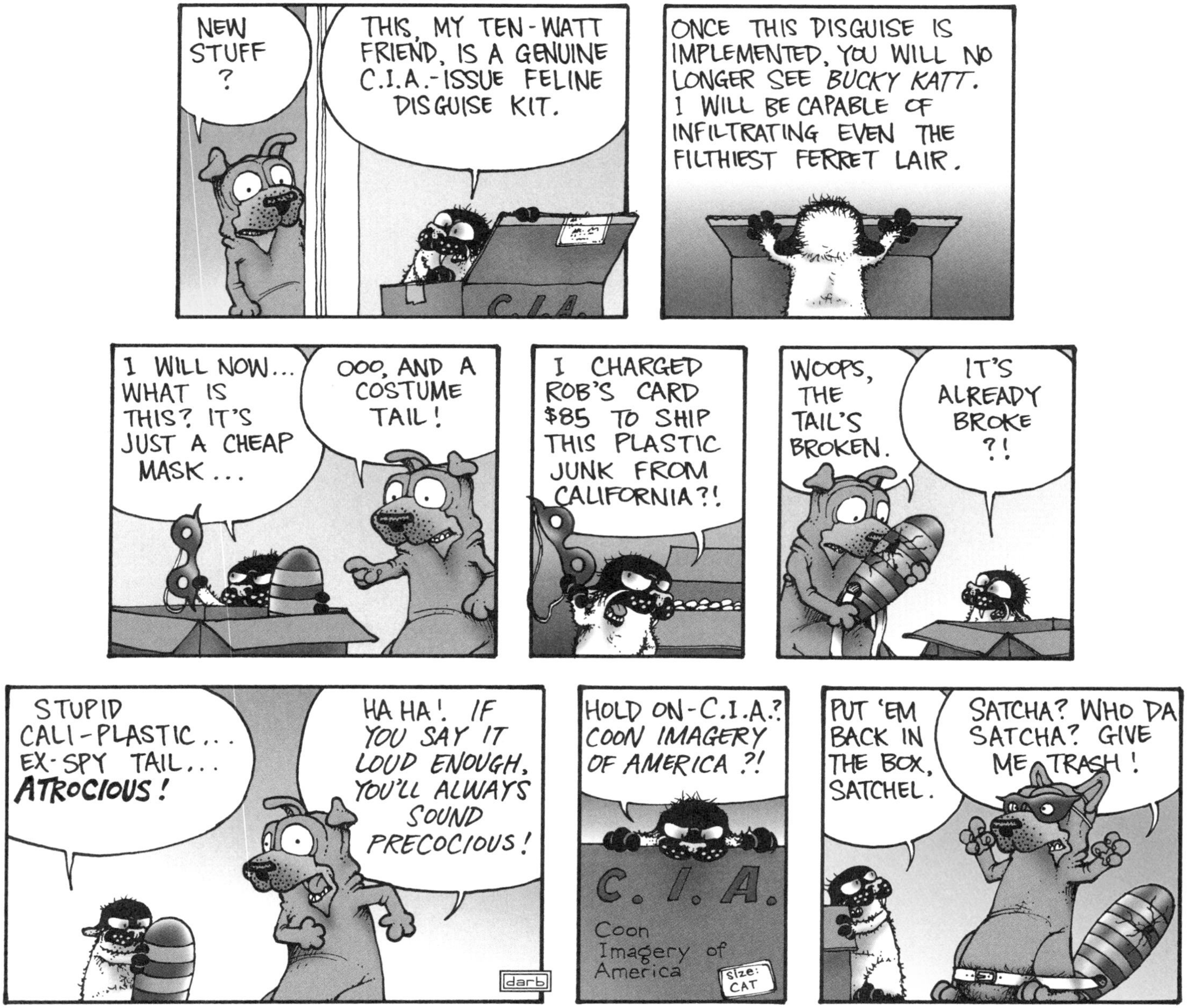
NEW STUFF ?
THIS, MY TEN-WATT FRIEND, IS A GENUINE C.I.A.-ISSUE FELINE DISGUISE KIT.
C.I.A.
ONCE THIS DISGUISE IS IMPLEMENTED, YOU WILL NO LONGER SEE *BUCKY KATT*. I WILL BE CAPABLE OF INFILTRATING EVEN THE FILTHIEST FERRET LAIR.
I WILL NOW... WHAT IS THIS? IT'S JUST A CHEAP MASK...
OOO, AND A COSTUME TAIL!
I CHARGED ROB'S CARD $85 TO SHIP THIS PLASTIC JUNK FROM CALIFORNIA?!
WOOPS, THE TAIL'S BROKEN.
IT'S ALREADY BROKE ?!
STUPID CALI-PLASTIC... EX-SPY TAIL... **ATROCIOUS!**
HA HA! IF YOU SAY IT LOUD ENOUGH, YOU'LL ALWAYS SOUND PRECOCIOUS!
darb
HOLD ON - C.I.A.? *COON IMAGERY OF AMERICA ?!*
C. I. A.
Coon Imagery of America
size: CAT
PUT 'EM BACK IN THE BOX, SATCHEL.
SATCHA? WHO DA SATCHA? GIVE ME TRASH!

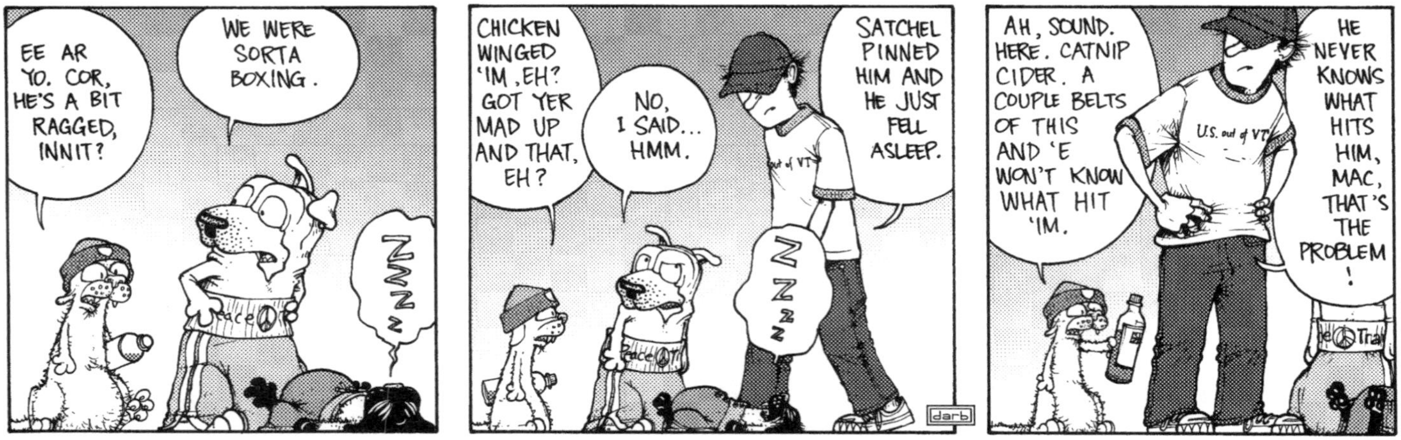
EE AR YO. COR, HE'S A BIT RAGGED, INNIT?
WE WERE SORTA BOXING.
ZZZz
CHICKEN WINGED 'IM, EH? GOT YER MAD UP AND THAT, EH?
NO, I SAID... HMM.
SATCHEL PINNED HIM AND HE JUST FELL ASLEEP.
ZZzz
darb
AH, SOUND. HERE. CATNIP CIDER. A COUPLE BELTS OF THIS AND 'E WON'T KNOW WHAT HIT 'IM.
U.S. out of VT
HE NEVER KNOWS WHAT HITS HIM, MAC, THAT'S THE PROBLEM!

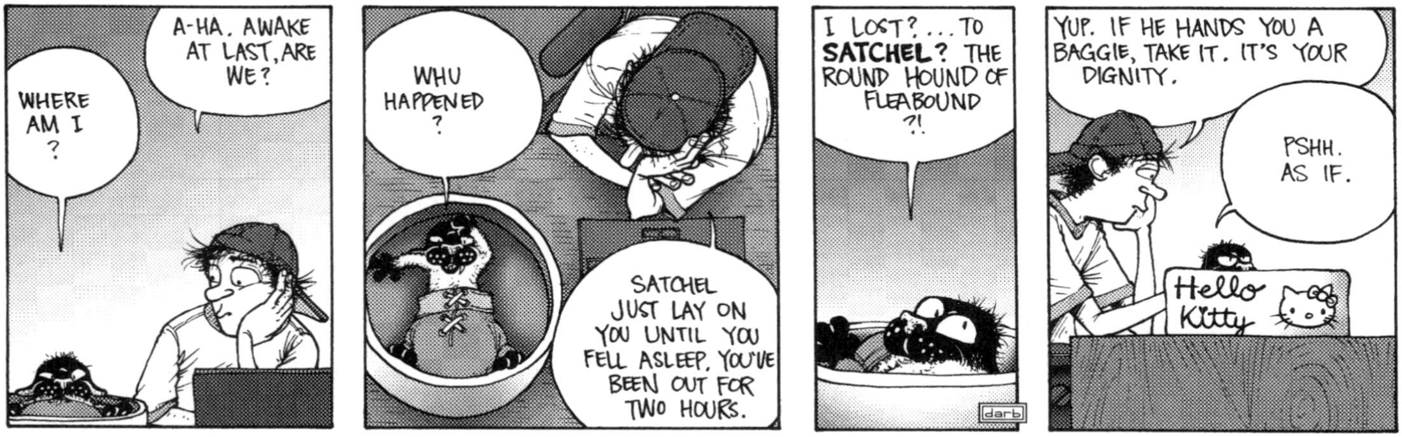
WHERE AM I?
A-HA. AWAKE AT LAST, ARE WE?
WHU HAPPENED?
SATCHEL JUST LAY ON YOU UNTIL YOU FELL ASLEEP. YOU'VE BEEN OUT FOR TWO HOURS.
I LOST?... TO SATCHEL? THE ROUND HOUND OF FLEABOUND?!
darb
YUP. IF HE HANDS YOU A BAGGIE, TAKE IT. IT'S YOUR DIGNITY.
PSHH. AS IF.
Hello Kitty

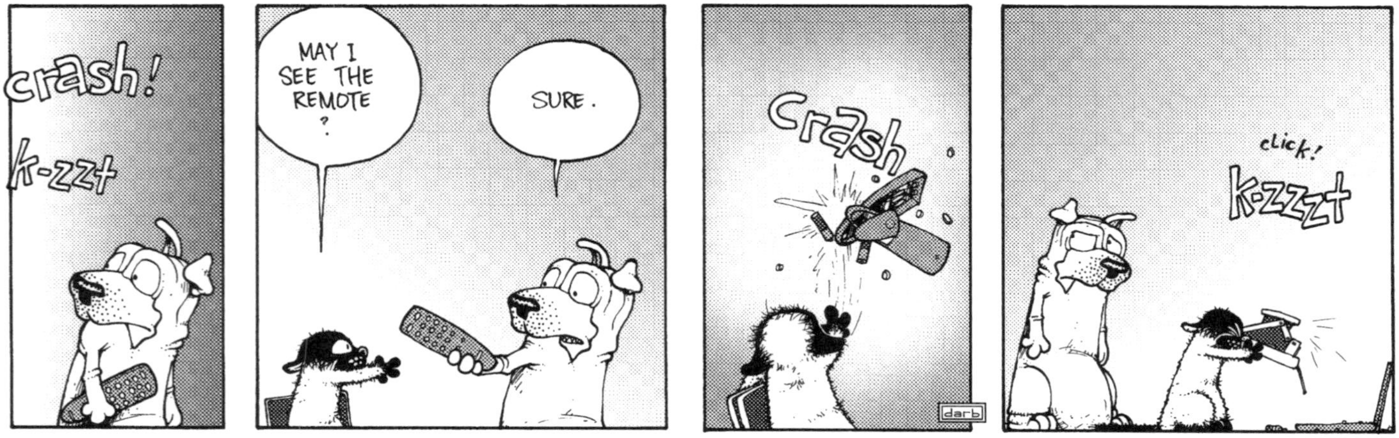
crash!
k-zzt
MAY I SEE THE REMOTE?
SURE.
crash
darb
click!
k-zzzt

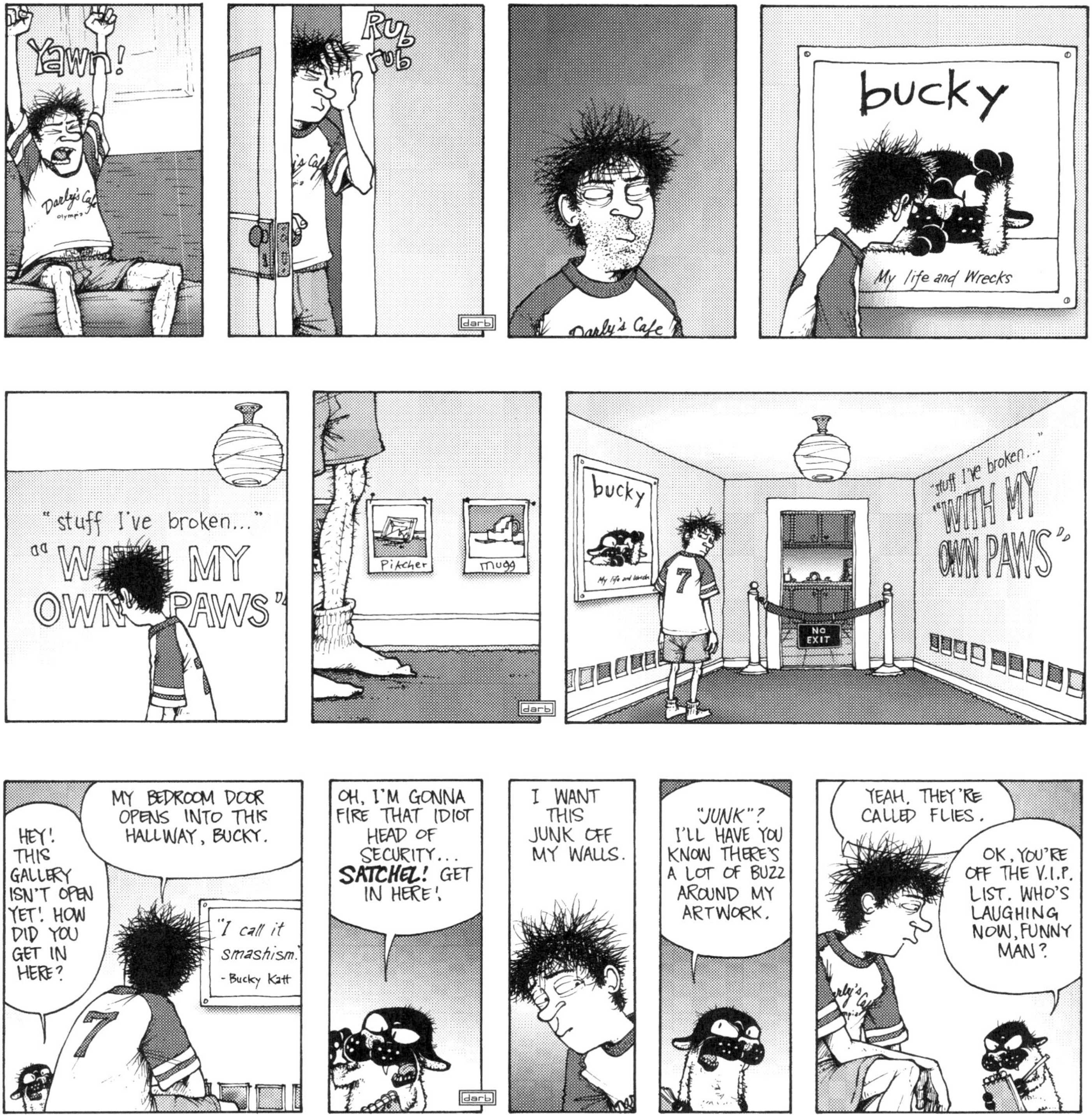

Yawn!
Rub rub
darb
bucky
My life and Wrecks
"stuff I've broken..."
MY
PAWS"
Pitcher
Mugg
darb
bucky
"stuff I've broken..."
"WITH MY OWN PAWS"
NO EXIT
HEY! THIS GALLERY ISN'T OPEN YET! HOW DID YOU GET IN HERE?
MY BEDROOM DOOR OPENS INTO THIS HALLWAY, BUCKY.
"I call it smashism." - Bucky Katt
OH, I'M GONNA FIRE THAT IDIOT HEAD OF SECURITY... SATCHEL! GET IN HERE!
darb
I WANT THIS JUNK OFF MY WALLS.
"JUNK"? I'LL HAVE YOU KNOW THERE'S A LOT OF BUZZ AROUND MY ARTWORK.
YEAH. THEY'RE CALLED FLIES.
OK, YOU'RE OFF THE V.I.P. LIST. WHO'S LAUGHING NOW, FUNNY MAN?

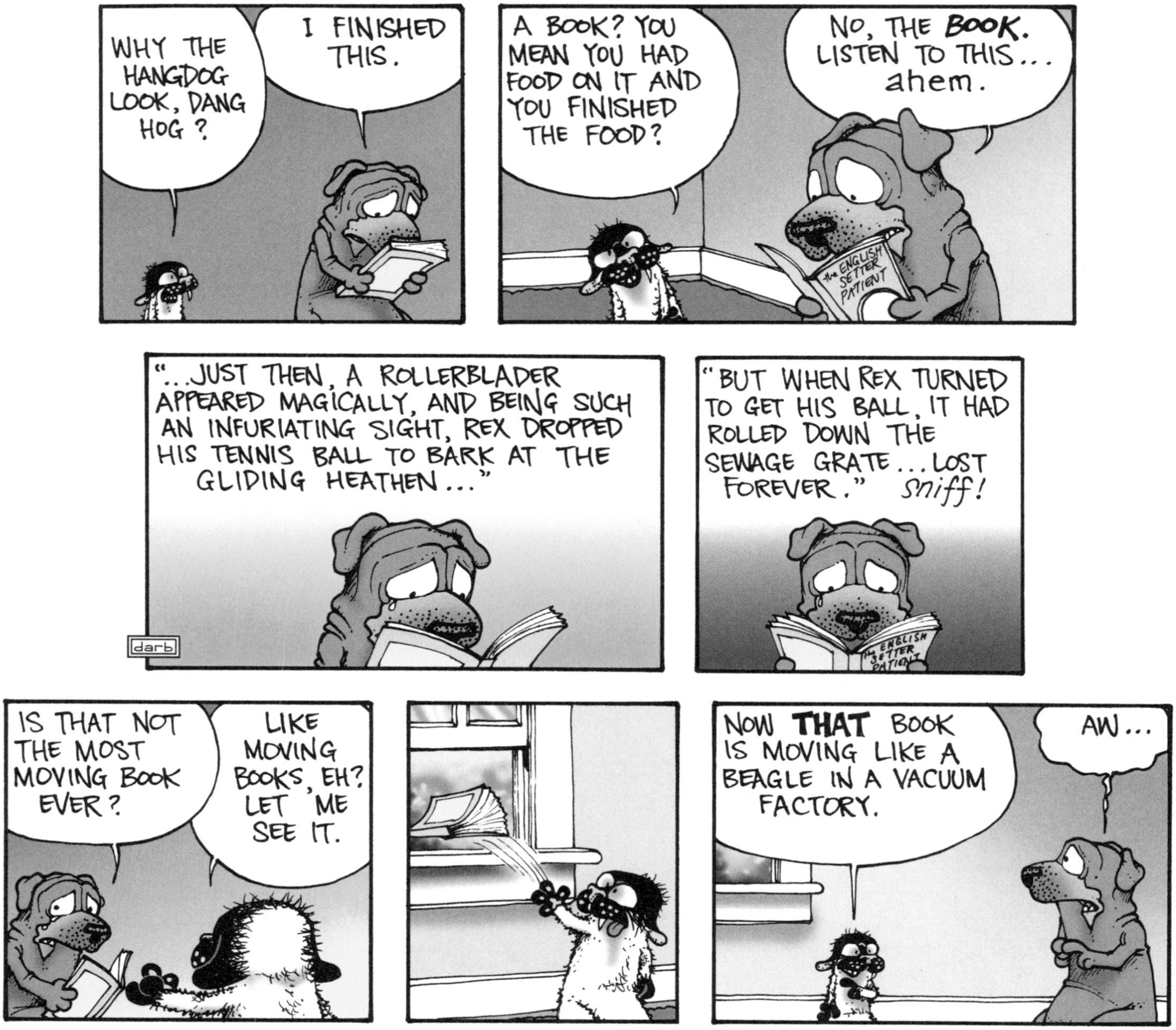
WHY THE HANGDOG LOOK, DANG HOG?
I FINISHED THIS.
A BOOK? YOU MEAN YOU HAD FOOD ON IT AND YOU FINISHED THE FOOD?
NO, THE BOOK. LISTEN TO THIS... ahem.
THE ENGLISH SETTER PATIENT
"...JUST THEN, A ROLLERBLADER APPEARED MAGICALLY, AND BEING SUCH AN INFURIATING SIGHT, REX DROPPED HIS TENNIS BALL TO BARK AT THE GLIDING HEATHEN..."
darb
"BUT WHEN REX TURNED TO GET HIS BALL, IT HAD ROLLED DOWN THE SEWAGE GRATE... LOST FOREVER." sniff!
IS THAT NOT THE MOST MOVING BOOK EVER?
LIKE MOVING BOOKS, EH? LET ME SEE IT.
NOW THAT BOOK IS MOVING LIKE A BEAGLE IN A VACUUM FACTORY.
AW...

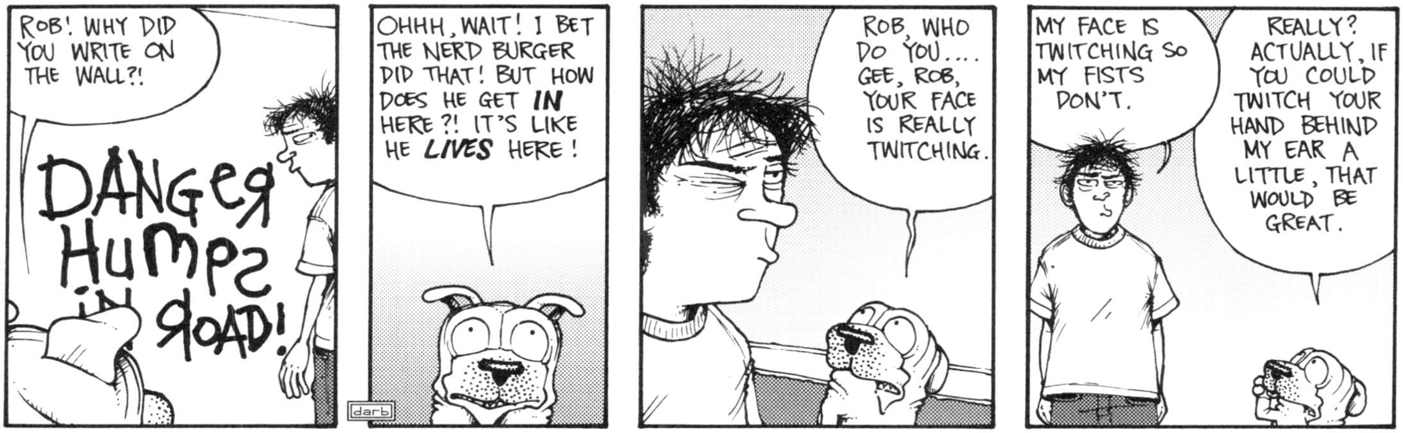
ROB! WHY DID YOU WRITE ON THE WALL?!
DANGER HUMPS IN ROAD!
OHHH, WAIT! I BET THE NERD BURGER DID THAT! BUT HOW DOES HE GET IN HERE?! IT'S LIKE HE LIVES HERE!
ROB, WHO DO YOU.... GEE, ROB, YOUR FACE IS REALLY TWITCHING.
MY FACE IS TWITCHING SO MY FISTS DON'T.
REALLY? ACTUALLY, IF YOU COULD TWITCH YOUR HAND BEHIND MY EAR A LITTLE, THAT WOULD BE GREAT.

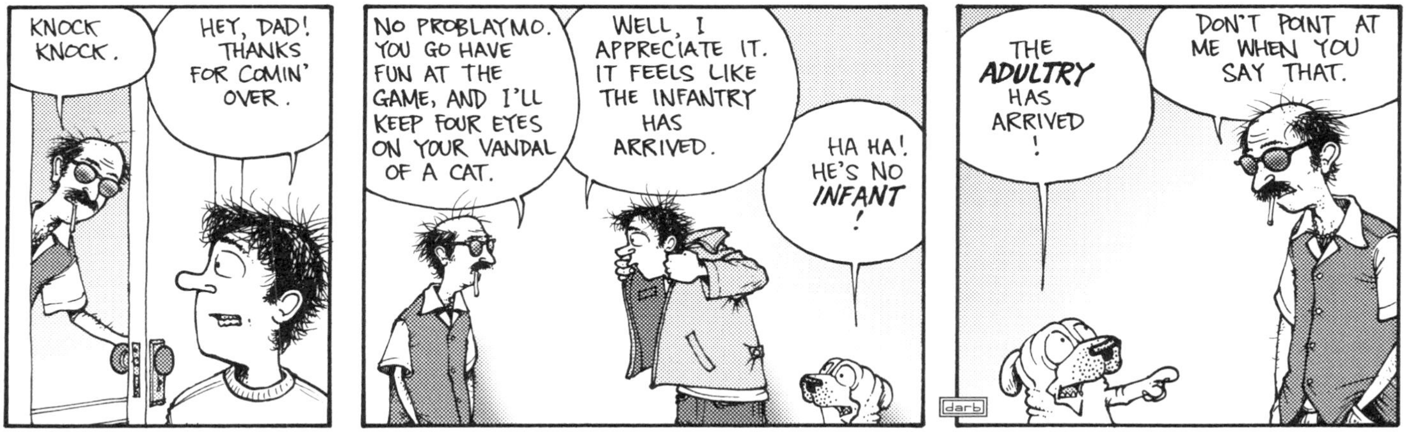
KNOCK KNOCK.
HEY, DAD! THANKS FOR COMIN' OVER.
NO PROBLAYMO. YOU GO HAVE FUN AT THE GAME, AND I'LL KEEP FOUR EYES ON YOUR VANDAL OF A CAT.
WELL, I APPRECIATE IT. IT FEELS LIKE THE INFANTRY HAS ARRIVED.
HA HA! HE'S NO INFANT!
THE ADULTRY HAS ARRIVED!
DON'T POINT AT ME WHEN YOU SAY THAT.

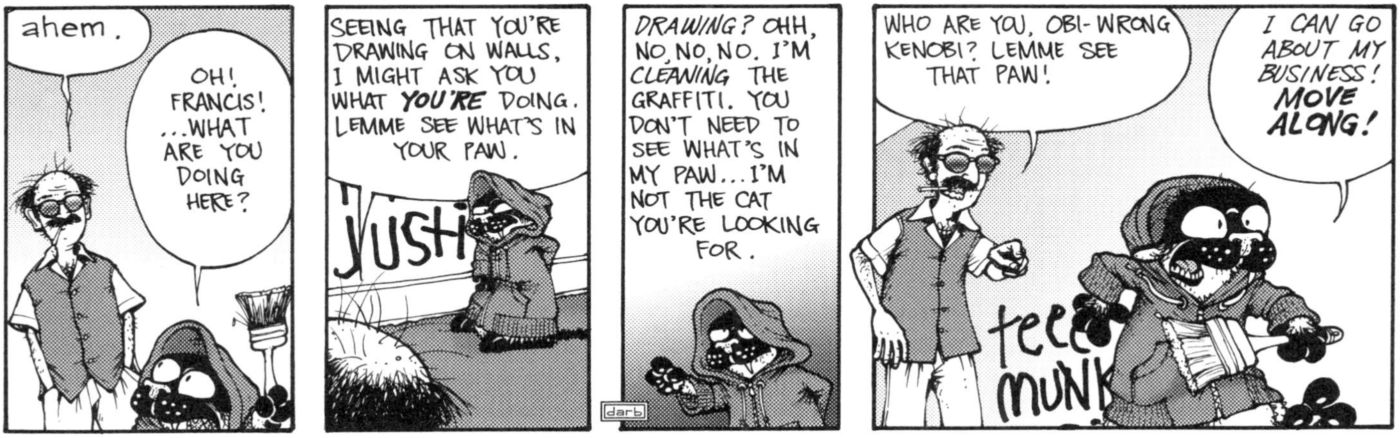
ahem.
OH! FRANCIS! ...WHAT ARE YOU DOING HERE?
SEEING THAT YOU'RE DRAWING ON WALLS, I MIGHT ASK YOU WHAT YOU'RE DOING. LEMME SEE WHAT'S IN YOUR PAW.
DRAWING? OHH, NO, NO, NO. I'M CLEANING THE GRAFFITI. YOU DON'T NEED TO SEE WHAT'S IN MY PAW... I'M NOT THE CAT YOU'RE LOOKING FOR.
WHO ARE YOU, OBI-WRONG KENOBI? LEMME SEE THAT PAW!
I CAN GO ABOUT MY BUSINESS! MOVE ALONG!

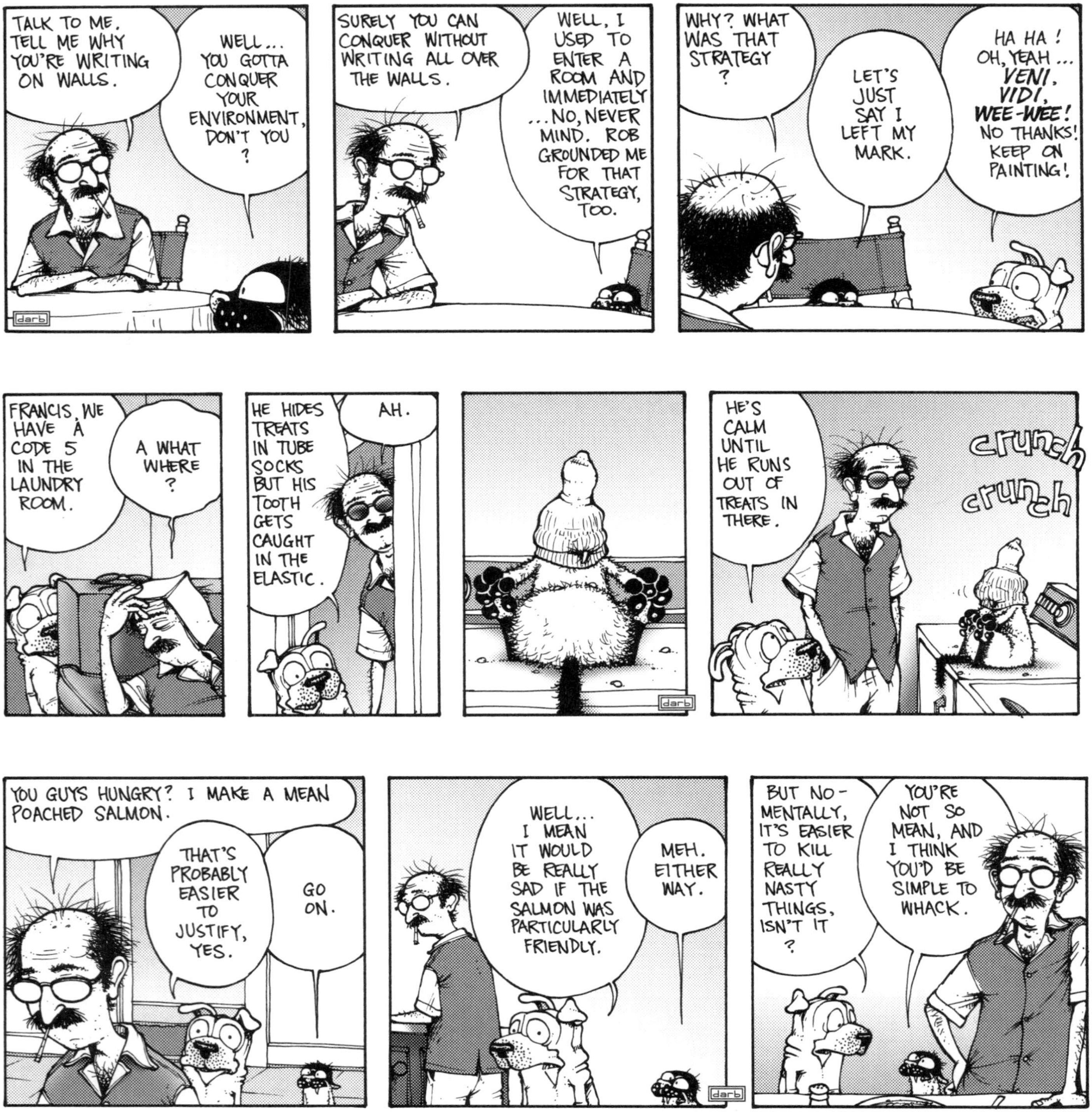
TALK TO ME. TELL ME WHY YOU'RE WRITING ON WALLS.
WELL... YOU GOTTA CONQUER YOUR ENVIRONMENT, DON'T YOU?
darb
SURELY YOU CAN CONQUER WITHOUT WRITING ALL OVER THE WALLS.
WELL, I USED TO ENTER A ROOM AND IMMEDIATELY ...NO, NEVER MIND. ROB GROUNDED ME FOR THAT STRATEGY, TOO.
WHY? WHAT WAS THAT STRATEGY?
LET'S JUST SAY I LEFT MY MARK.
HA HA! OH, YEAH... VENI. VIDI. WEE-WEE! NO THANKS! KEEP ON PAINTING!
FRANCIS, WE HAVE A CODE 5 IN THE LAUNDRY ROOM.
A WHAT WHERE?
HE HIDES TREATS IN TUBE SOCKS BUT HIS TOOTH GETS CAUGHT IN THE ELASTIC.
AH.
darb
HE'S CALM UNTIL HE RUNS OUT OF TREATS IN THERE.
crunch
crunch
YOU GUYS HUNGRY? I MAKE A MEAN POACHED SALMON.
THAT'S PROBABLY EASIER TO JUSTIFY, YES.
GO ON.
WELL... I MEAN IT WOULD BE REALLY SAD IF THE SALMON WAS PARTICULARLY FRIENDLY.
MEH. EITHER WAY.
darb
BUT NO- MENTALLY, IT'S EASIER TO KILL REALLY NASTY THINGS, ISN'T IT?
YOU'RE NOT SO MEAN, AND I THINK YOU'D BE SIMPLE TO WHACK.

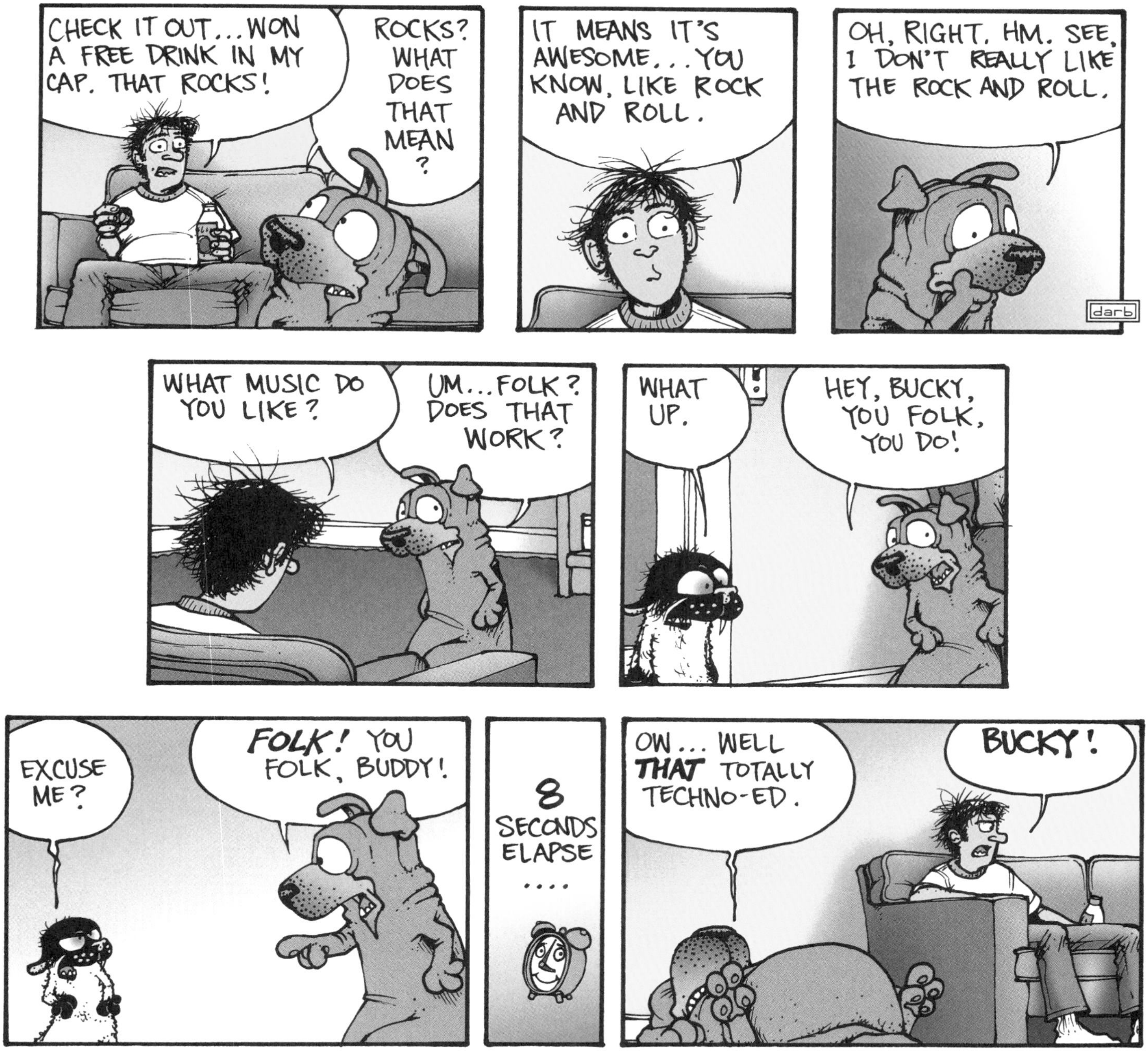
CHECK IT OUT... WON A FREE DRINK IN MY CAP. THAT ROCKS!
ROCKS? WHAT DOES THAT MEAN?
IT MEANS IT'S AWESOME... YOU KNOW, LIKE ROCK AND ROLL.
OH, RIGHT. HM. SEE, I DON'T REALLY LIKE THE ROCK AND ROLL.
darb
WHAT MUSIC DO YOU LIKE?
UM... FOLK? DOES THAT WORK?
WHAT UP.
HEY, BUCKY, YOU FOLK, YOU DO!
EXCUSE ME?
FOLK! YOU FOLK, BUDDY!
8 SECONDS ELAPSE ....
OW... WELL THAT TOTALLY TECHNO-ED.
BUCKY!